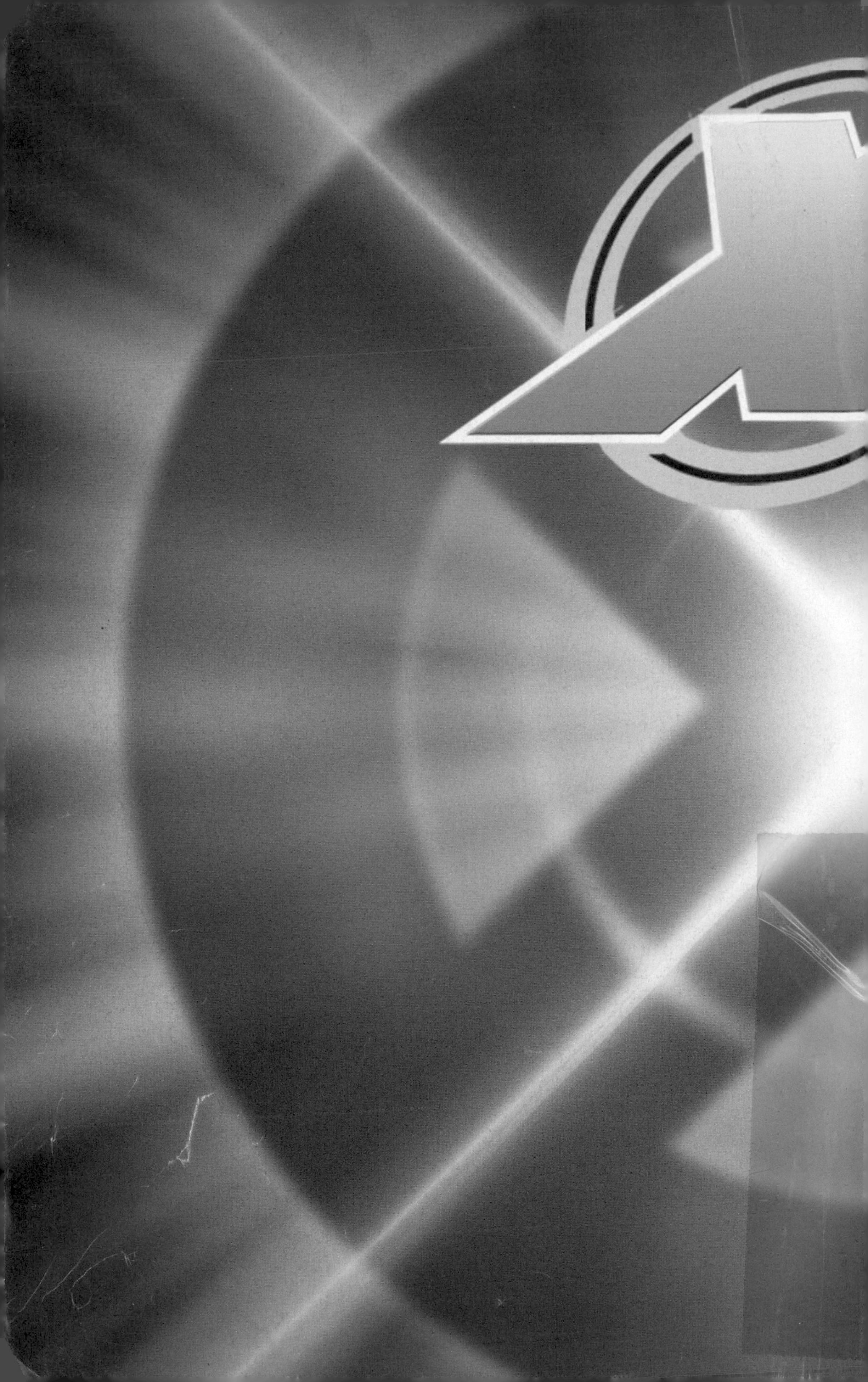

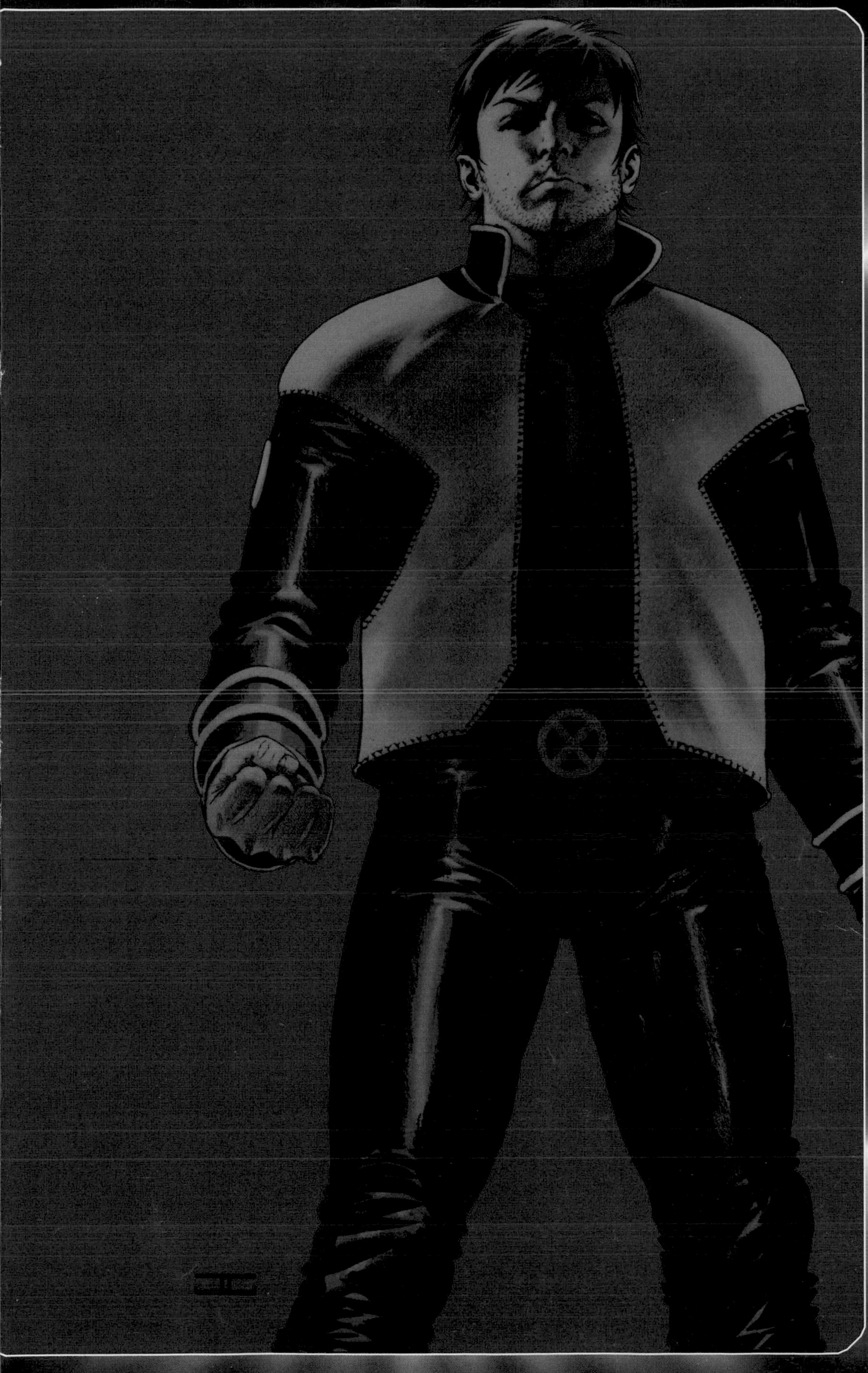

19 VARIANT

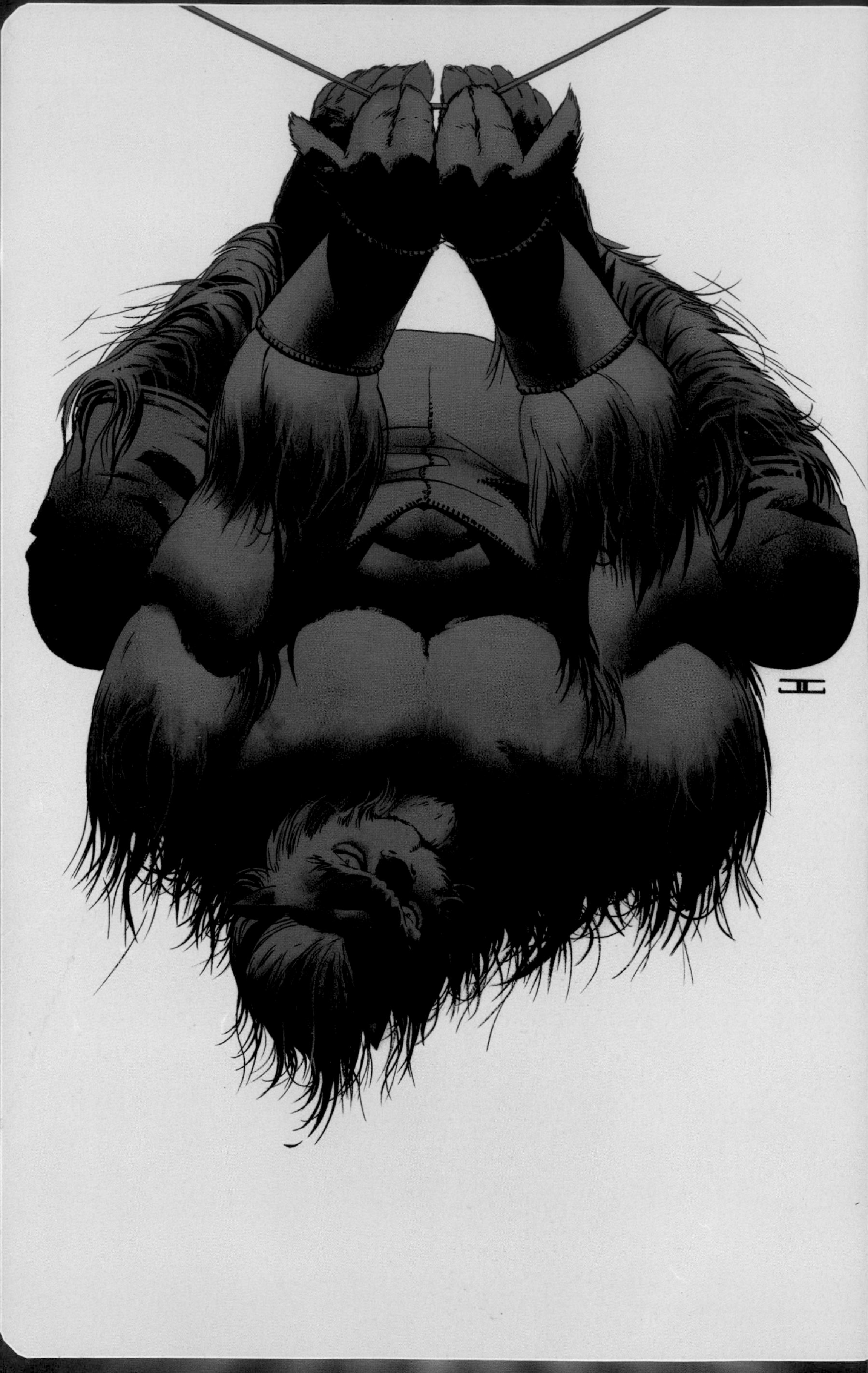

20 VARIANT

ASTONISHING X-MEN

UNSTOPPABLE

writer_**JOSS WHEDON**

artist_**JOHN CASSADAY**

colorist_**LAURA MARTIN**
letterers_**CHRIS ELIOPOULOS**
WITH **JOE CARAMAGNA**

assistant editors_**SEAN RYAN & WILL PANZO**
associate editor_**ANDY SCHMIDT**
editors_**MIKE MARTS & NICK LOWE**

collection editor_**JENNIFER GRÜNWALD**
assistant editors
_**CORY LEVINE & JOHN DENNING**
editor, special projects_**MARK D. BEAZLEY**
senior editor, special projects
_**JEFF YOUNGQUIST**

senior vice president of sales_**DAVID GABRIEL**
vice president of creative
_**TOM MARVELLI**

editor in chief_**JOE QUESADA**
publisher_**DAN BUCKLEY**

PREVIOUSLY:

The oracles of Breakworld foresaw a future where their world was destroyed by a mutant from Earth. So they sent one of their own, ORD, to take care of the problem. His solution was to develop a "cure" for mutancy that would eliminate the danger to his homeworld. In the process of creating this "cure," Ord resurrected the deceased X-Man COLOSSUS to be used as a research subject.

The X-Men stopped Ord from wiping out the Earth's mutants and he was then incarcerated by S.W.O.R.D. (Sentient Worlds Observation and Response Department), an organization led by AGENT BRAND. Irony reared its ugly head when S.W.O.R.D. precognitives discovered that the mutant destined to destroy Breakworld was the mutant Ord brought back to life — Colossus.

Ord broke out of S.W.O.R.D. imprisonment with the help of the sentient robot DANGER, and attacked the X-Men, who, at the same time, were falling apart at the seams. EMMA FROST, under the influence of CASSANDRA NOVA and suffering from extreme survivor's guilt, mentally took apart the X-Men. They were able to save their teammate and themselves, but not without consequence. CYCLOPS lost his optic blasts and KITTY PRYDE is still suffering from the emotional anguish Emma caused her.

All of this was thrown on the back burner as S.W.O.R.D. has just teleported Ord, Danger and the X-Men (along with X-student HISAKO) aboard a starship.

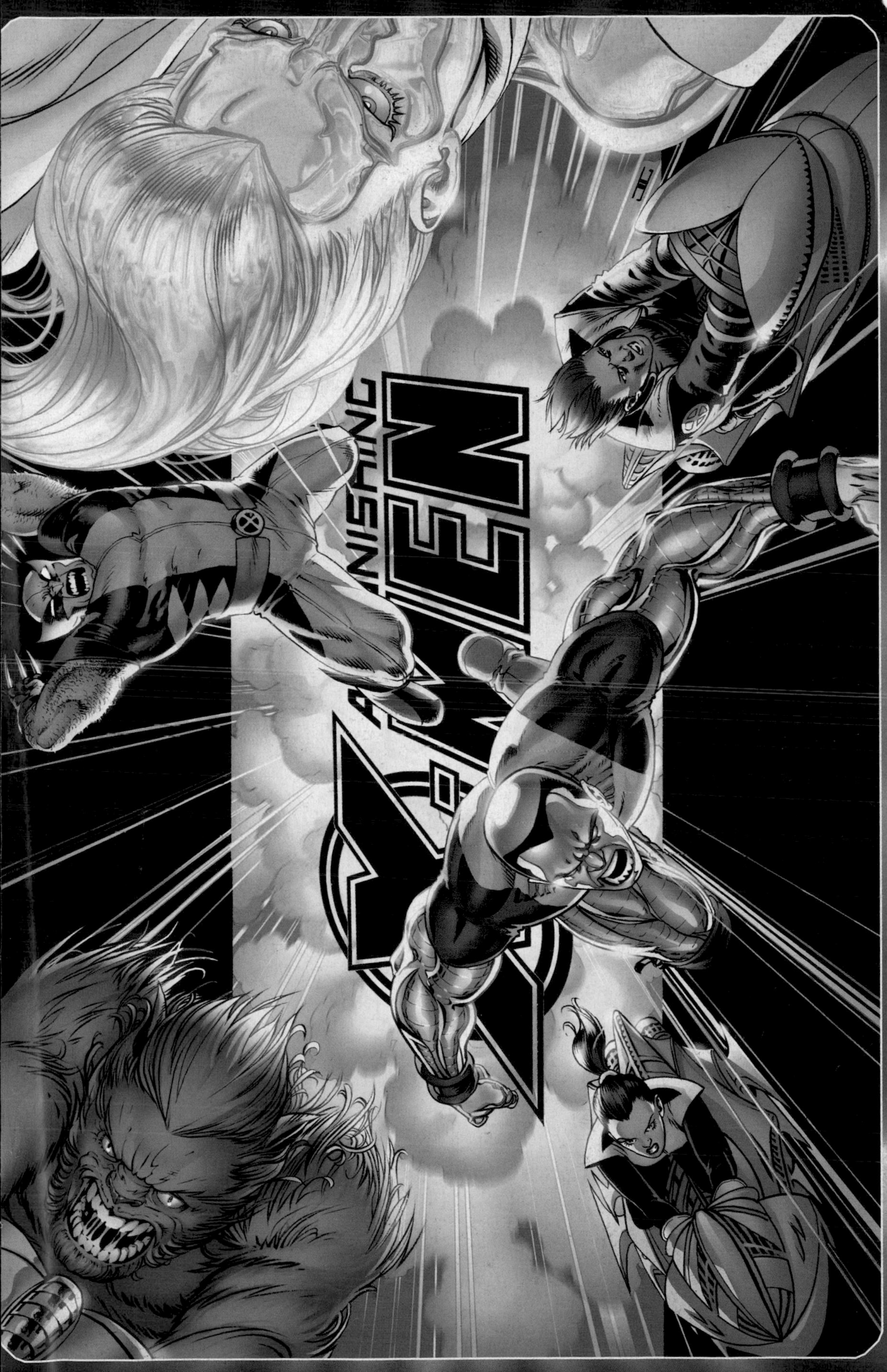

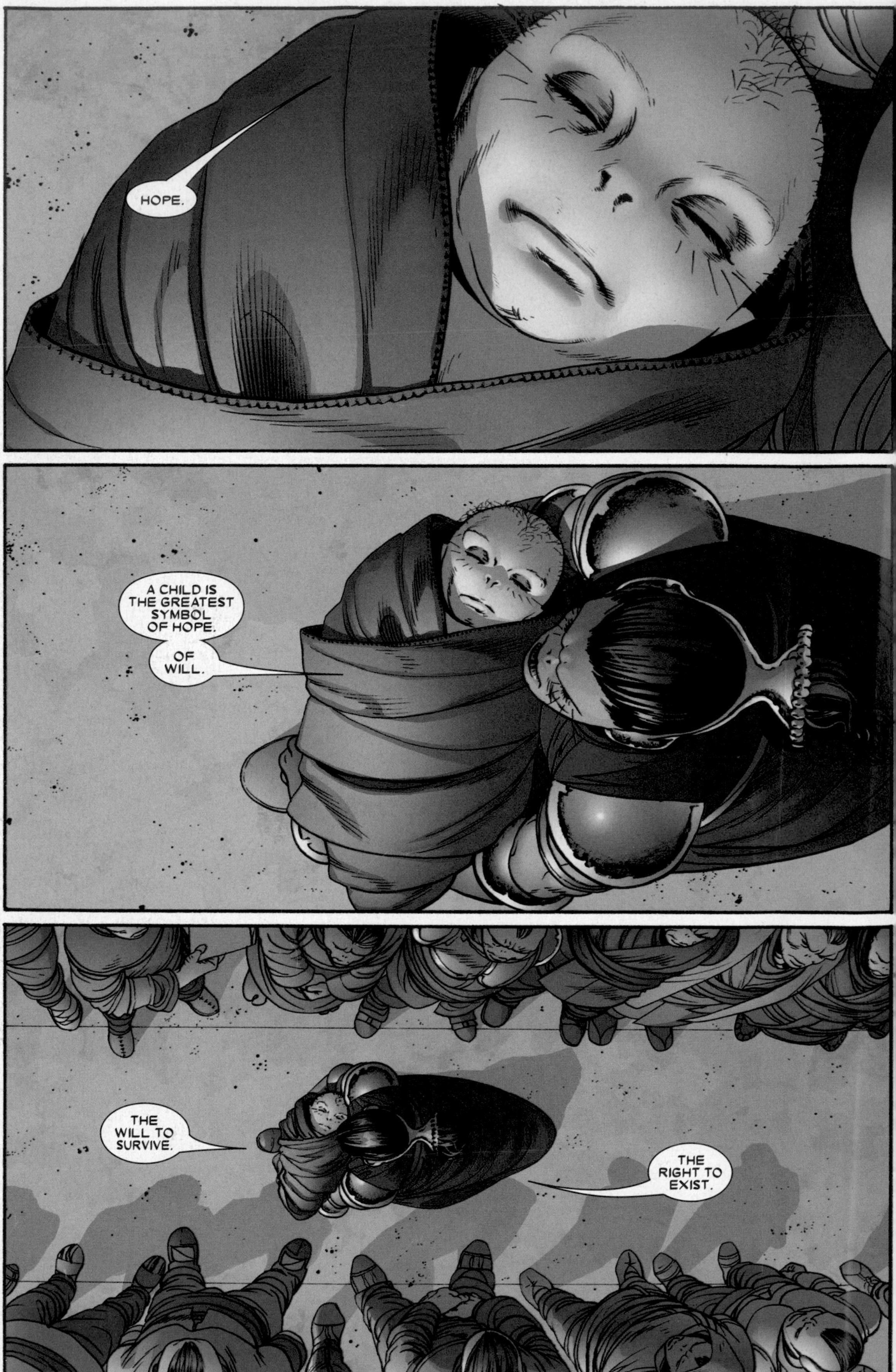
HOPE.
A CHILD IS THE GREATEST SYMBOL OF HOPE.
OF WILL.
THE WILL TO SURVIVE.
THE RIGHT TO EXIST.

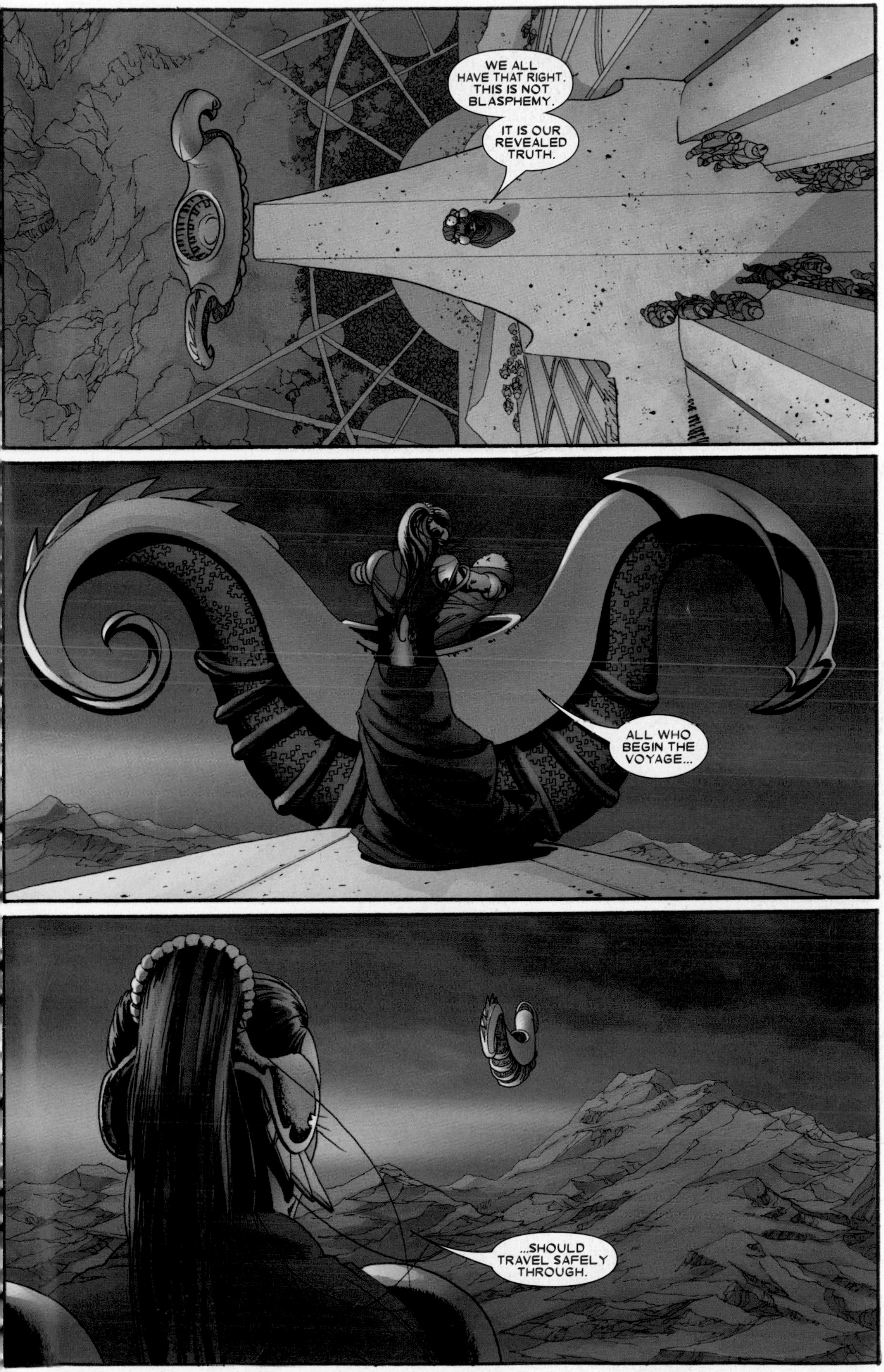
WE ALL HAVE THAT RIGHT. THIS IS NOT BLASPHEMY.
IT IS OUR REVEALED TRUTH.
ALL WHO BEGIN THE VOYAGE...
...SHOULD TRAVEL SAFELY THROUGH.

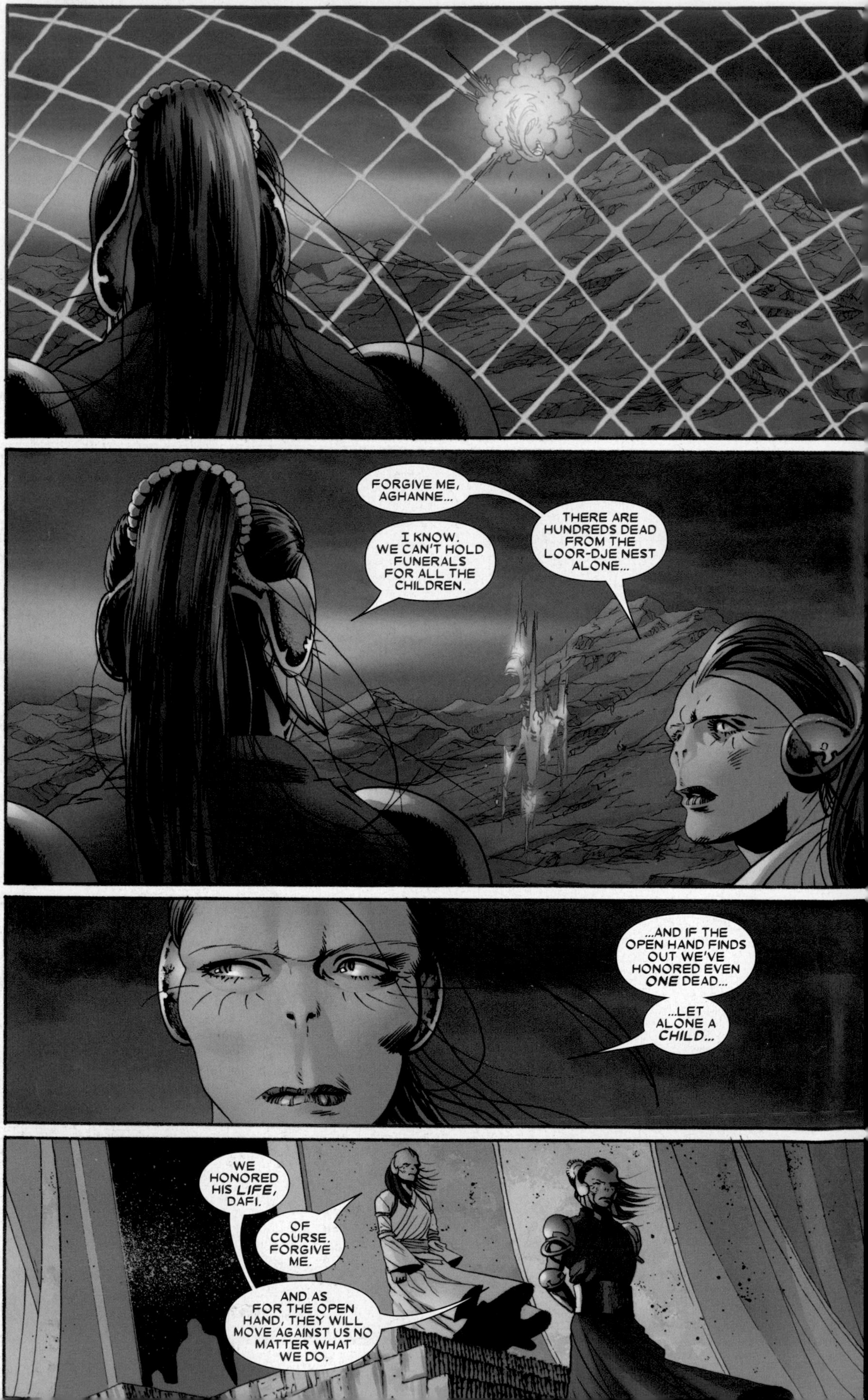
FORGIVE ME, AGHANNE...
THERE ARE HUNDREDS DEAD FROM THE LOOR-DJE NEST ALONE...
I KNOW. WE CAN'T HOLD FUNERALS FOR ALL THE CHILDREN.
...AND IF THE OPEN HAND FINDS OUT WE'VE HONORED EVEN ONE DEAD...
...LET ALONE A CHILD...
WE HONORED HIS LIFE, DAFI.
OF COURSE. FORGIVE ME.
AND AS FOR THE OPEN HAND, THEY WILL MOVE AGAINST US NO MATTER WHAT WE DO.

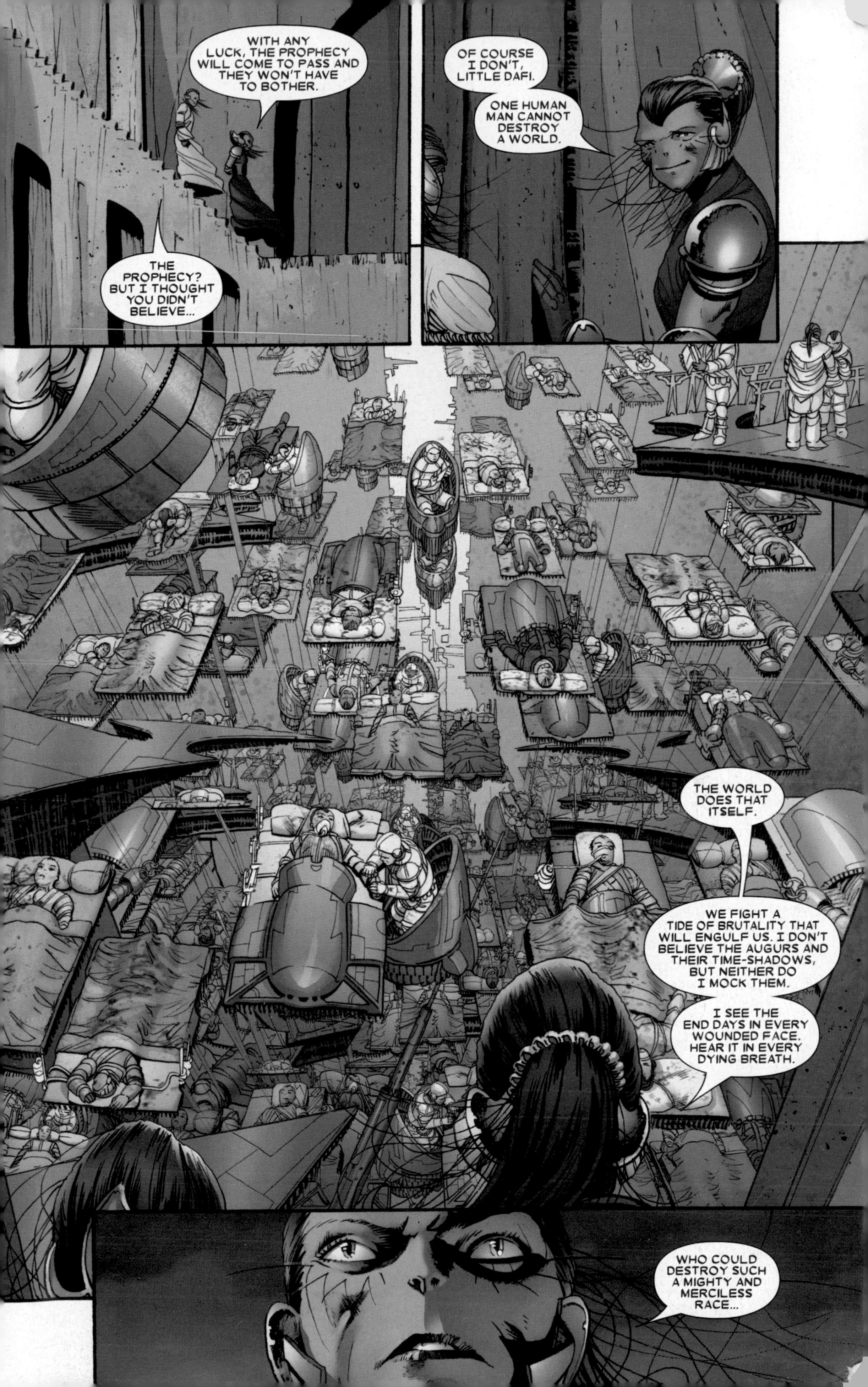
WITH ANY LUCK, THE PROPHECY WILL COME TO PASS AND THEY WON'T HAVE TO BOTHER.
THE PROPHECY? BUT I THOUGHT YOU DIDN'T BELIEVE...
OF COURSE I DON'T, LITTLE DAFI.
ONE HUMAN MAN CANNOT DESTROY A WORLD.
THE WORLD DOES THAT ITSELF.
WE FIGHT A TIDE OF BRUTALITY THAT WILL ENGULF US. I DON'T BELIEVE THE AUGURS AND THEIR TIME-SHADOWS, BUT NEITHER DO I MOCK THEM.
I SEE THE END DAYS IN EVERY WOUNDED FACE. HEAR IT IN EVERY DYING BREATH.
WHO COULD DESTROY SUCH A MIGHTY AND MERCILESS RACE...

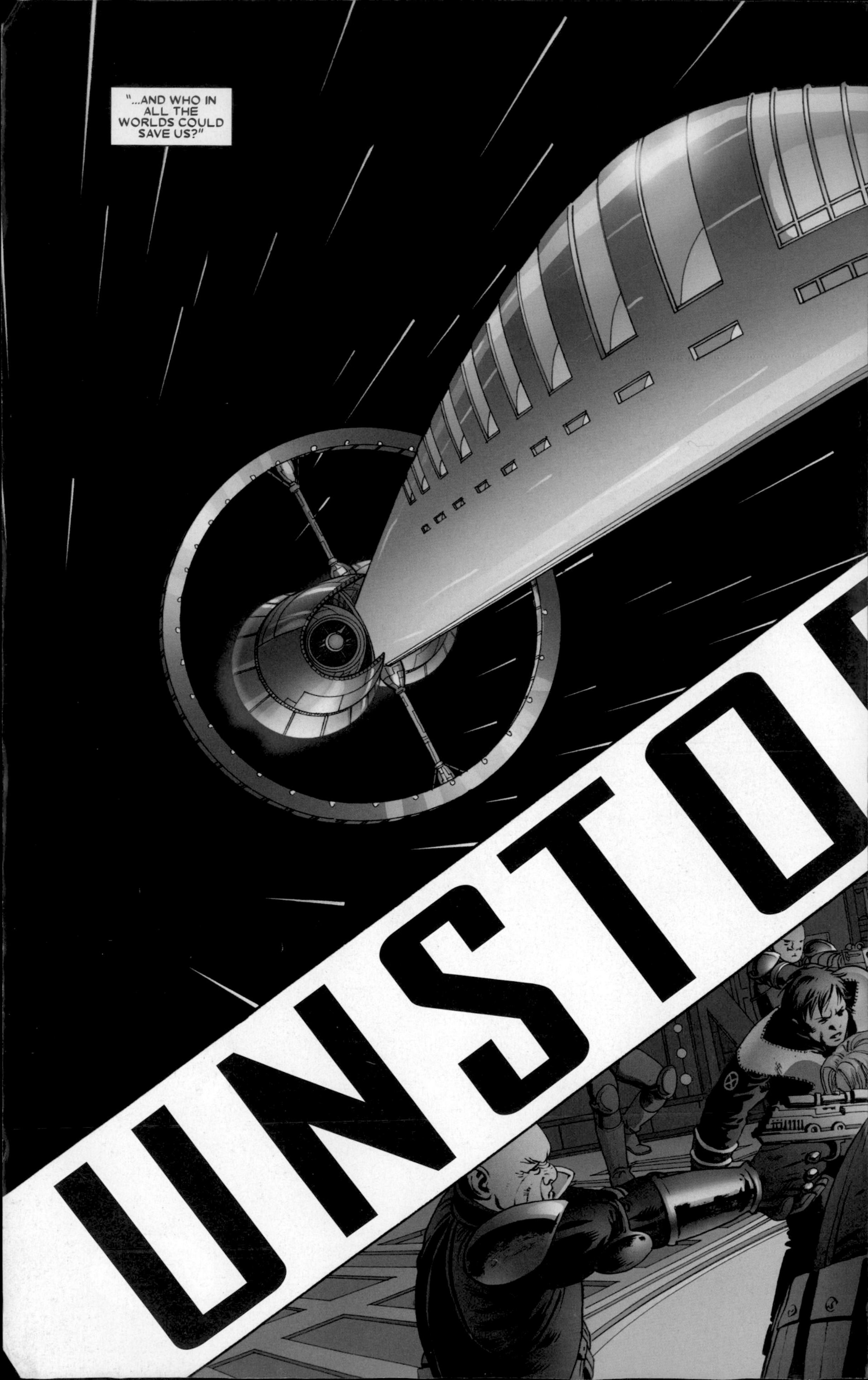
"...AND WHO IN ALL THE WORLDS COULD SAVE US?"
UNSTO

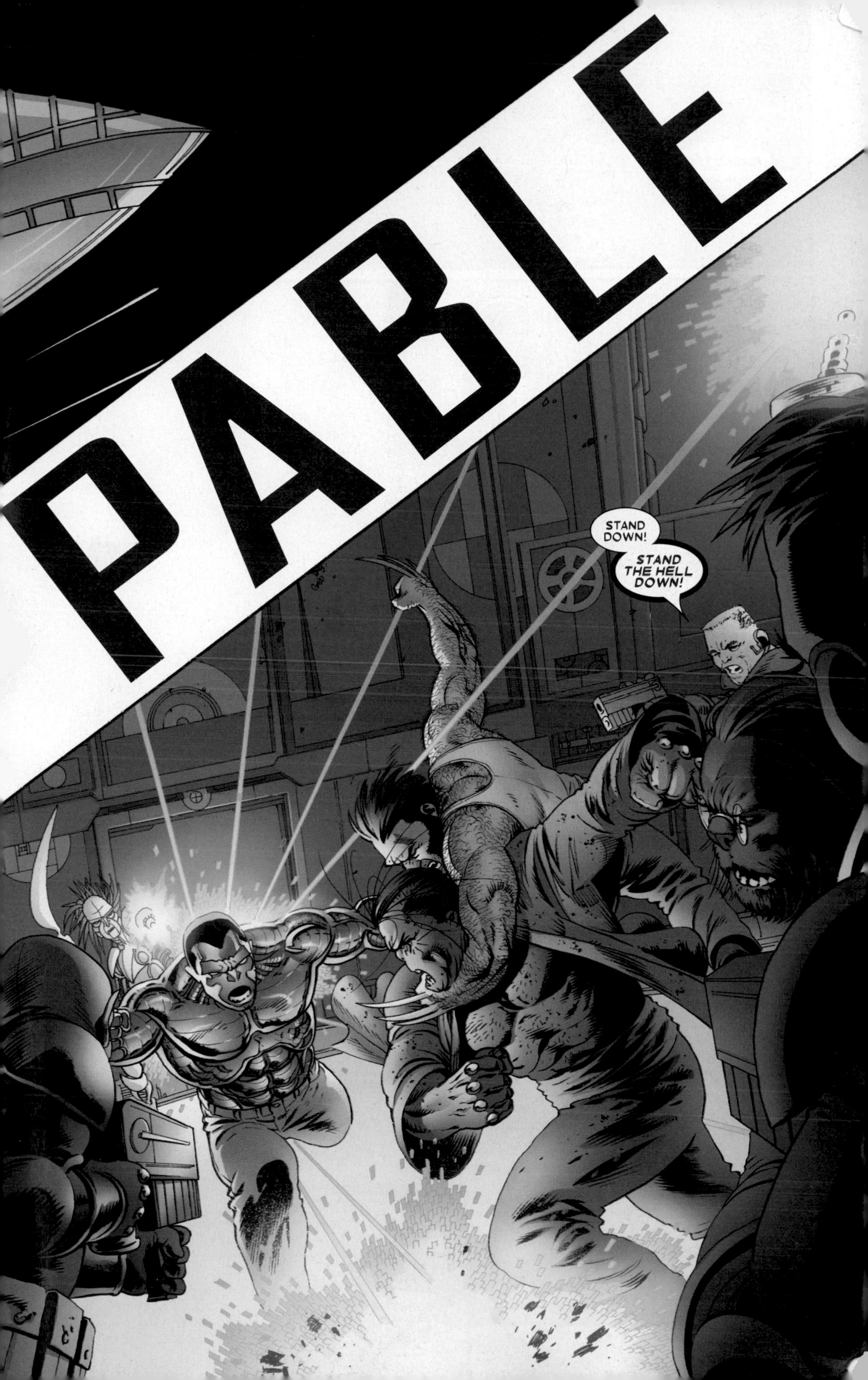
PABLE
STAND DOWN!
STAND THE HELL DOWN!

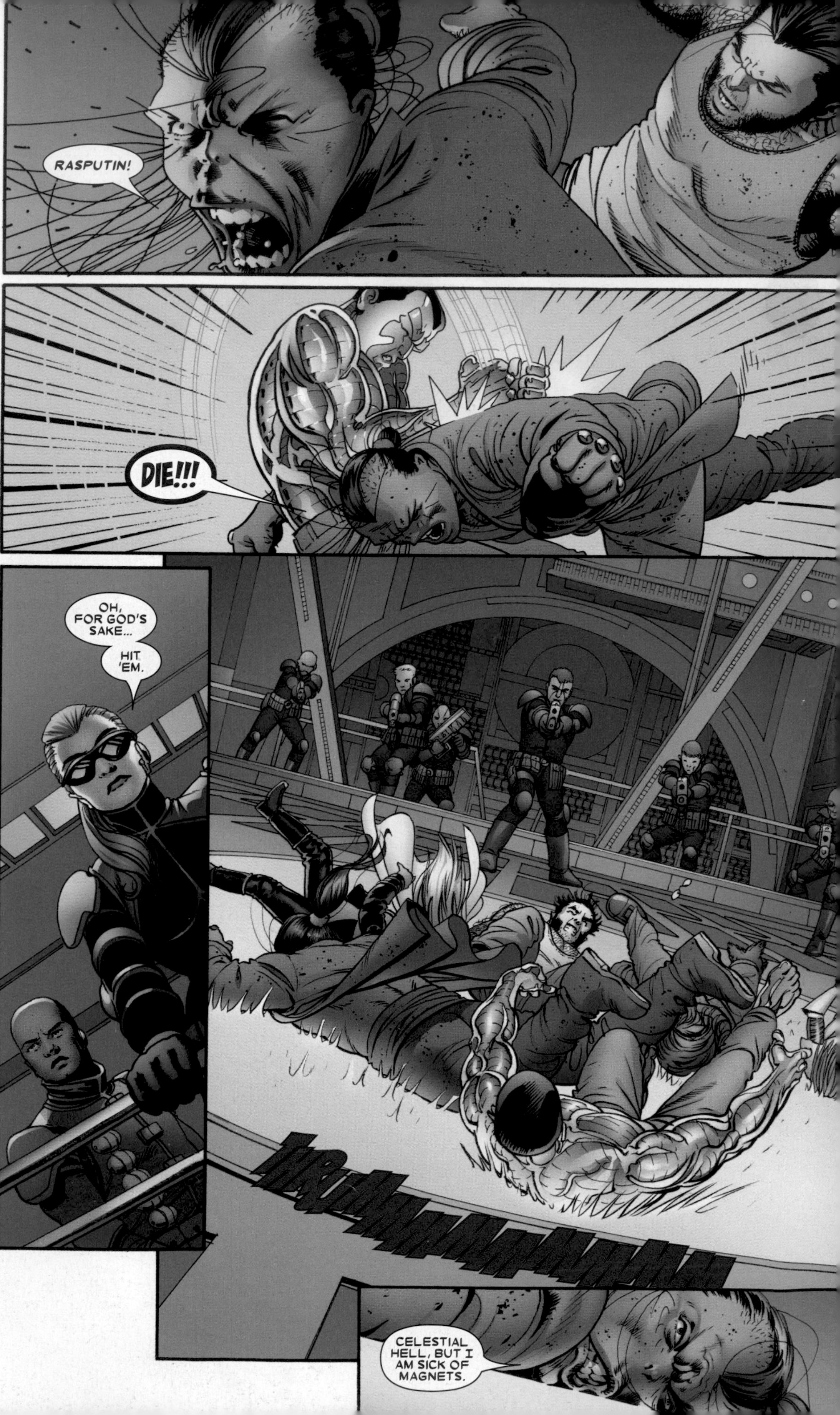
RASPUTIN!
DIE!!!
OH, FOR GOD'S SAKE...
HIT 'EM.
CELESTIAL HELL, BUT I AM SICK OF MAGNETS.

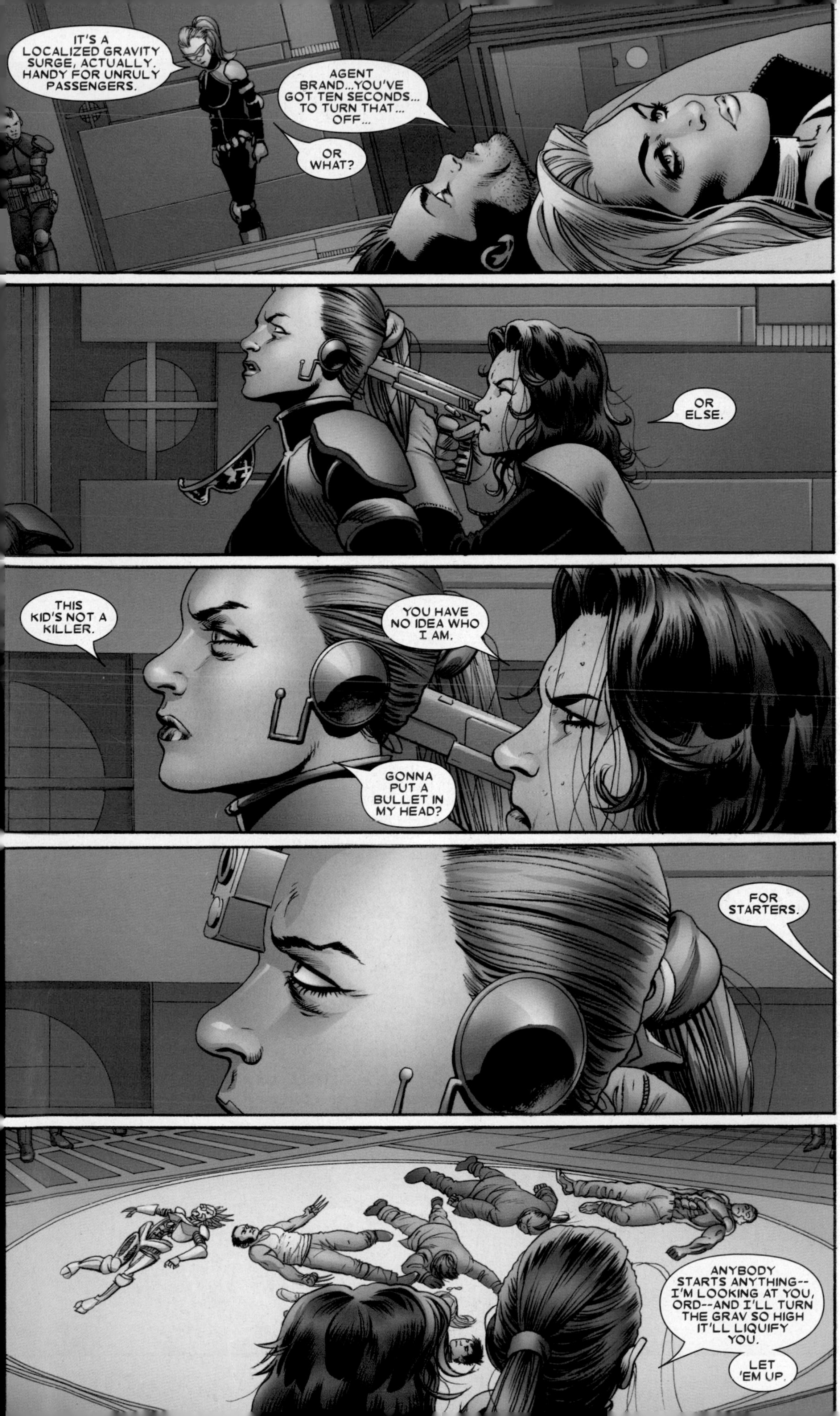
IT'S A LOCALIZED GRAVITY SURGE, ACTUALLY. HANDY FOR UNRULY PASSENGERS.
AGENT BRAND...YOU'VE GOT TEN SECONDS... TO TURN THAT... OFF...
OR WHAT?
OR ELSE.
THIS KID'S NOT A KILLER.
YOU HAVE NO IDEA WHO I AM.
GONNA PUT A BULLET IN MY HEAD?
FOR STARTERS.
ANYBODY STARTS ANYTHING-- I'M LOOKING AT YOU, ORD--AND I'LL TURN THE GRAV SO HIGH IT'LL LIQUIFY YOU.
LET 'EM UP.

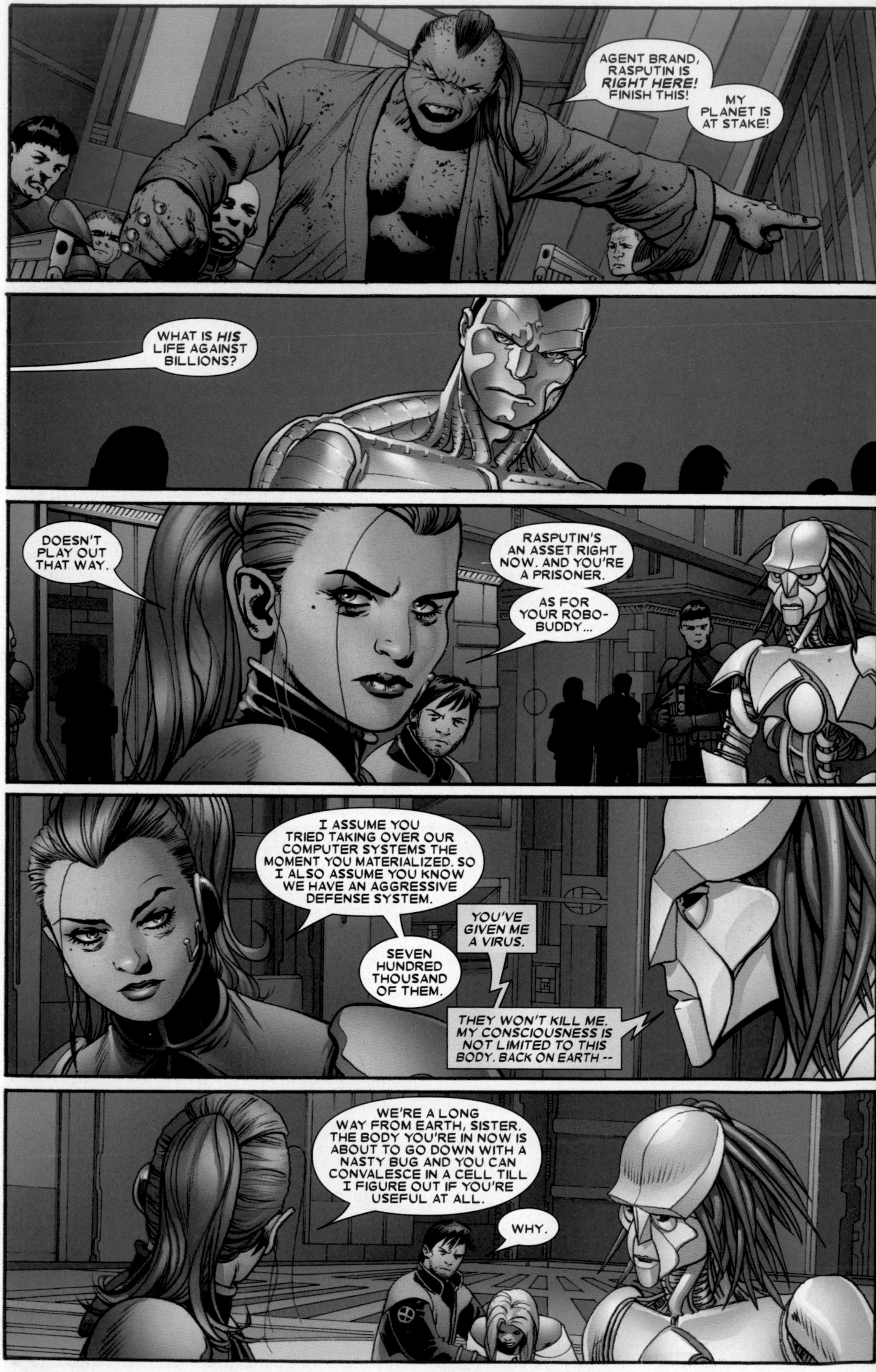
AGENT BRAND, RASPUTIN IS *RIGHT HERE!* FINISH THIS!
MY PLANET IS AT STAKE!
WHAT IS *HIS* LIFE AGAINST BILLIONS?
DOESN'T PLAY OUT THAT WAY.
RASPUTIN'S AN ASSET RIGHT NOW. AND YOU'RE A PRISONER.
AS FOR YOUR ROBO-BUDDY...
I ASSUME YOU TRIED TAKING OVER OUR COMPUTER SYSTEMS THE MOMENT YOU MATERIALIZED. SO I ALSO ASSUME YOU KNOW WE HAVE AN AGGRESSIVE DEFENSE SYSTEM.
SEVEN HUNDRED THOUSAND OF THEM.
YOU'VE GIVEN ME A VIRUS.
THEY WON'T KILL ME. MY CONSCIOUSNESS IS NOT LIMITED TO THIS BODY. BACK ON EARTH --
WE'RE A LONG WAY FROM EARTH, SISTER. THE BODY YOU'RE IN NOW IS ABOUT TO GO DOWN WITH A NASTY BUG AND YOU CAN CONVALESCE IN A CELL TILL I FIGURE OUT IF YOU'RE USEFUL AT ALL.
WHY.

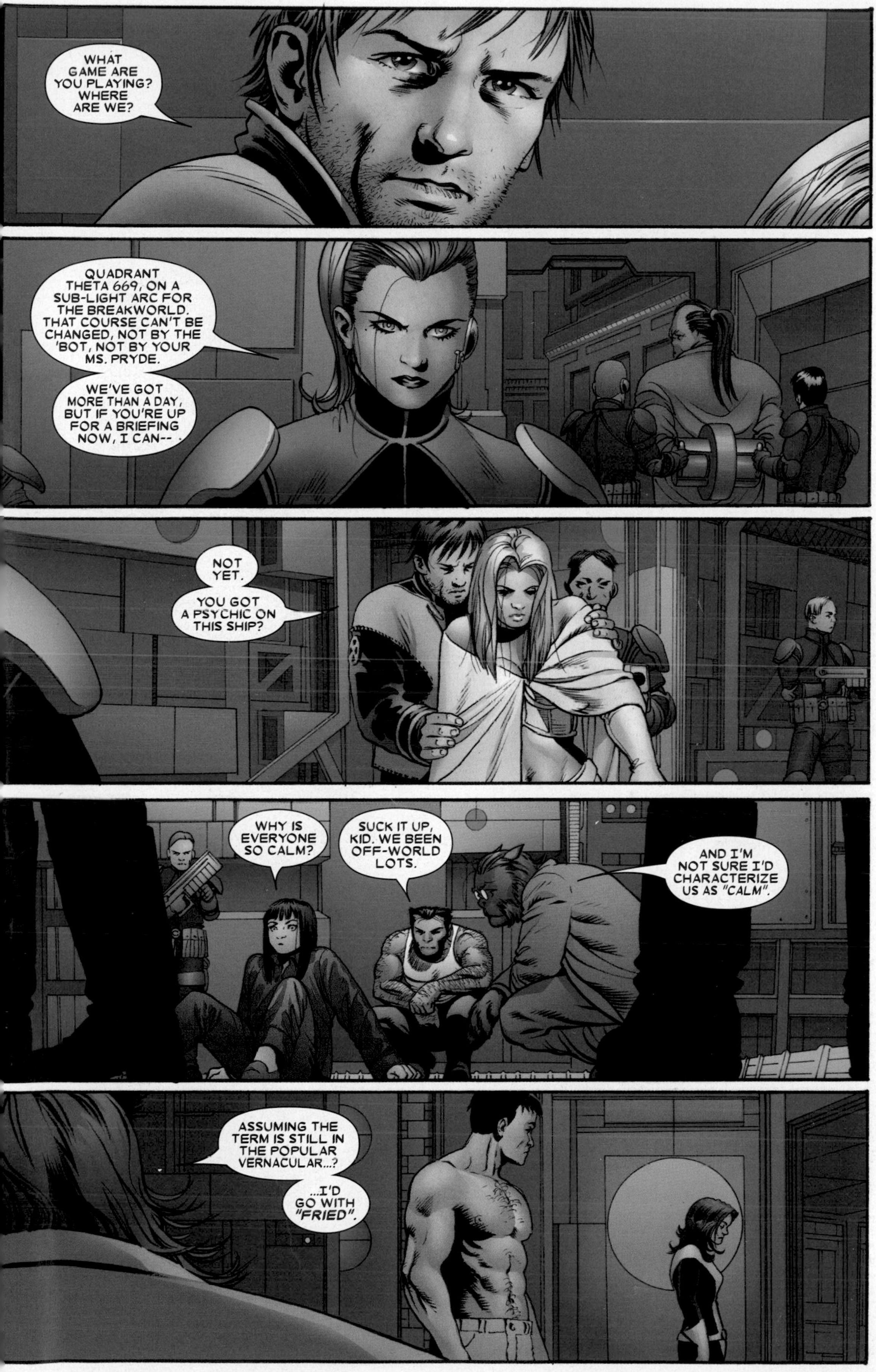
WHAT GAME ARE YOU PLAYING? WHERE ARE WE?
QUADRANT THETA 669, ON A SUB-LIGHT ARC FOR THE BREAKWORLD. THAT COURSE CAN'T BE CHANGED, NOT BY THE 'BOT, NOT BY YOUR MS. PRYDE.
WE'VE GOT MORE THAN A DAY, BUT IF YOU'RE UP FOR A BRIEFING NOW, I CAN--
NOT YET.
YOU GOT A PSYCHIC ON THIS SHIP?
WHY IS EVERYONE SO CALM?
SUCK IT UP, KID. WE BEEN OFF-WORLD LOTS.
AND I'M NOT SURE I'D CHARACTERIZE US AS "CALM".
ASSUMING THE TERM IS STILL IN THE POPULAR VERNACULAR...?
...I'D GO WITH "FRIED".

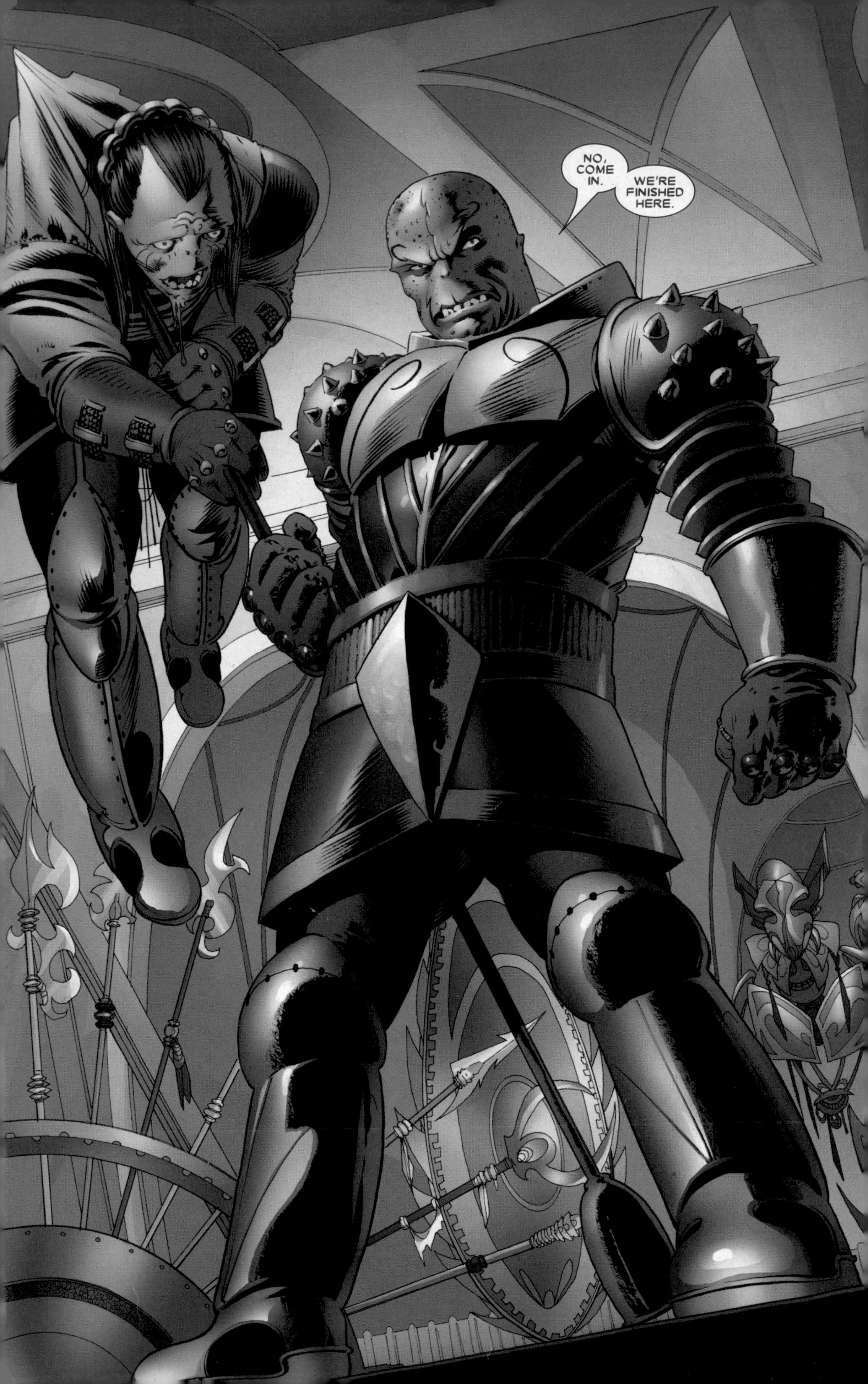
NO, COME IN.
WE'RE FINISHED HERE.

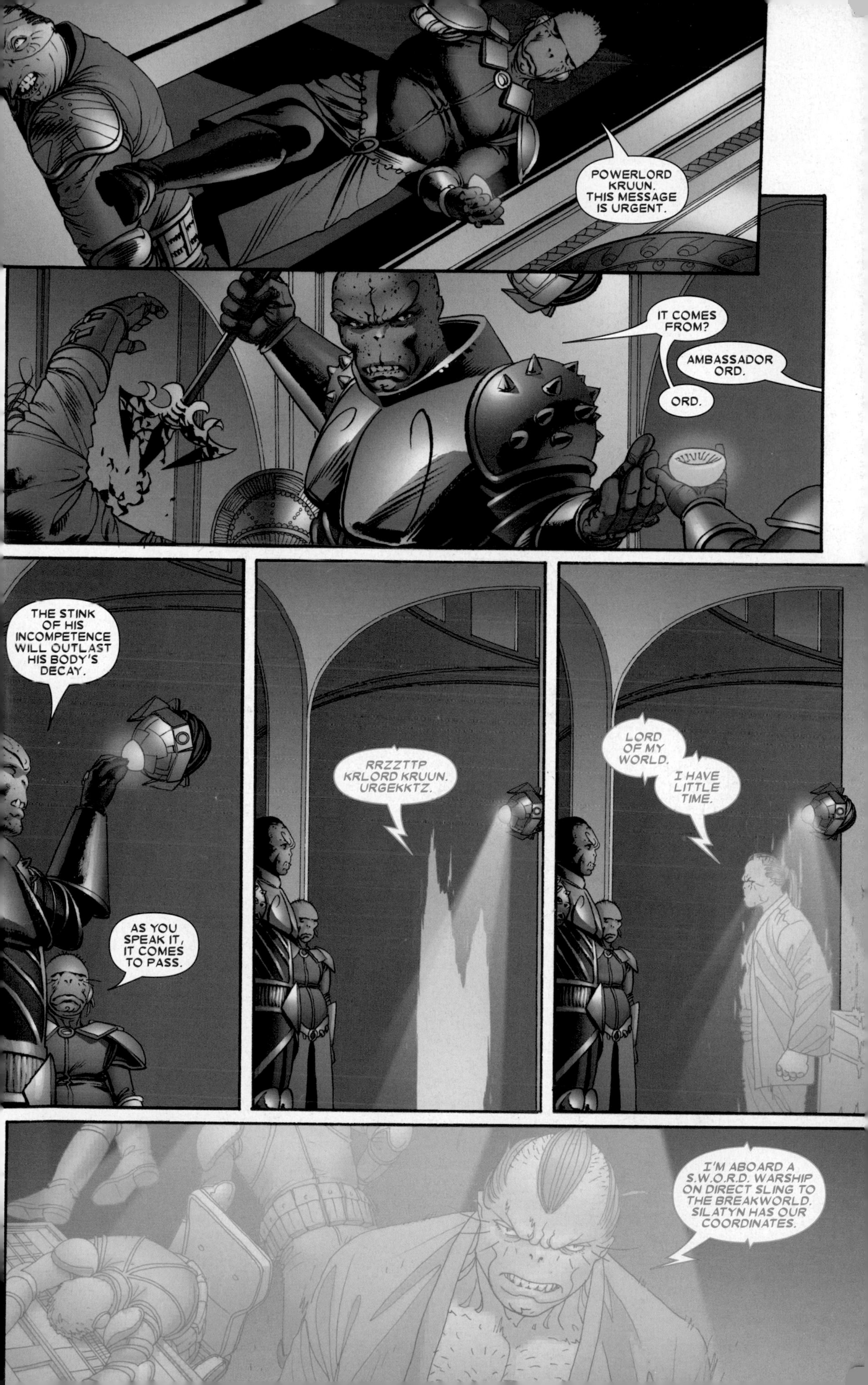
POWERLORD KRUUN. THIS MESSAGE IS URGENT.
IT COMES FROM?
AMBASSADOR ORD.
ORD.
THE STINK OF HIS INCOMPETENCE WILL OUTLAST HIS BODY'S DECAY.
AS YOU SPEAK IT, IT COMES TO PASS.
RRZZTTP KRLORD KRUUN. URGEKKTZ.
LORD OF MY WORLD.
I HAVE LITTLE TIME.
I'M ABOARD A S.W.O.R.D. WARSHIP ON DIRECT SLING TO THE BREAKWORLD. SILATYN HAS OUR COORDINATES.

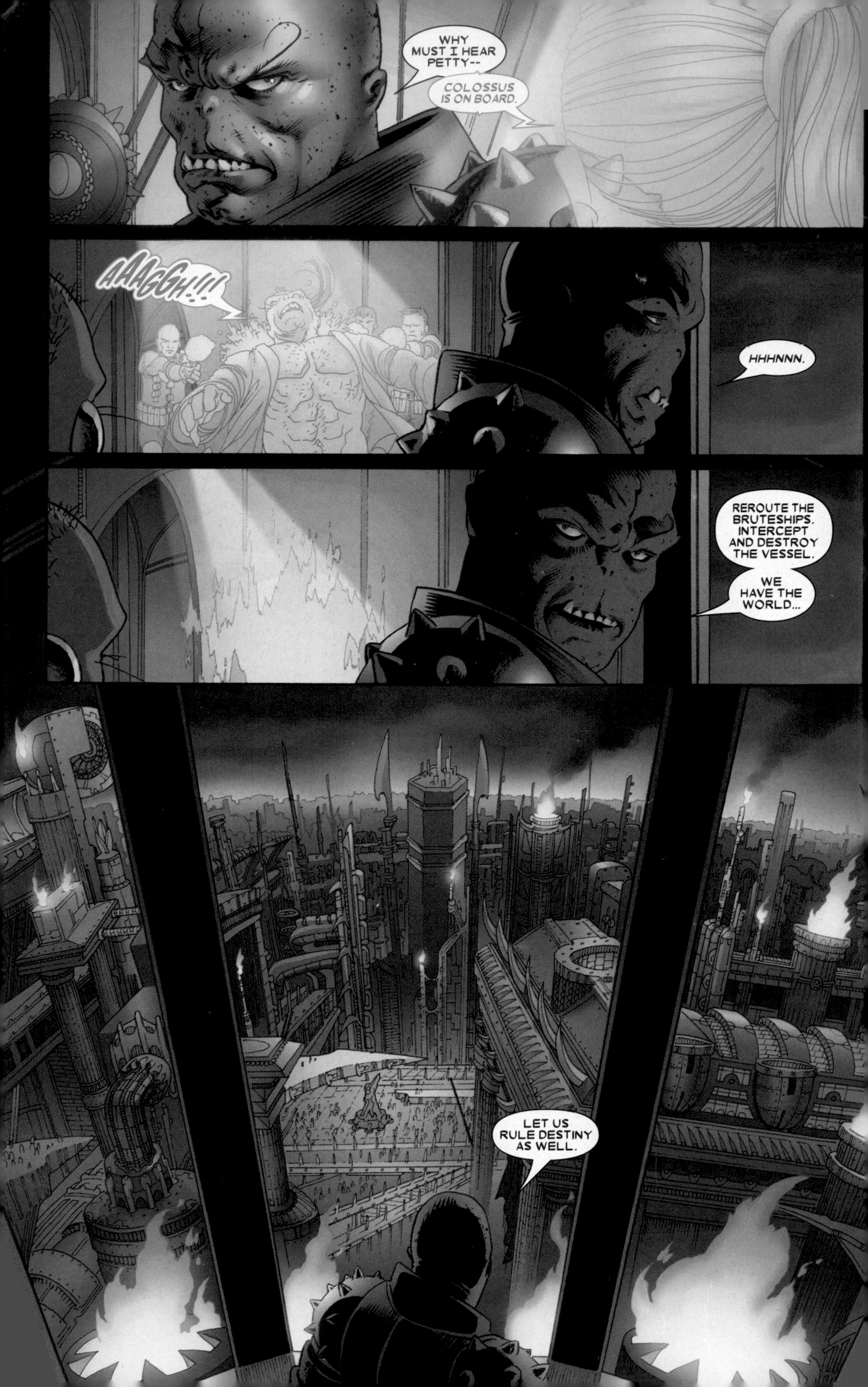
WHY MUST I HEAR PETTY--
COLOSSUS IS ON BOARD.
AAAGGH!!!
HHHNNN.
REROUTE THE BRUTESHIPS. INTERCEPT AND DESTROY THE VESSEL.
WE HAVE THE WORLD...
LET US RULE DESTINY AS WELL.

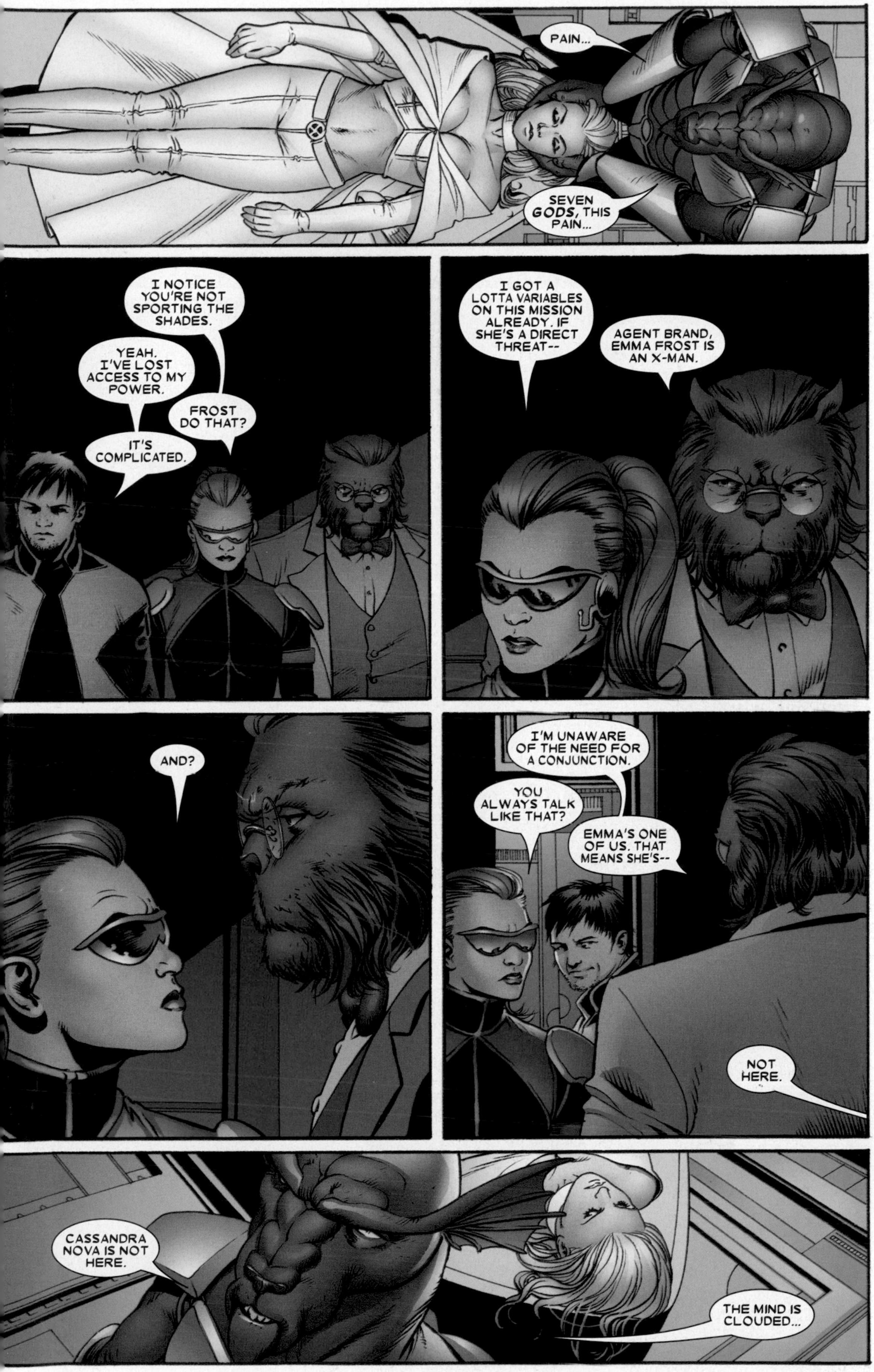
PAIN...
SEVEN GODS, THIS PAIN...
I NOTICE YOU'RE NOT SPORTING THE SHADES.
YEAH. I'VE LOST ACCESS TO MY POWER.
FROST DO THAT?
IT'S COMPLICATED.
I GOT A LOTTA VARIABLES ON THIS MISSION ALREADY. IF SHE'S A DIRECT THREAT--
AGENT BRAND, EMMA FROST IS AN X-MAN.
AND?
I'M UNAWARE OF THE NEED FOR A CONJUNCTION.
YOU ALWAYS TALK LIKE THAT?
EMMA'S ONE OF US. THAT MEANS SHE'S--
NOT HERE.
CASSANDRA NOVA IS NOT HERE.
THE MIND IS CLOUDED...

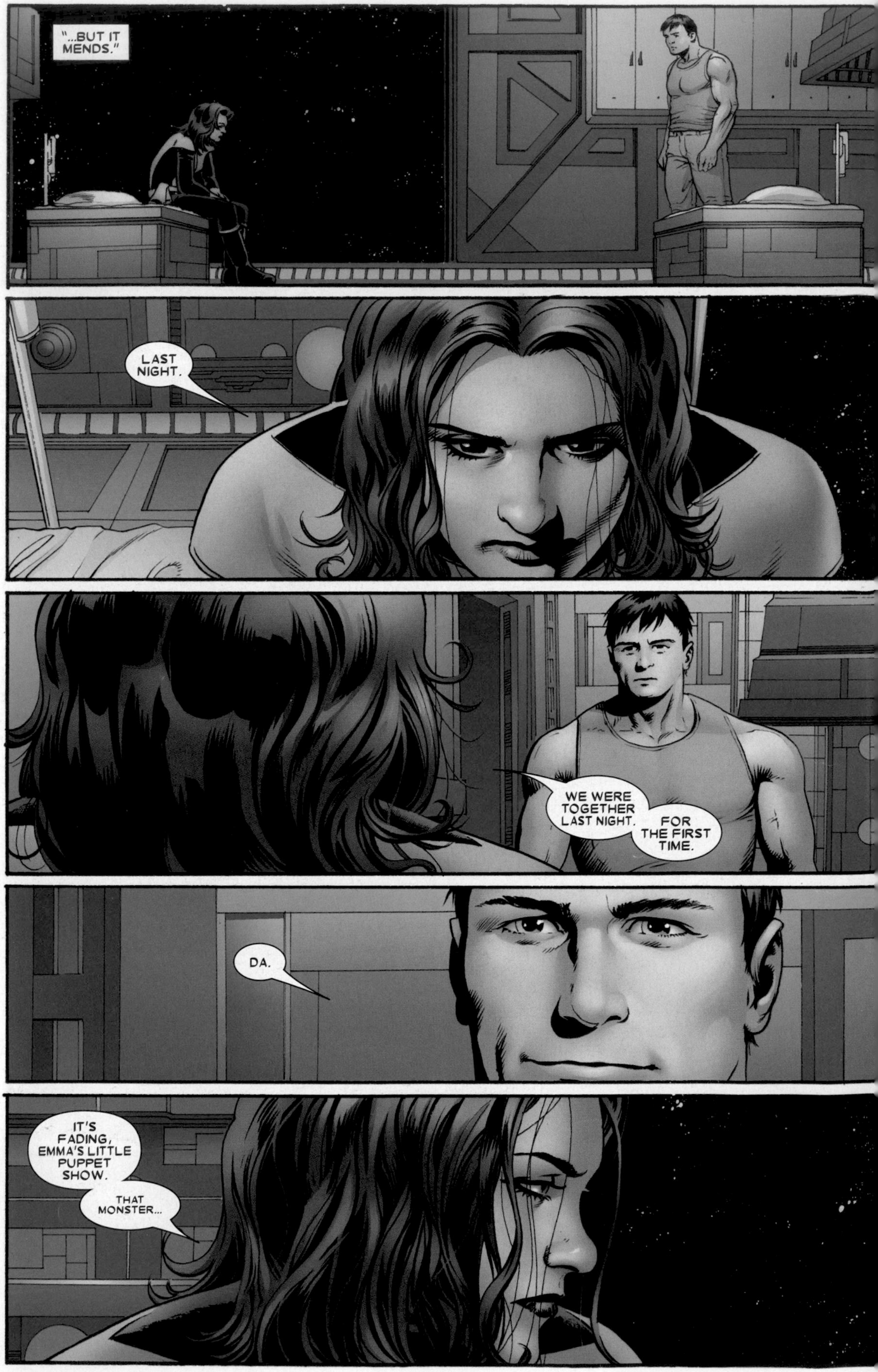
"...BUT IT MENDS."
LAST NIGHT.
WE WERE TOGETHER LAST NIGHT.
FOR THE FIRST TIME.
DA.
IT'S FADING, EMMA'S LITTLE PUPPET SHOW.
THAT MONSTER...

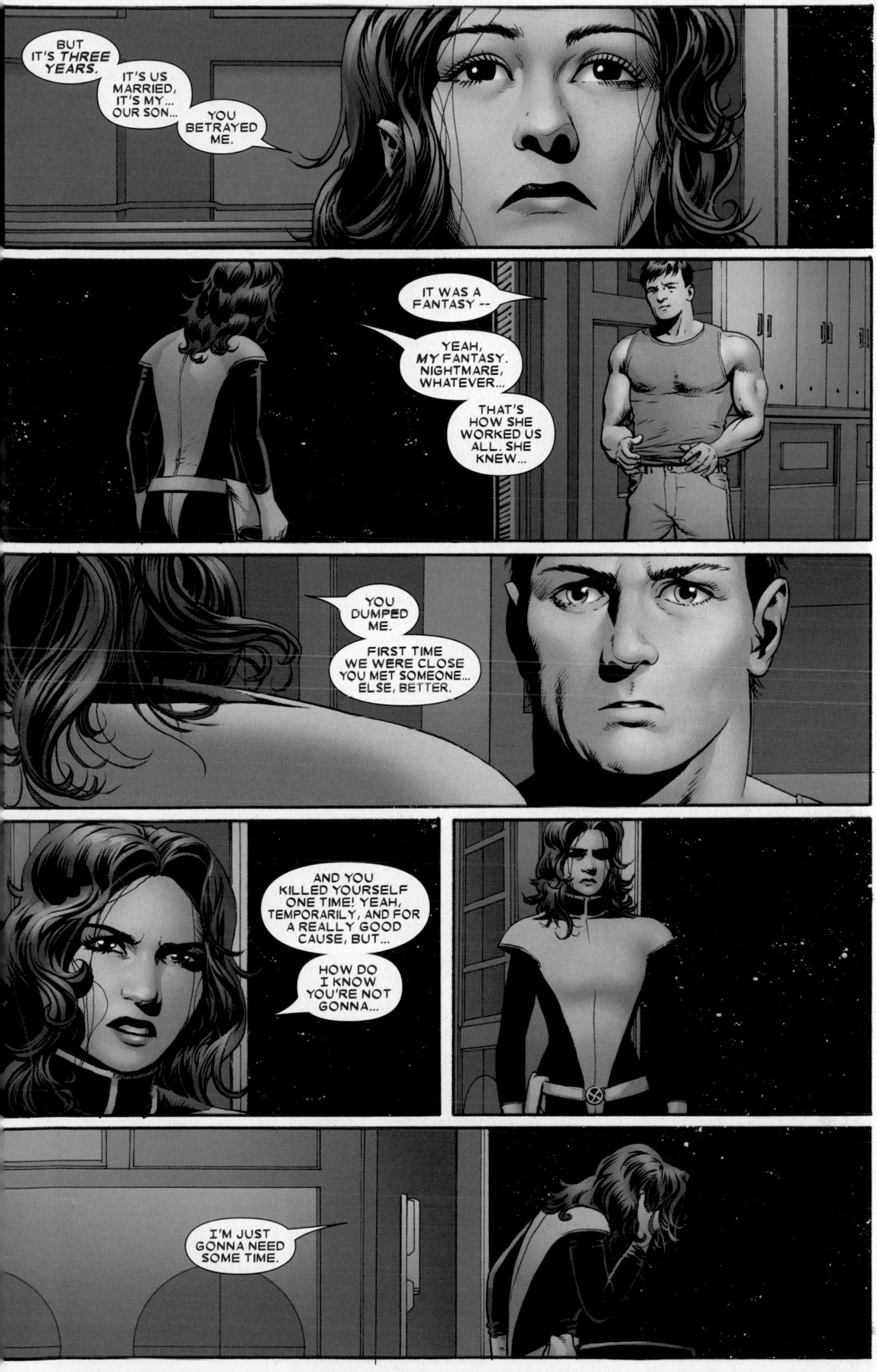
BUT IT'S THREE YEARS.
IT'S US MARRIED, IT'S MY... OUR SON...
YOU BETRAYED ME.
IT WAS A FANTASY --
YEAH, MY FANTASY. NIGHTMARE, WHATEVER...
THAT'S HOW SHE WORKED US ALL. SHE KNEW...
YOU DUMPED ME.
FIRST TIME WE WERE CLOSE YOU MET SOMEONE... ELSE, BETTER.
AND YOU KILLED YOURSELF ONE TIME! YEAH, TEMPORARILY, AND FOR A REALLY GOOD CAUSE, BUT...
HOW DO I KNOW YOU'RE NOT GONNA...
I'M JUST GONNA NEED SOME TIME.

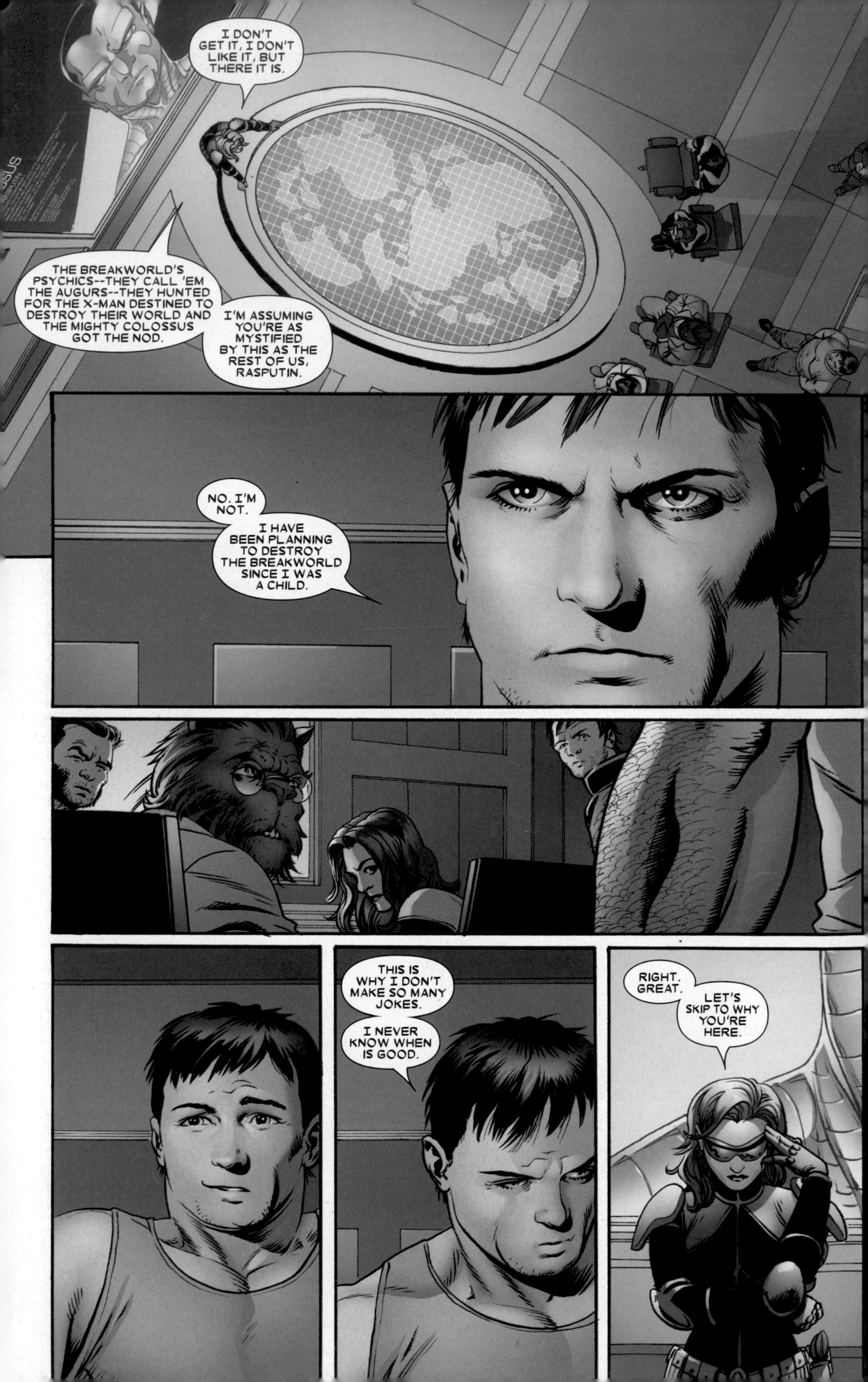

I DON'T GET IT, I DON'T LIKE IT, BUT THERE IT IS.
THE BREAKWORLD'S PSYCHICS--THEY CALL 'EM THE AUGURS--THEY HUNTED FOR THE X-MAN DESTINED TO DESTROY THEIR WORLD AND THE MIGHTY COLOSSUS GOT THE NOD.
I'M ASSUMING YOU'RE AS MYSTIFIED BY THIS AS THE REST OF US, RASPUTIN.
NO. I'M NOT.
I HAVE BEEN PLANNING TO DESTROY THE BREAKWORLD SINCE I WAS A CHILD.
THIS IS WHY I DON'T MAKE SO MANY JOKES.
I NEVER KNOW WHEN IS GOOD.
RIGHT. GREAT.
LET'S SKIP TO WHY YOU'RE HERE.

YOU KIDNAPPED US.

WE'RE NOT PAST THAT YET?

IT WAS FOUR HOURS AGO.

THE MOMENT THE AUGURS PINPOINTED RASPUTIN, AN ARMADA WAS SENT TOWARDS EARTH.

ON THE WAY TO HIS CELL, ORD BROKE FREE AND CONTACTED THE BREAKWORLD.

THAT ARMADA IS NOW HEADED TOWARDS US.

JUST LIKE YOU PLANNED.

JUST LIKE I PLANNED.

I WONDERED WHY YOU WERE SO SPECIFIC ABOUT OUR COORDINATES IN FRONT OF THE GUY.

I NEEDED TO DRAW THEM AWAY FROM EARTH. NOW THE BEST WAY TO KEEP THEM FROM BLOWING THIS SHIP INTO FRAGMENTS IS TO GET TO THE BREAKWORLD BEFORE THEY CAN.

AT CURRENT SPEED, WE SHOULD JUST MAKE IT.

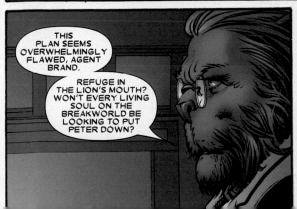

THIS PLAN SEEMS OVERWHELMINGLY FLAWED, AGENT BRAND.

REFUGE IN THE LION'S MOUTH? WON'T EVERY LIVING SOUL ON THE BREAKWORLD BE LOOKING TO PUT PETER DOWN?

YOU THINK I HAVEN'T THOUGHT OF THAT, COOKIE MONSTER?

WHEN ARE YOU GUYS GONNA FIGURE OUT THAT THIS IS BIGGER THAN ALL OF YOU?

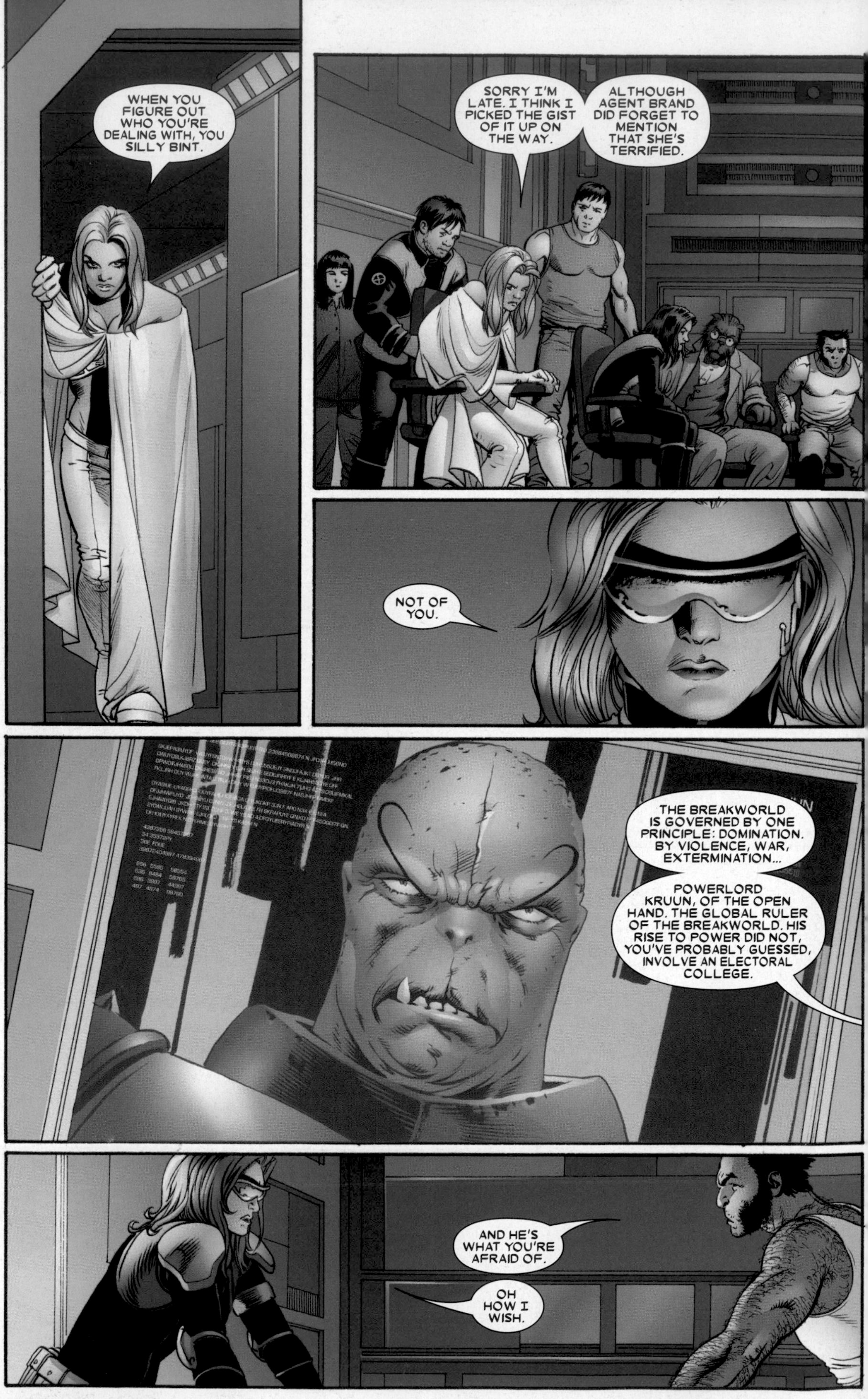
WHEN YOU FIGURE OUT WHO YOU'RE DEALING WITH, YOU SILLY BINT.
SORRY I'M LATE. I THINK I PICKED THE GIST OF IT UP ON THE WAY.
ALTHOUGH AGENT BRAND DID FORGET TO MENTION THAT SHE'S TERRIFIED.
NOT OF YOU.
THE BREAKWORLD IS GOVERNED BY ONE PRINCIPLE: DOMINATION. BY VIOLENCE, WAR, EXTERMINATION...
POWERLORD KRUUN, OF THE OPEN HAND. THE GLOBAL RULER OF THE BREAKWORLD. HIS RISE TO POWER DID NOT, YOU'VE PROBABLY GUESSED, INVOLVE AN ELECTORAL COLLEGE.
AND HE'S WHAT YOU'RE AFRAID OF.
OH HOW I WISH.

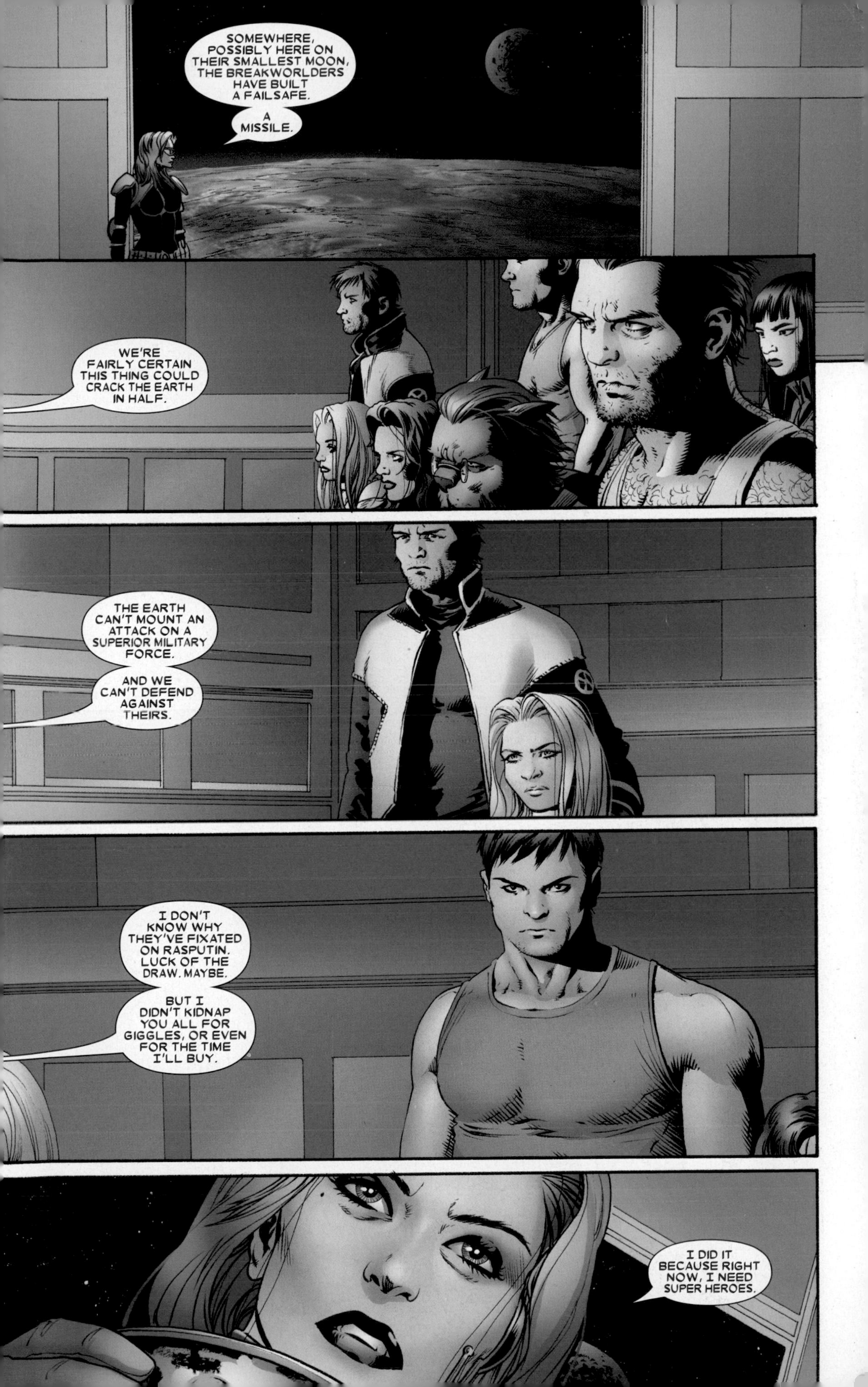
SOMEWHERE, POSSIBLY HERE ON THEIR SMALLEST MOON, THE BREAKWORLDERS HAVE BUILT A FAILSAFE.
A MISSILE.
WE'RE FAIRLY CERTAIN THIS THING COULD CRACK THE EARTH IN HALF.
THE EARTH CAN'T MOUNT AN ATTACK ON A SUPERIOR MILITARY FORCE.
AND WE CAN'T DEFEND AGAINST THEIRS.
I DON'T KNOW WHY THEY'VE FIXATED ON RASPUTIN. LUCK OF THE DRAW, MAYBE.
BUT I DIDN'T KIDNAP YOU ALL FOR GIGGLES, OR EVEN FOR THE TIME I'LL BUY.
I DID IT BECAUSE RIGHT NOW, I NEED SUPER HEROES.

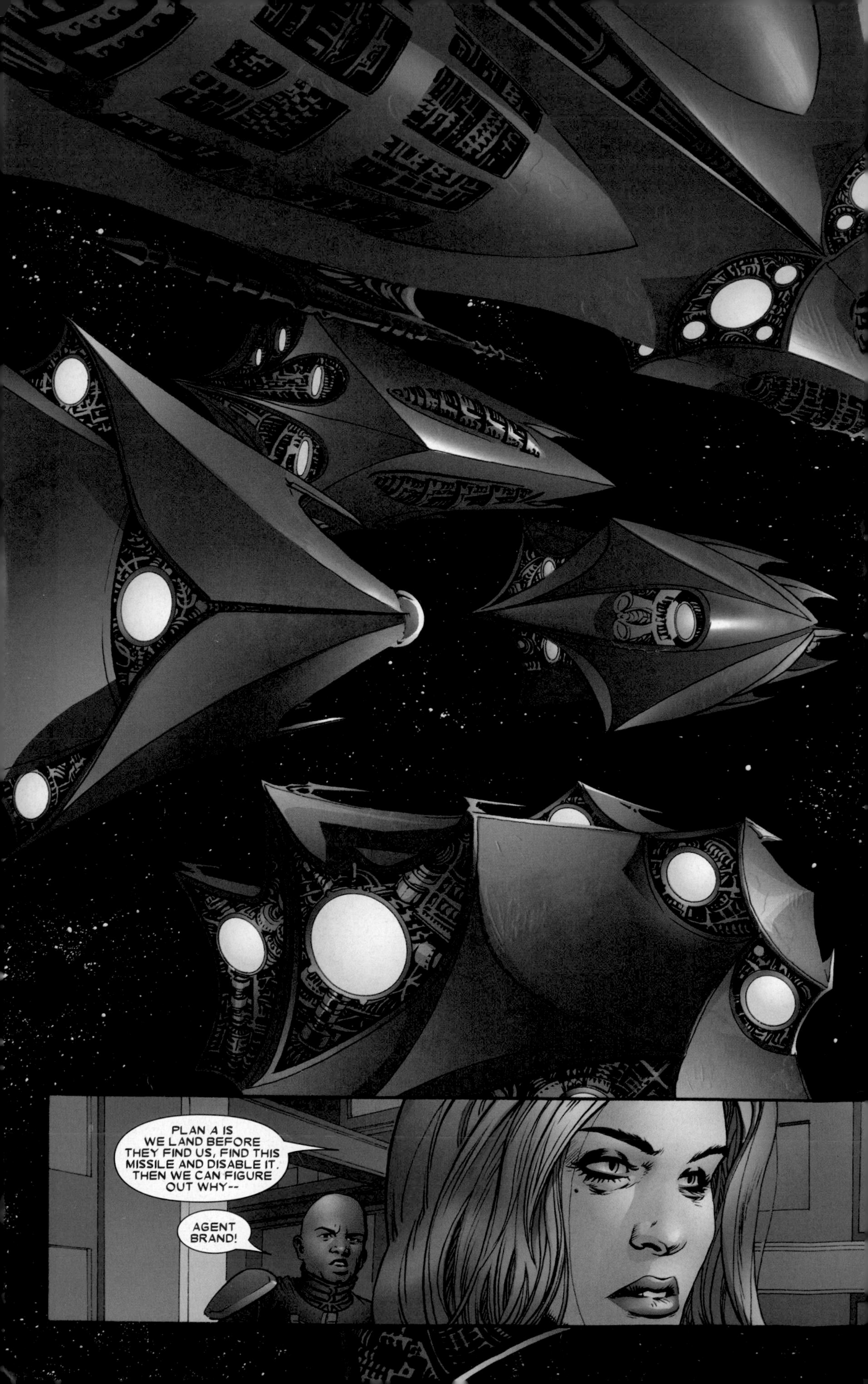
PLAN A IS WE LAND BEFORE THEY FIND US, FIND THIS MISSILE AND DISABLE IT. THEN WE CAN FIGURE OUT WHY--
AGENT BRAND!

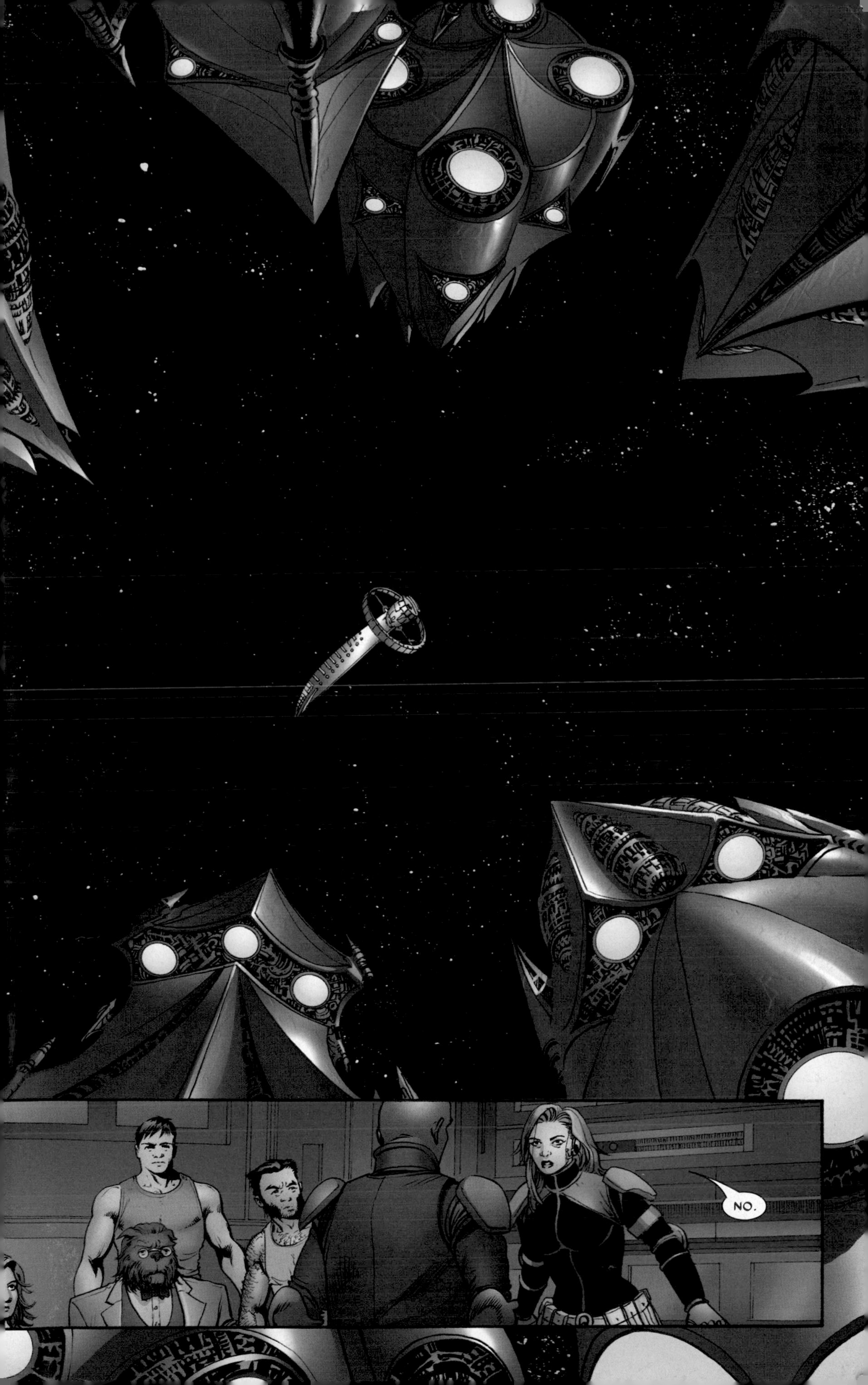
NO.

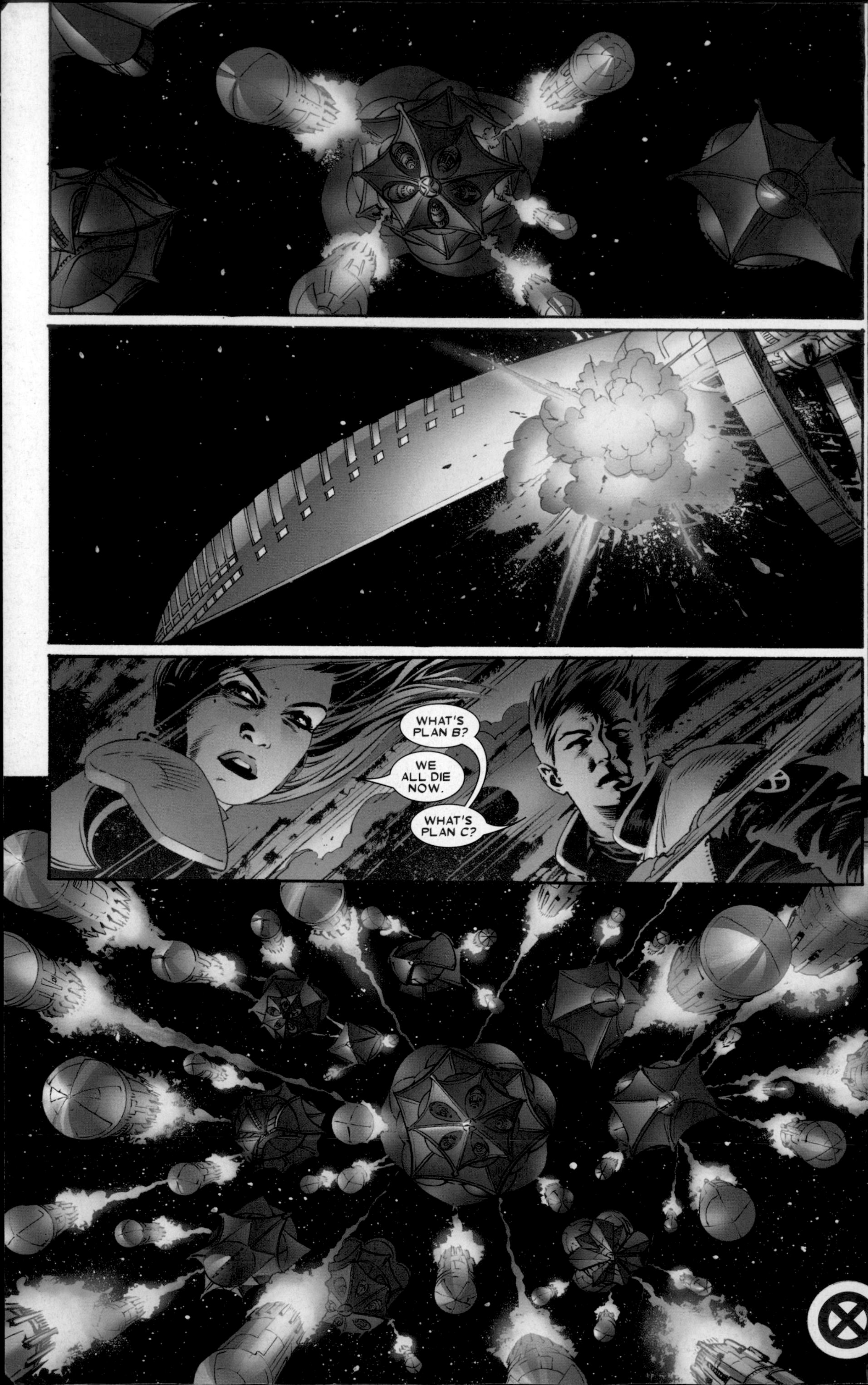
WHAT'S PLAN B?
WE ALL DIE NOW.
WHAT'S PLAN C?

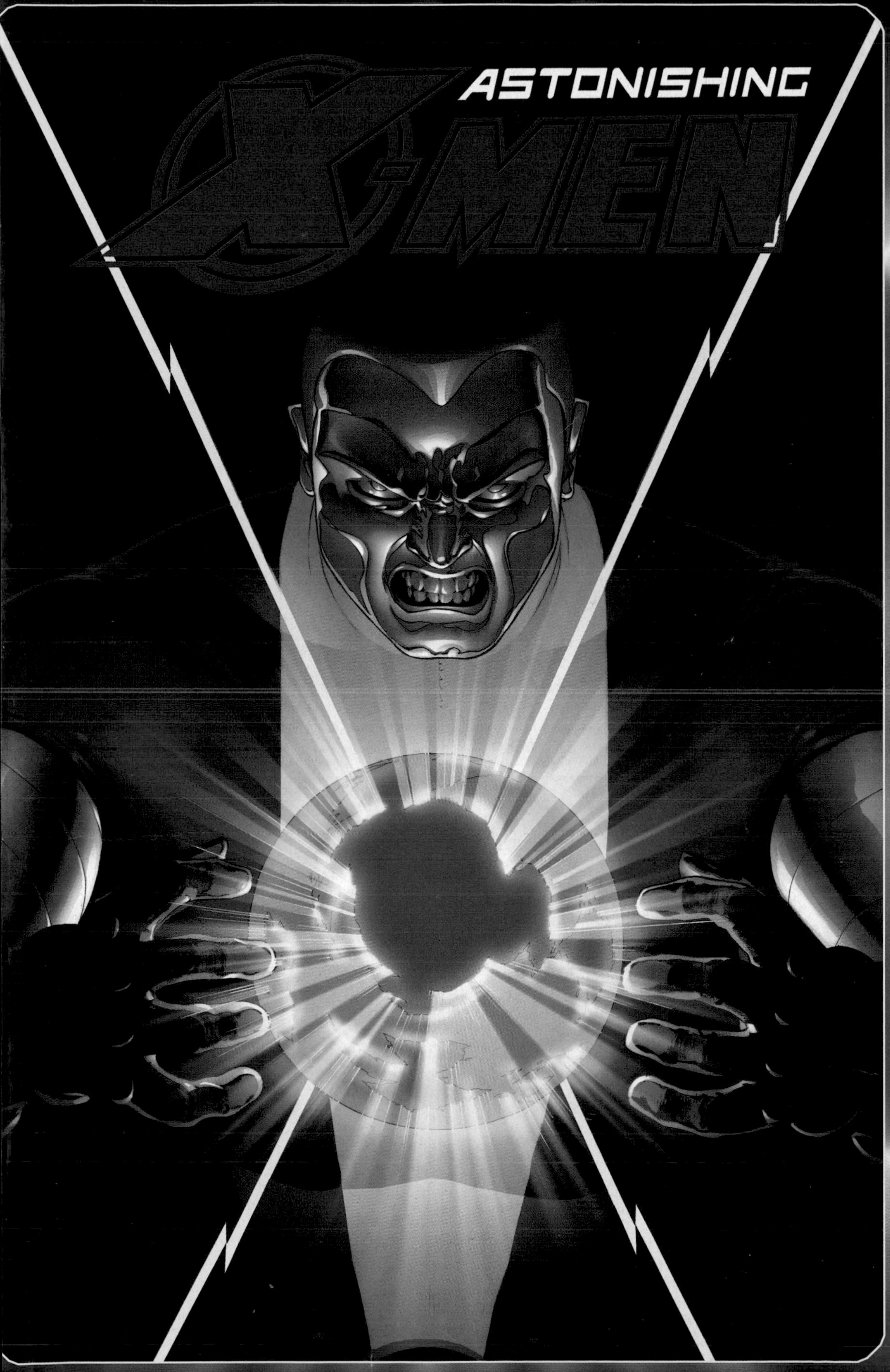
ASTONISHING
X-MEN

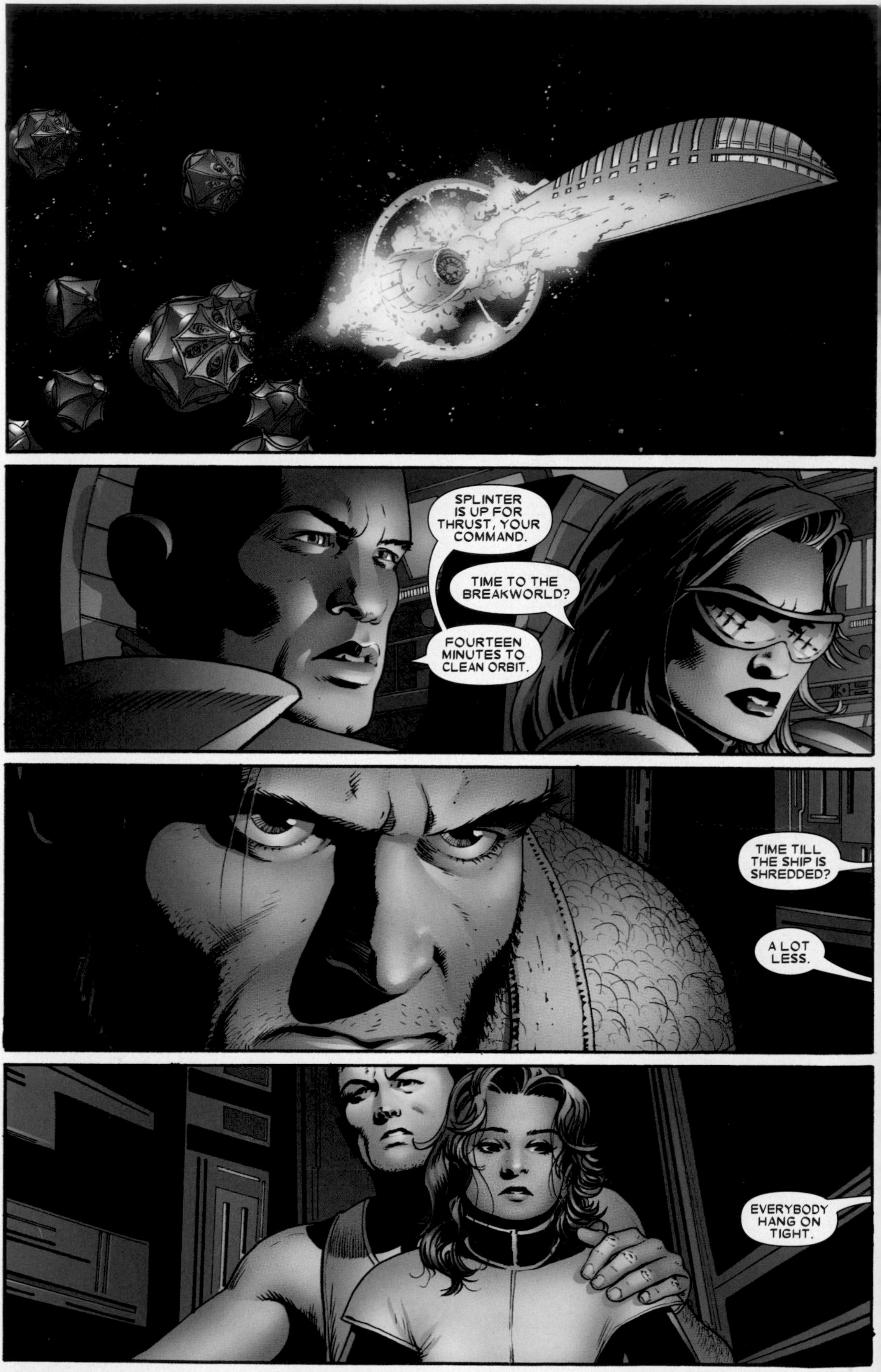
SPLINTER IS UP FOR THRUST, YOUR COMMAND.
TIME TO THE BREAKWORLD?
FOURTEEN MINUTES TO CLEAN ORBIT.
TIME TILL THE SHIP IS SHREDDED?
A LOT LESS.
EVERYBODY HANG ON TIGHT.

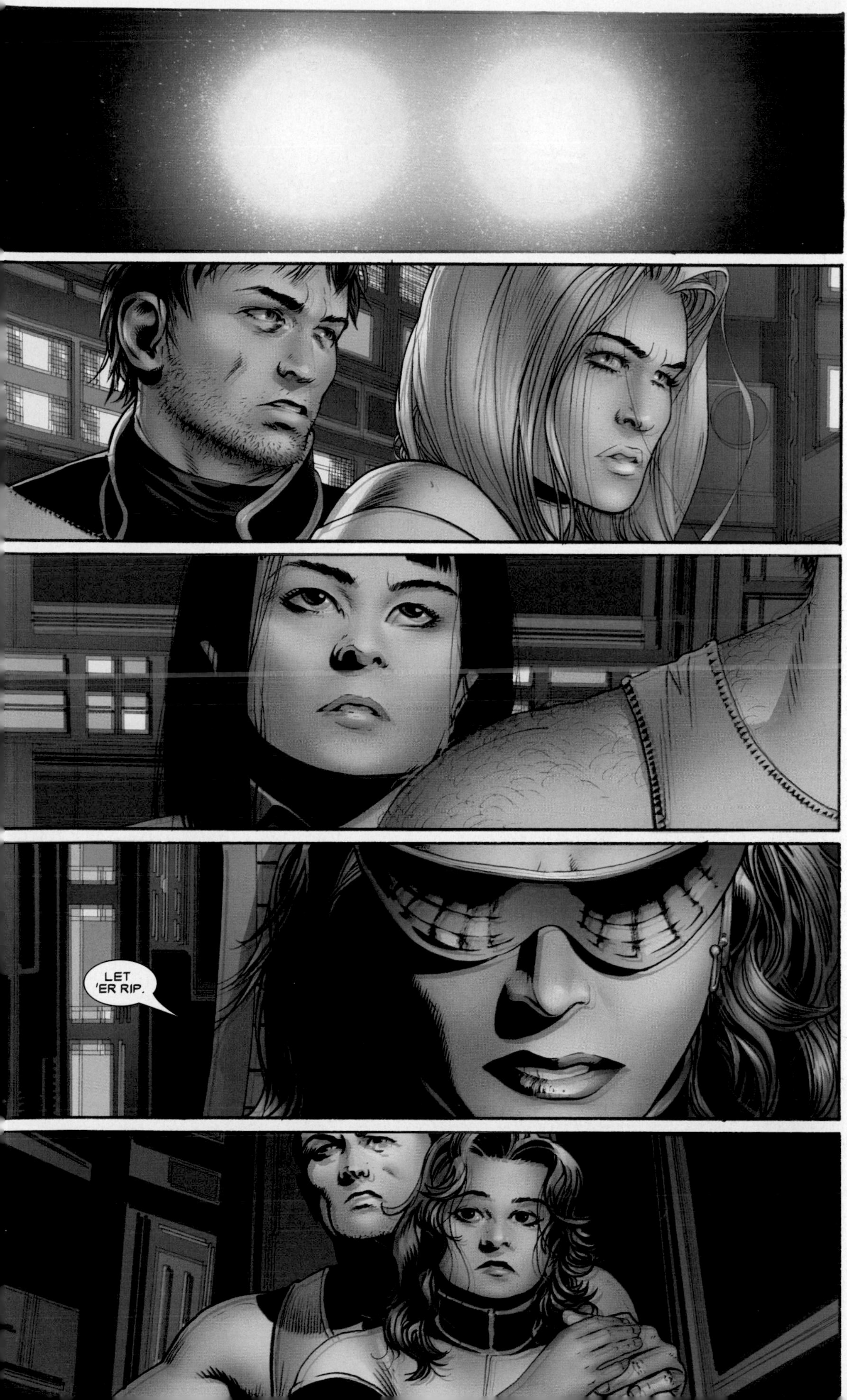
LET 'ER RIP.

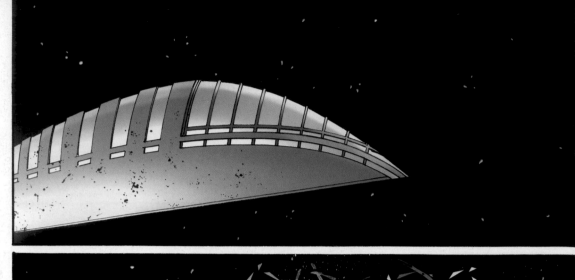

"UNBREACHABLE HULL, PRECISE MANEUVERABILITY, ENOUGH POWER AT SHORT-RANGE TO OUTRUN ANYONE."

PRETTIEST SHIP IN THE FLEET.

NOT TO BE PICKY, AGENT BRAND, BUT IF THIS SPLINTER IS SUCH A WONDERFUL SHIP...

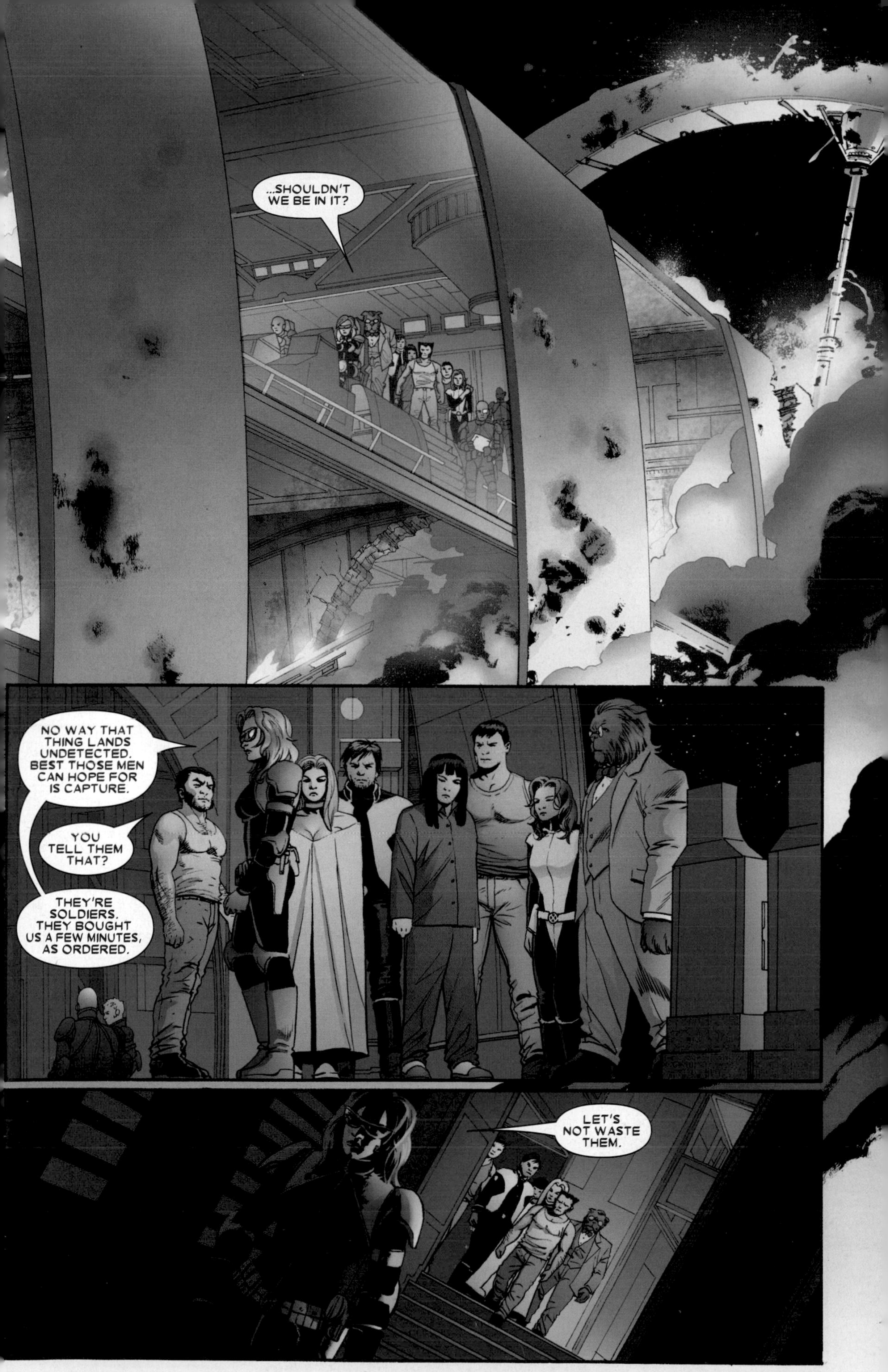
...SHOULDN'T WE BE IN IT?
NO WAY THAT THING LANDS UNDETECTED. BEST THOSE MEN CAN HOPE FOR IS CAPTURE.
YOU TELL THEM THAT?
THEY'RE SOLDIERS. THEY BOUGHT US A FEW MINUTES, AS ORDERED.
LET'S NOT WASTE THEM.

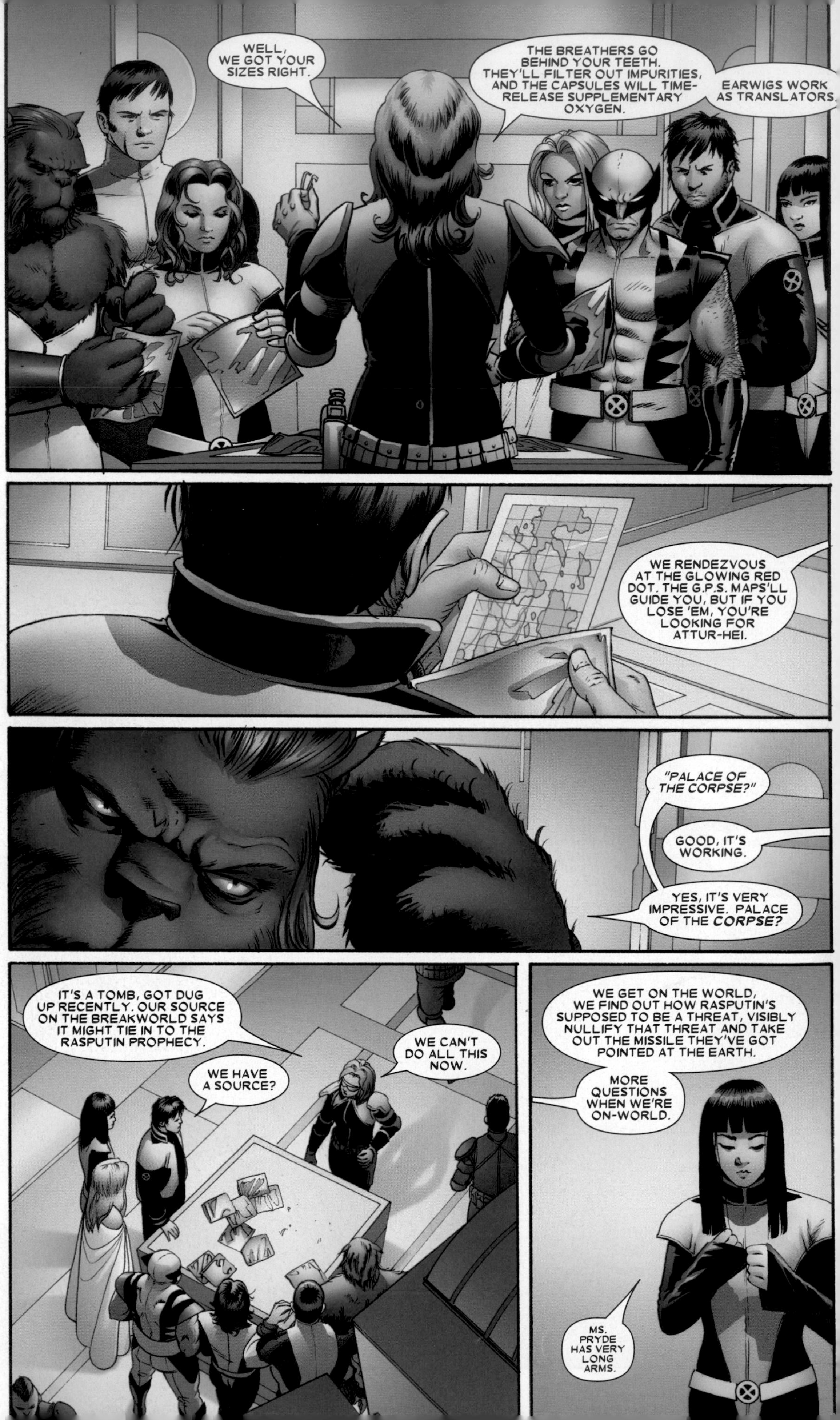
WELL, WE GOT YOUR SIZES RIGHT.
THE BREATHERS GO BEHIND YOUR TEETH. THEY'LL FILTER OUT IMPURITIES, AND THE CAPSULES WILL TIME-RELEASE SUPPLEMENTARY OXYGEN.
EARWIGS WORK AS TRANSLATORS.
WE RENDEZVOUS AT THE GLOWING RED DOT. THE G.P.S. MAPS'LL GUIDE YOU, BUT IF YOU LOSE 'EM, YOU'RE LOOKING FOR ATTUR-HEI.
"PALACE OF THE CORPSE?"
GOOD, IT'S WORKING.
YES, IT'S VERY IMPRESSIVE. PALACE OF THE *CORPSE?*
IT'S A TOMB, GOT DUG UP RECENTLY. OUR SOURCE ON THE BREAKWORLD SAYS IT MIGHT TIE IN TO THE RASPUTIN PROPHECY.
WE HAVE A SOURCE?
WE CAN'T DO ALL THIS NOW.
WE GET ON THE WORLD, WE FIND OUT HOW RASPUTIN'S SUPPOSED TO BE A THREAT, VISIBLY NULLIFY THAT THREAT AND TAKE OUT THE MISSILE THEY'VE GOT POINTED AT THE EARTH.
MORE QUESTIONS WHEN WE'RE ON-WORLD.
MS. PRYDE HAS VERY LONG ARMS.

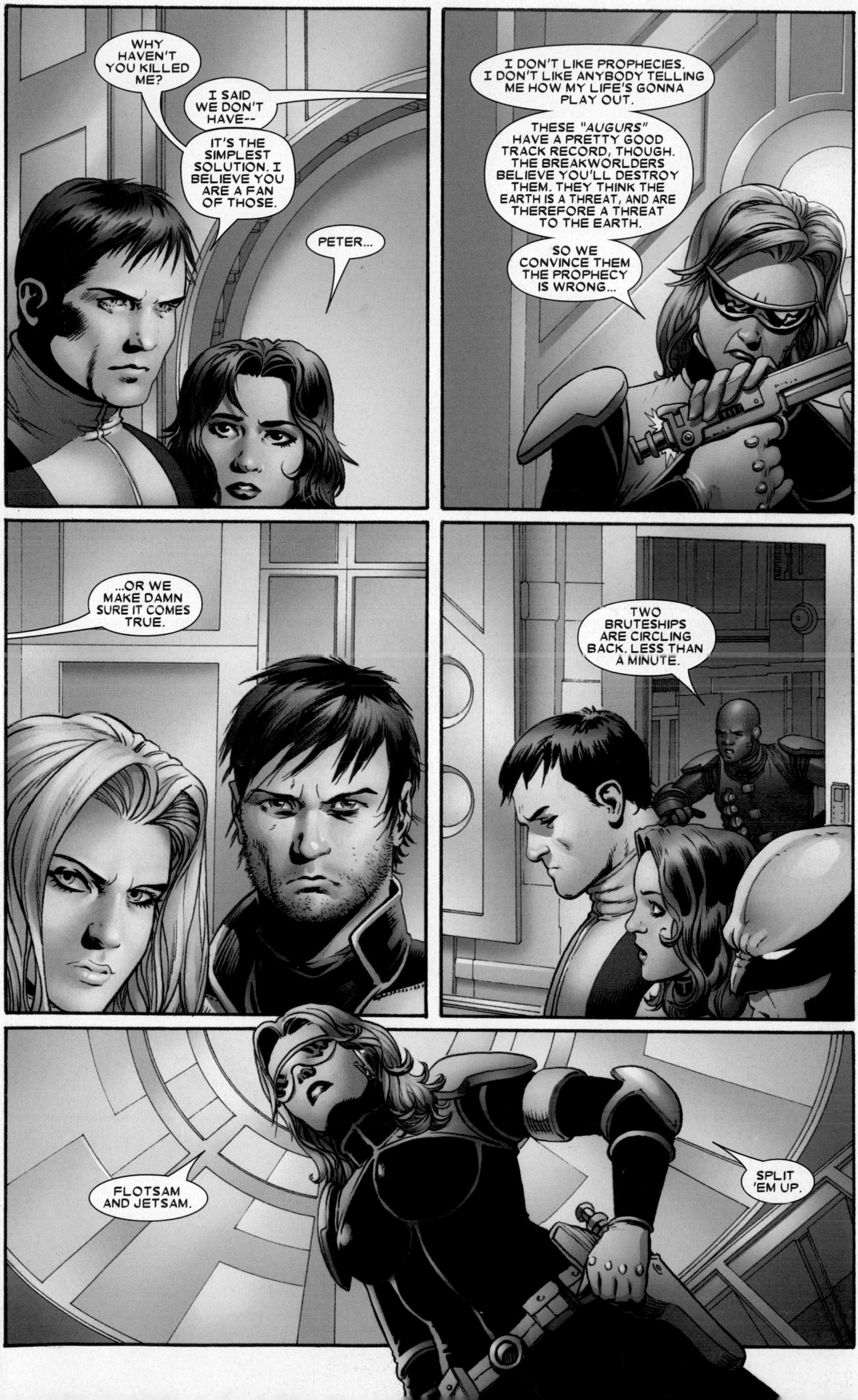
WHY HAVEN'T YOU KILLED ME?
I SAID WE DON'T HAVE--
IT'S THE SIMPLEST SOLUTION. I BELIEVE YOU ARE A FAN OF THOSE.
PETER...
I DON'T LIKE PROPHECIES. I DON'T LIKE ANYBODY TELLING ME HOW MY LIFE'S GONNA PLAY OUT.
THESE "AUGURS" HAVE A PRETTY GOOD TRACK RECORD, THOUGH. THE BREAKWORLDERS BELIEVE YOU'LL DESTROY THEM. THEY THINK THE EARTH IS A THREAT, AND ARE THEREFORE A THREAT TO THE EARTH.
SO WE CONVINCE THEM THE PROPHECY IS WRONG...
...OR WE MAKE DAMN SURE IT COMES TRUE.
TWO BRUTESHIPS ARE CIRCLING BACK. LESS THAN A MINUTE.
FLOTSAM AND JETSAM.
SPLIT 'EM UP.

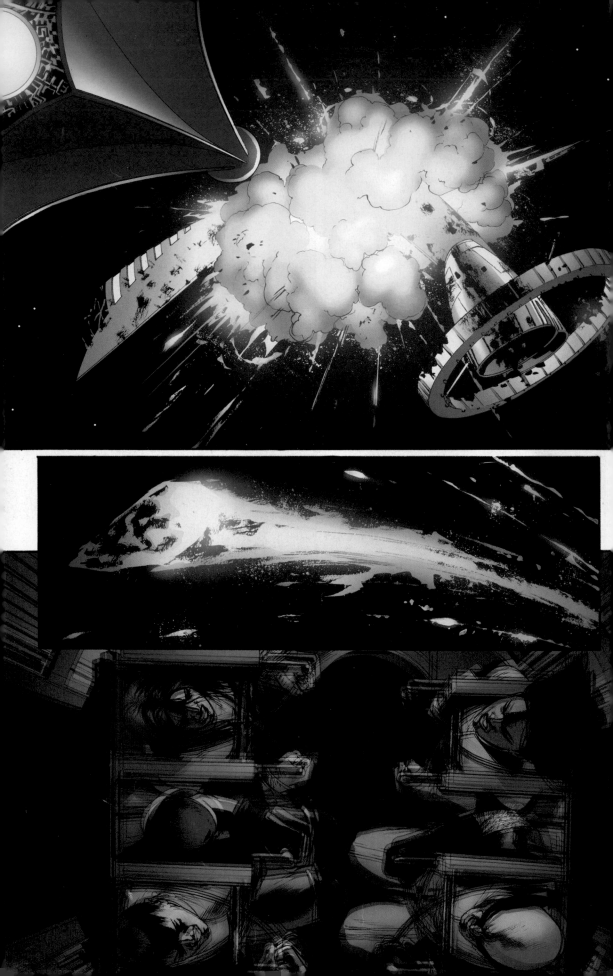

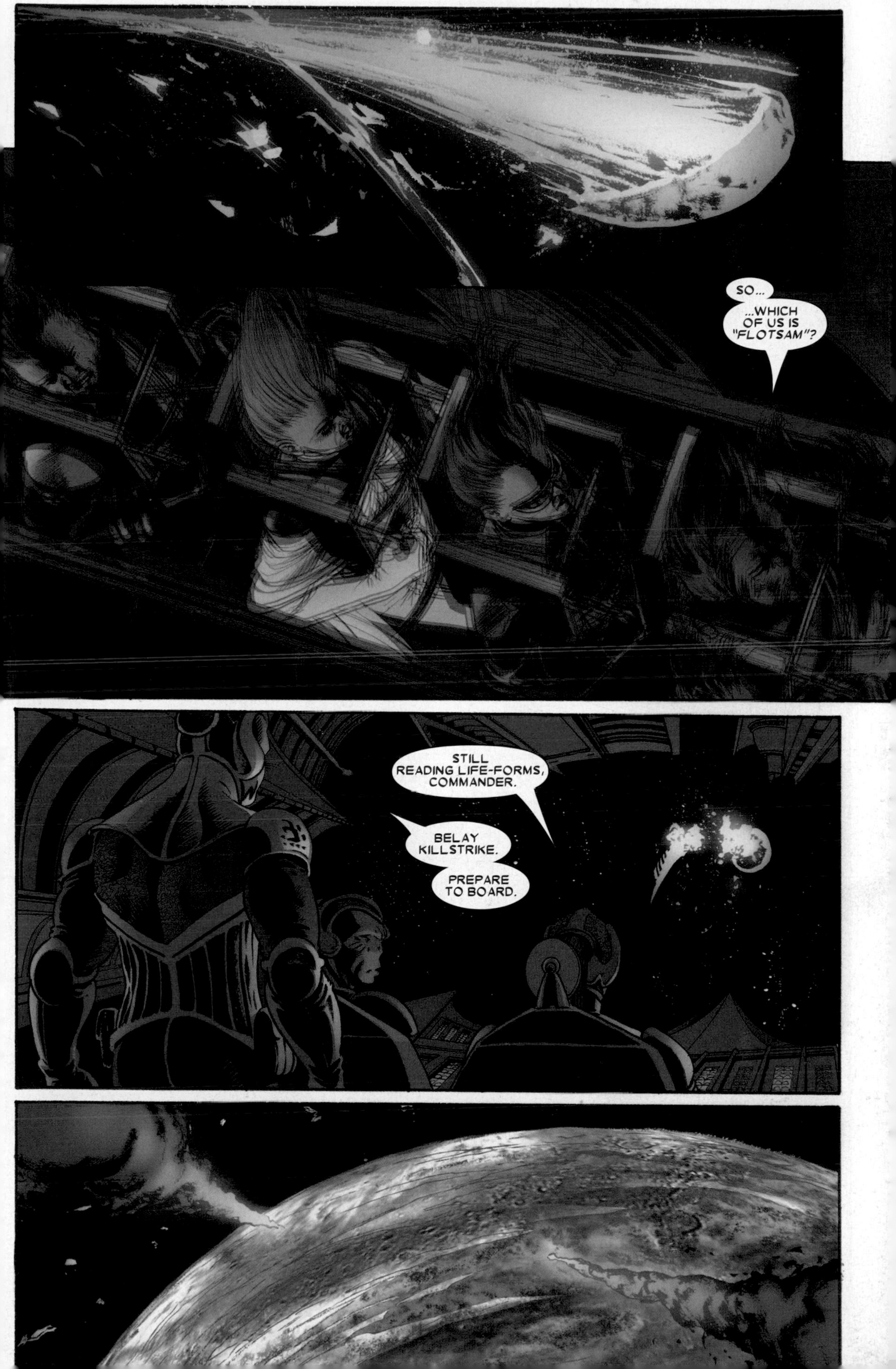
SO...
...WHICH OF US IS "FLOTSAM"?
STILL READING LIFE-FORMS, COMMANDER.
BELAY KILLSTRIKE.
PREPARE TO BOARD.

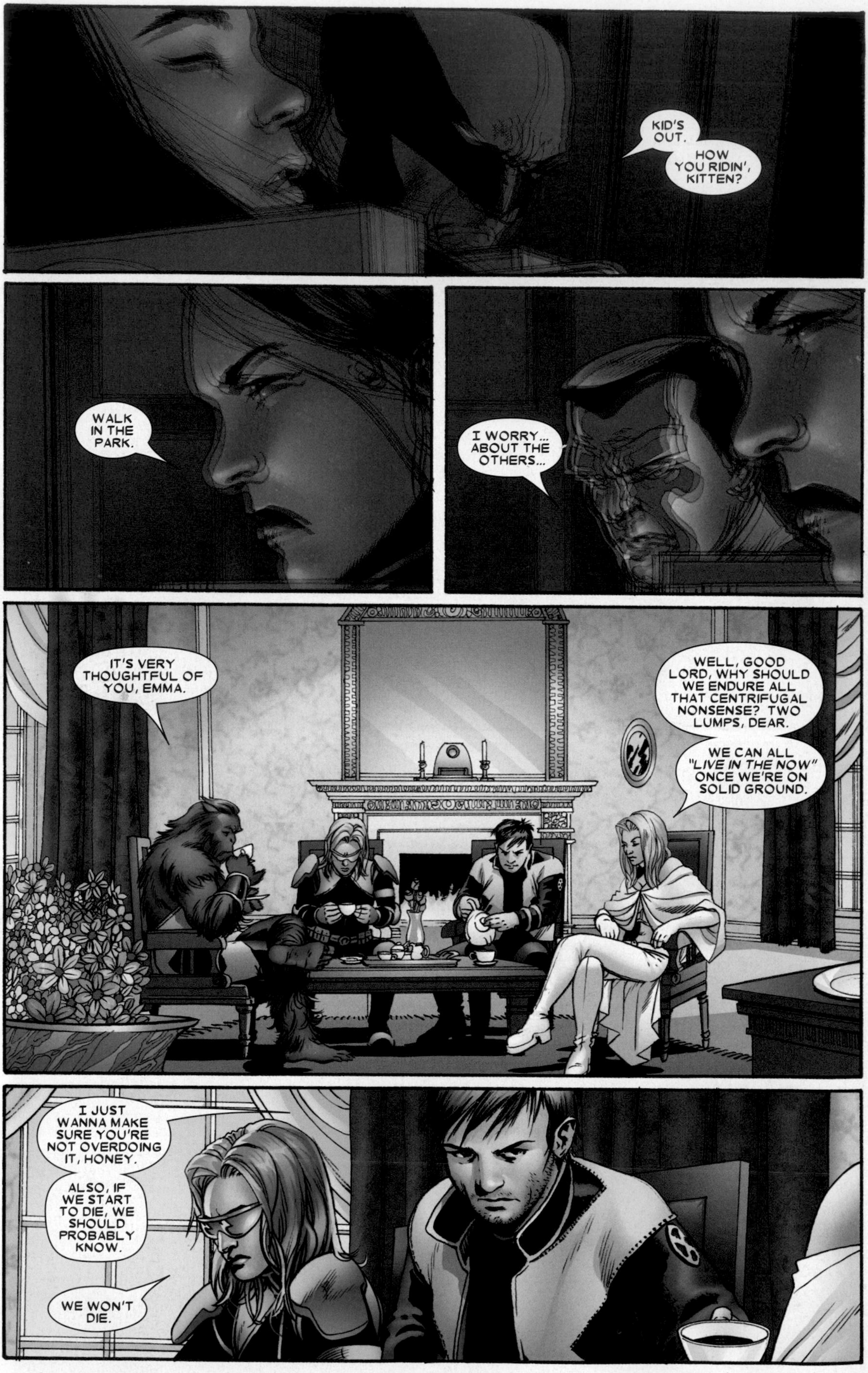
KID'S OUT.
HOW YOU RIDIN', KITTEN?
WALK IN THE PARK.
I WORRY... ABOUT THE OTHERS...
IT'S VERY THOUGHTFUL OF YOU, EMMA.
WELL, GOOD LORD, WHY SHOULD WE ENDURE ALL THAT CENTRIFUGAL NONSENSE? TWO LUMPS, DEAR.
WE CAN ALL "LIVE IN THE NOW" ONCE WE'RE ON SOLID GROUND.
I JUST WANNA MAKE SURE YOU'RE NOT OVERDOING IT, HONEY.
ALSO, IF WE START TO DIE, WE SHOULD PROBABLY KNOW.
WE WON'T DIE.

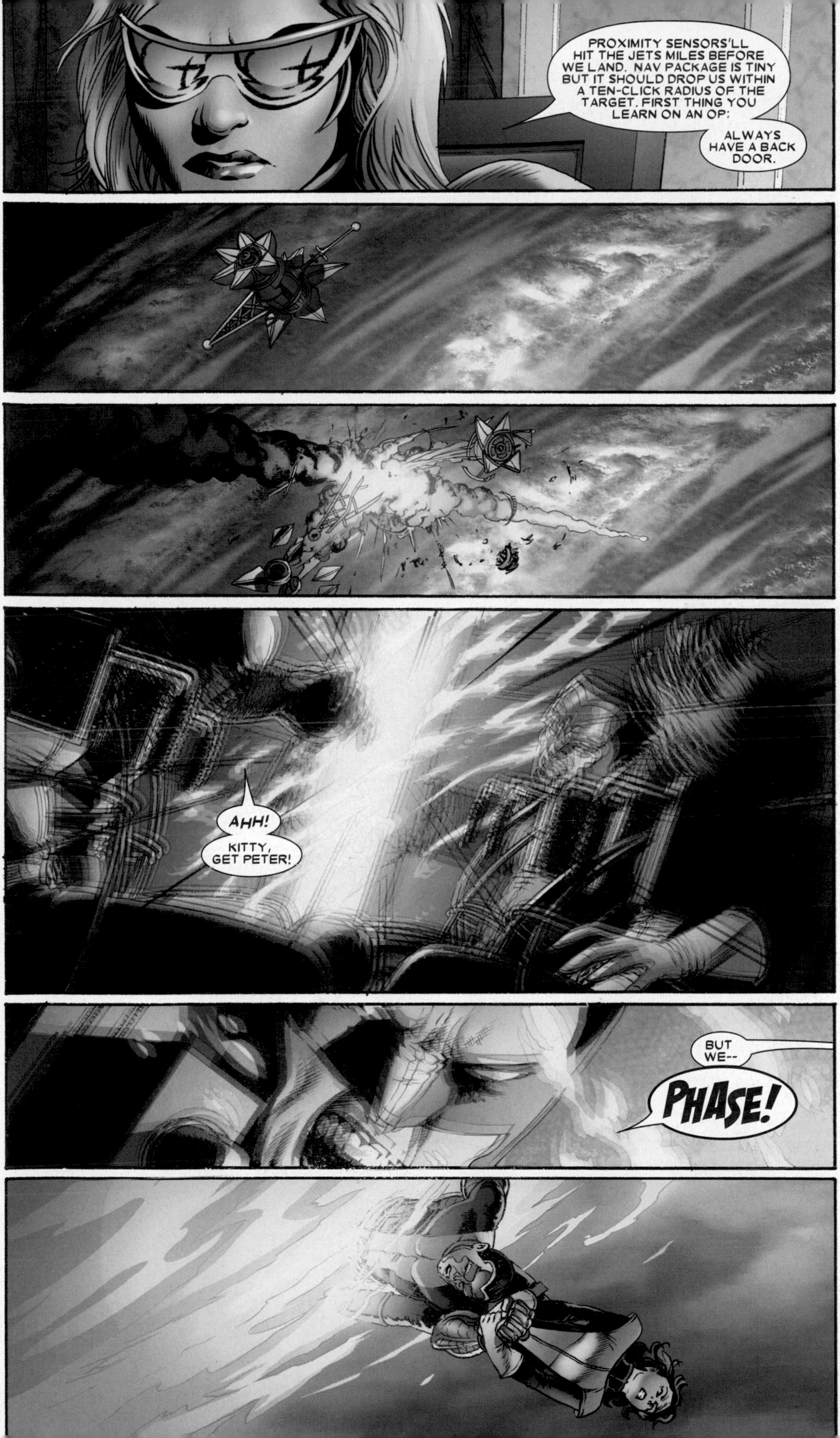
PROXIMITY SENSORS'LL HIT THE JETS MILES BEFORE WE LAND. NAV PACKAGE IS TINY BUT IT SHOULD DROP US WITHIN A TEN-CLICK RADIUS OF THE TARGET. FIRST THING YOU LEARN ON AN OP:
ALWAYS HAVE A BACK DOOR.
AHH!
KITTY, GET PETER!
BUT WE--
PHASE!

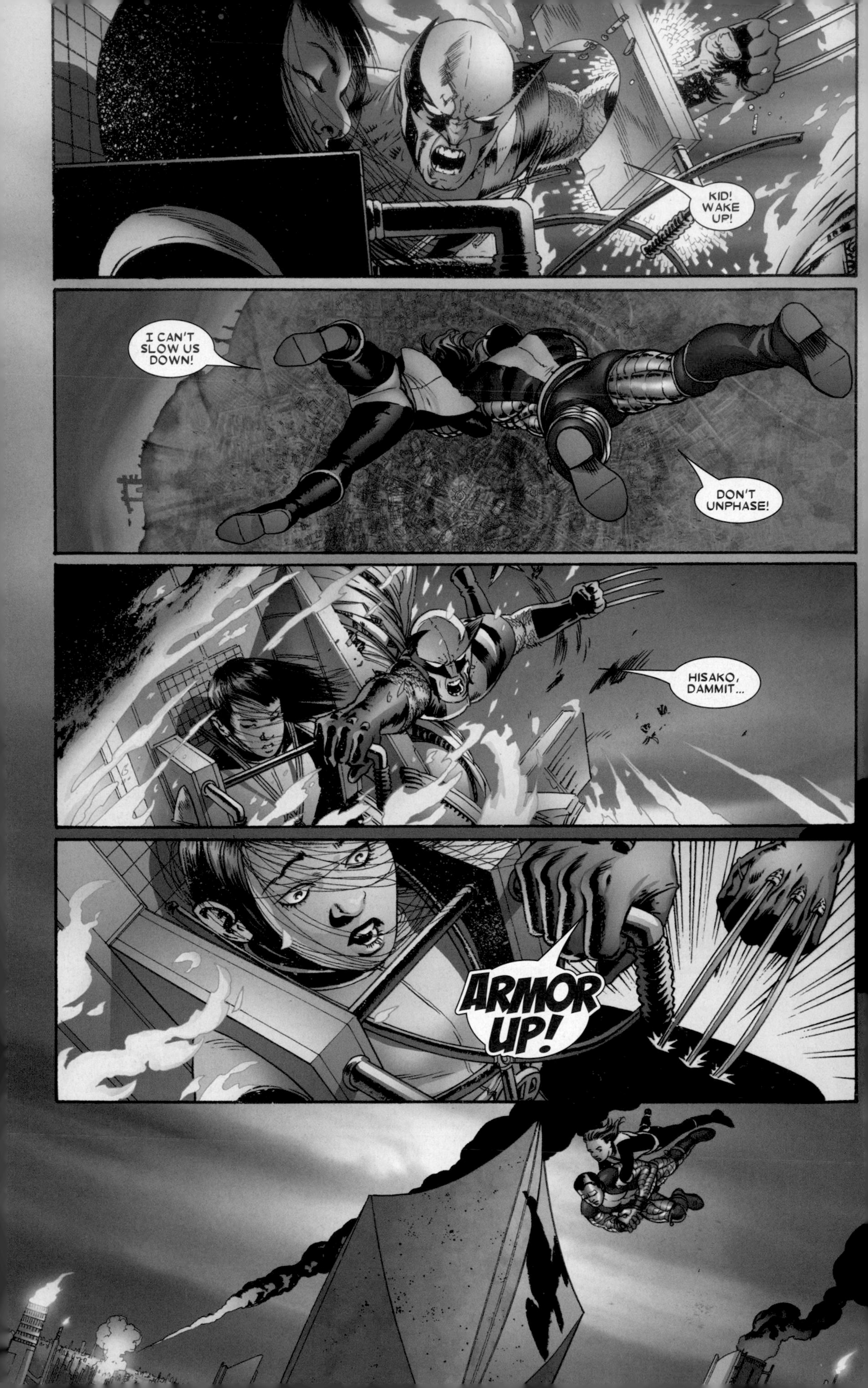
KID! WAKE UP!
I CAN'T SLOW US DOWN!
DON'T UNPHASE!
HISAKO, DAMMIT...
ARMOR UP!

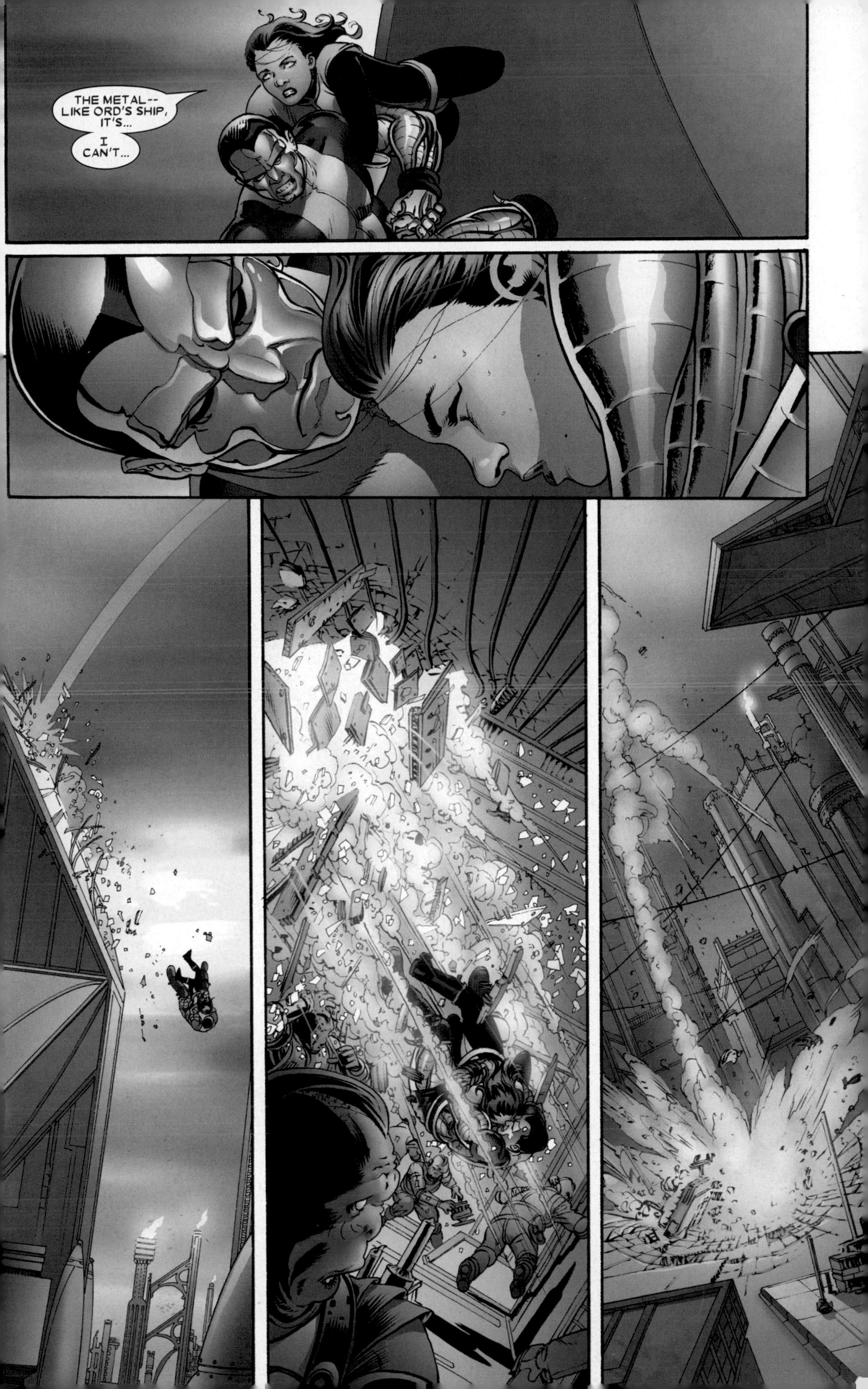
THE METAL--
LIKE ORD'S SHIP, IT'S...
I CAN'T...

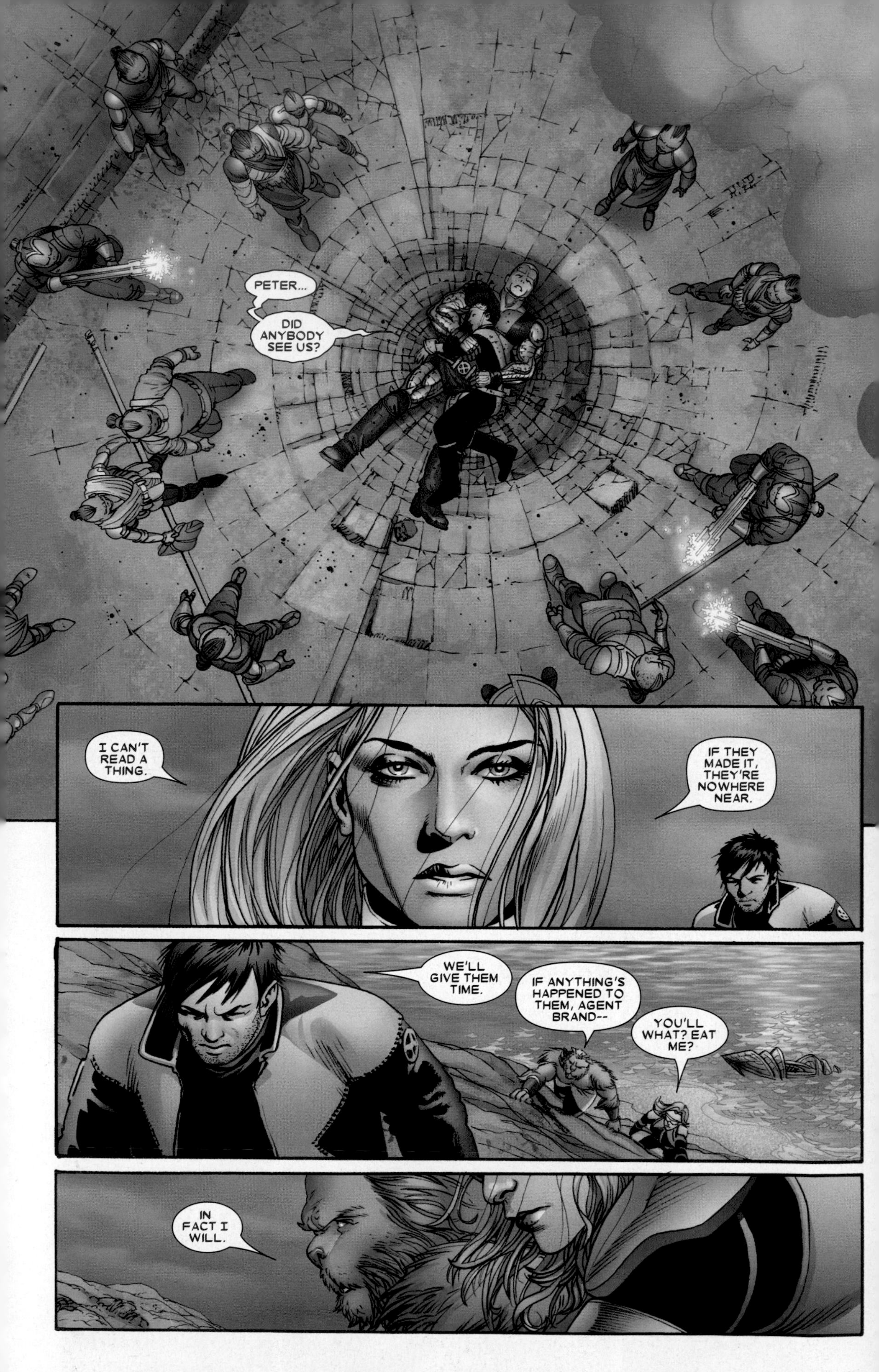
PETER...
DID ANYBODY SEE US?
I CAN'T READ A THING.
IF THEY MADE IT, THEY'RE NOWHERE NEAR.
WE'LL GIVE THEM TIME.
IF ANYTHING'S HAPPENED TO THEM, AGENT BRAND--
YOU'LL WHAT? EAT ME?
IN FACT I WILL.

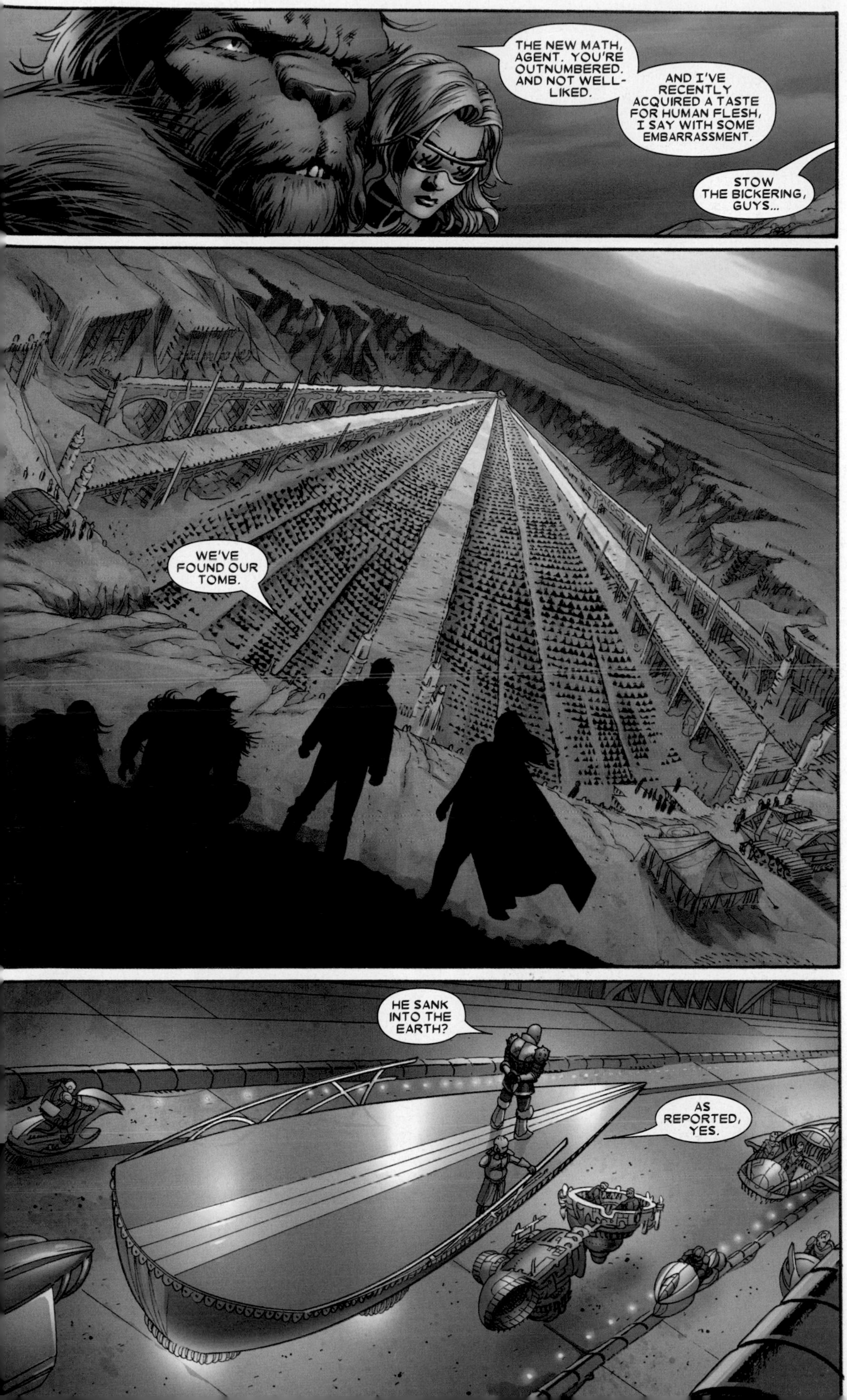
THE NEW MATH, AGENT. YOU'RE OUTNUMBERED. AND NOT WELL-LIKED.
AND I'VE RECENTLY ACQUIRED A TASTE FOR HUMAN FLESH, I SAY WITH SOME EMBARRASSMENT.
STOW THE BICKERING, GUYS...
WE'VE FOUND OUR TOMB.
HE SANK INTO THE EARTH?
AS REPORTED, YES.

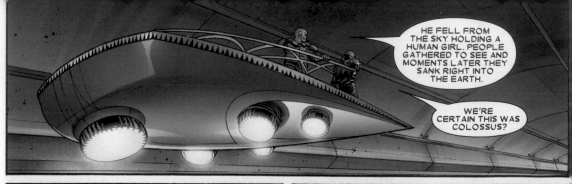

HE FELL FROM THE SKY HOLDING A HUMAN GIRL. PEOPLE GATHERED TO SEE AND MOMENTS LATER THEY SANK RIGHT INTO THE EARTH.

WE'RE CERTAIN THIS WAS COLOSSUS?

THE PEOPLE WERE. THEY PANICKED. AND IT SPREADS. THEY BELIEVE HE'S GONE INTO THE EARTH TO INFECT IT.

THAT THE PROPHECY HAS BEGUN.

AND FOR ALL WE KNOW THEY COULD BE RIGHT.

IT DOESN'T FIT EXACTLY, BUT THIS IS NOT AN EXACT SCIENCE. WE COULD HAVE MISINTERPRETED THE ATTUR-HYN.

LET'S HOPE THE PRISONERS HAVE SOMETHING USEFUL TO SAY.

IT'S THE GIRL. THIS IS HER POWER: TO MOVE THROUGH SOLID OBJECTS. COLOSSUS WILL BE SOMEWHERE ABOVE GROUND. HE CAN BE STOPPED.

BUT NOT BY YOU.

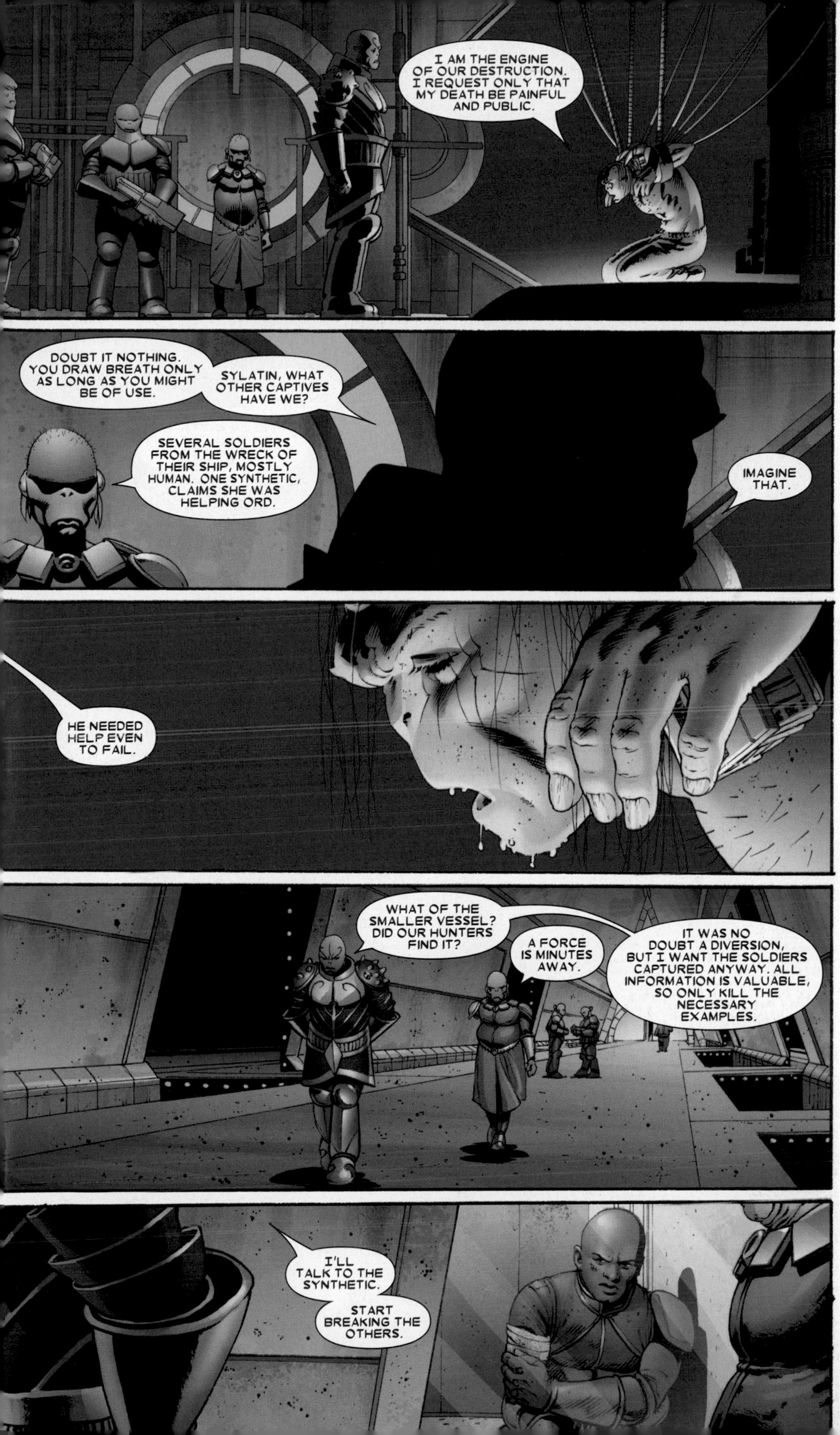
I AM THE ENGINE OF OUR DESTRUCTION. I REQUEST ONLY THAT MY DEATH BE PAINFUL AND PUBLIC.
DOUBT IT NOTHING. YOU DRAW BREATH ONLY AS LONG AS YOU MIGHT BE OF USE.
SYLATIN, WHAT OTHER CAPTIVES HAVE WE?
SEVERAL SOLDIERS FROM THE WRECK OF THEIR SHIP, MOSTLY HUMAN. ONE SYNTHETIC, CLAIMS SHE WAS HELPING ORD.
IMAGINE THAT.
HE NEEDED HELP EVEN TO FAIL.
WHAT OF THE SMALLER VESSEL? DID OUR HUNTERS FIND IT?
A FORCE IS MINUTES AWAY.
IT WAS NO DOUBT A DIVERSION, BUT I WANT THE SOLDIERS CAPTURED ANYWAY. ALL INFORMATION IS VALUABLE, SO ONLY KILL THE NECESSARY EXAMPLES.
I'LL TALK TO THE SYNTHETIC.
START BREAKING THE OTHERS.

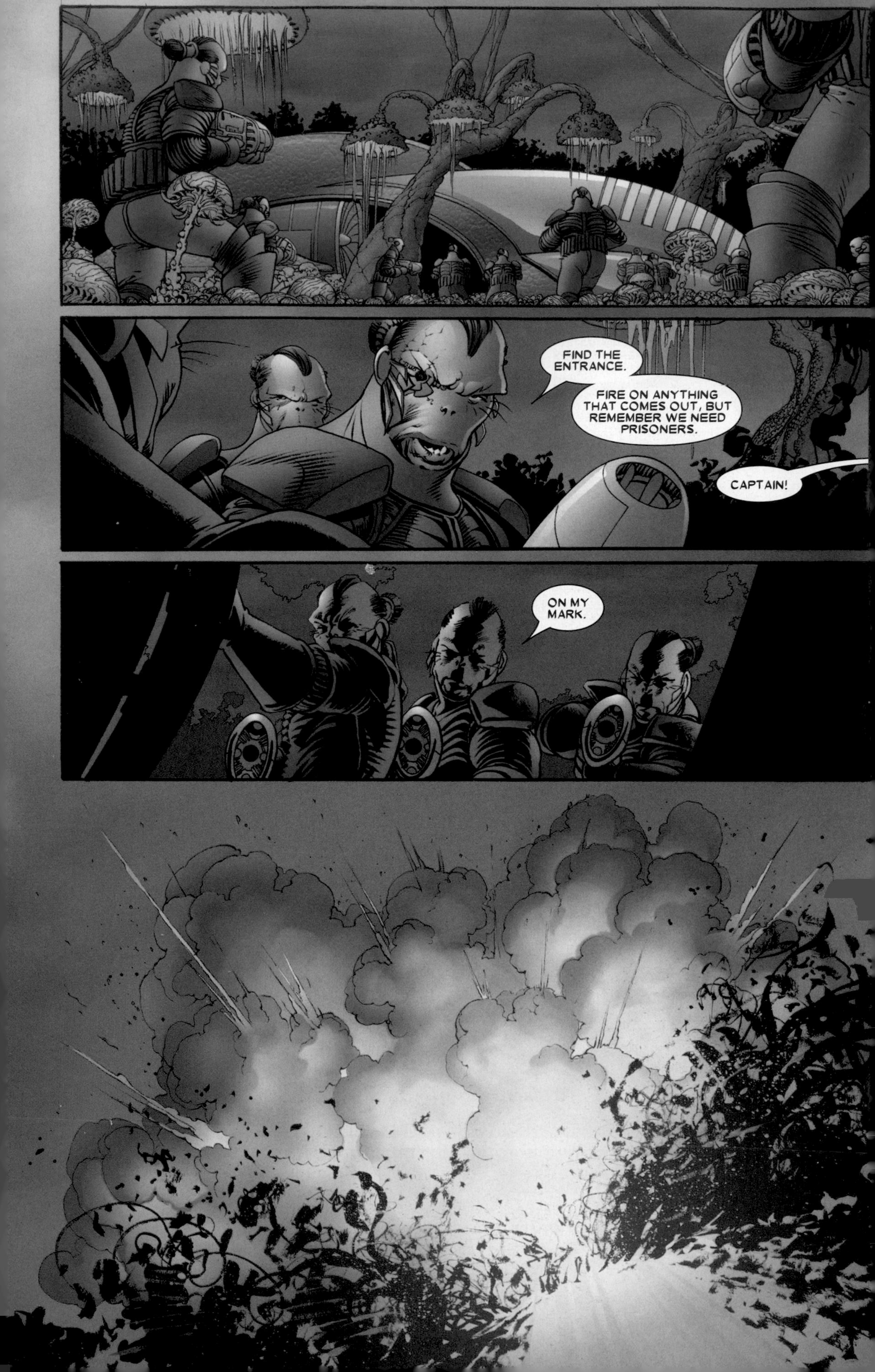
FIND THE ENTRANCE.
FIRE ON ANYTHING THAT COMES OUT, BUT REMEMBER WE NEED PRISONERS.
CAPTAIN!
ON MY MARK.

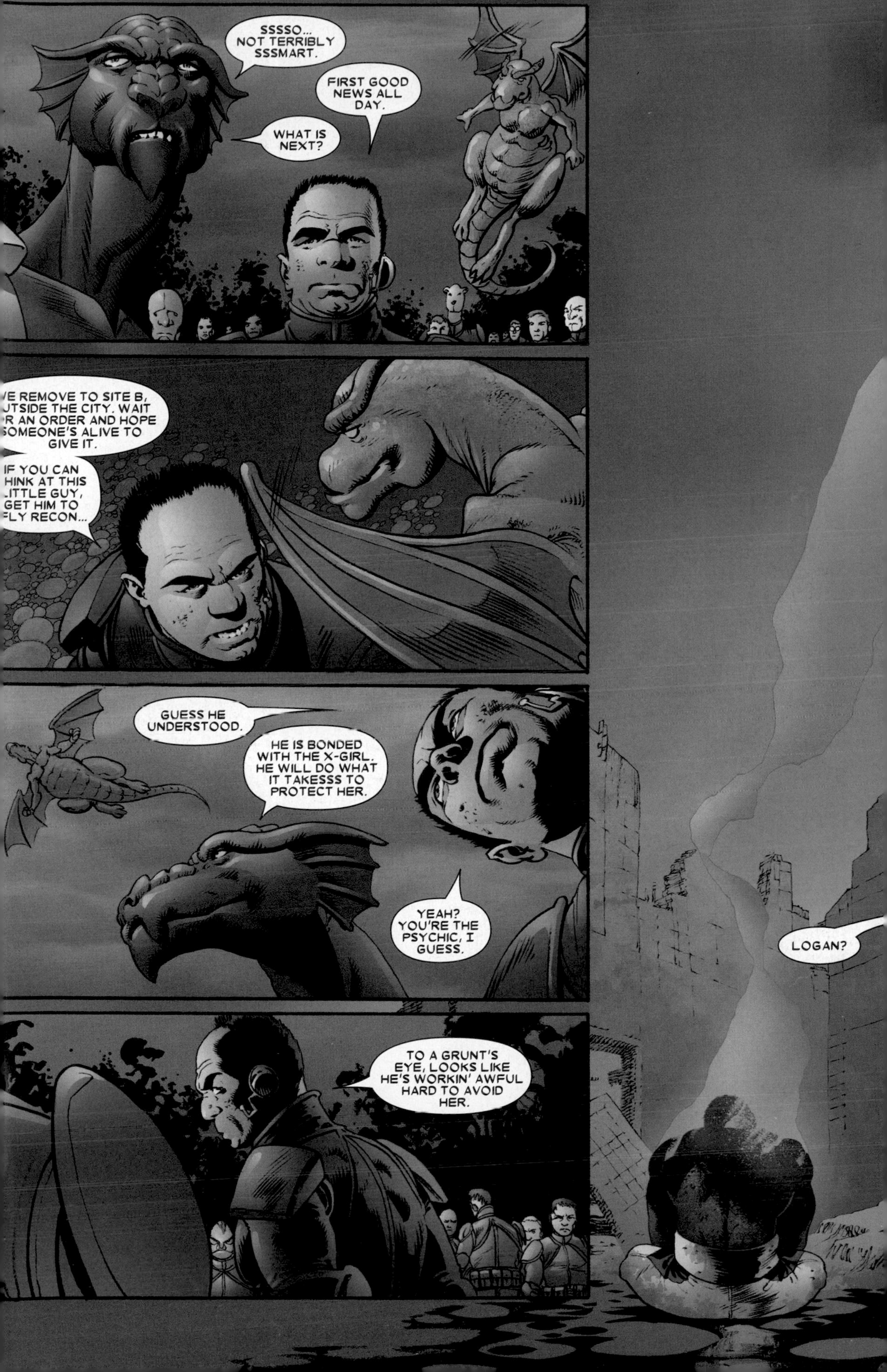
SSSSO... NOT TERRIBLY SSSMART.
FIRST GOOD NEWS ALL DAY.
WHAT IS NEXT?
WE REMOVE TO SITE B, OUTSIDE THE CITY. WAIT FOR AN ORDER AND HOPE SOMEONE'S ALIVE TO GIVE IT.
IF YOU CAN THINK AT THIS LITTLE GUY, GET HIM TO FLY RECON...
GUESS HE UNDERSTOOD.
HE IS BONDED WITH THE X-GIRL. HE WILL DO WHAT IT TAKESSS TO PROTECT HER.
YEAH? YOU'RE THE PSYCHIC, I GUESS.
TO A GRUNT'S EYE, LOOKS LIKE HE'S WORKIN' AWFUL HARD TO AVOID HER.
LOGAN?

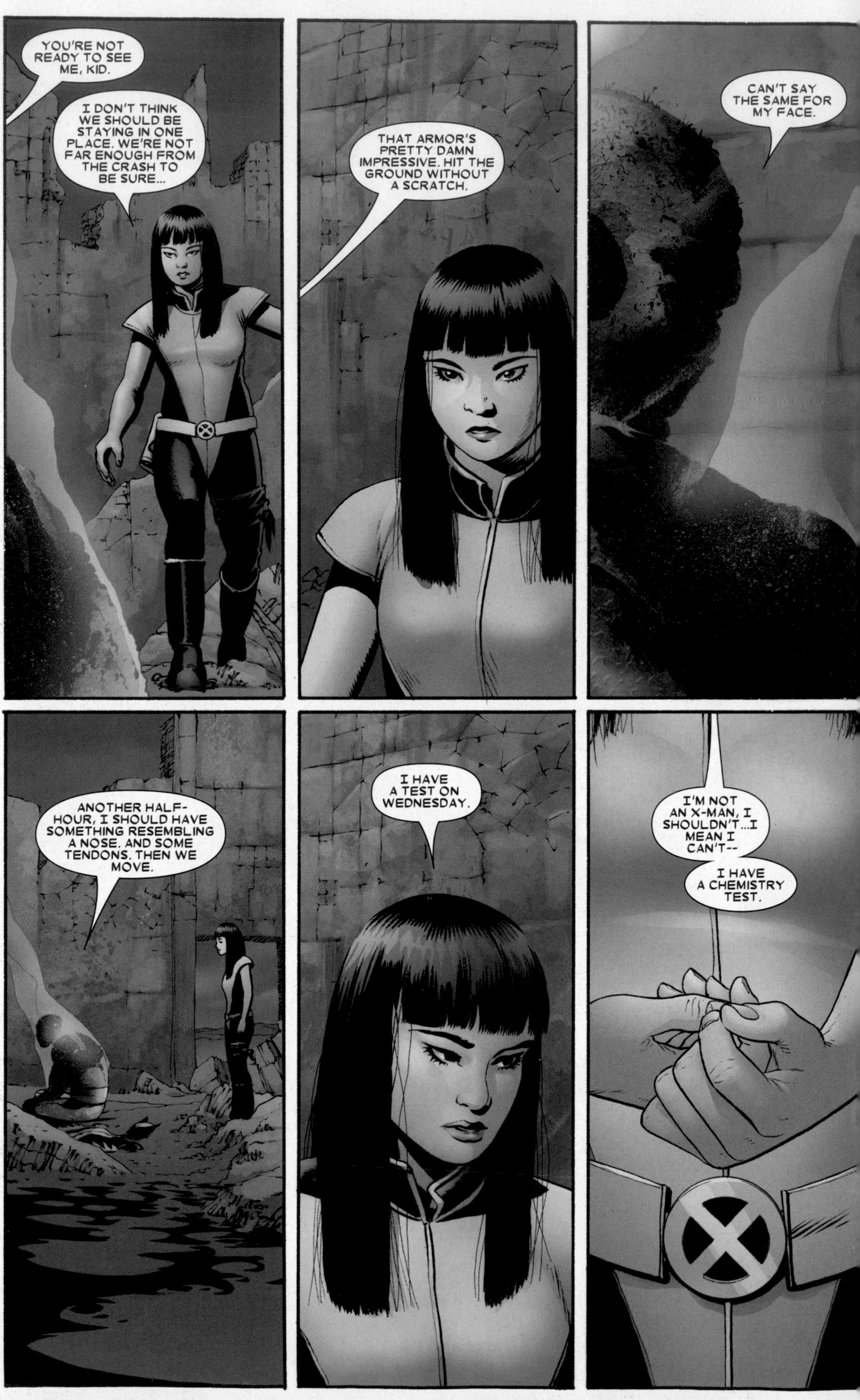
YOU'RE NOT READY TO SEE ME, KID.
I DON'T THINK WE SHOULD BE STAYING IN ONE PLACE. WE'RE NOT FAR ENOUGH FROM THE CRASH TO BE SURE...
THAT ARMOR'S PRETTY DAMN IMPRESSIVE. HIT THE GROUND WITHOUT A SCRATCH.
CAN'T SAY THE SAME FOR MY FACE.
ANOTHER HALF-HOUR, I SHOULD HAVE SOMETHING RESEMBLING A NOSE. AND SOME TENDONS. THEN WE MOVE.
I HAVE A TEST ON WEDNESDAY.
I'M NOT AN X-MAN, I SHOULDN'T...I MEAN I CAN'T--
I HAVE A CHEMISTRY TEST.

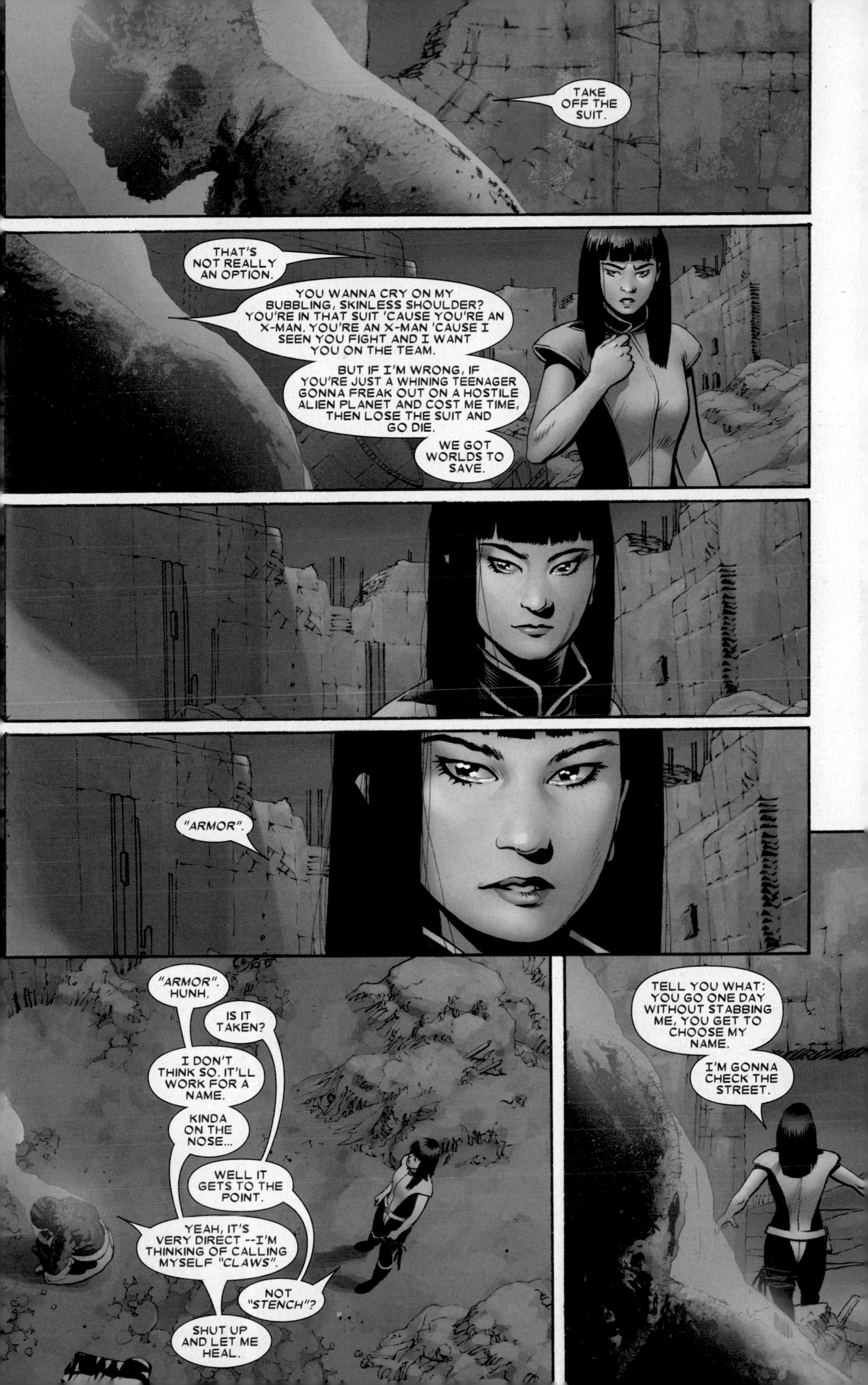
TAKE OFF THE SUIT.
THAT'S NOT REALLY AN OPTION.
YOU WANNA CRY ON MY BUBBLING, SKINLESS SHOULDER? YOU'RE IN THAT SUIT 'CAUSE YOU'RE AN X-MAN. YOU'RE AN X-MAN 'CAUSE I SEEN YOU FIGHT AND I WANT YOU ON THE TEAM.
BUT IF I'M WRONG, IF YOU'RE JUST A WHINING TEENAGER GONNA FREAK OUT ON A HOSTILE ALIEN PLANET AND COST ME TIME, THEN LOSE THE SUIT AND GO DIE.
WE GOT WORLDS TO SAVE.
"ARMOR".
"ARMOR". HUNH.
IS IT TAKEN?
I DON'T THINK SO. IT'LL WORK FOR A NAME.
KINDA ON THE NOSE...
WELL IT GETS TO THE POINT.
YEAH, IT'S VERY DIRECT --I'M THINKING OF CALLING MYSELF "CLAWS".
NOT "STENCH"?
SHUT UP AND LET ME HEAL.
TELL YOU WHAT: YOU GO ONE DAY WITHOUT STABBING ME, YOU GET TO CHOOSE MY NAME.
I'M GONNA CHECK THE STREET.

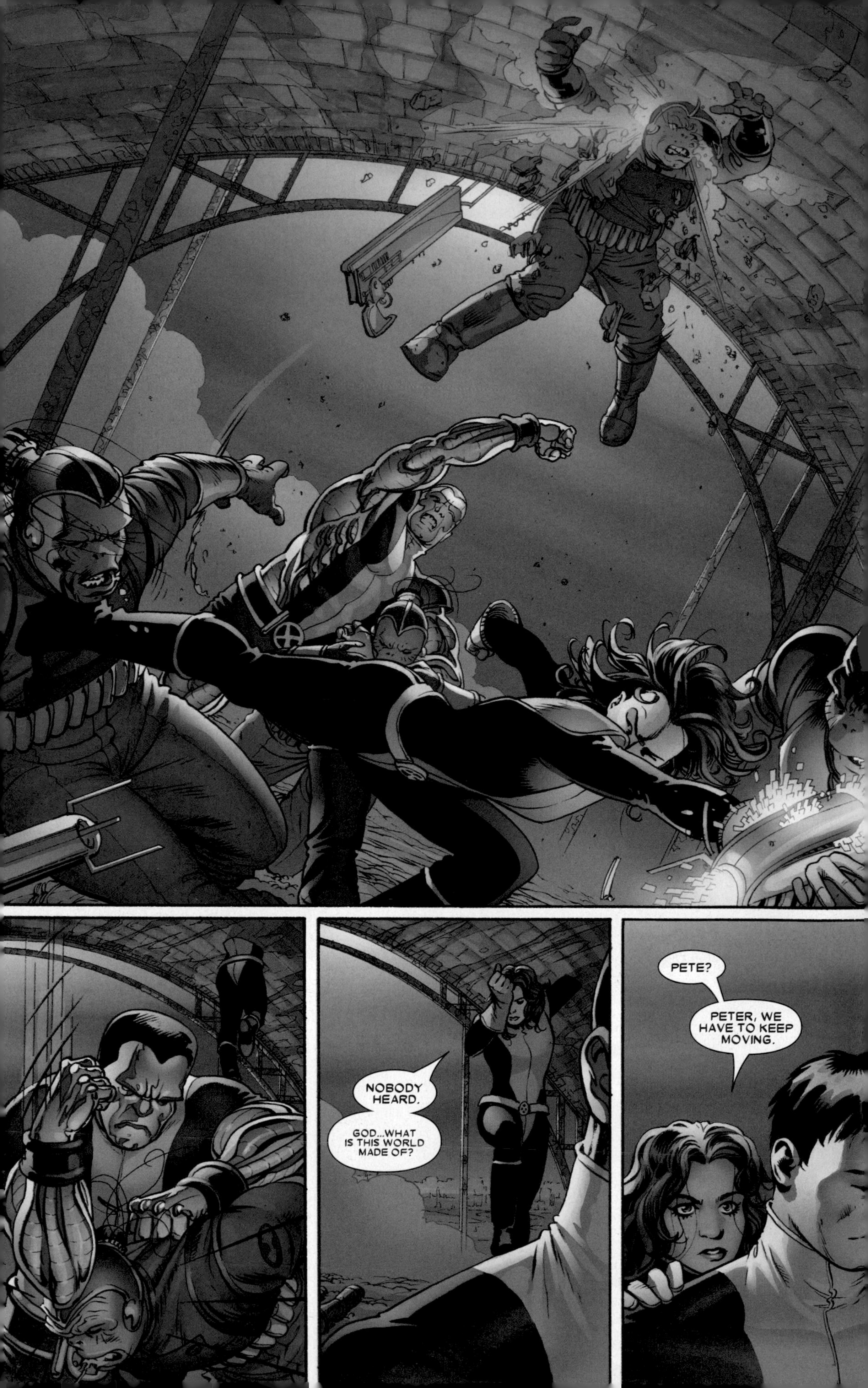
NOBODY HEARD.
GOD...WHAT IS THIS WORLD MADE OF?
PETE?
PETER, WE HAVE TO KEEP MOVING.

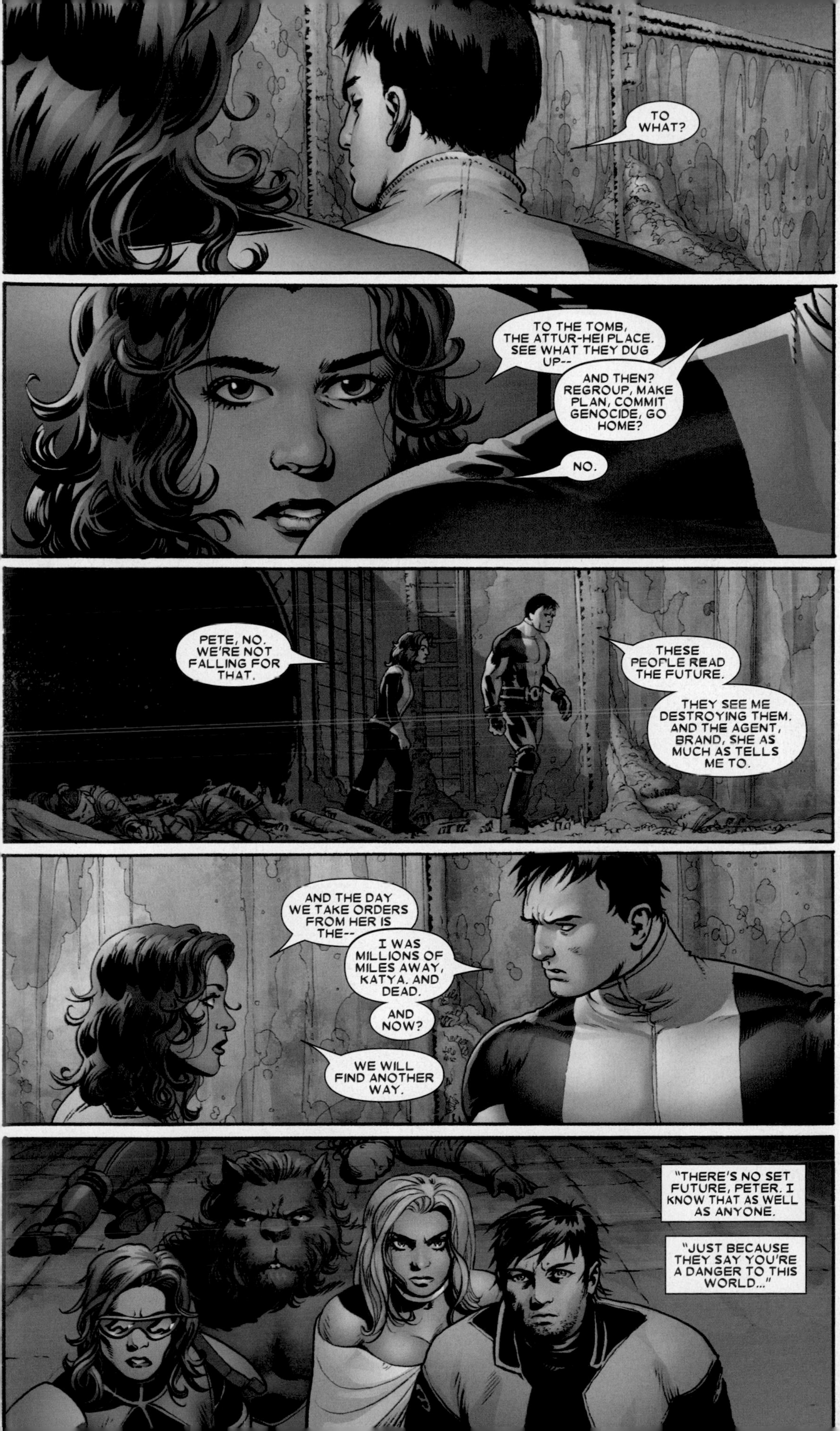
TO WHAT?
TO THE TOMB, THE ATTUR-HEI PLACE. SEE WHAT THEY DUG UP--
AND THEN? REGROUP, MAKE PLAN, COMMIT GENOCIDE, GO HOME?
NO.
PETE, NO. WE'RE NOT FALLING FOR THAT.
THESE PEOPLE READ THE FUTURE.
THEY SEE ME DESTROYING THEM. AND THE AGENT, BRAND, SHE AS MUCH AS TELLS ME TO.
AND THE DAY WE TAKE ORDERS FROM HER IS THE--
I WAS MILLIONS OF MILES AWAY, KATYA. AND DEAD.
AND NOW?
WE WILL FIND ANOTHER WAY.
"THERE'S NO SET FUTURE, PETER. I KNOW THAT AS WELL AS ANYONE.
"JUST BECAUSE THEY SAY YOU'RE A DANGER TO THIS WORLD..."

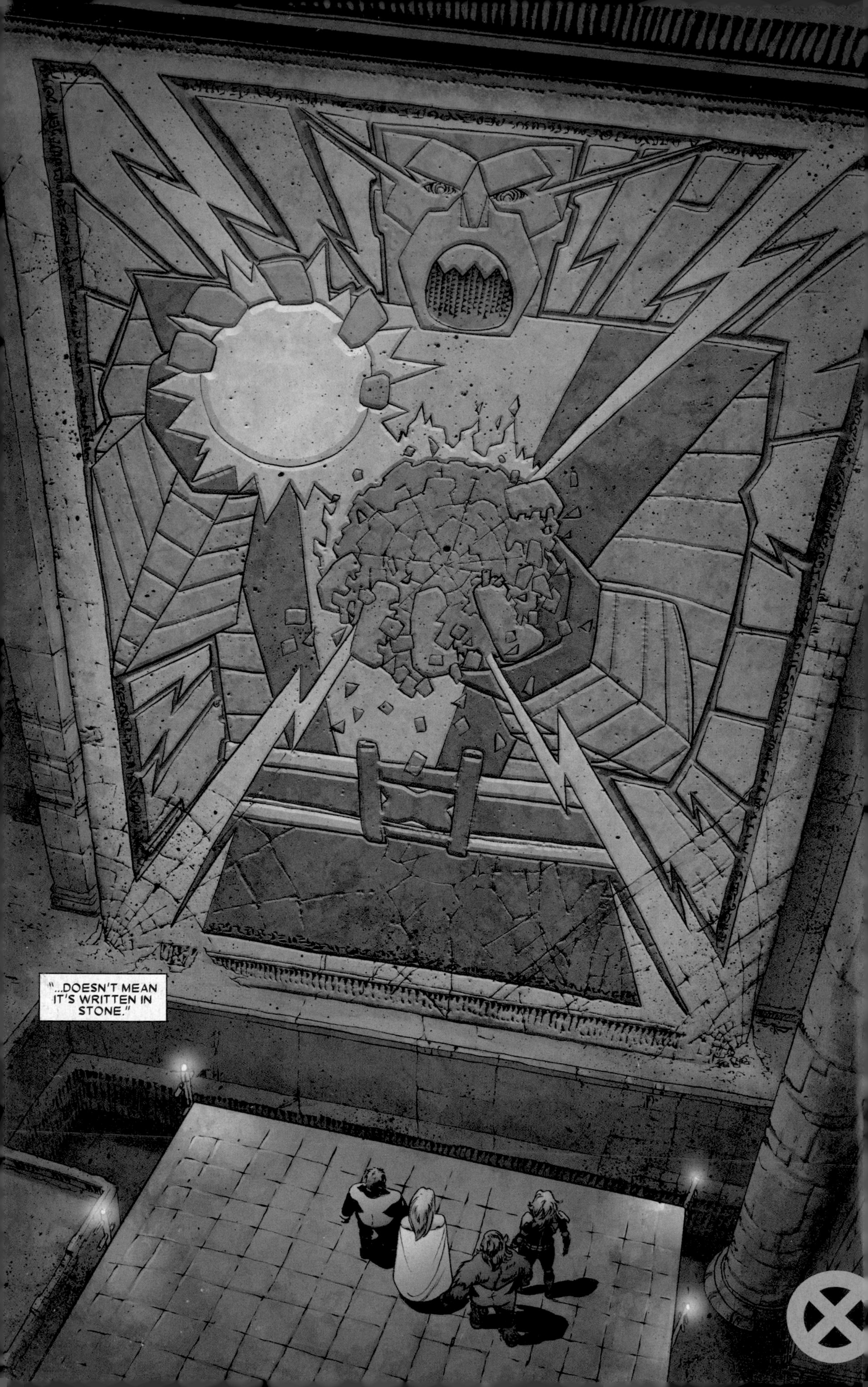
"...DOESN'T MEAN IT'S WRITTEN IN STONE."

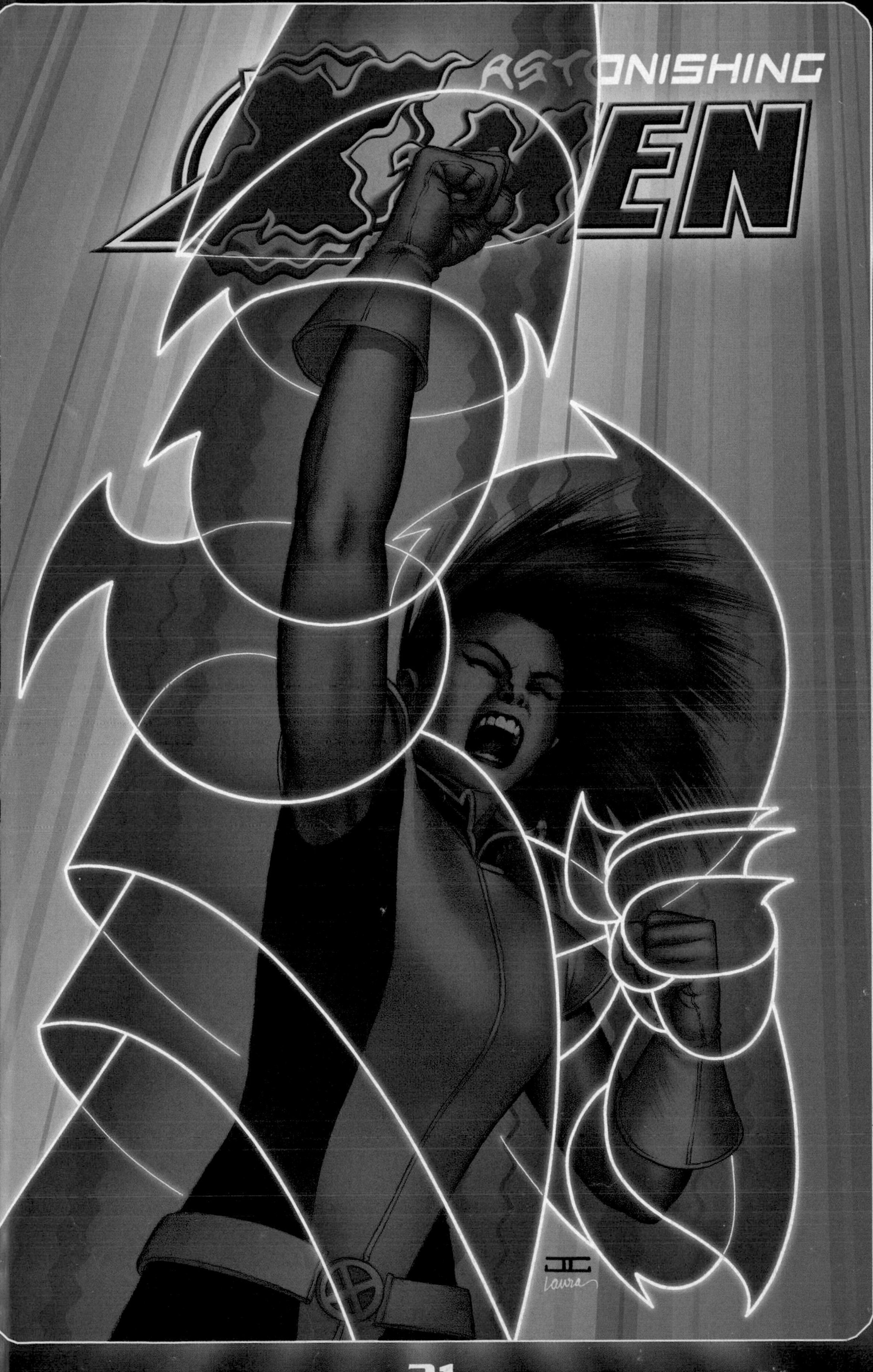

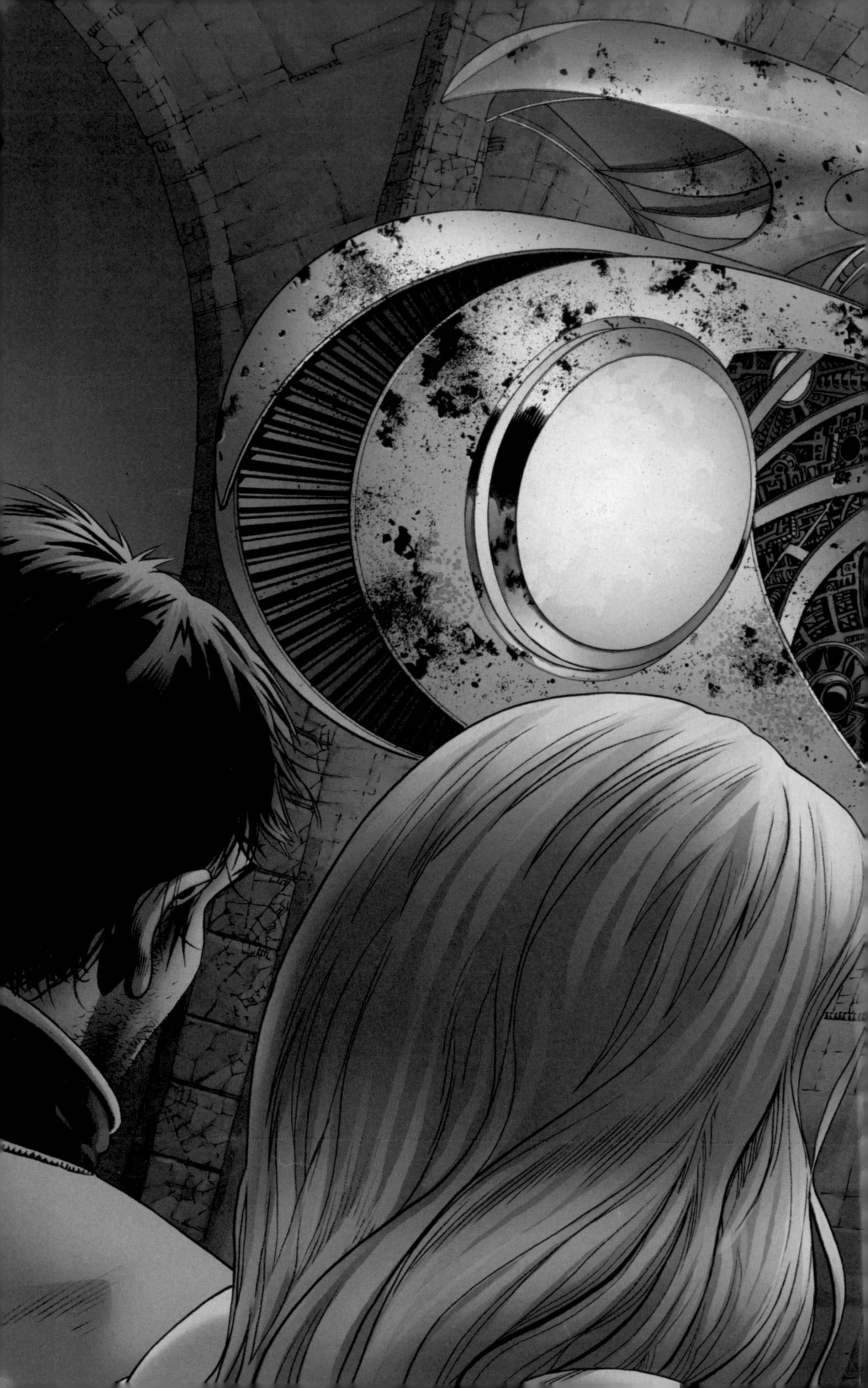

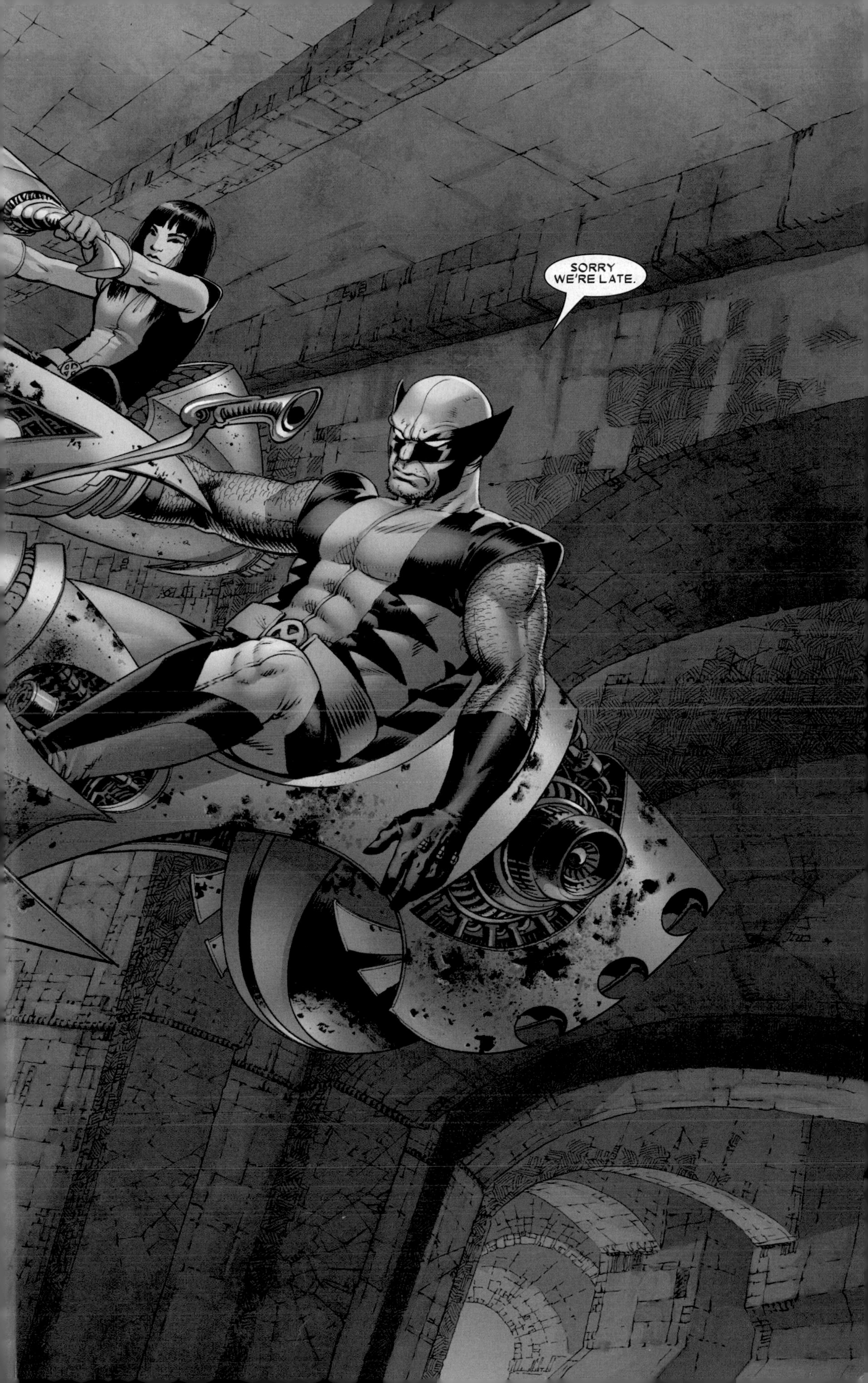
SORRY WE'RE LATE.

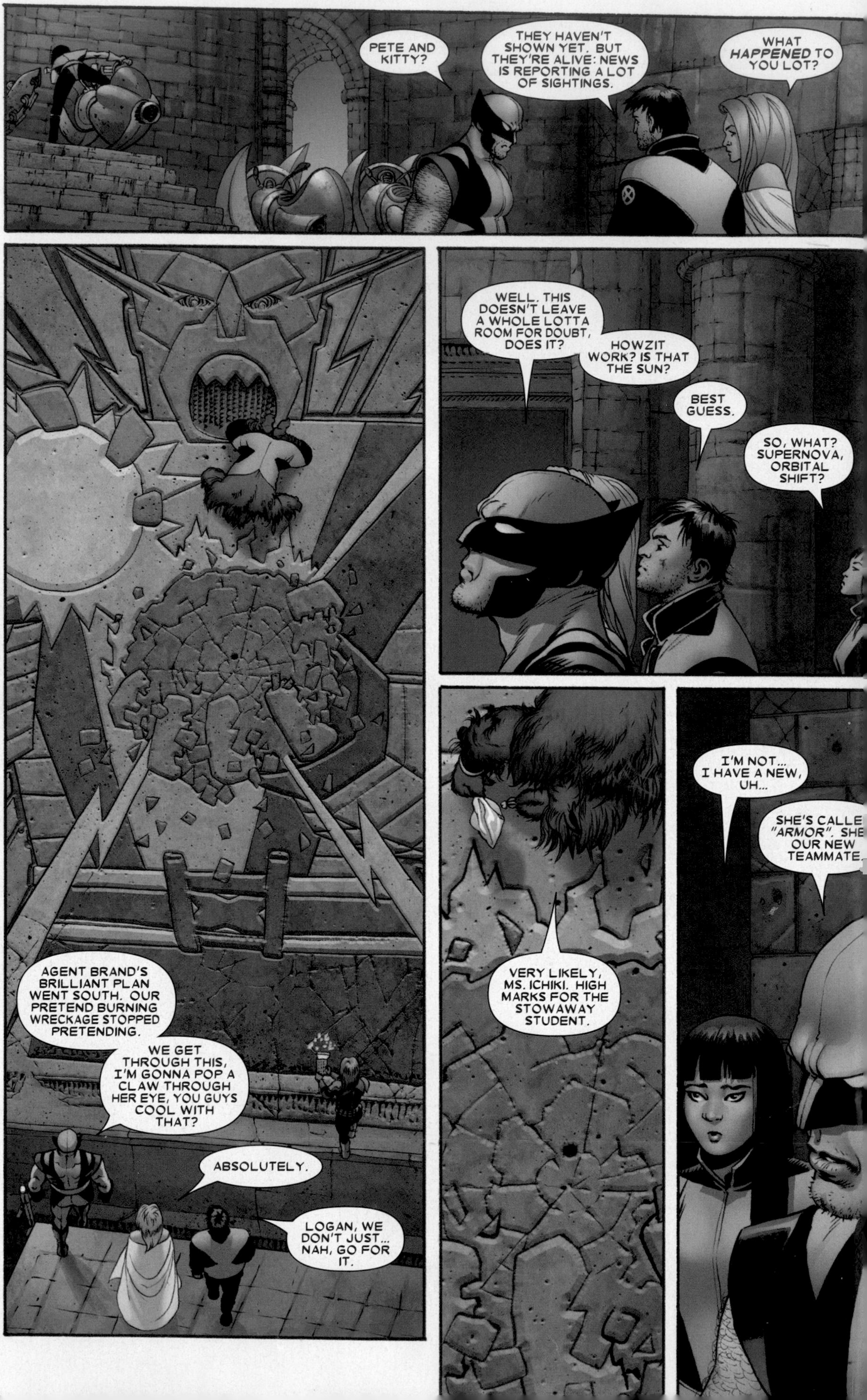
PETE AND KITTY?
THEY HAVEN'T SHOWN YET. BUT THEY'RE ALIVE: NEWS IS REPORTING A LOT OF SIGHTINGS.
WHAT HAPPENED TO YOU LOT?
AGENT BRAND'S BRILLIANT PLAN WENT SOUTH. OUR PRETEND BURNING WRECKAGE STOPPED PRETENDING.
WE GET THROUGH THIS, I'M GONNA POP A CLAW THROUGH HER EYE, YOU GUYS COOL WITH THAT?
ABSOLUTELY.
LOGAN, WE DON'T JUST... NAH, GO FOR IT.
WELL. THIS DOESN'T LEAVE A WHOLE LOTTA ROOM FOR DOUBT, DOES IT?
HOWZIT WORK? IS THAT THE SUN?
BEST GUESS.
SO, WHAT? SUPERNOVA, ORBITAL SHIFT?
VERY LIKELY, MS. ICHIKI. HIGH MARKS FOR THE STOWAWAY STUDENT.
I'M NOT... I HAVE A NEW, UH...
SHE'S CALLE "ARMOR". SHE OUR NEW TEAMMATE.

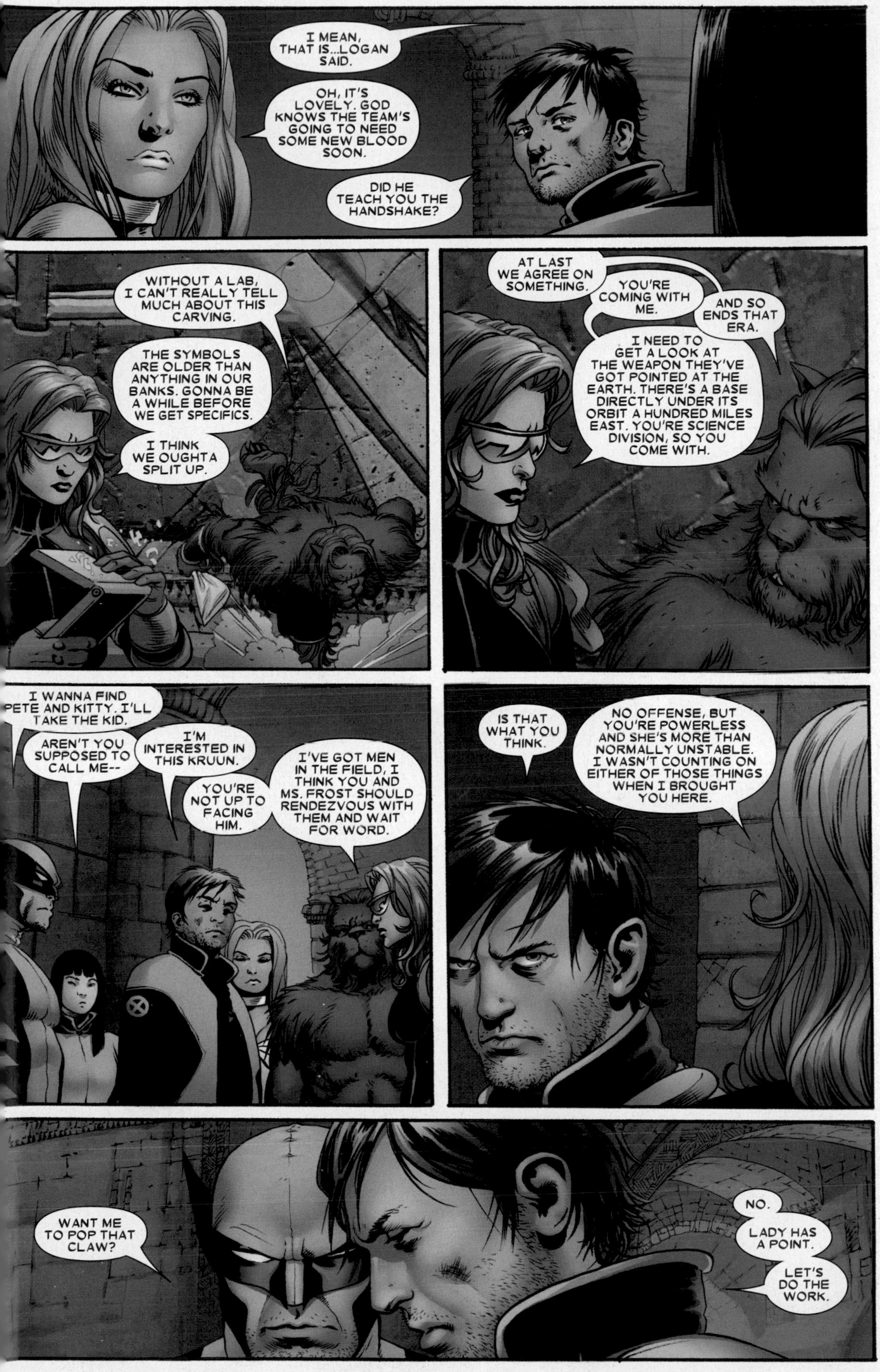
I MEAN, THAT IS...LOGAN SAID.
OH, IT'S LOVELY. GOD KNOWS THE TEAM'S GOING TO NEED SOME NEW BLOOD SOON.
DID HE TEACH YOU THE HANDSHAKE?
WITHOUT A LAB, I CAN'T REALLY TELL MUCH ABOUT THIS CARVING.
THE SYMBOLS ARE OLDER THAN ANYTHING IN OUR BANKS. GONNA BE A WHILE BEFORE WE GET SPECIFICS.
I THINK WE OUGHTA SPLIT UP.
AT LAST WE AGREE ON SOMETHING.
YOU'RE COMING WITH ME.
AND SO ENDS THAT ERA.
I NEED TO GET A LOOK AT THE WEAPON THEY'VE GOT POINTED AT THE EARTH. THERE'S A BASE DIRECTLY UNDER ITS ORBIT A HUNDRED MILES EAST. YOU'RE SCIENCE DIVISION, SO YOU COME WITH.
I WANNA FIND PETE AND KITTY. I'LL TAKE THE KID.
AREN'T YOU SUPPOSED TO CALL ME--
I'M INTERESTED IN THIS KRUUN.
YOU'RE NOT UP TO FACING HIM.
I'VE GOT MEN IN THE FIELD, I THINK YOU AND MS. FROST SHOULD RENDEZVOUS WITH THEM AND WAIT FOR WORD.
IS THAT WHAT YOU THINK.
NO OFFENSE, BUT YOU'RE POWERLESS AND SHE'S MORE THAN NORMALLY UNSTABLE. I WASN'T COUNTING ON EITHER OF THOSE THINGS WHEN I BROUGHT YOU HERE.
WANT ME TO POP THAT CLAW?
NO.
LADY HAS A POINT.
LET'S DO THE WORK.

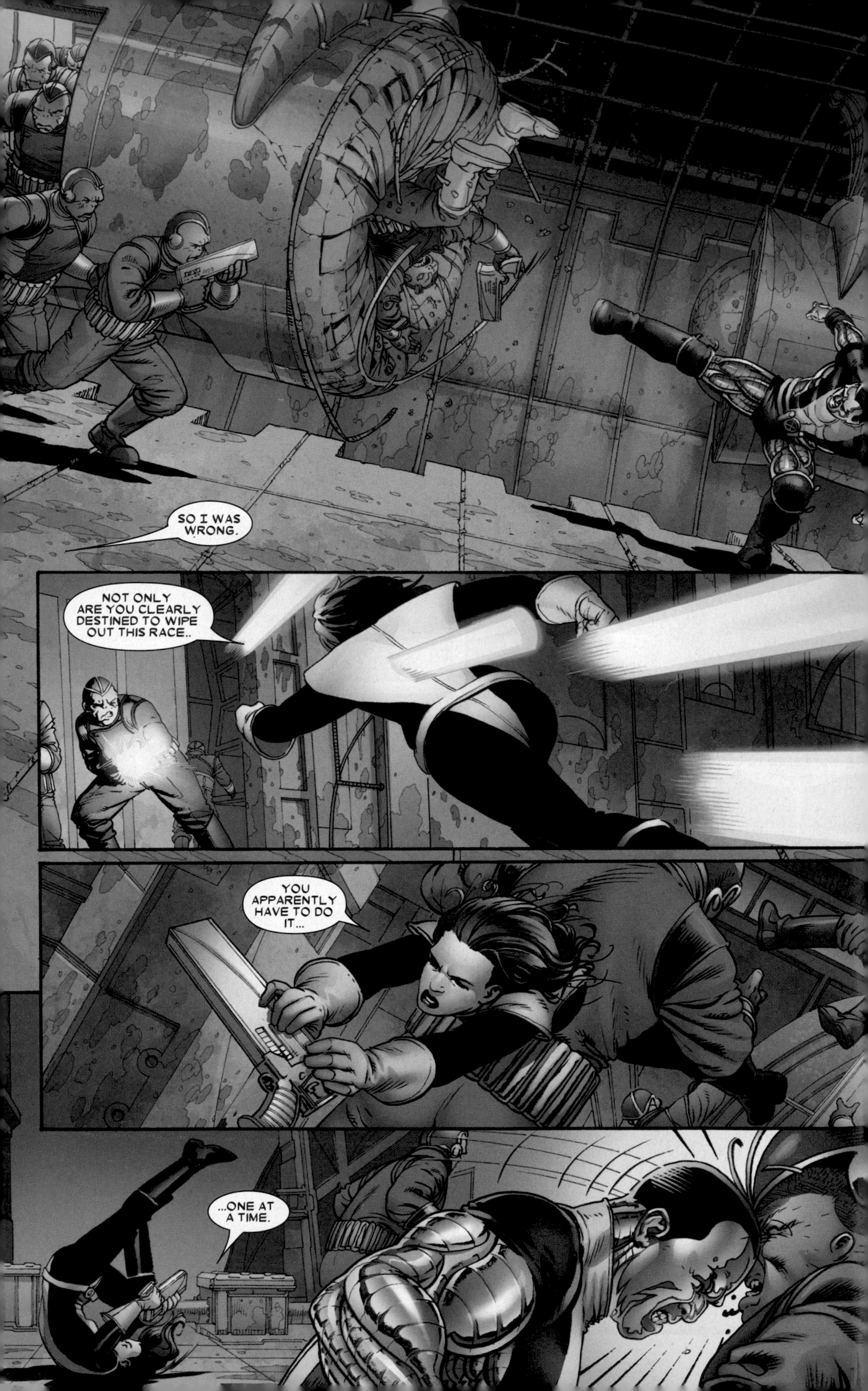
SO I WAS WRONG.
NOT ONLY ARE YOU CLEARLY DESTINED TO WIPE OUT THIS RACE..
YOU APPARENTLY HAVE TO DO IT...
...ONE AT A TIME.

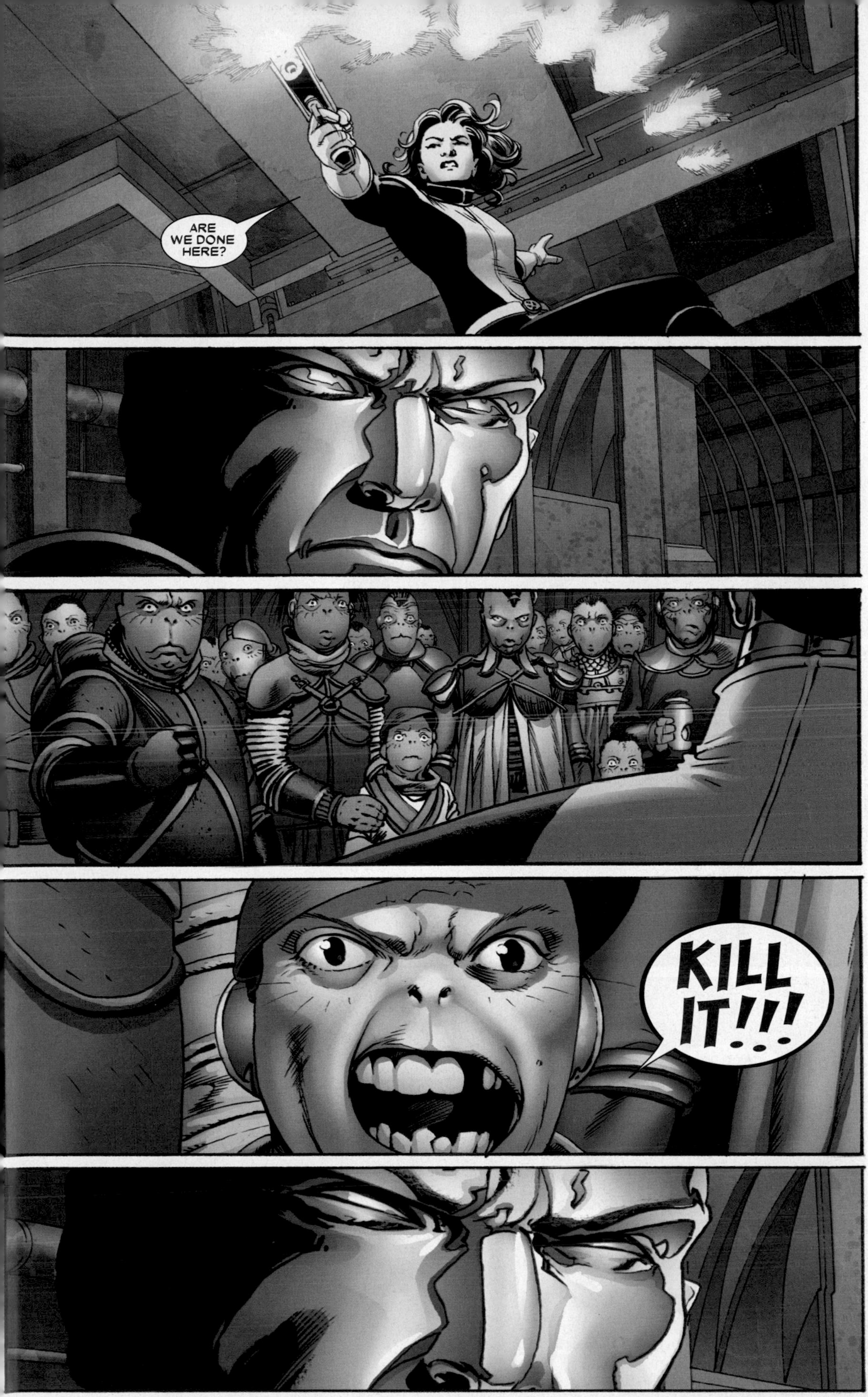
ARE WE DONE HERE?
KILL IT!!!

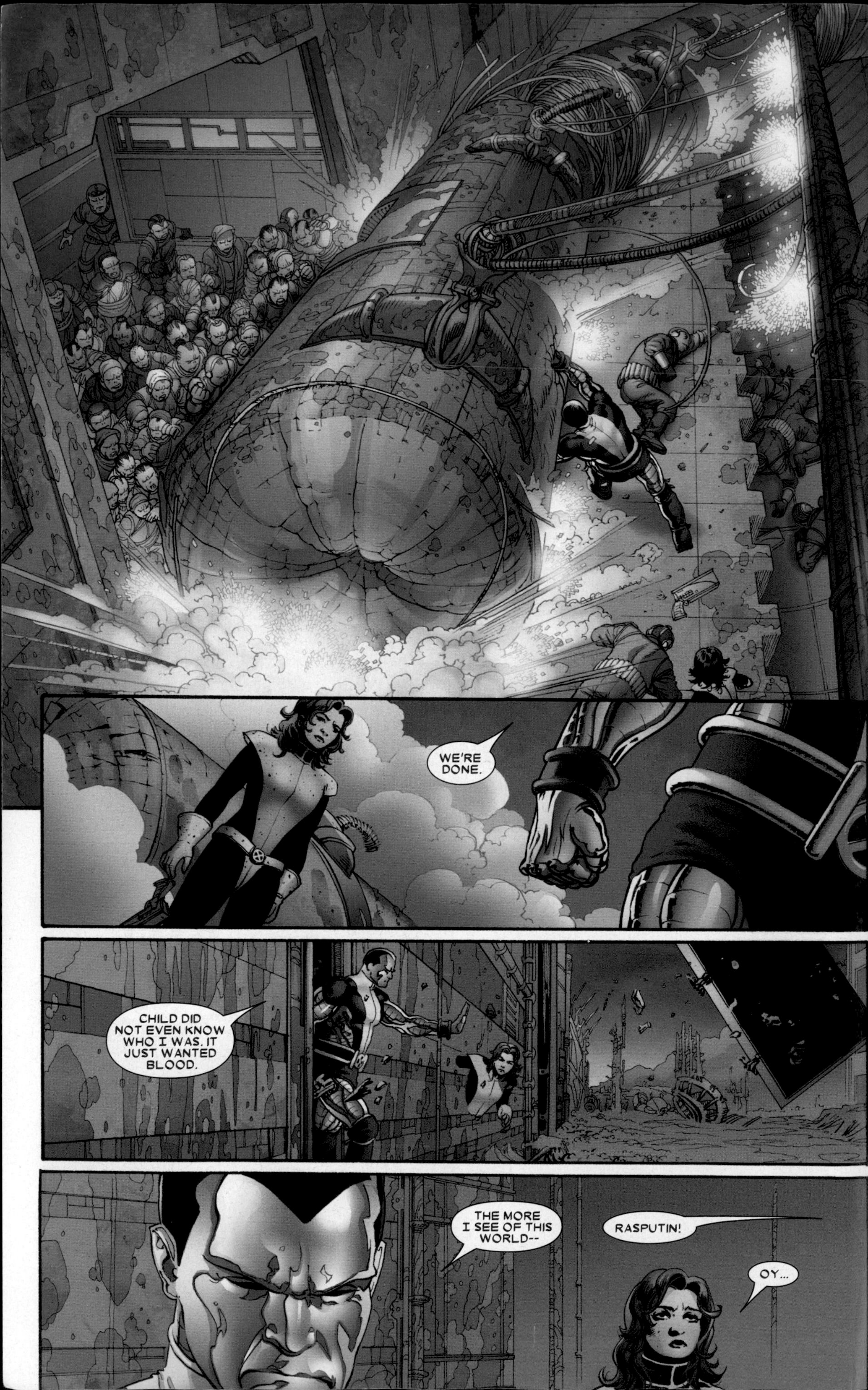
WE'RE DONE.
CHILD DID NOT EVEN KNOW WHO I WAS. IT JUST WANTED BLOOD.
THE MORE I SEE OF THIS WORLD--
RASPUTIN!
OY...

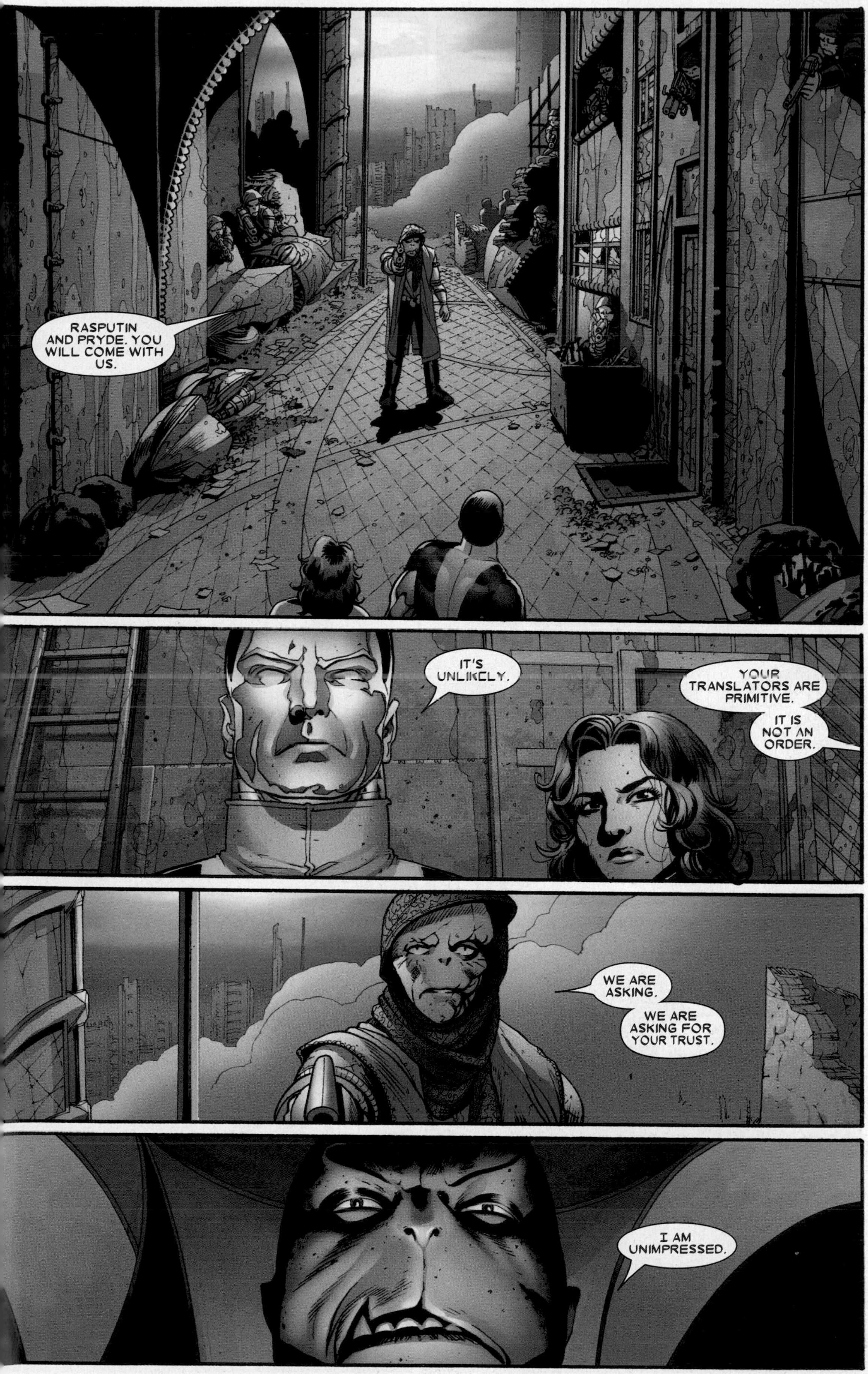
RASPUTIN AND PRYDE. YOU WILL COME WITH US.
IT'S UNLIKELY.
YOUR TRANSLATORS ARE PRIMITIVE.
IT IS NOT AN ORDER.
WE ARE ASKING.
WE ARE ASKING FOR YOUR TRUST.
I AM UNIMPRESSED.

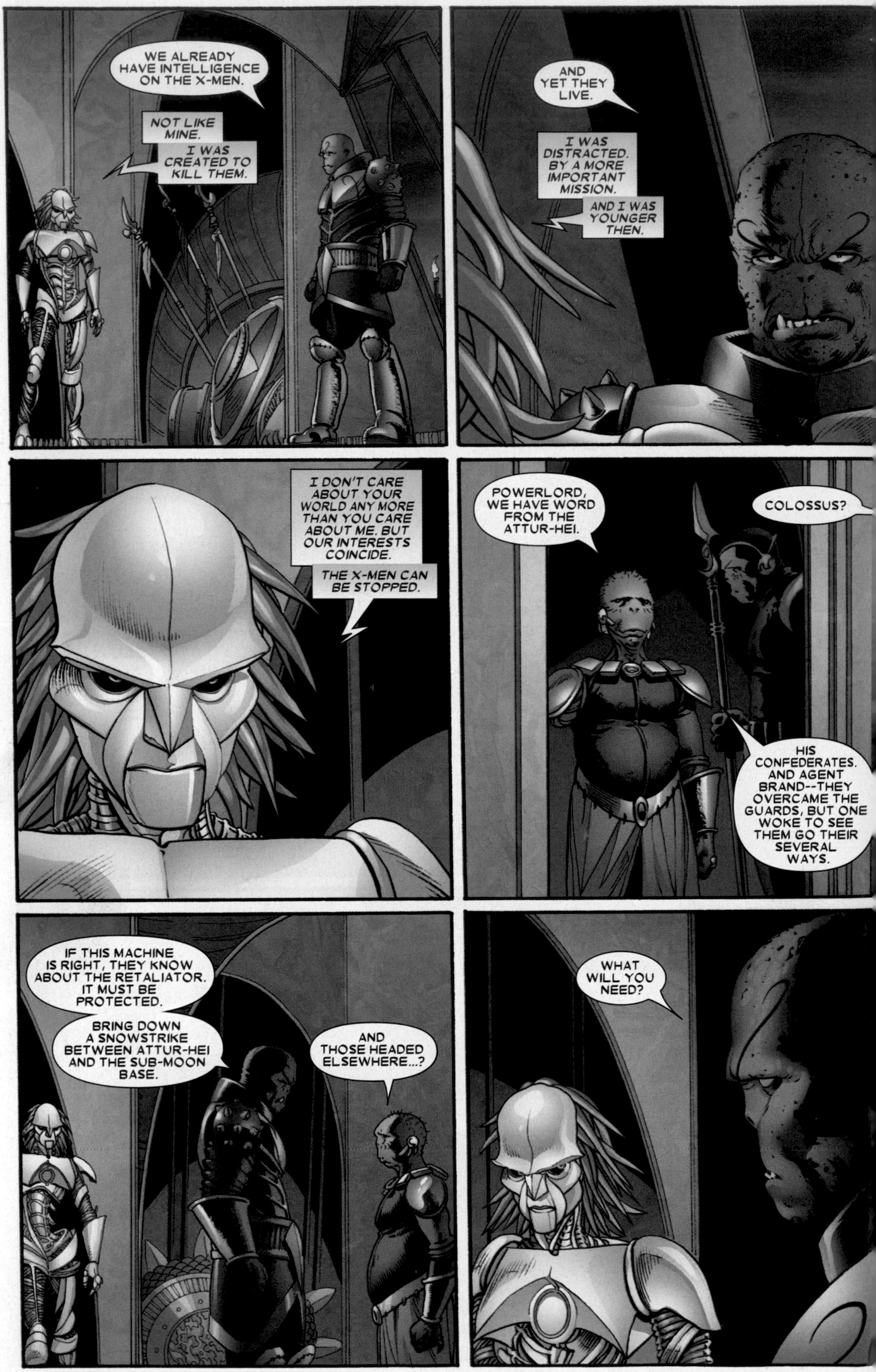
WE ALREADY HAVE INTELLIGENCE ON THE X-MEN.
NOT LIKE MINE.
I WAS CREATED TO KILL THEM.
AND YET THEY LIVE.
I WAS DISTRACTED. BY A MORE IMPORTANT MISSION.
AND I WAS YOUNGER THEN.
I DON'T CARE ABOUT YOUR WORLD ANY MORE THAN YOU CARE ABOUT ME. BUT OUR INTERESTS COINCIDE.
THE X-MEN CAN BE STOPPED.
POWERLORD, WE HAVE WORD FROM THE ATTUR-HEI.
COLOSSUS?
HIS CONFEDERATES. AND AGENT BRAND--THEY OVERCAME THE GUARDS, BUT ONE WOKE TO SEE THEM GO THEIR SEVERAL WAYS.
IF THIS MACHINE IS RIGHT, THEY KNOW ABOUT THE RETALIATOR. IT MUST BE PROTECTED.
BRING DOWN A SNOWSTRIKE BETWEEN ATTUR-HEI AND THE SUB-MOON BASE.
AND THOSE HEADED ELSEWHERE...?
WHAT WILL YOU NEED?

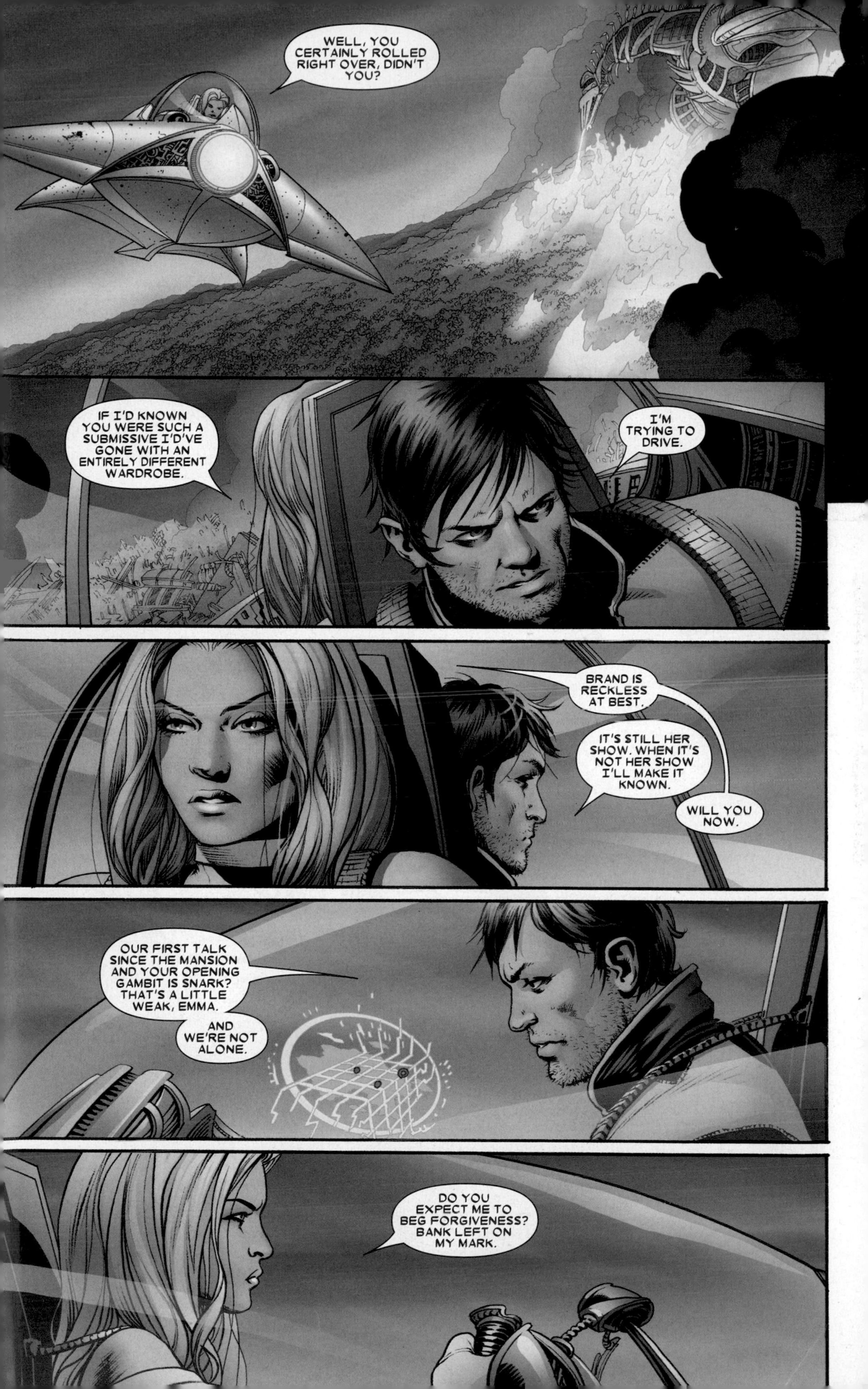
WELL, YOU CERTAINLY ROLLED RIGHT OVER, DIDN'T YOU?
IF I'D KNOWN YOU WERE SUCH A SUBMISSIVE I'D'VE GONE WITH AN ENTIRELY DIFFERENT WARDROBE.
I'M TRYING TO DRIVE.
BRAND IS RECKLESS AT BEST.
IT'S STILL HER SHOW. WHEN IT'S NOT HER SHOW I'LL MAKE IT KNOWN.
WILL YOU NOW.
OUR FIRST TALK SINCE THE MANSION AND YOUR OPENING GAMBIT IS SNARK? THAT'S A LITTLE WEAK, EMMA.
AND WE'RE NOT ALONE.
DO YOU EXPECT ME TO BEG FORGIVENESS? BANK LEFT ON MY MARK.

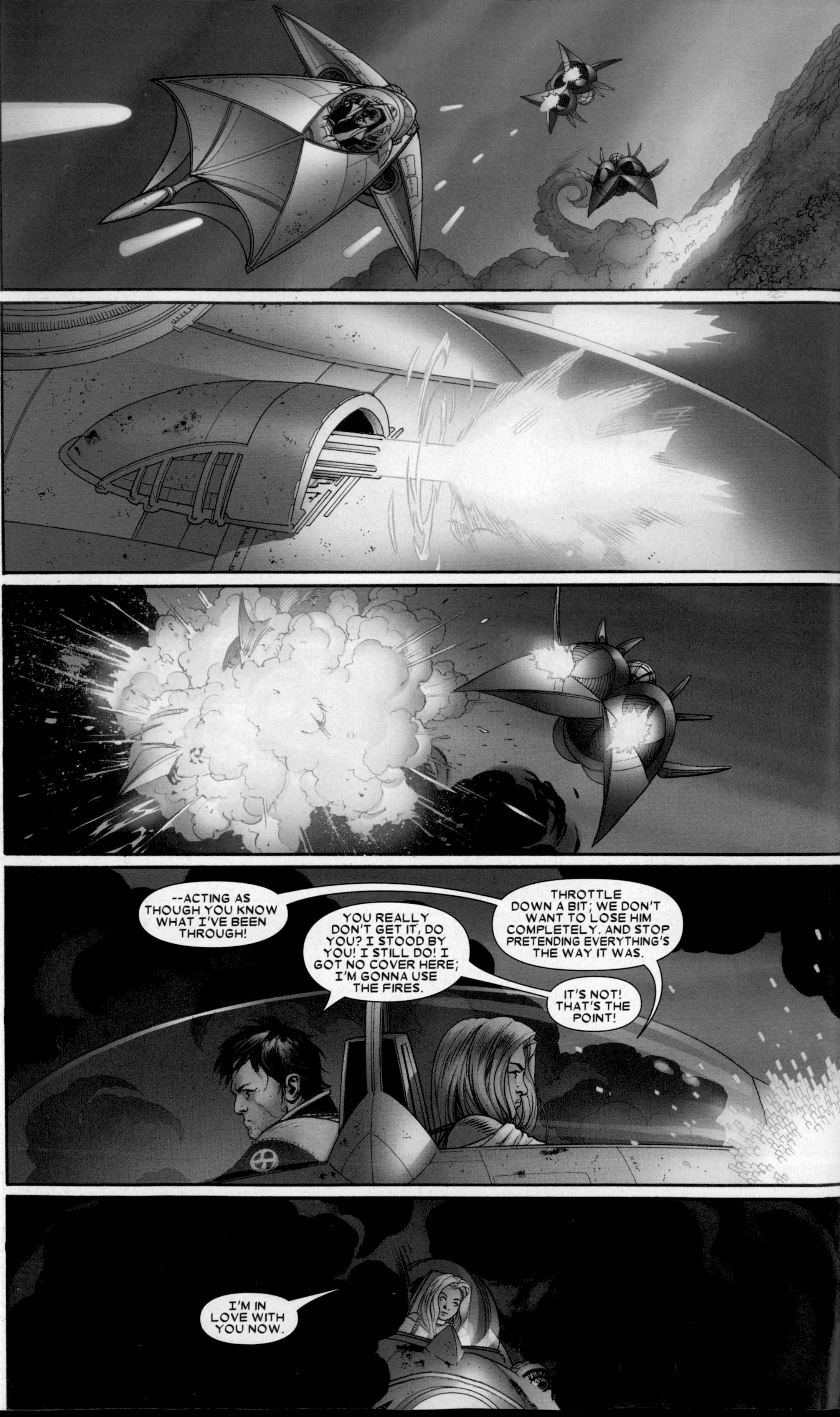
--ACTING AS THOUGH YOU KNOW WHAT I'VE BEEN THROUGH!
THROTTLE DOWN A BIT; WE DON'T WANT TO LOSE HIM COMPLETELY. AND STOP PRETENDING EVERYTHING'S THE WAY IT WAS.
YOU REALLY DON'T GET IT, DO YOU? I STOOD BY YOU! I STILL DO! I GOT NO COVER HERE; I'M GONNA USE THE FIRES.
IT'S NOT! THAT'S THE POINT!
I'M IN LOVE WITH YOU NOW.

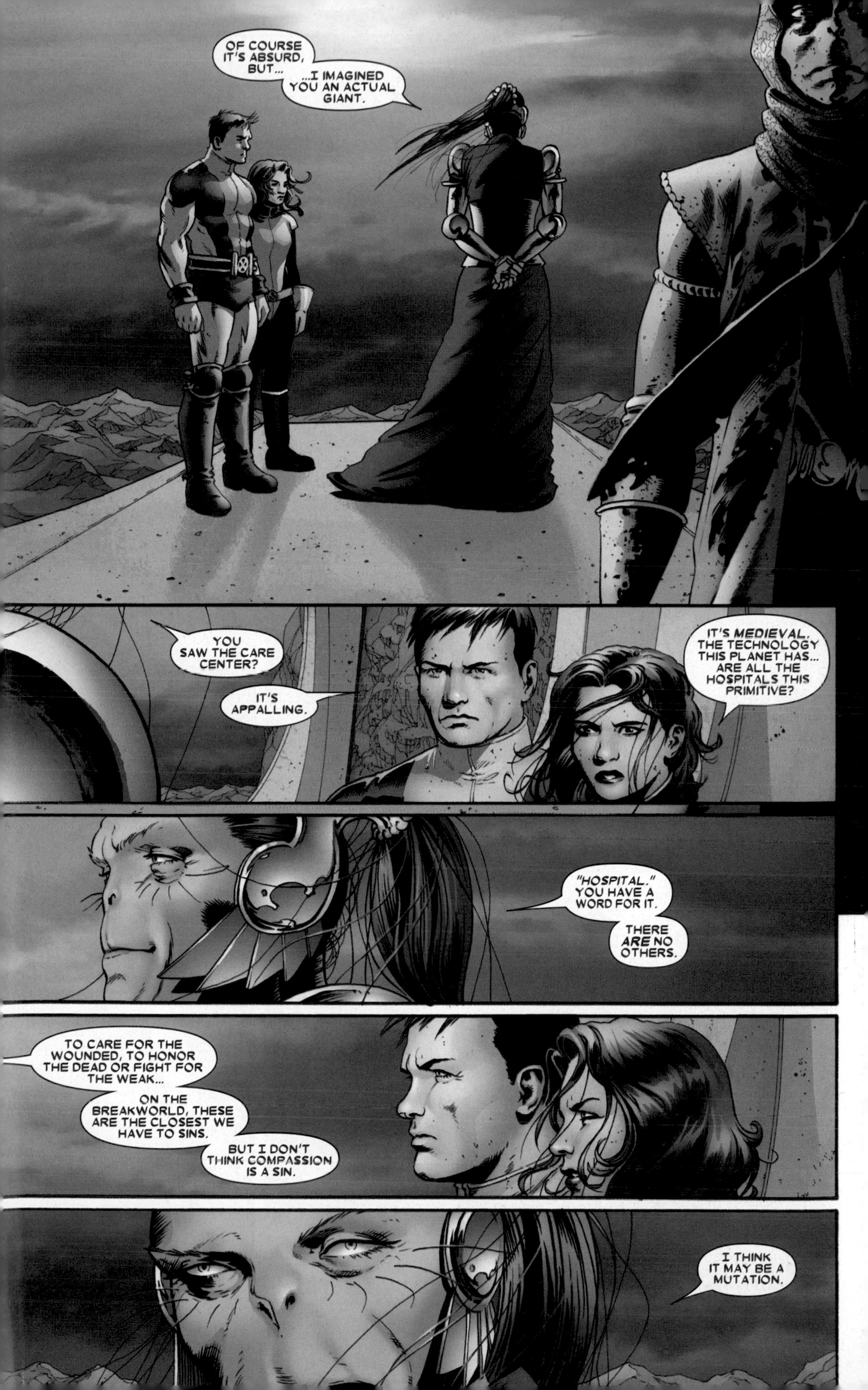
OF COURSE IT'S ABSURD, BUT...
...I IMAGINED YOU AN ACTUAL GIANT.
YOU SAW THE CARE CENTER?
IT'S APPALLING.
IT'S MEDIEVAL. THE TECHNOLOGY THIS PLANET HAS... ARE ALL THE HOSPITALS THIS PRIMITIVE?
"HOSPITAL." YOU HAVE A WORD FOR IT.
THERE ARE NO OTHERS.
TO CARE FOR THE WOUNDED, TO HONOR THE DEAD OR FIGHT FOR THE WEAK...
ON THE BREAKWORLD, THESE ARE THE CLOSEST WE HAVE TO SINS.
BUT I DON'T THINK COMPASSION IS A SIN.
I THINK IT MAY BE A MUTATION.

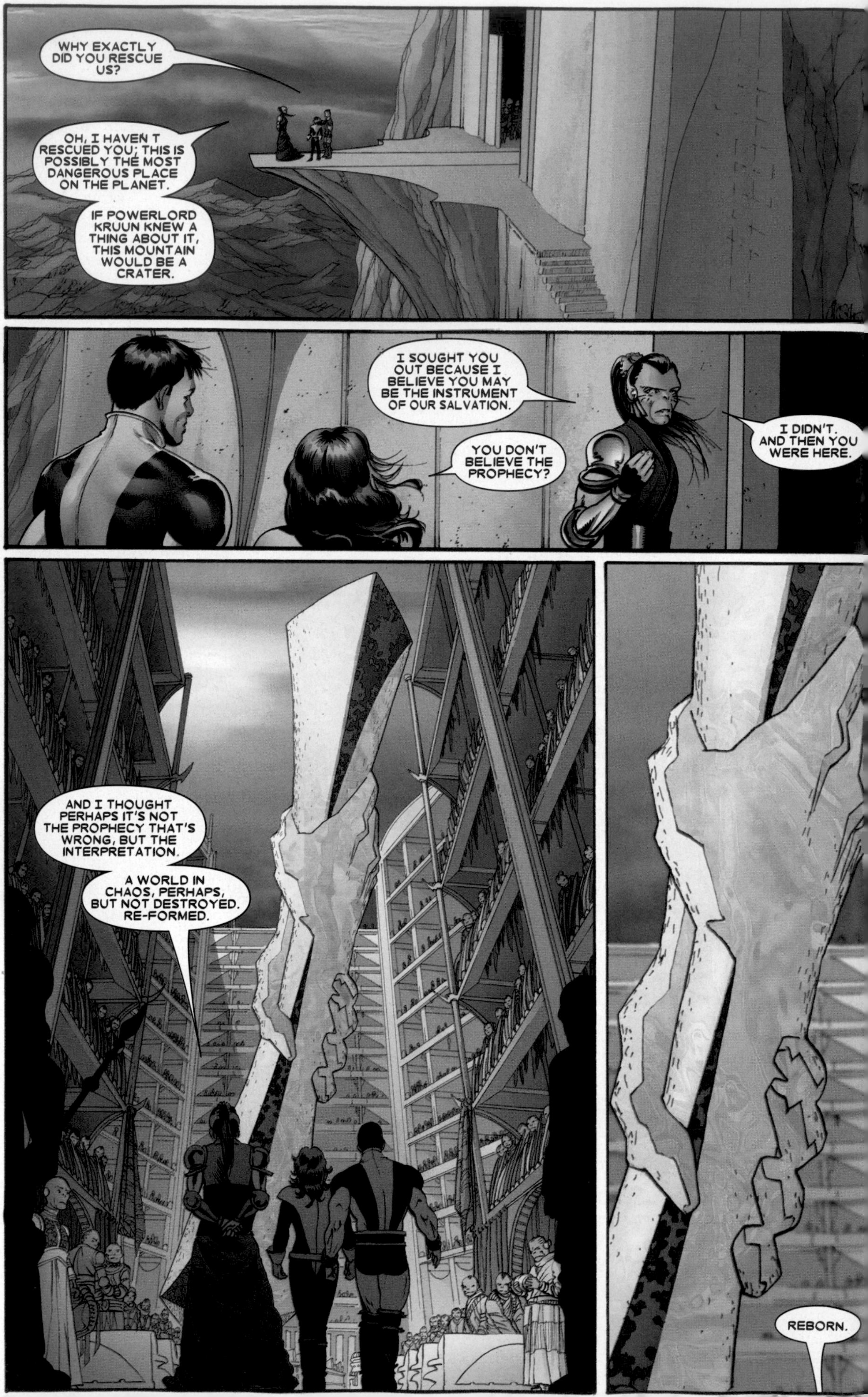
WHY EXACTLY DID YOU RESCUE US?
OH, I HAVEN'T RESCUED YOU; THIS IS POSSIBLY THE MOST DANGEROUS PLACE ON THE PLANET.
IF POWERLORD KRUUN KNEW A THING ABOUT IT, THIS MOUNTAIN WOULD BE A CRATER.
I SOUGHT YOU OUT BECAUSE I BELIEVE YOU MAY BE THE INSTRUMENT OF OUR SALVATION.
YOU DON'T BELIEVE THE PROPHECY?
I DIDN'T. AND THEN YOU WERE HERE.
AND I THOUGHT PERHAPS IT'S NOT THE PROPHECY THAT'S WRONG, BUT THE INTERPRETATION.
A WORLD IN CHAOS, PERHAPS, BUT NOT DESTROYED. RE-FORMED.
REBORN.

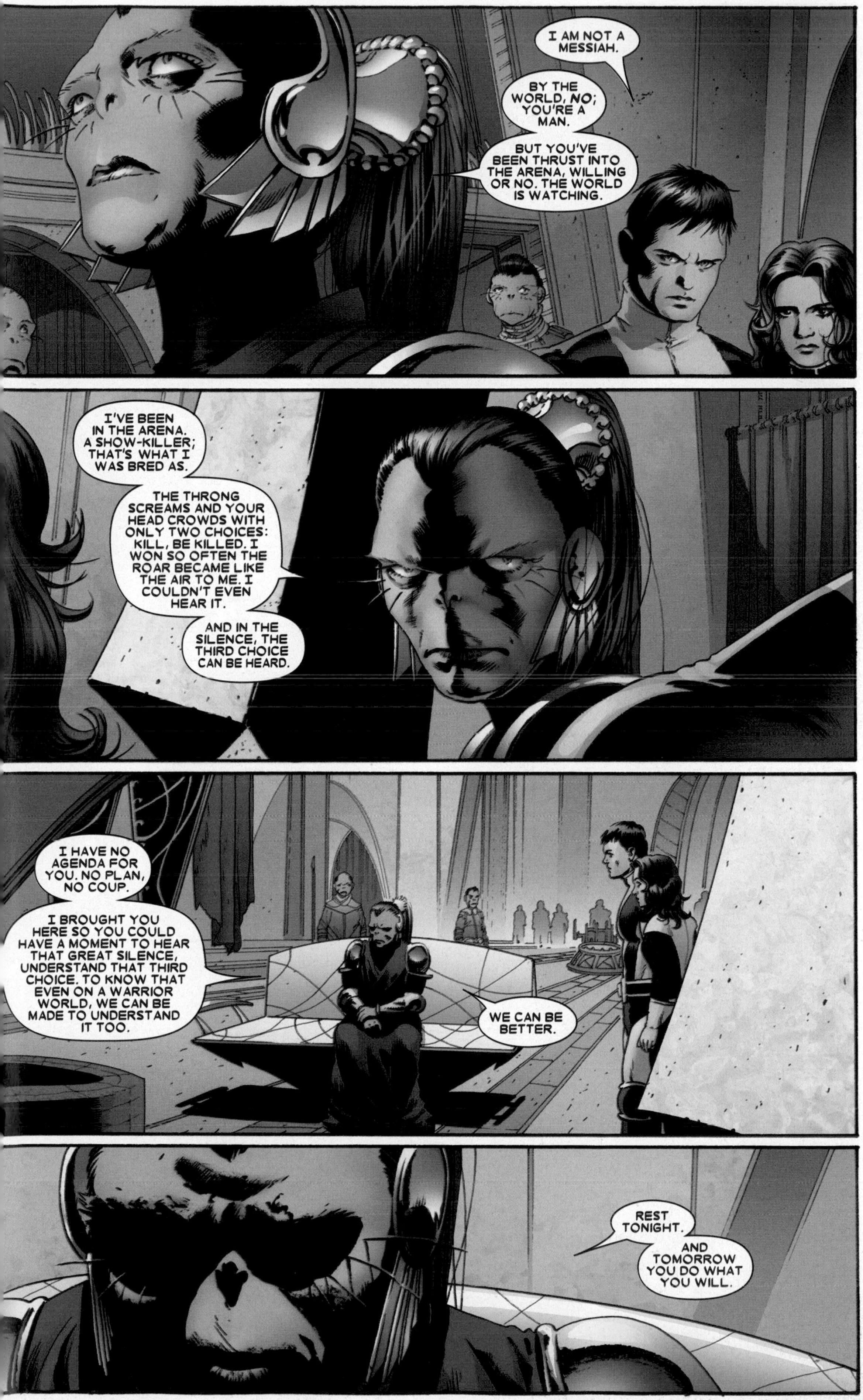
I AM NOT A MESSIAH.
BY THE WORLD, NO; YOU'RE A MAN.
BUT YOU'VE BEEN THRUST INTO THE ARENA, WILLING OR NO. THE WORLD IS WATCHING.
I'VE BEEN IN THE ARENA. A SHOW-KILLER; THAT'S WHAT I WAS BRED AS.
THE THRONG SCREAMS AND YOUR HEAD CROWDS WITH ONLY TWO CHOICES: KILL, BE KILLED. I WON SO OFTEN THE ROAR BECAME LIKE THE AIR TO ME. I COULDN'T EVEN HEAR IT.
AND IN THE SILENCE, THE THIRD CHOICE CAN BE HEARD.
I HAVE NO AGENDA FOR YOU. NO PLAN, NO COUP.
I BROUGHT YOU HERE SO YOU COULD HAVE A MOMENT TO HEAR THAT GREAT SILENCE, UNDERSTAND THAT THIRD CHOICE. TO KNOW THAT EVEN ON A WARRIOR WORLD, WE CAN BE MADE TO UNDERSTAND IT TOO.
WE CAN BE BETTER.
REST TONIGHT.
AND TOMORROW YOU DO WHAT YOU WILL.

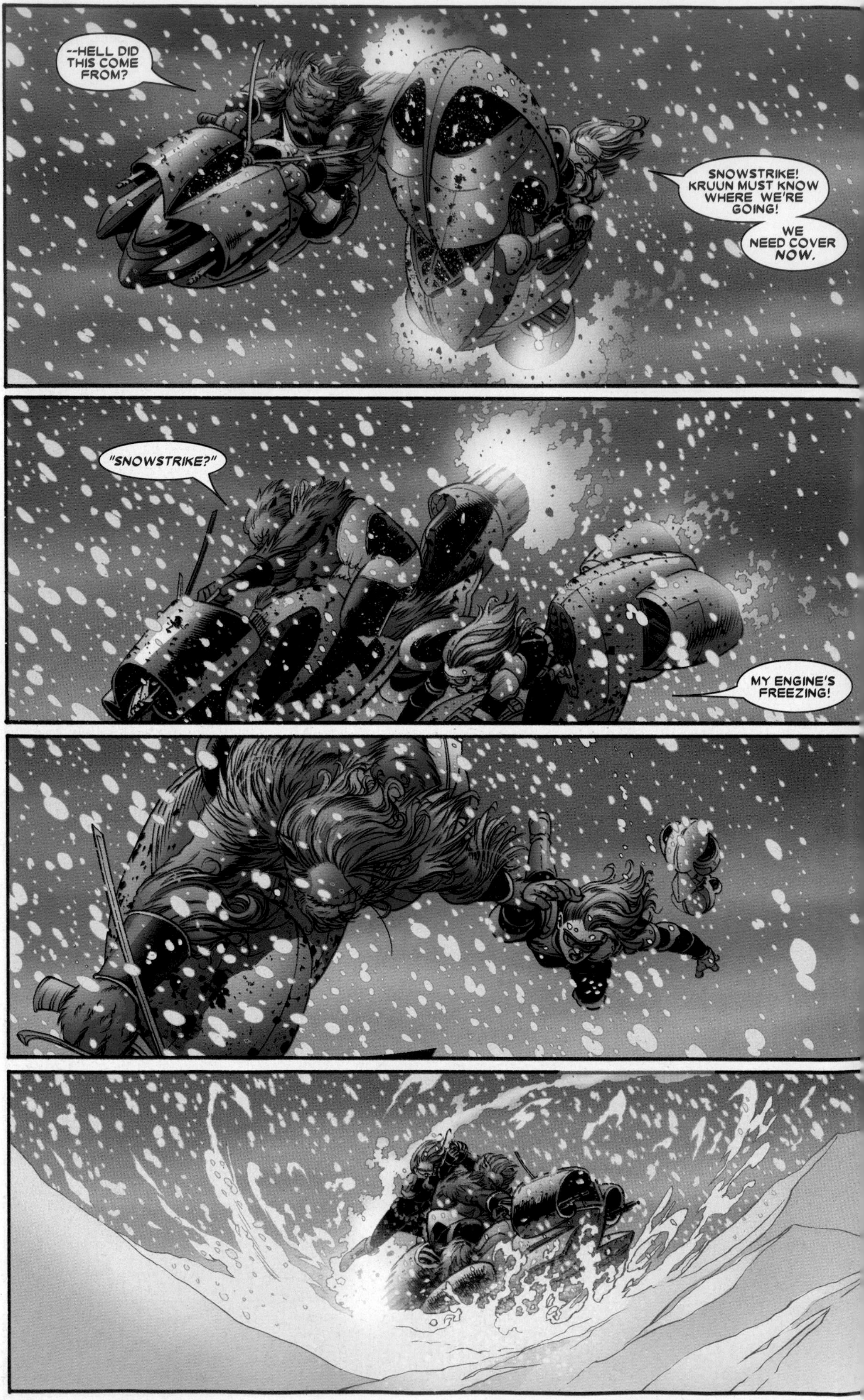
--HELL DID THIS COME FROM?
SNOWSTRIKE! KRUUN MUST KNOW WHERE WE'RE GOING!
WE NEED COVER NOW.
"SNOWSTRIKE?"
MY ENGINE'S FREEZING!

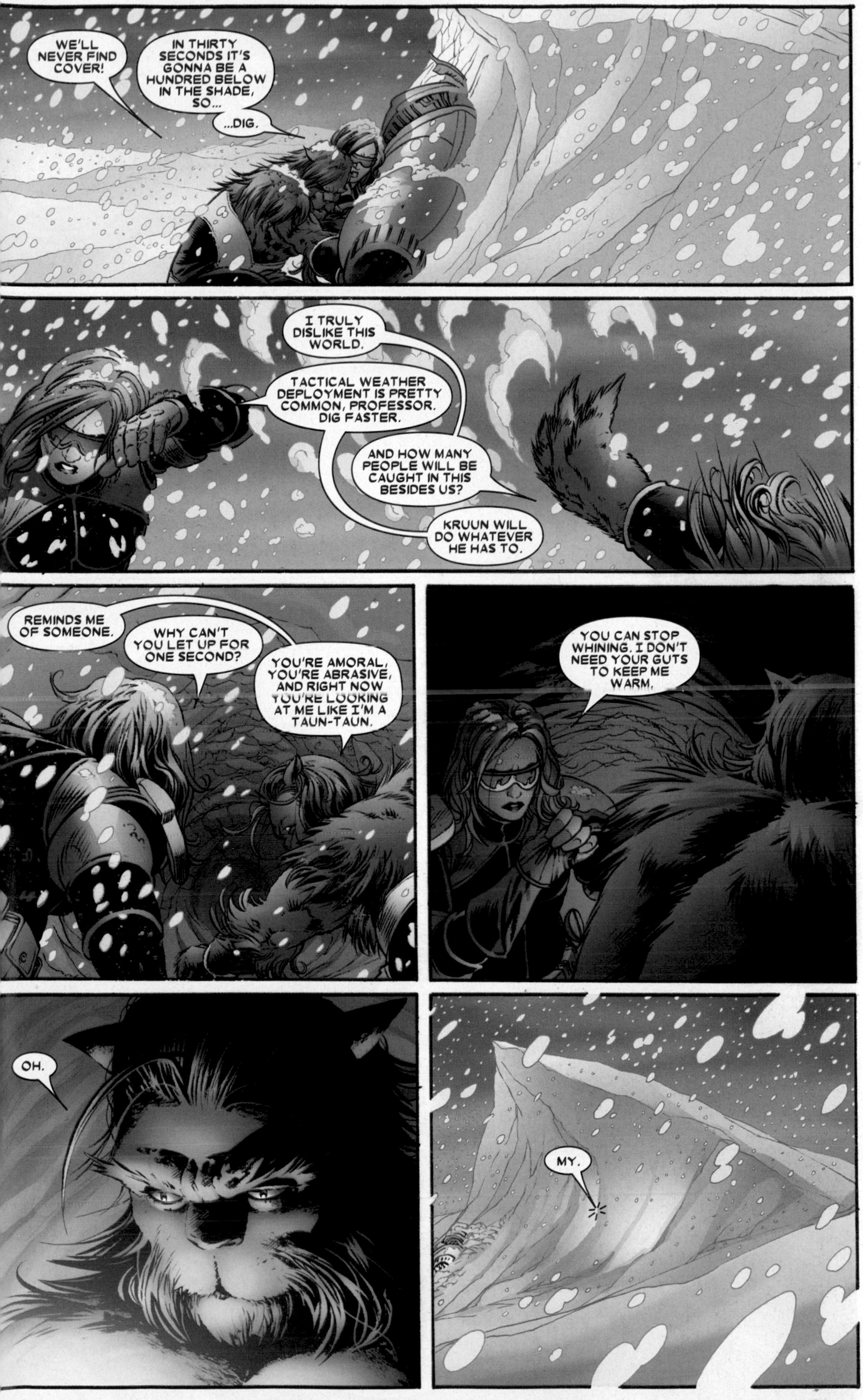
WE'LL NEVER FIND COVER!
IN THIRTY SECONDS IT'S GONNA BE A HUNDRED BELOW IN THE SHADE, SO...
...DIG.
I TRULY DISLIKE THIS WORLD.
TACTICAL WEATHER DEPLOYMENT IS PRETTY COMMON, PROFESSOR. DIG FASTER.
AND HOW MANY PEOPLE WILL BE CAUGHT IN THIS BESIDES US?
KRUUN WILL DO WHATEVER HE HAS TO.
REMINDS ME OF SOMEONE.
WHY CAN'T YOU LET UP FOR ONE SECOND?
YOU'RE AMORAL, YOU'RE ABRASIVE, AND RIGHT NOW YOU'RE LOOKING AT ME LIKE I'M A TAUN-TAUN.
YOU CAN STOP WHINING. I DON'T NEED YOUR GUTS TO KEEP ME WARM.
OH.
MY.

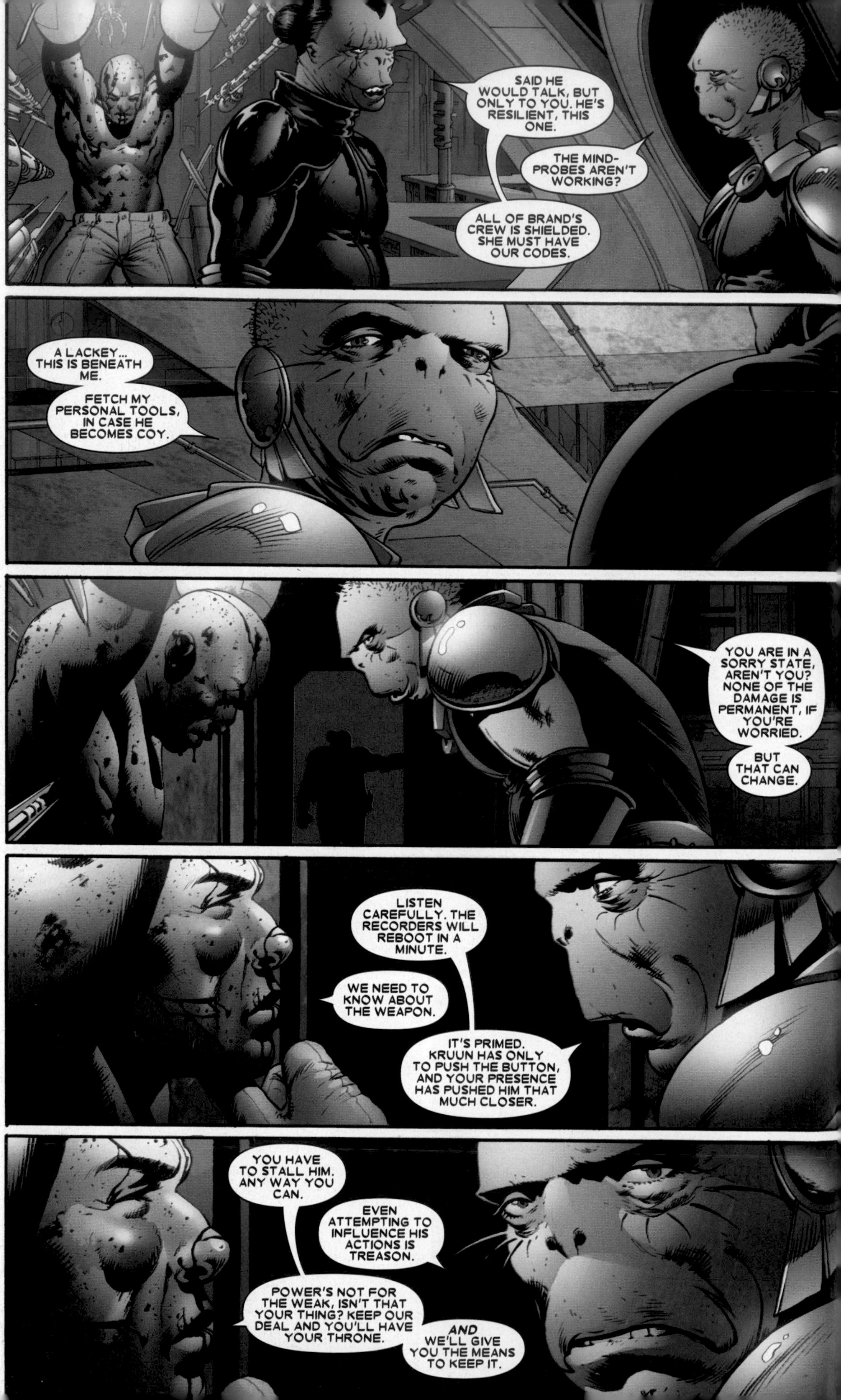
SAID HE WOULD TALK, BUT ONLY TO YOU. HE'S RESILIENT, THIS ONE.
THE MIND-PROBES AREN'T WORKING?
ALL OF BRAND'S CREW IS SHIELDED. SHE MUST HAVE OUR CODES.
A LACKEY... THIS IS BENEATH ME.
FETCH MY PERSONAL TOOLS, IN CASE HE BECOMES COY.
YOU ARE IN A SORRY STATE, AREN'T YOU? NONE OF THE DAMAGE IS PERMANENT, IF YOU'RE WORRIED.
BUT THAT CAN CHANGE.
LISTEN CAREFULLY. THE RECORDERS WILL REBOOT IN A MINUTE.
WE NEED TO KNOW ABOUT THE WEAPON.
IT'S PRIMED. KRUUN HAS ONLY TO PUSH THE BUTTON, AND YOUR PRESENCE HAS PUSHED HIM THAT MUCH CLOSER.
YOU HAVE TO STALL HIM. ANY WAY YOU CAN.
EVEN ATTEMPTING TO INFLUENCE HIS ACTIONS IS TREASON.
POWER'S NOT FOR THE WEAK, ISN'T THAT YOUR THING? KEEP OUR DEAL AND YOU'LL HAVE YOUR THRONE.
AND WE'LL GIVE YOU THE MEANS TO KEEP IT.

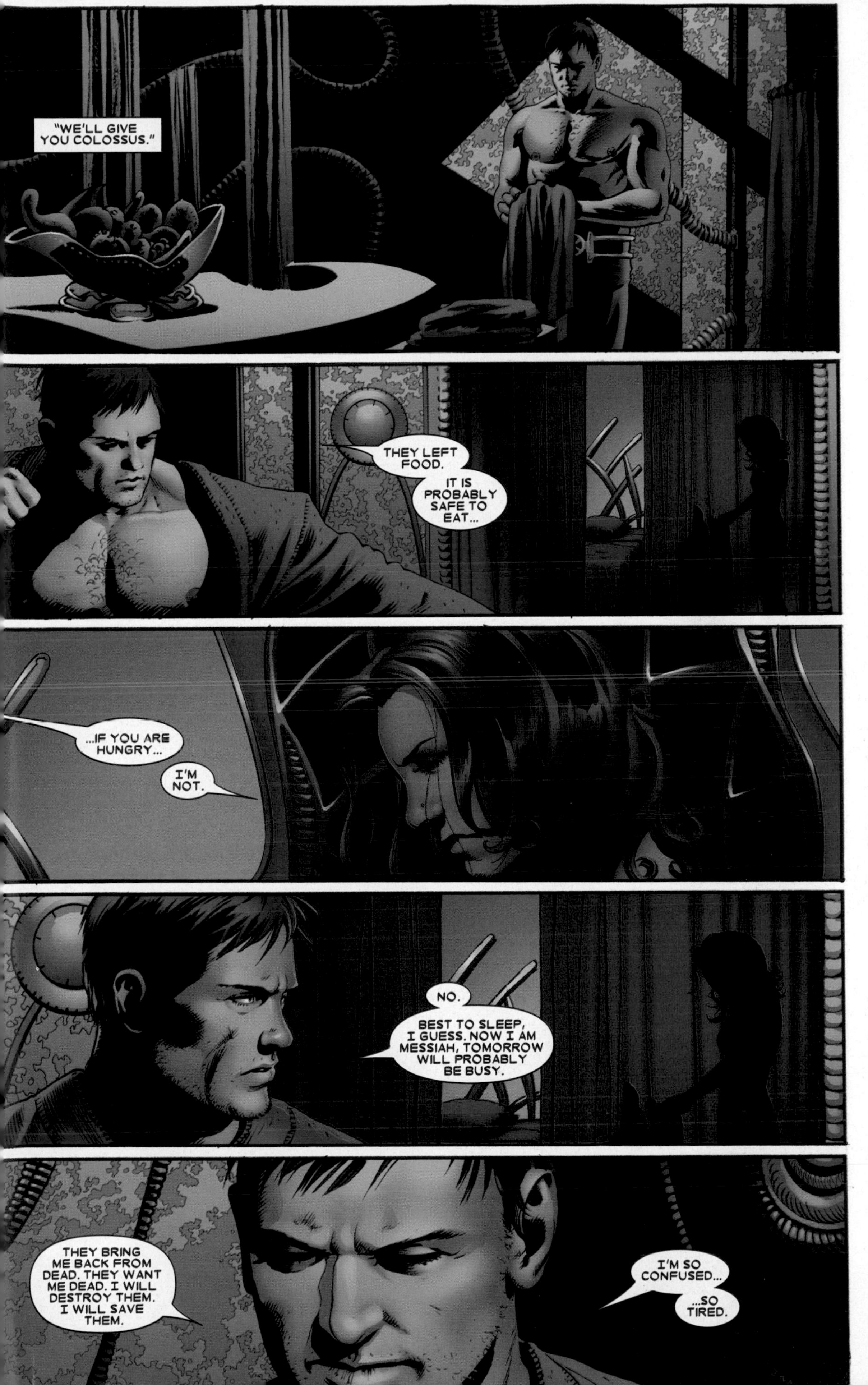
"WE'LL GIVE YOU COLOSSUS."
THEY LEFT FOOD.
IT IS PROBABLY SAFE TO EAT...
...IF YOU ARE HUNGRY...
I'M NOT.
NO.
BEST TO SLEEP, I GUESS. NOW I AM MESSIAH, TOMORROW WILL PROBABLY BE BUSY.
THEY BRING ME BACK FROM DEAD. THEY WANT ME DEAD. I WILL DESTROY THEM. I WILL SAVE THEM.
I'M SO CONFUSED...
...SO TIRED.

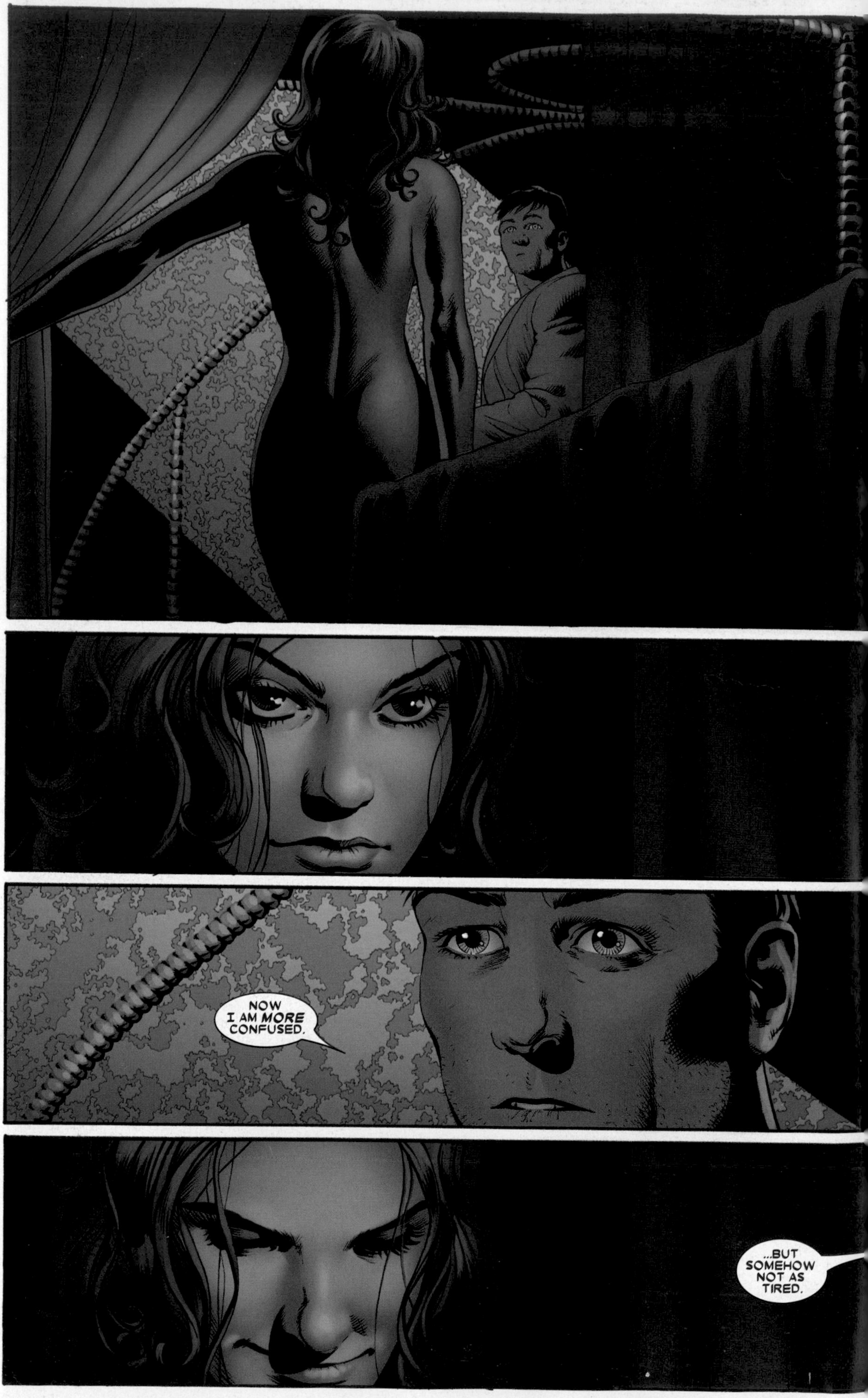
NOW I AM MORE CONFUSED.
...BUT SOMEHOW NOT AS TIRED.

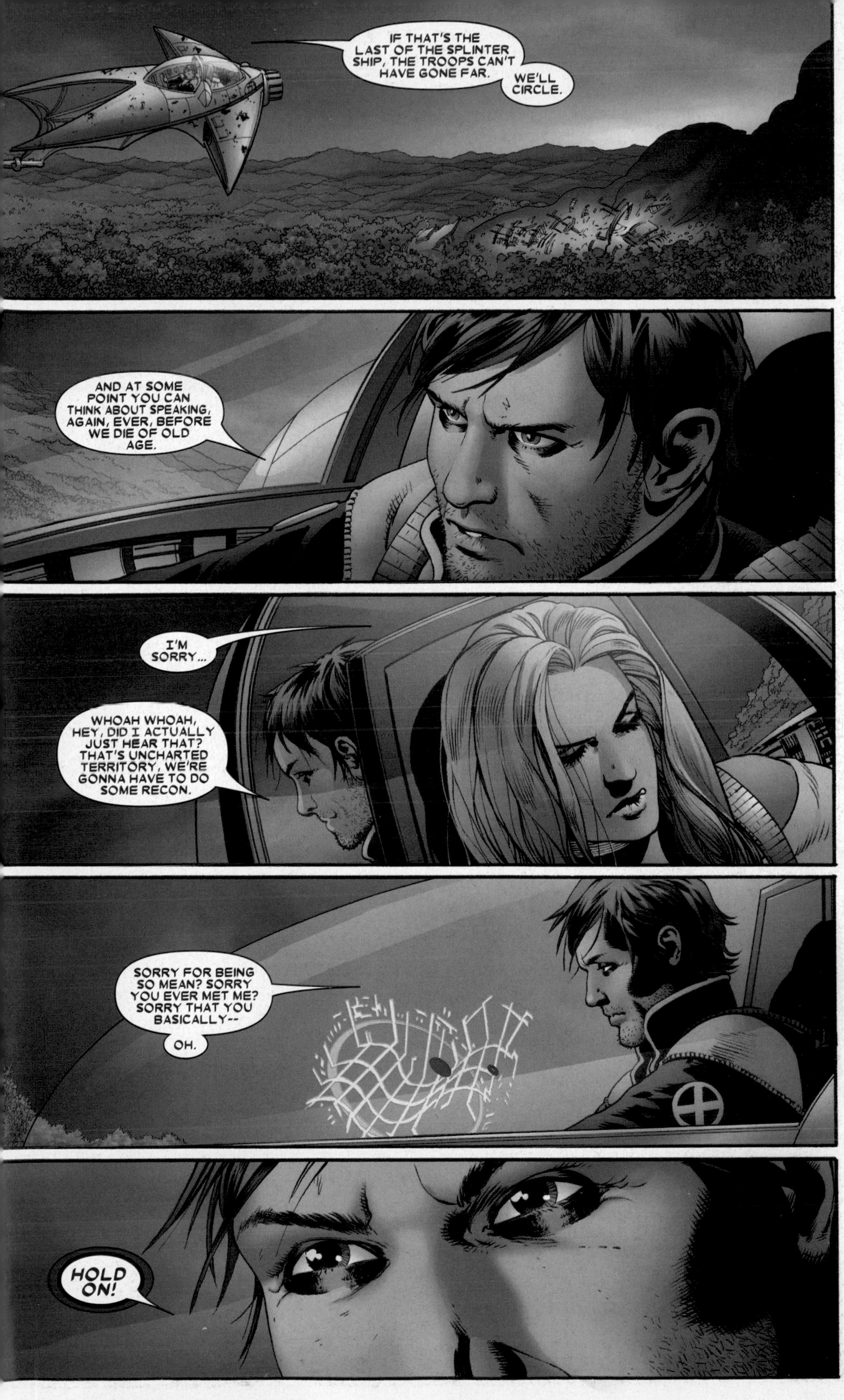
IF THAT'S THE LAST OF THE SPLINTER SHIP, THE TROOPS CAN'T HAVE GONE FAR.
WE'LL CIRCLE.
AND AT SOME POINT YOU CAN THINK ABOUT SPEAKING, AGAIN, EVER, BEFORE WE DIE OF OLD AGE.
I'M SORRY...
WHOAH WHOAH, HEY, DID I ACTUALLY JUST HEAR THAT? THAT'S UNCHARTED TERRITORY, WE'RE GONNA HAVE TO DO SOME RECON.
SORRY FOR BEING SO MEAN? SORRY YOU EVER MET ME? SORRY THAT YOU BASICALLY--
OH.
HOLD ON!

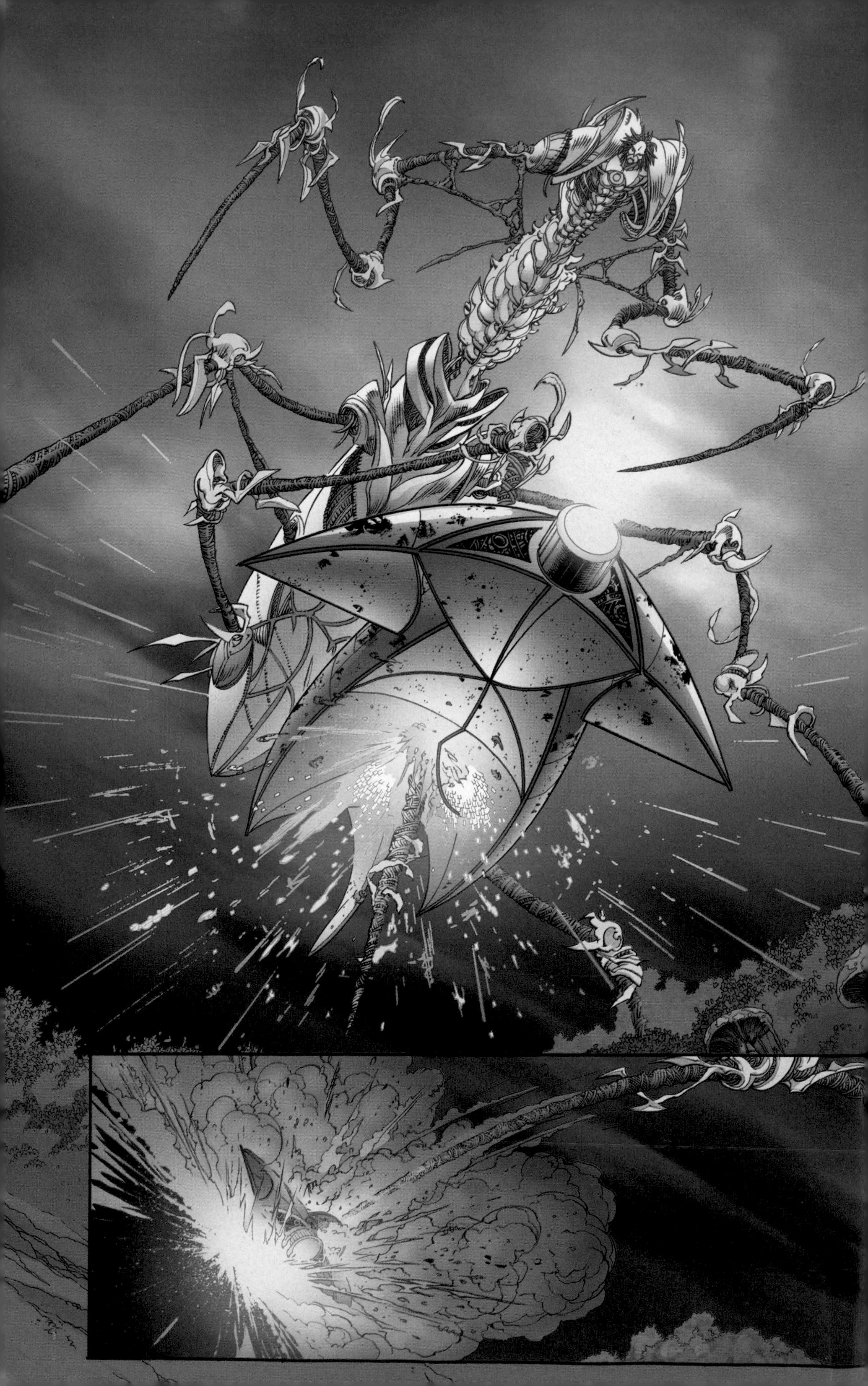

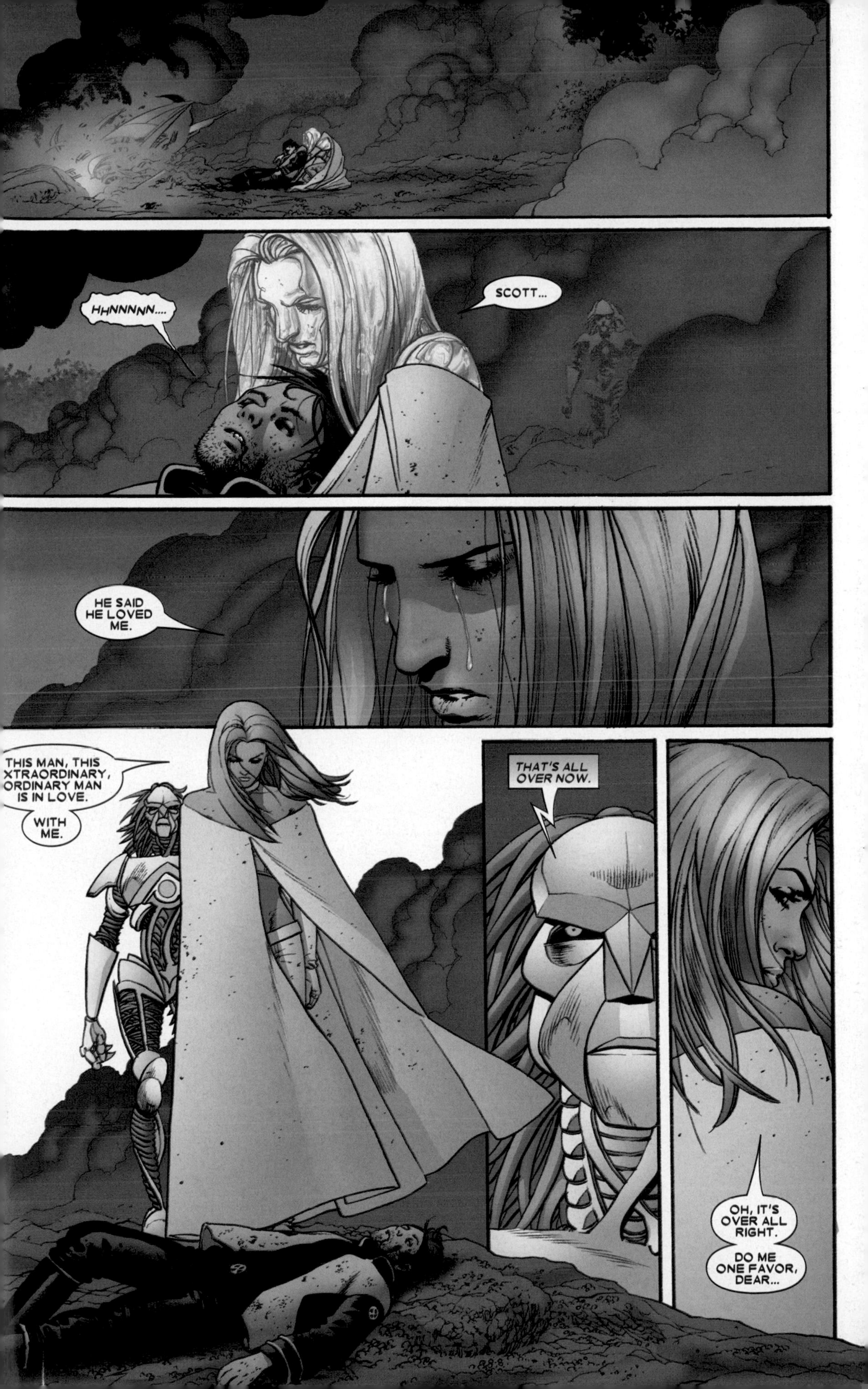
HHNNNNN....
SCOTT...
HE SAID HE LOVED ME.
THIS MAN, THIS XTRAORDINARY, ORDINARY MAN IS IN LOVE.
WITH ME.
THAT'S ALL OVER NOW.
OH, IT'S OVER ALL RIGHT.
DO ME ONE FAVOR, DEAR...

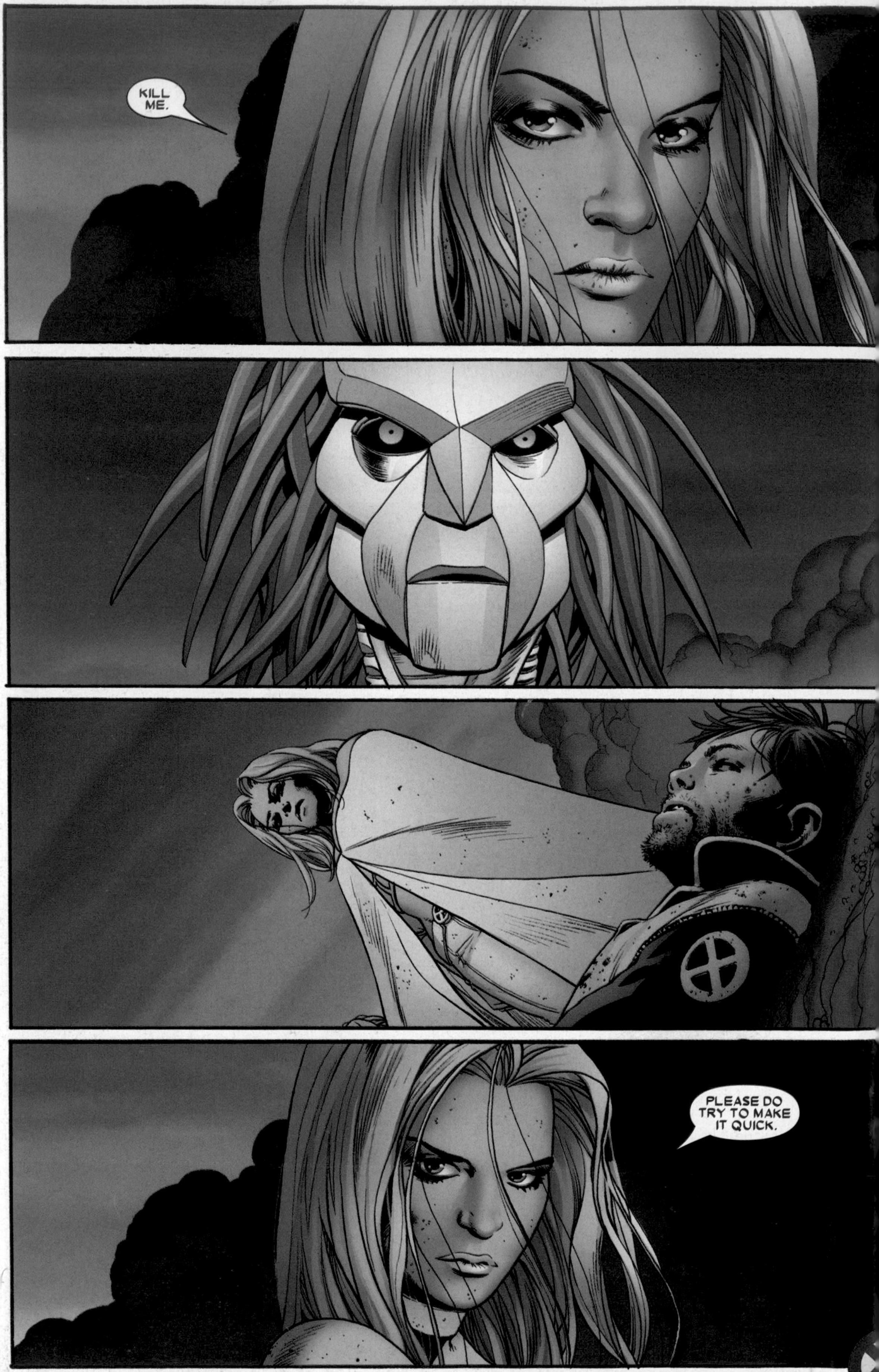
KILL ME.
PLEASE DO TRY TO MAKE IT QUICK.

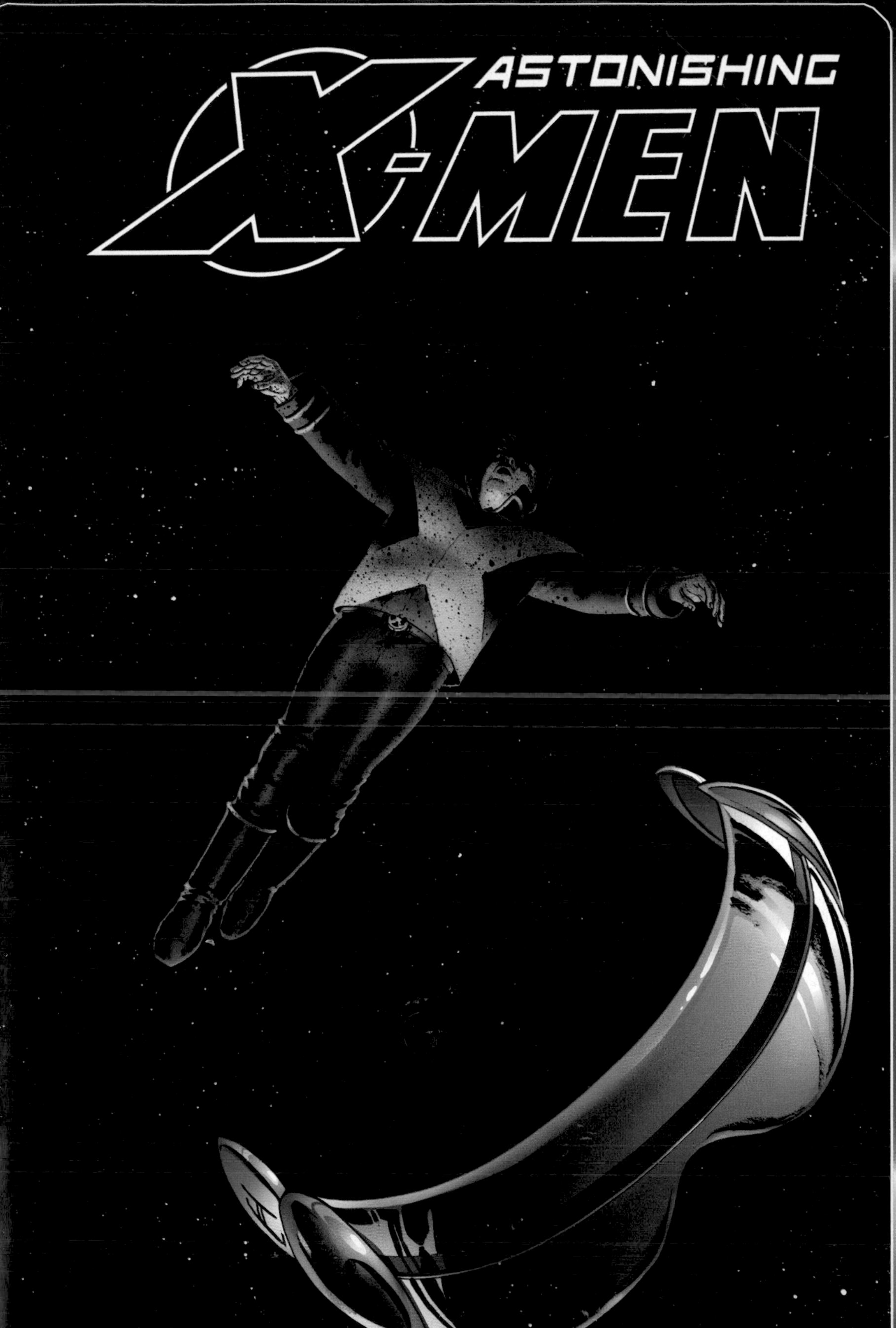
ASTONISHING
X-MEN

22

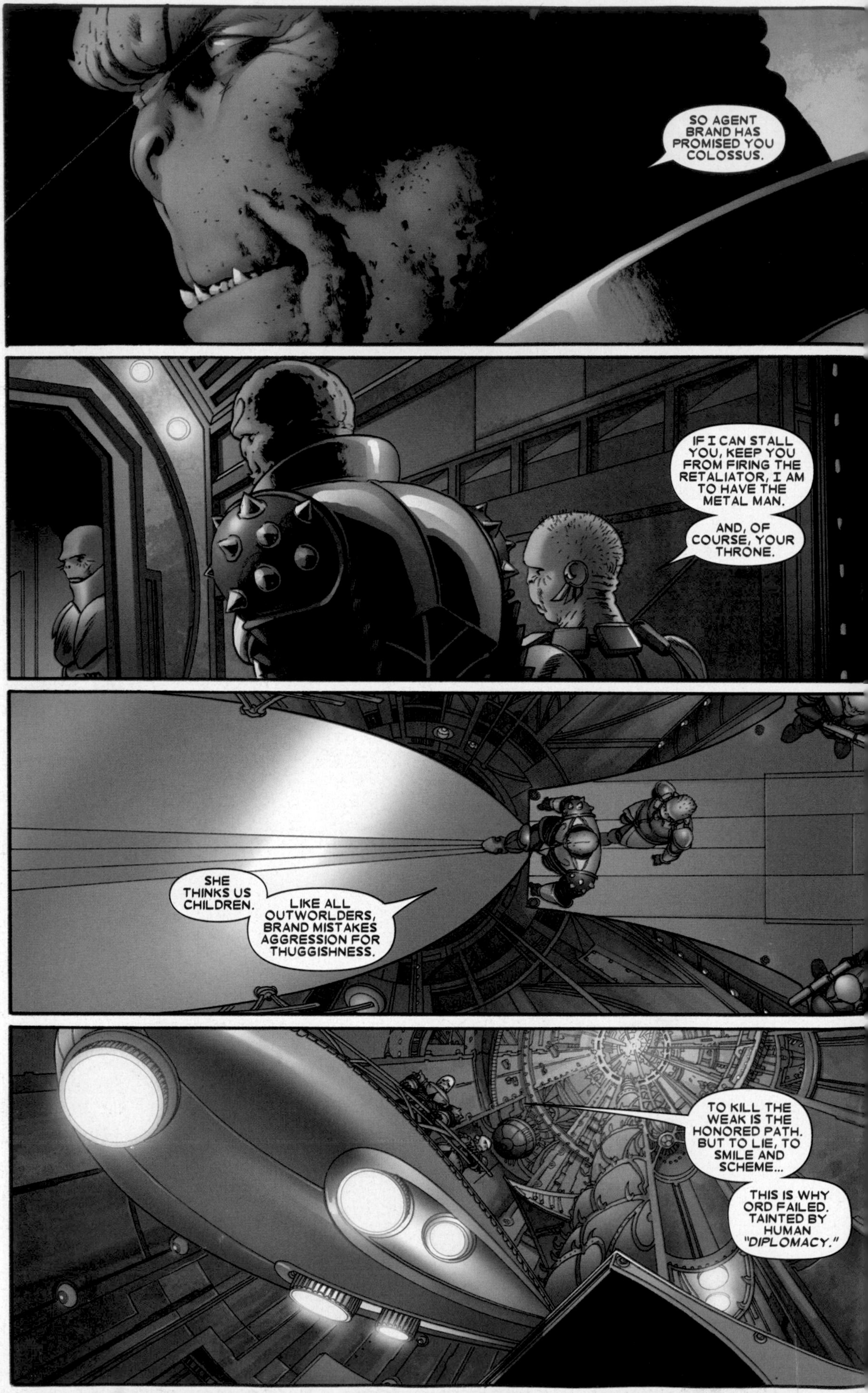
SO AGENT BRAND HAS PROMISED YOU COLOSSUS.
IF I CAN STALL YOU, KEEP YOU FROM FIRING THE RETALIATOR, I AM TO HAVE THE METAL MAN.
AND, OF COURSE, YOUR THRONE.
SHE THINKS US CHILDREN.
LIKE ALL OUTWORLDERS, BRAND MISTAKES AGGRESSION FOR THUGGISHNESS.
TO KILL THE WEAK IS THE HONORED PATH. BUT TO LIE, TO SMILE AND SCHEME...
THIS IS WHY ORD FAILED. TAINTED BY HUMAN "DIPLOMACY."

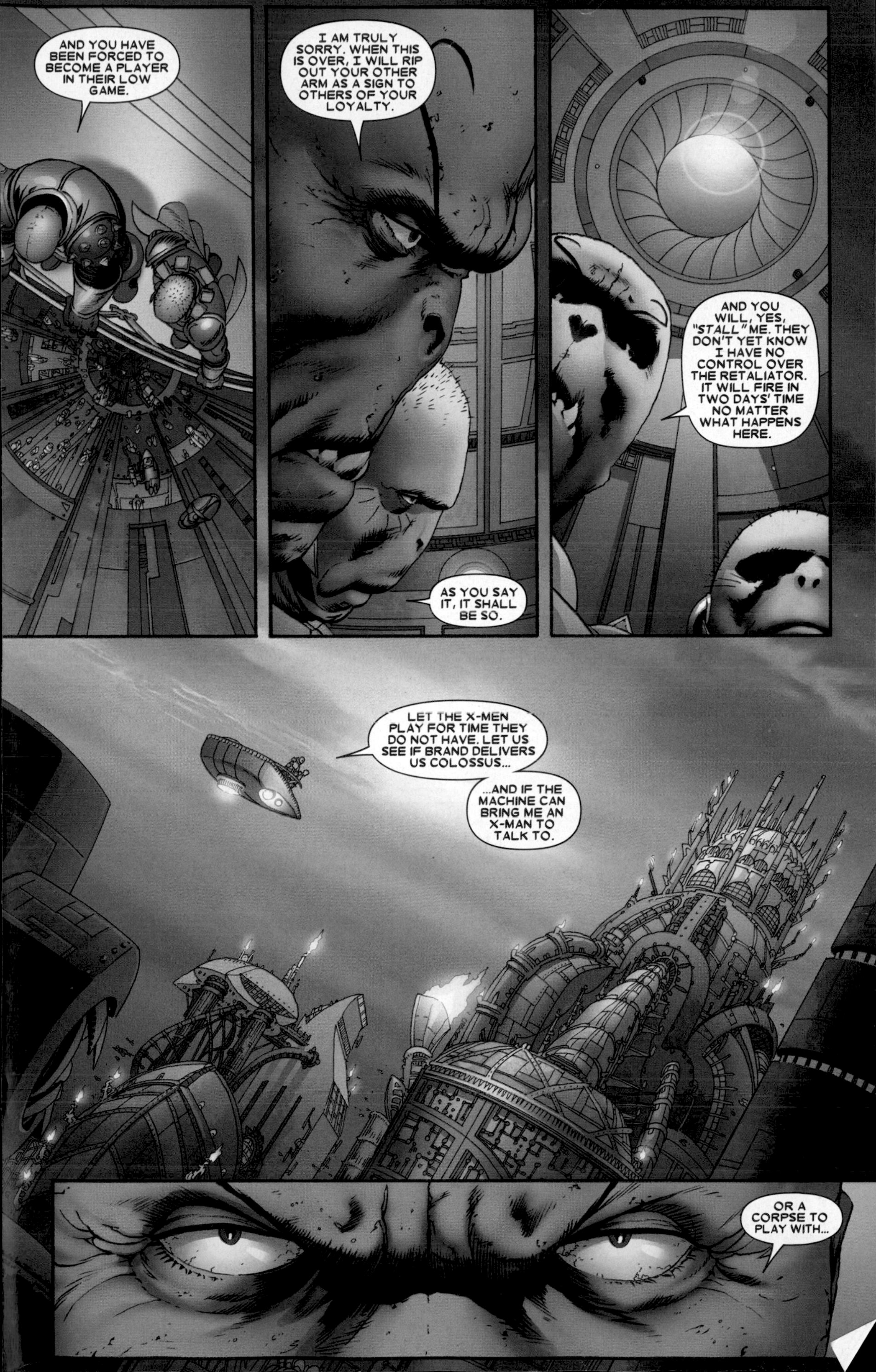
AND YOU HAVE BEEN FORCED TO BECOME A PLAYER IN THEIR LOW GAME.
I AM TRULY SORRY. WHEN THIS IS OVER, I WILL RIP OUT YOUR OTHER ARM AS A SIGN TO OTHERS OF YOUR LOYALTY.
AS YOU SAY IT, IT SHALL BE SO.
AND YOU WILL, YES, "STALL" ME. THEY DON'T YET KNOW I HAVE NO CONTROL OVER THE RETALIATOR. IT WILL FIRE IN TWO DAYS' TIME NO MATTER WHAT HAPPENS HERE.
LET THE X-MEN PLAY FOR TIME THEY DO NOT HAVE. LET US SEE IF BRAND DELIVERS US COLOSSUS...
...AND IF THE MACHINE CAN BRING ME AN X-MAN TO TALK TO.
OR A CORPSE TO PLAY WITH...

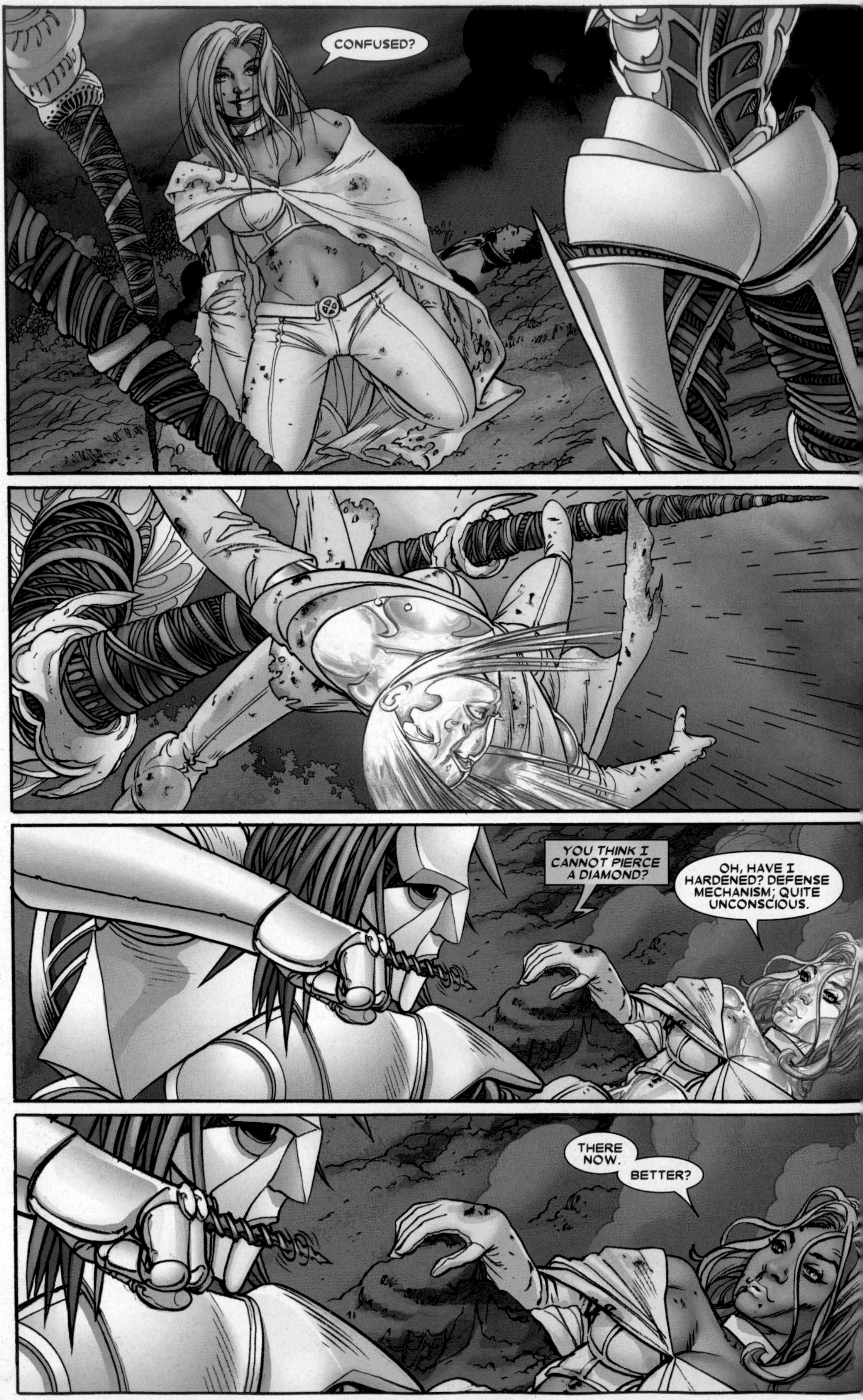
CONFUSED?
YOU THINK I CANNOT PIERCE A DIAMOND?
OH, HAVE I HARDENED? DEFENSE MECHANISM; QUITE UNCONSCIOUS.
THERE NOW.
BETTER?

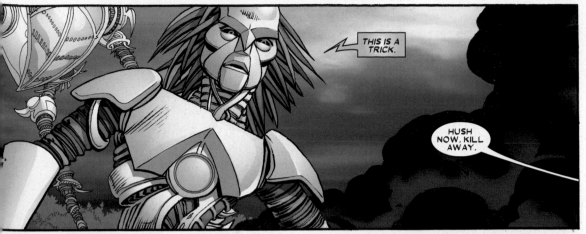

THIS IS A TRICK.

HUSH NOW. KILL AWAY.

KRUUN WILL WANT YOU ALIVE.

NONSENSE. HE'LL BE THRILLED. SHOWER YOU WITH GARLANDS AND WEAR MY SKIN LIKE A SHAWL.

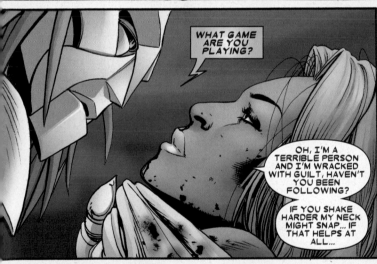

WHAT GAME ARE YOU PLAYING?

OH, I'M A TERRIBLE PERSON AND I'M WRACKED WITH GUILT, HAVEN'T YOU BEEN FOLLOWING?

IF YOU SHAKE HARDER MY NECK MIGHT SNAP... IF THAT HELPS AT ALL...

SHALL I TELL YOU WHY YOU HAVEN'T KILLED ME YET?

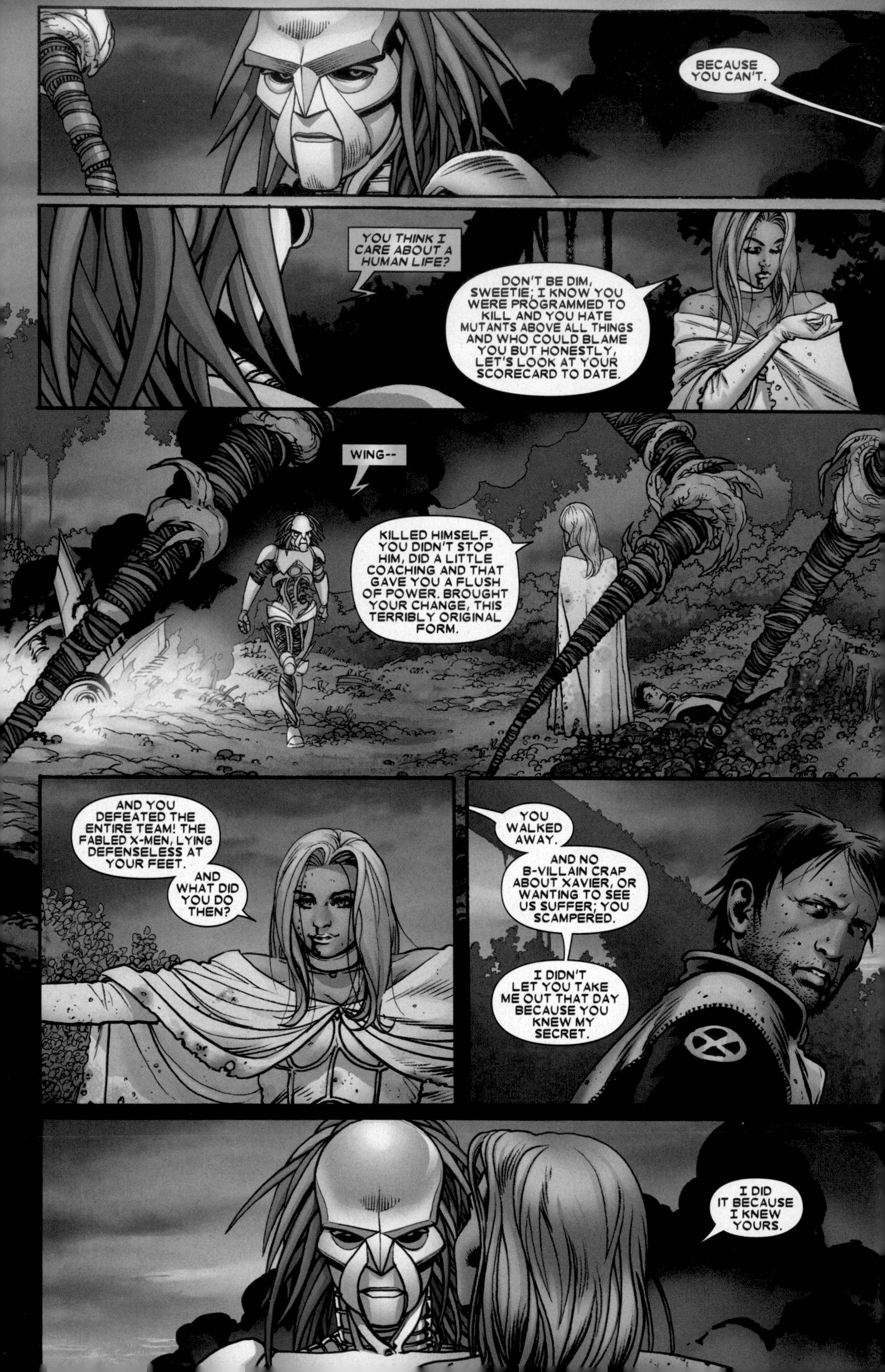
BECAUSE YOU CAN'T.
YOU THINK I CARE ABOUT A HUMAN LIFE?
DON'T BE DIM, SWEETIE; I KNOW YOU WERE PROGRAMMED TO KILL AND YOU HATE MUTANTS ABOVE ALL THINGS AND WHO COULD BLAME YOU BUT HONESTLY, LET'S LOOK AT YOUR SCORECARD TO DATE.
WING--
KILLED HIMSELF. YOU DIDN'T STOP HIM, DID A LITTLE COACHING AND THAT GAVE YOU A FLUSH OF POWER. BROUGHT YOUR CHANGE, THIS TERRIBLY ORIGINAL FORM.
AND YOU DEFEATED THE ENTIRE TEAM! THE FABLED X-MEN, LYING DEFENSELESS AT YOUR FEET.
AND WHAT DID YOU DO THEN?
YOU WALKED AWAY.
AND NO B-VILLAIN CRAP ABOUT XAVIER, OR WANTING TO SEE US SUFFER; YOU SCAMPERED.
I DIDN'T LET YOU TAKE ME OUT THAT DAY BECAUSE YOU KNEW MY SECRET.
I DID IT BECAUSE I KNEW YOURS.

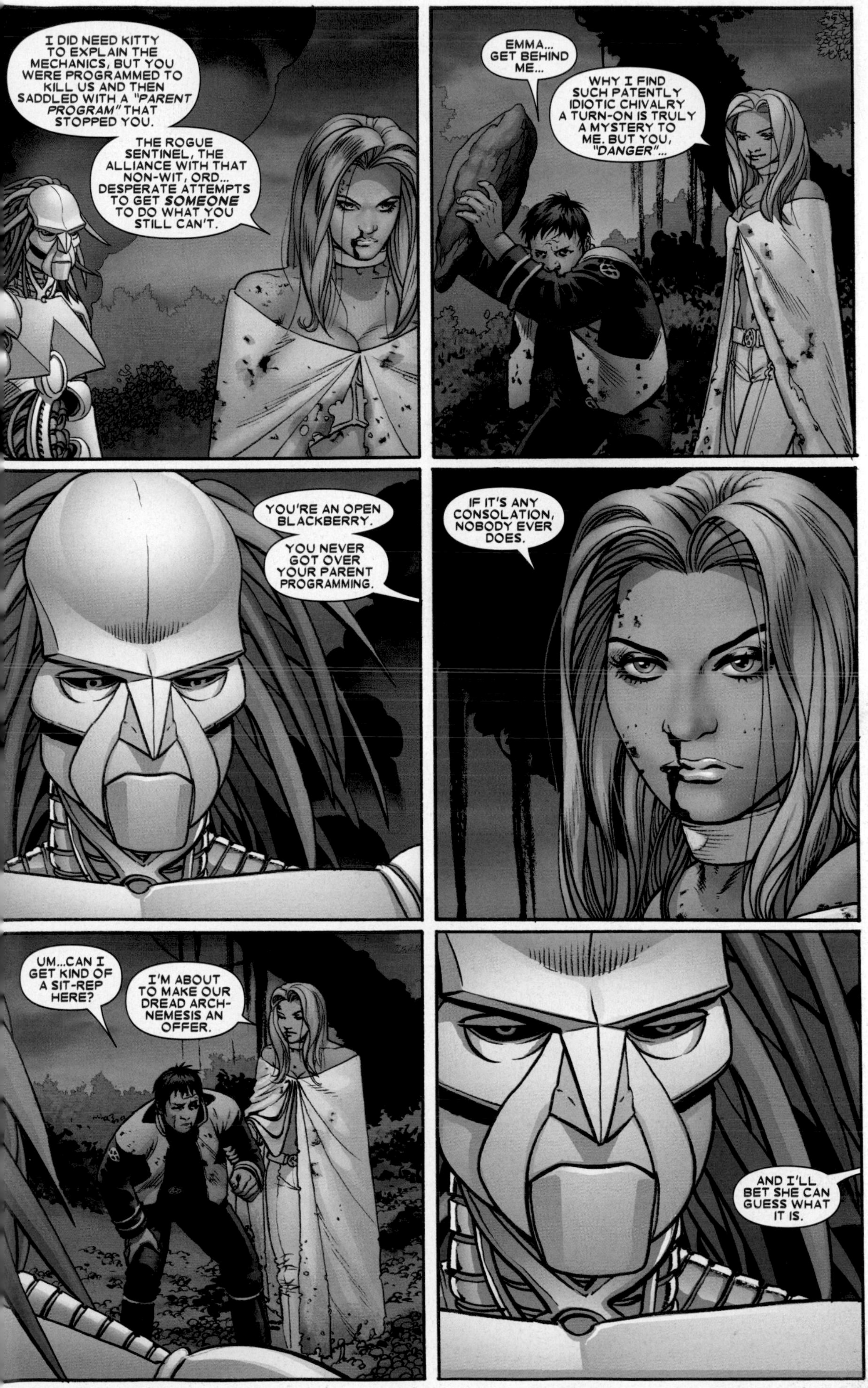
I DID NEED KITTY TO EXPLAIN THE MECHANICS, BUT YOU WERE PROGRAMMED TO KILL US AND THEN SADDLED WITH A "PARENT PROGRAM" THAT STOPPED YOU.
THE ROGUE SENTINEL, THE ALLIANCE WITH THAT NON-WIT, ORD... DESPERATE ATTEMPTS TO GET SOMEONE TO DO WHAT YOU STILL CAN'T.
EMMA... GET BEHIND ME...
WHY I FIND SUCH PATENTLY IDIOTIC CHIVALRY A TURN-ON IS TRULY A MYSTERY TO ME. BUT YOU, "DANGER"...
YOU'RE AN OPEN BLACKBERRY.
YOU NEVER GOT OVER YOUR PARENT PROGRAMMING.
IF IT'S ANY CONSOLATION, NOBODY EVER DOES.
UM...CAN I GET KIND OF A SIT-REP HERE?
I'M ABOUT TO MAKE OUR DREAD ARCH-NEMESIS AN OFFER.
AND I'LL BET SHE CAN GUESS WHAT IT IS.

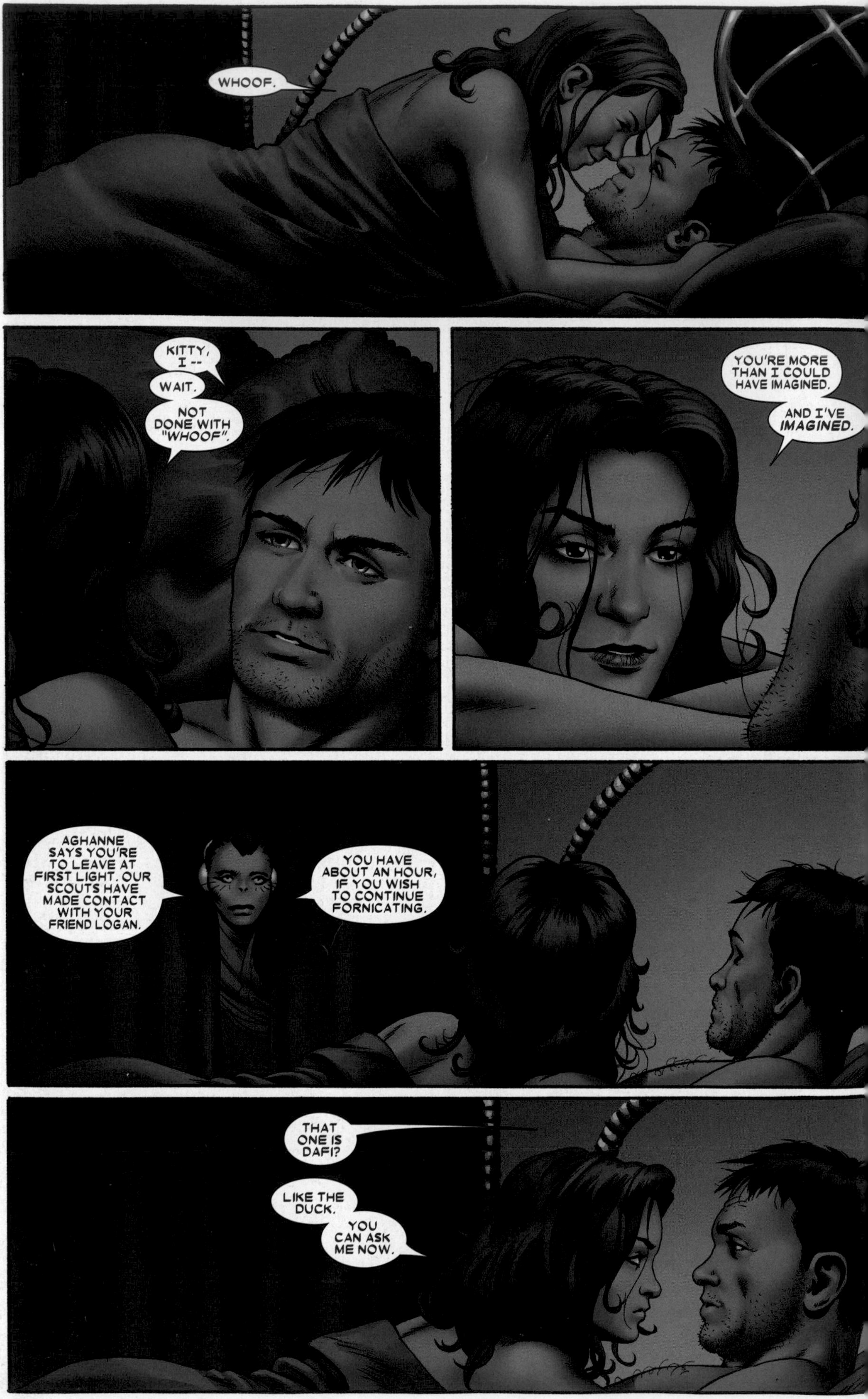
WHOOF.
KITTY, I --
WAIT.
NOT DONE WITH "WHOOF".
YOU'RE MORE THAN I COULD HAVE IMAGINED.
AND I'VE *IMAGINED.*
AGHANNE SAYS YOU'RE TO LEAVE AT FIRST LIGHT. OUR SCOUTS HAVE MADE CONTACT WITH YOUR FRIEND LOGAN.
YOU HAVE ABOUT AN HOUR, IF YOU WISH TO CONTINUE FORNICATING.
THAT ONE IS DAFI?
LIKE THE DUCK.
YOU CAN ASK ME NOW.

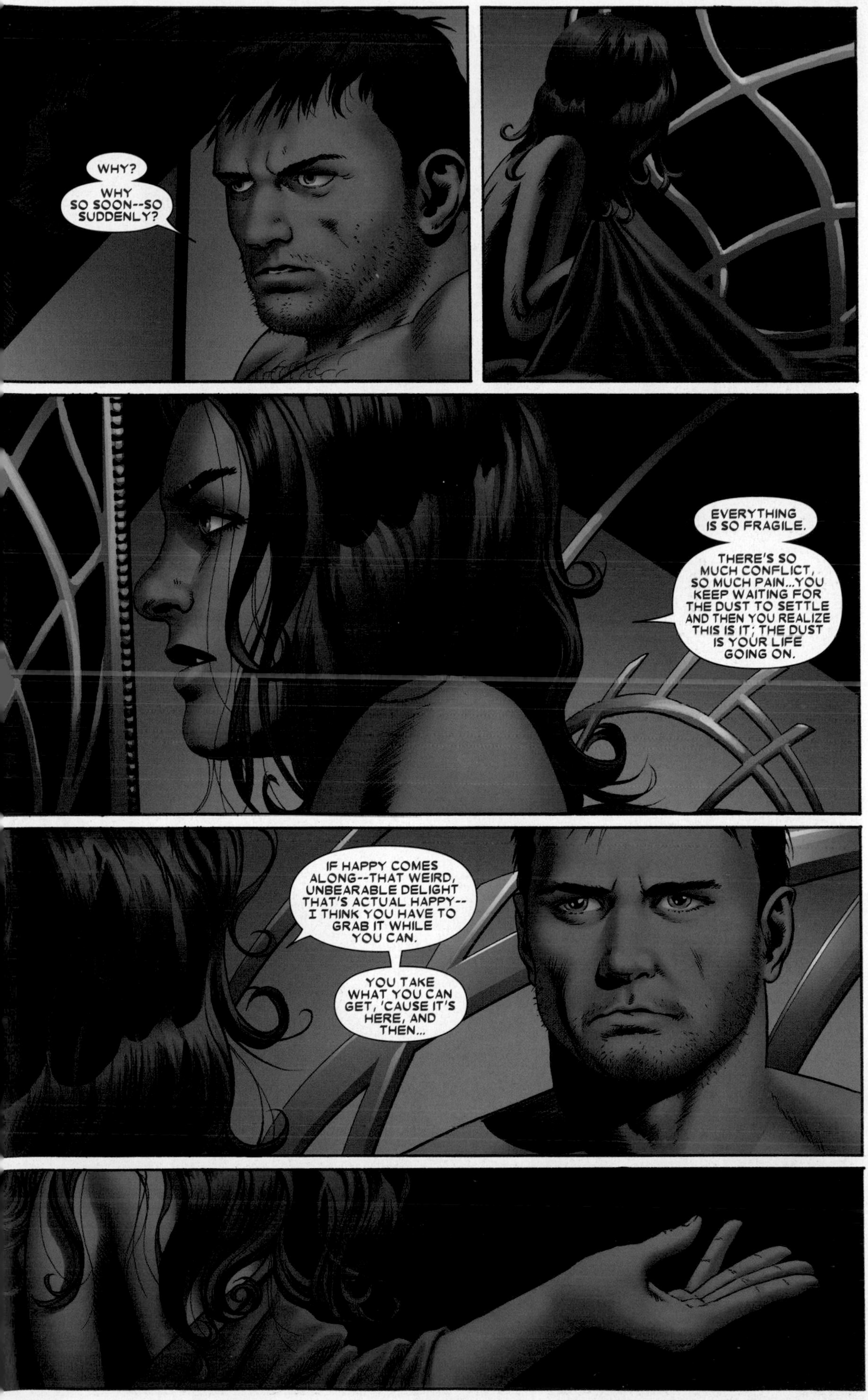
WHY?
WHY SO SOON--SO SUDDENLY?
EVERYTHING IS SO FRAGILE.
THERE'S SO MUCH CONFLICT, SO MUCH PAIN...YOU KEEP WAITING FOR THE DUST TO SETTLE AND THEN YOU REALIZE THIS IS IT; THE DUST IS YOUR LIFE GOING ON.
IF HAPPY COMES ALONG--THAT WEIRD, UNBEARABLE DELIGHT THAT'S ACTUAL HAPPY-- I THINK YOU HAVE TO GRAB IT WHILE YOU CAN.
YOU TAKE WHAT YOU CAN GET, 'CAUSE IT'S HERE, AND THEN...

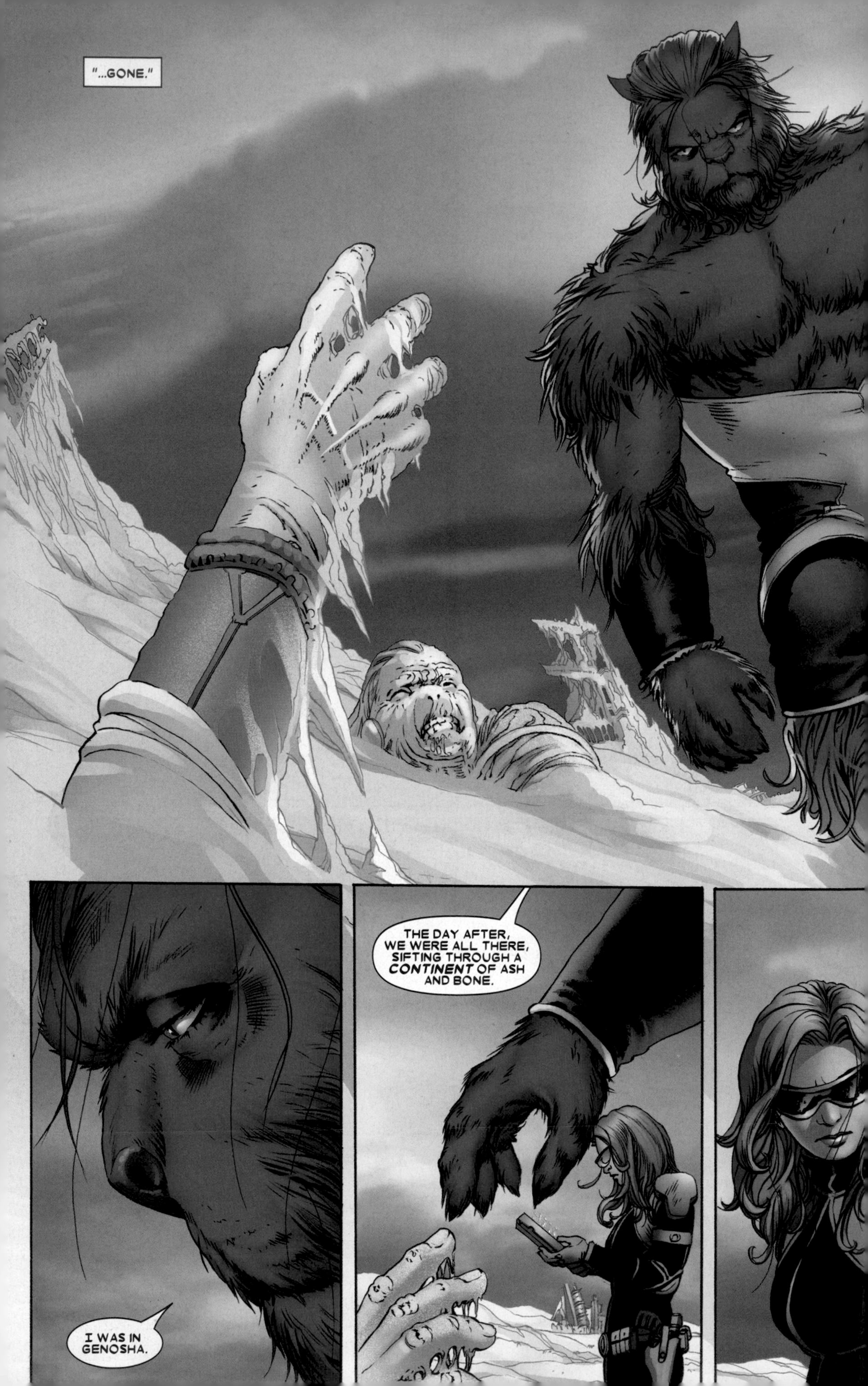
"...GONE."
I WAS IN GENOSHA.
THE DAY AFTER, WE WERE ALL THERE, SIFTING THROUGH A *CONTINENT* OF ASH AND BONE.

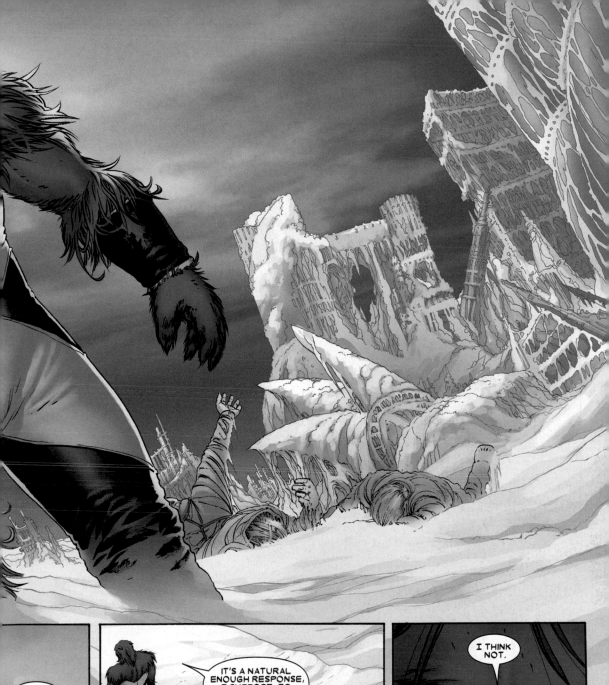

I MADE JOKES.

WE NEED A SHIP.

IT'S A NATURAL ENOUGH RESPONSE, I SUPPOSE, TO UNIMAGINABLE HORROR--

LET'S THINK DEEP THOUGHTS LATER, PROFESSOR. THERE *WILL* BE SURVIVORS AND WE *DON'T* WANT TO MEET THEM.

WE NEED TO RAID THAT SHIPYARD AND GET TO THE DAMN MOONBASE.

I THINK NOT.

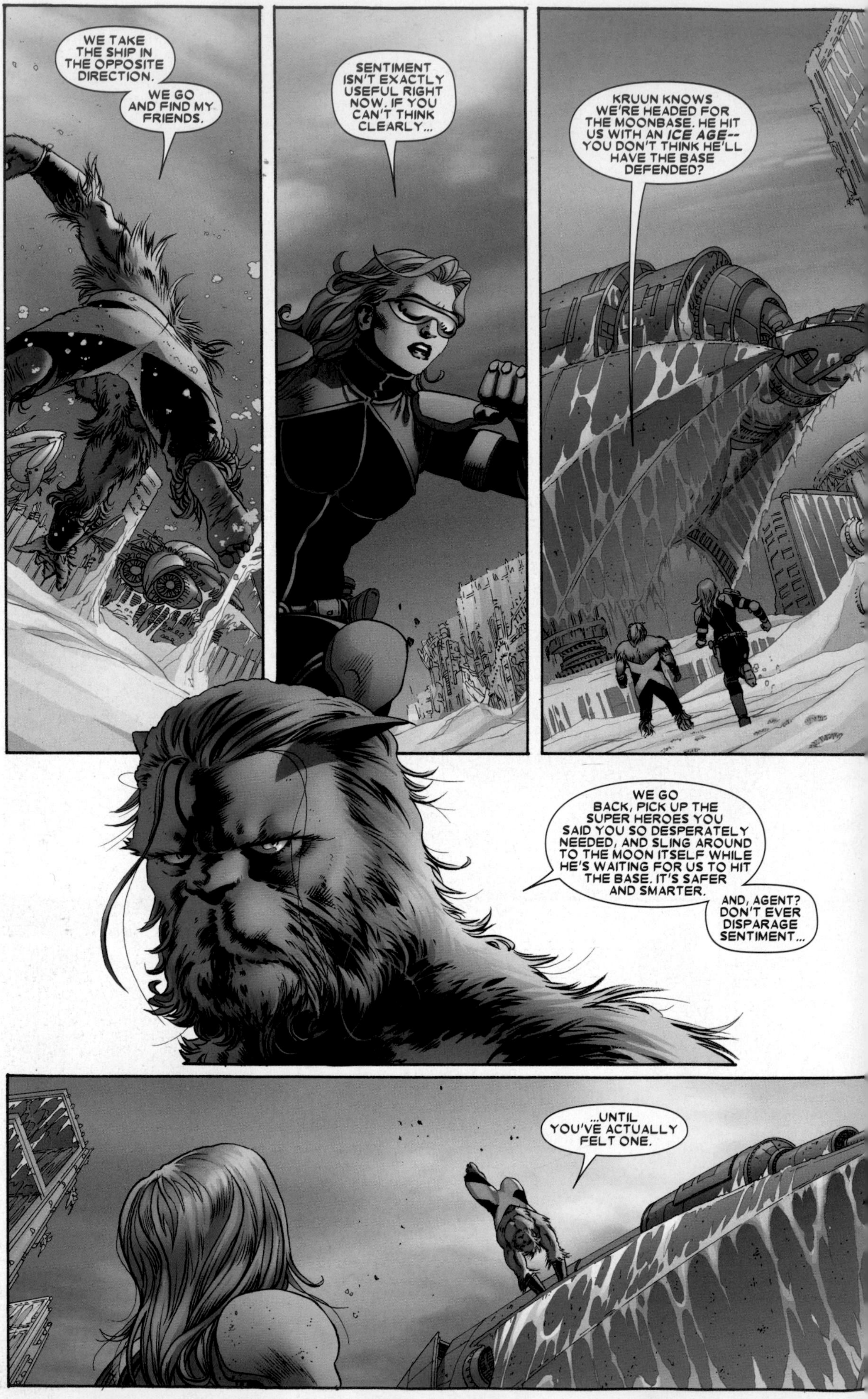
WE TAKE THE SHIP IN THE OPPOSITE DIRECTION.
WE GO AND FIND MY FRIENDS.
SENTIMENT ISN'T EXACTLY USEFUL RIGHT NOW. IF YOU CAN'T THINK CLEARLY...
KRUUN KNOWS WE'RE HEADED FOR THE MOONBASE. HE HIT US WITH AN *ICE AGE*-- YOU DON'T THINK HE'LL HAVE THE BASE DEFENDED?
WE GO BACK, PICK UP THE SUPER HEROES YOU SAID YOU SO DESPERATELY NEEDED, AND SLING AROUND TO THE MOON ITSELF WHILE HE'S WAITING FOR US TO HIT THE BASE. IT'S SAFER AND SMARTER.
AND, AGENT? DON'T EVER DISPARAGE SENTIMENT...
...UNTIL YOU'VE ACTUALLY FELT ONE.

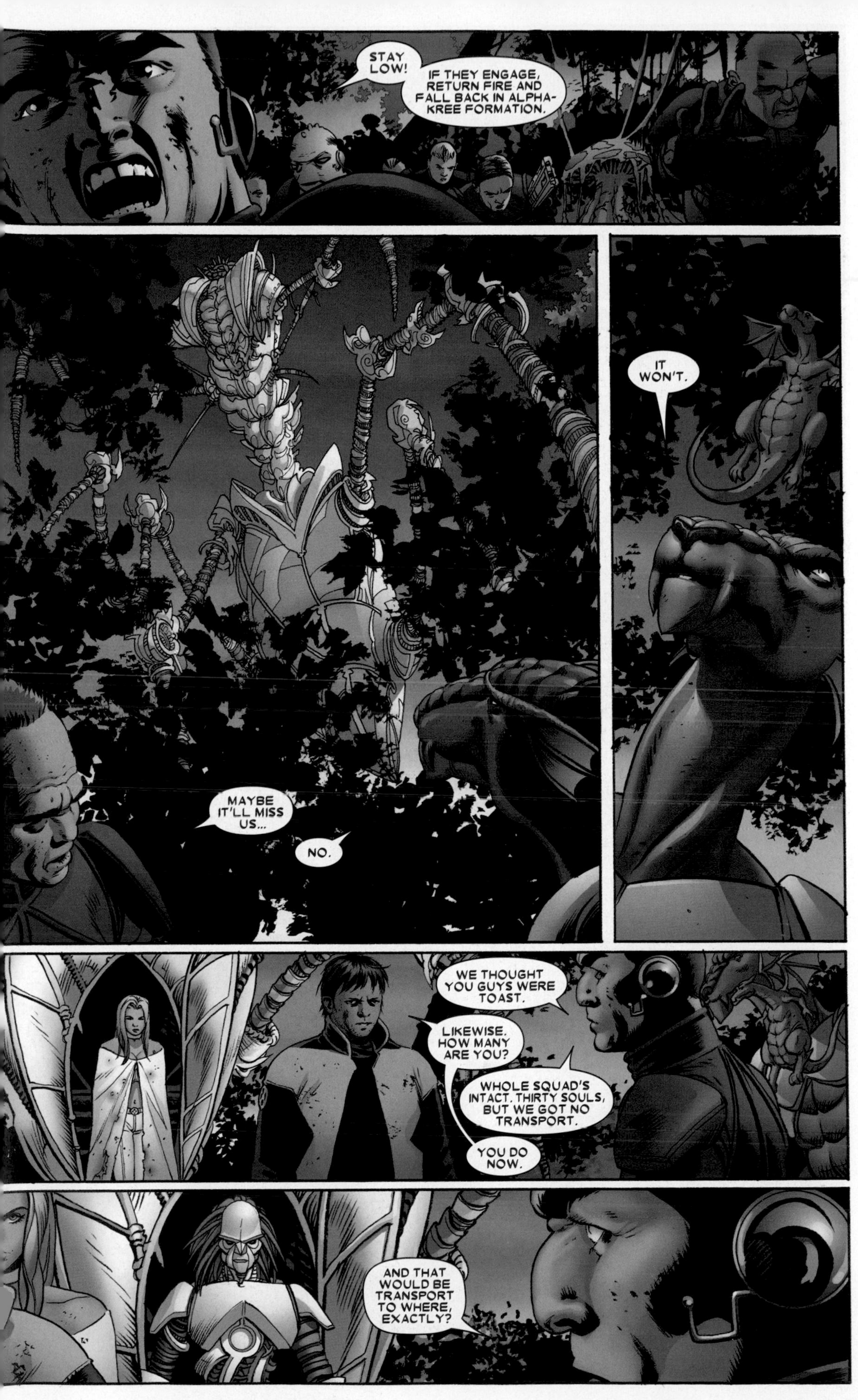
STAY LOW!
IF THEY ENGAGE, RETURN FIRE AND FALL BACK IN ALPHA-KREE FORMATION.
IT WON'T.
MAYBE IT'LL MISS US...
NO.
WE THOUGHT YOU GUYS WERE TOAST.
LIKEWISE. HOW MANY ARE YOU?
WHOLE SQUAD'S INTACT. THIRTY SOULS, BUT WE GOT NO TRANSPORT.
YOU DO NOW.
AND THAT WOULD BE TRANSPORT TO WHERE, EXACTLY?

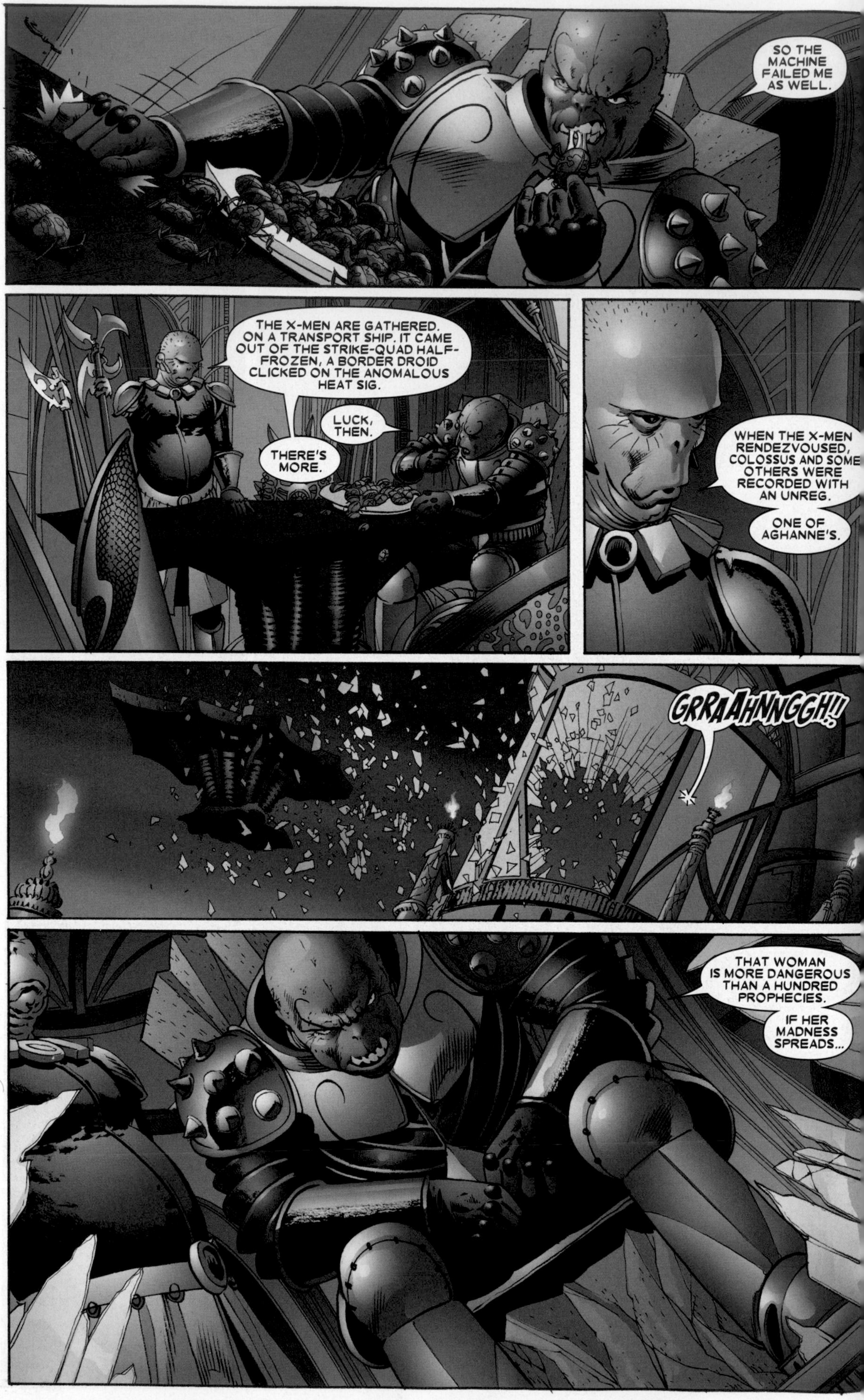
SO THE MACHINE FAILED ME AS WELL.
THE X-MEN ARE GATHERED. ON A TRANSPORT SHIP. IT CAME OUT OF THE STRIKE-QUAD HALF-FROZEN, A BORDER DROID CLICKED ON THE ANOMALOUS HEAT SIG.
LUCK, THEN.
THERE'S MORE.
WHEN THE X-MEN RENDEZVOUSED, COLOSSUS AND SOME OTHERS WERE RECORDED WITH AN UNREG.
ONE OF AGHANNE'S.
GRRAAHNNGGH!!
THAT WOMAN IS MORE DANGEROUS THAN A HUNDRED PROPHECIES.
IF HER MADNESS SPREADS...

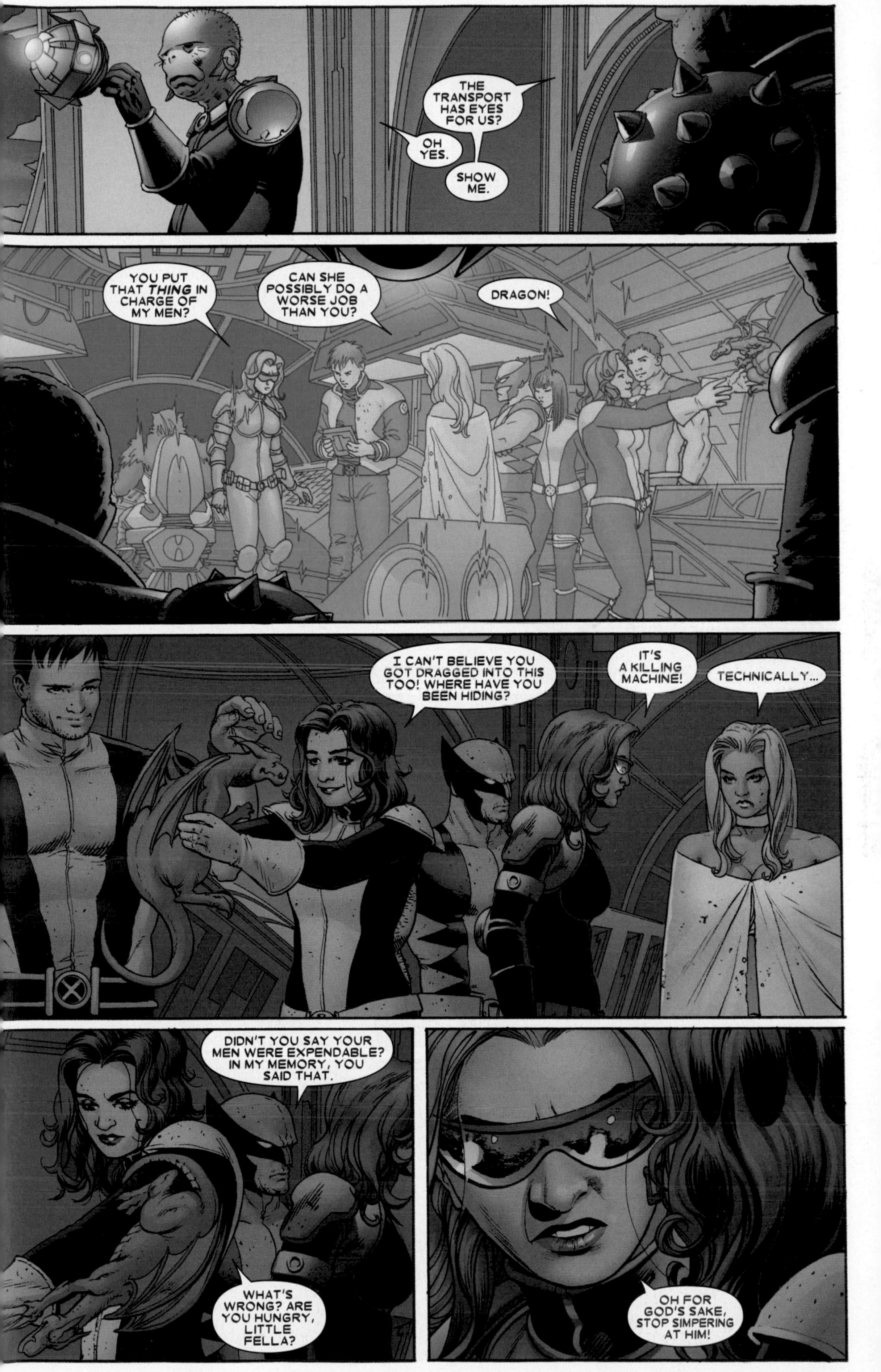
THE TRANSPORT HAS EYES FOR US?
OH YES.
SHOW ME.
YOU PUT THAT *THING* IN CHARGE OF MY MEN?
CAN SHE POSSIBLY DO A WORSE JOB THAN YOU?
DRAGON!
I CAN'T BELIEVE YOU GOT DRAGGED INTO THIS TOO! WHERE HAVE YOU BEEN HIDING?
IT'S A KILLING MACHINE!
TECHNICALLY...
DIDN'T YOU SAY YOUR MEN WERE EXPENDABLE? IN MY MEMORY, YOU SAID THAT.
WHAT'S WRONG? ARE YOU HUNGRY, LITTLE FELLA?
OH FOR GOD'S SAKE, STOP SIMPERING AT HIM!

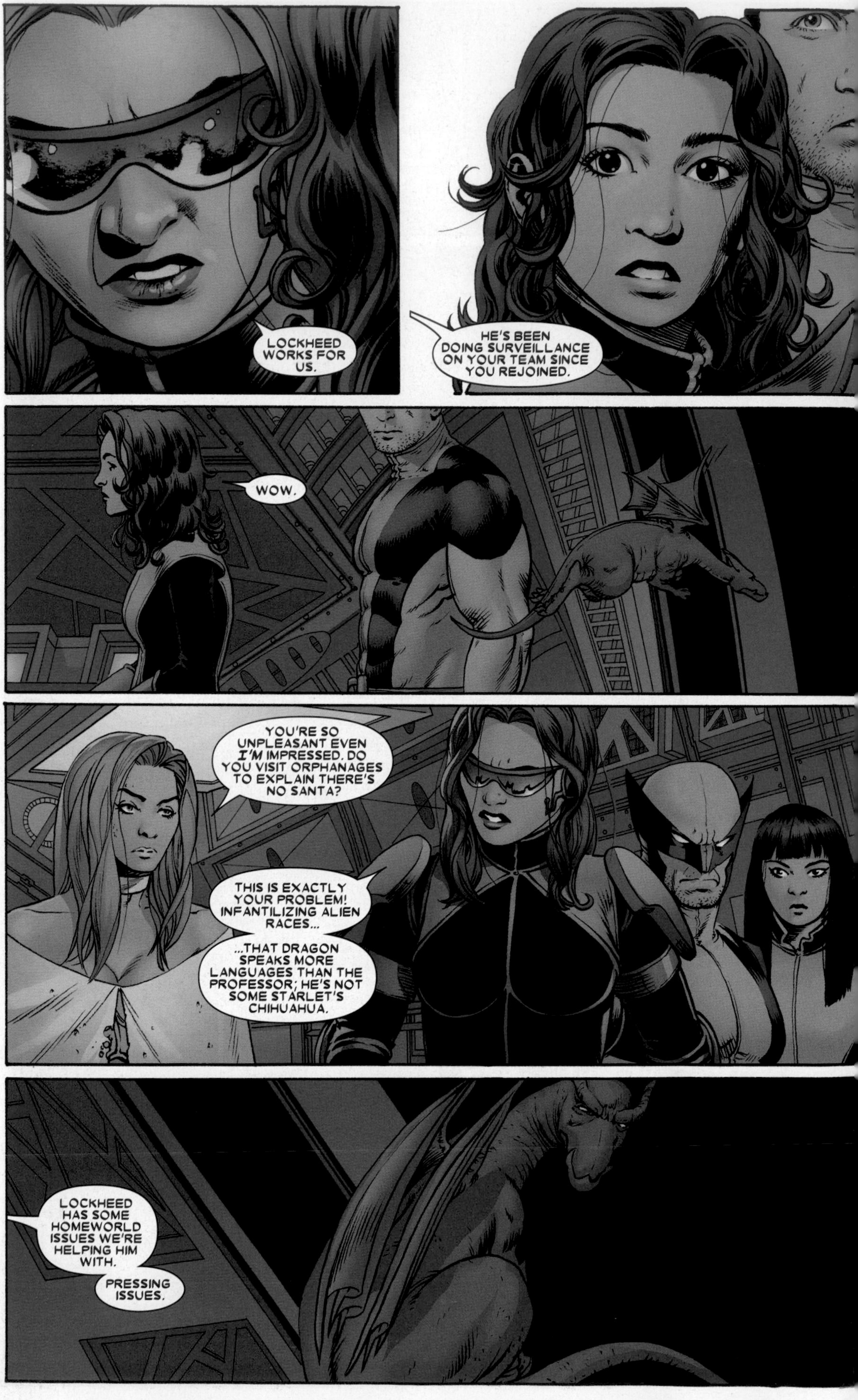
LOCKHEED WORKS FOR US.
HE'S BEEN DOING SURVEILLANCE ON YOUR TEAM SINCE YOU REJOINED.
WOW.
YOU'RE SO UNPLEASANT EVEN I'M IMPRESSED. DO YOU VISIT ORPHANAGES TO EXPLAIN THERE'S NO SANTA?
THIS IS EXACTLY YOUR PROBLEM! INFANTILIZING ALIEN RACES...
...THAT DRAGON SPEAKS MORE LANGUAGES THAN THE PROFESSOR; HE'S NOT SOME STARLET'S CHIHUAHUA.
LOCKHEED HAS SOME HOMEWORLD ISSUES WE'RE HELPING HIM WITH.
PRESSING ISSUES.

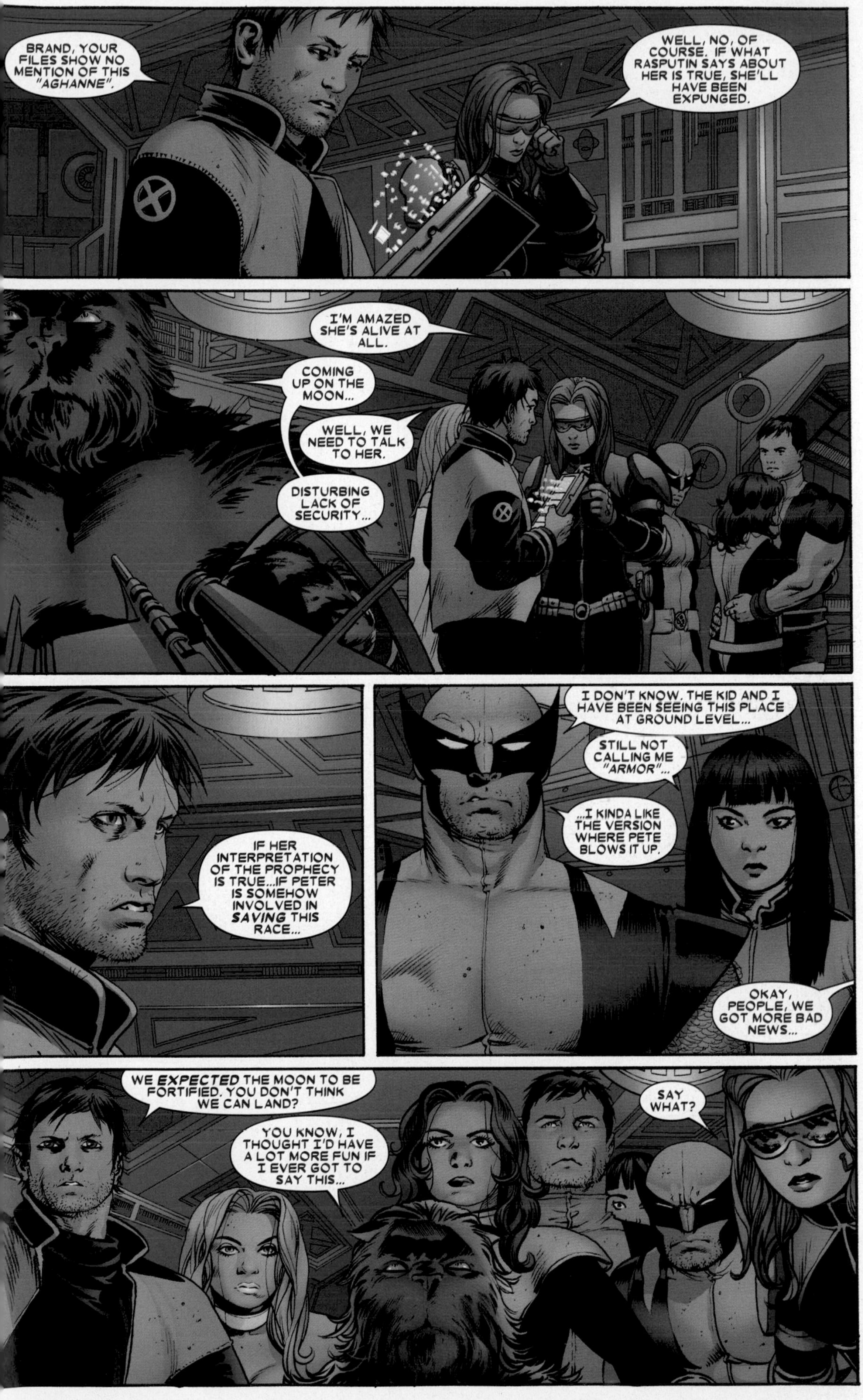
BRAND, YOUR FILES SHOW NO MENTION OF THIS "AGHANNE".
WELL, NO, OF COURSE. IF WHAT RASPUTIN SAYS ABOUT HER IS TRUE, SHE'LL HAVE BEEN EXPUNGED.
I'M AMAZED SHE'S ALIVE AT ALL.
COMING UP ON THE MOON...
WELL, WE NEED TO TALK TO HER.
DISTURBING LACK OF SECURITY...
IF HER INTERPRETATION OF THE PROPHECY IS TRUE...IF PETER IS SOMEHOW INVOLVED IN SAVING THIS RACE...
I DON'T KNOW. THE KID AND I HAVE BEEN SEEING THIS PLACE AT GROUND LEVEL...
STILL NOT CALLING ME "ARMOR"...
...I KINDA LIKE THE VERSION WHERE PETE BLOWS IT UP.
OKAY, PEOPLE, WE GOT MORE BAD NEWS...
WE EXPECTED THE MOON TO BE FORTIFIED. YOU DON'T THINK WE CAN LAND?
YOU KNOW, I THOUGHT I'D HAVE A LOT MORE FUN IF I EVER GOT TO SAY THIS...
SAY WHAT?

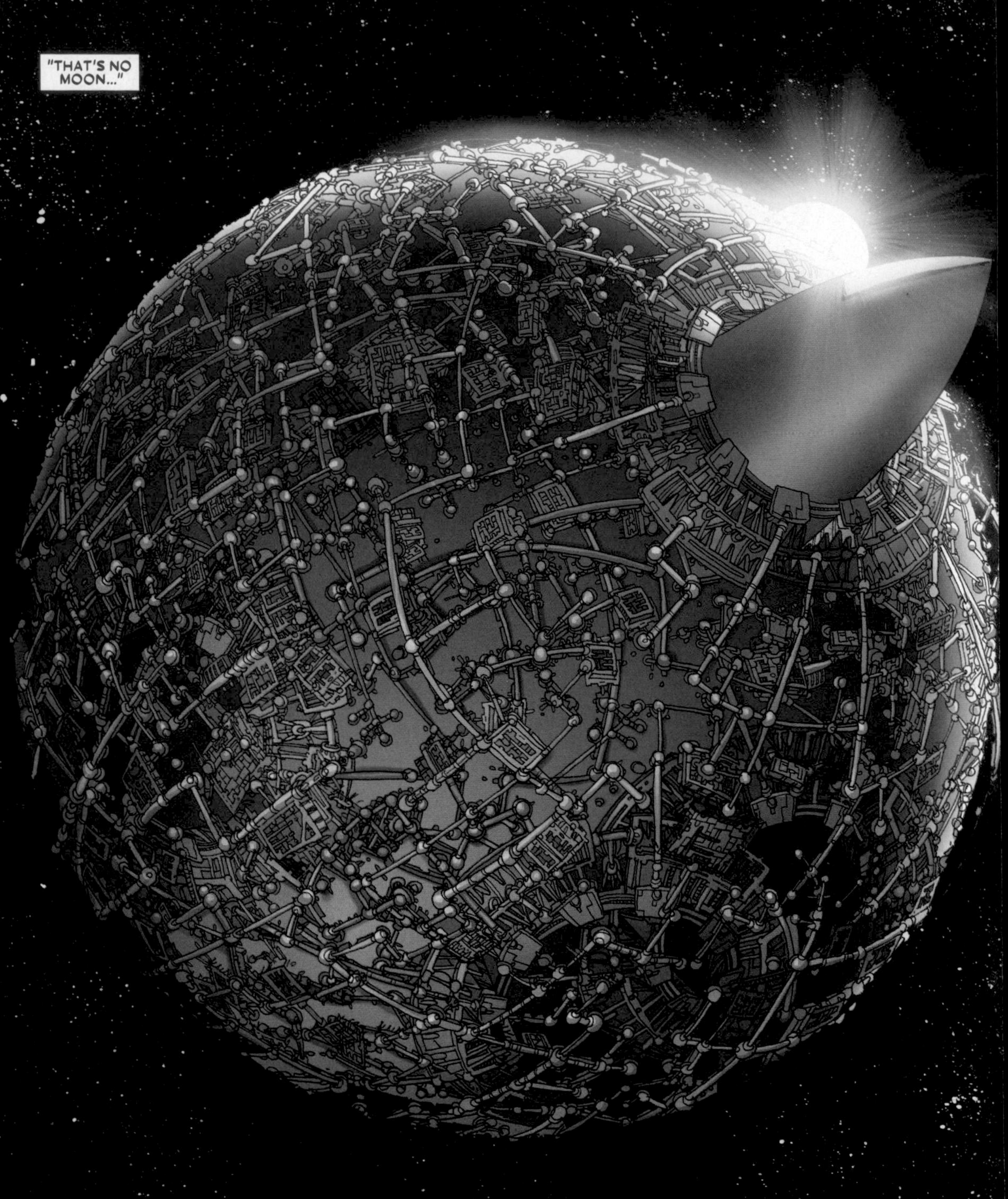
"THAT'S NO MOON..."

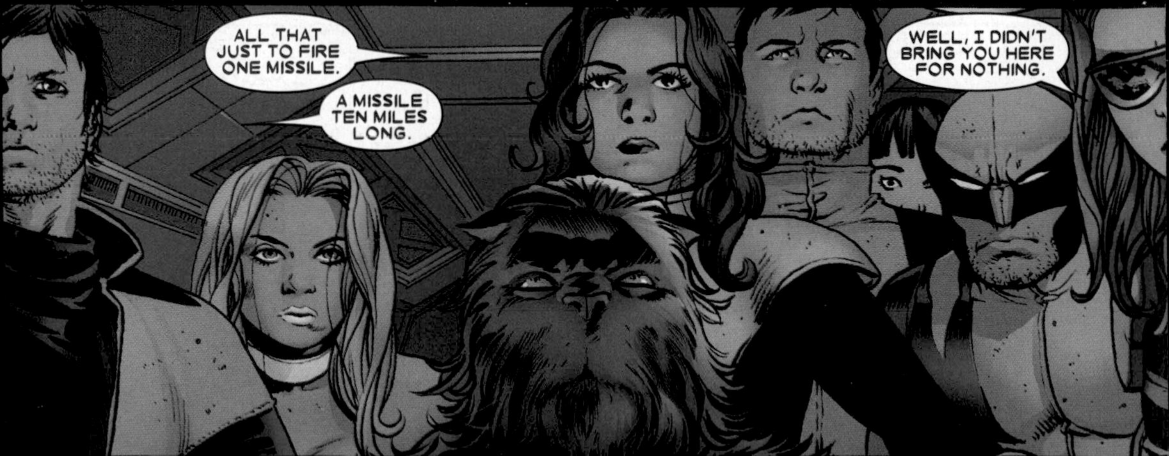
ALL THAT JUST TO FIRE ONE MISSILE.
A MISSILE TEN MILES LONG.
WELL, I DIDN'T BRING YOU HERE FOR NOTHING.

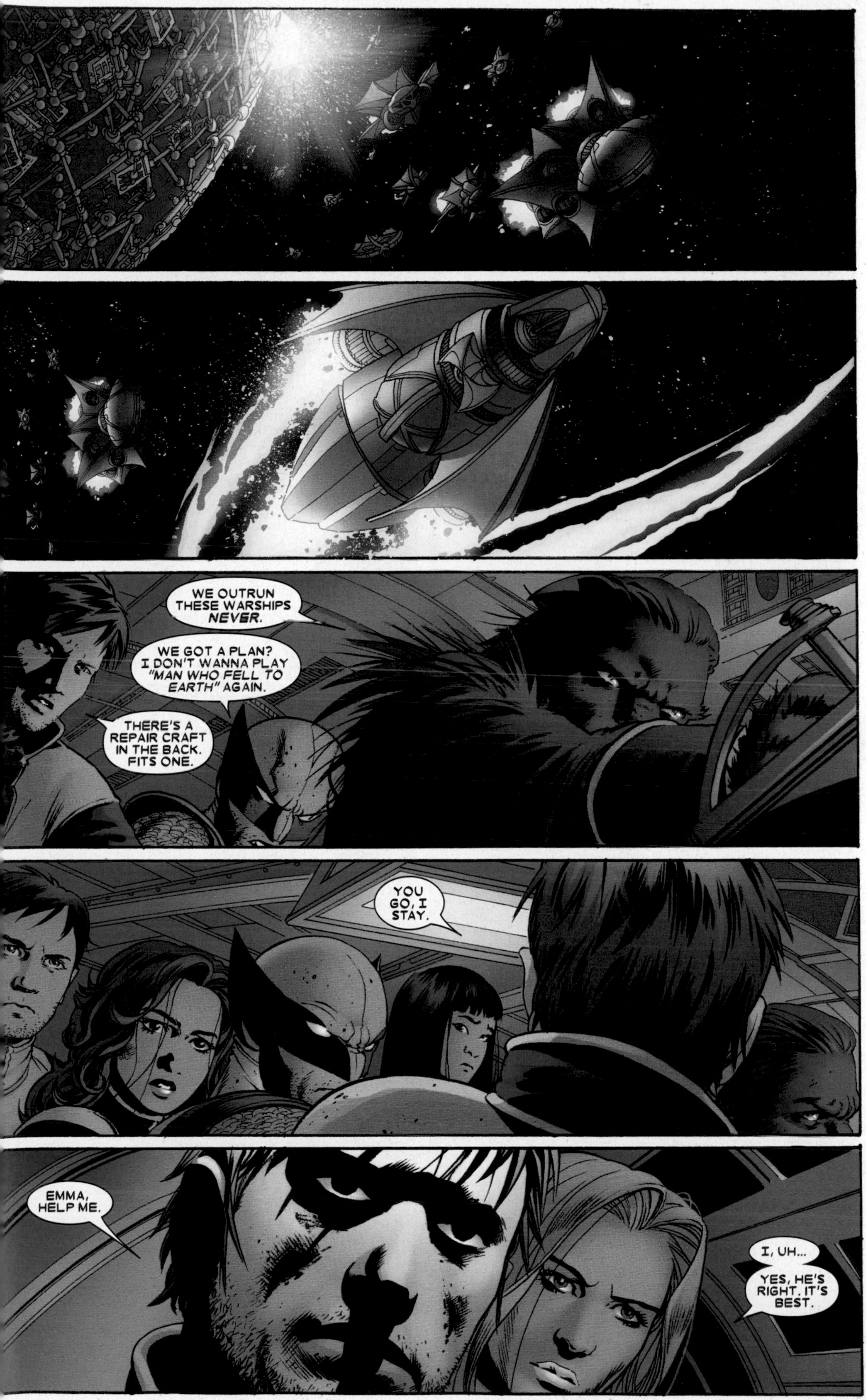
WE OUTRUN THESE WARSHIPS *NEVER*.
WE GOT A PLAN? I DON'T WANNA PLAY *"MAN WHO FELL TO EARTH"* AGAIN.
THERE'S A REPAIR CRAFT IN THE BACK. FITS ONE.
YOU GO, I STAY.
EMMA, HELP ME.
I, UH...
YES, HE'S RIGHT. IT'S BEST.

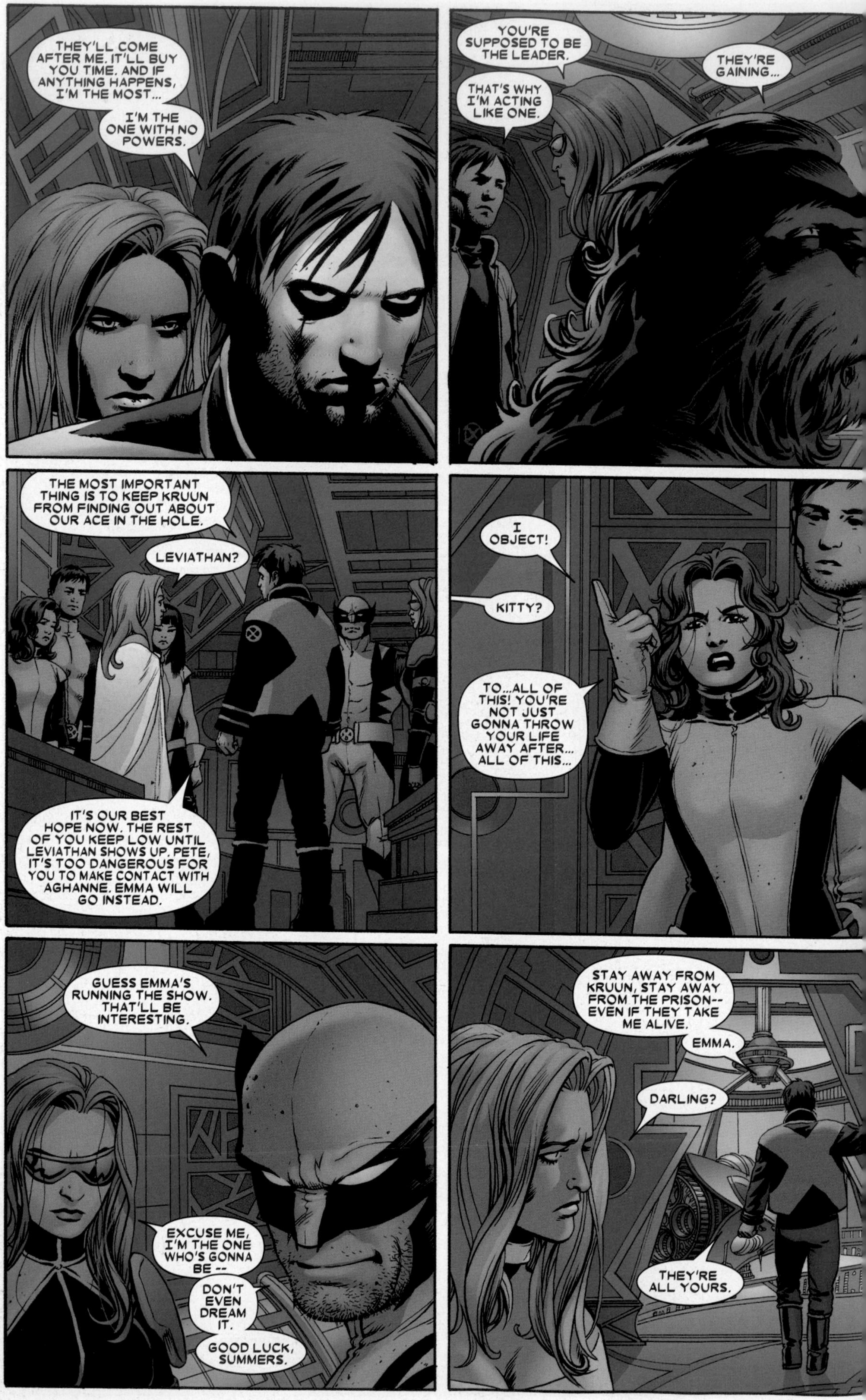
THEY'LL COME AFTER ME. IT'LL BUY YOU TIME. AND IF ANYTHING HAPPENS, I'M THE MOST...
I'M THE ONE WITH NO POWERS.
YOU'RE SUPPOSED TO BE THE LEADER.
THAT'S WHY I'M ACTING LIKE ONE.
THEY'RE GAINING...
THE MOST IMPORTANT THING IS TO KEEP KRUUN FROM FINDING OUT ABOUT OUR ACE IN THE HOLE.
LEVIATHAN?
IT'S OUR BEST HOPE NOW. THE REST OF YOU KEEP LOW UNTIL LEVIATHAN SHOWS UP. PETE, IT'S TOO DANGEROUS FOR YOU TO MAKE CONTACT WITH AGHANNE. EMMA WILL GO INSTEAD.
I OBJECT!
KITTY?
TO...ALL OF THIS! YOU'RE NOT JUST GONNA THROW YOUR LIFE AWAY AFTER... ALL OF THIS...
GUESS EMMA'S RUNNING THE SHOW. THAT'LL BE INTERESTING.
EXCUSE ME, I'M THE ONE WHO'S GONNA BE --
DON'T EVEN DREAM IT.
GOOD LUCK, SUMMERS.
STAY AWAY FROM KRUUN, STAY AWAY FROM THE PRISON-- EVEN IF THEY TAKE ME ALIVE.
EMMA.
DARLING?
THEY'RE ALL YOURS.

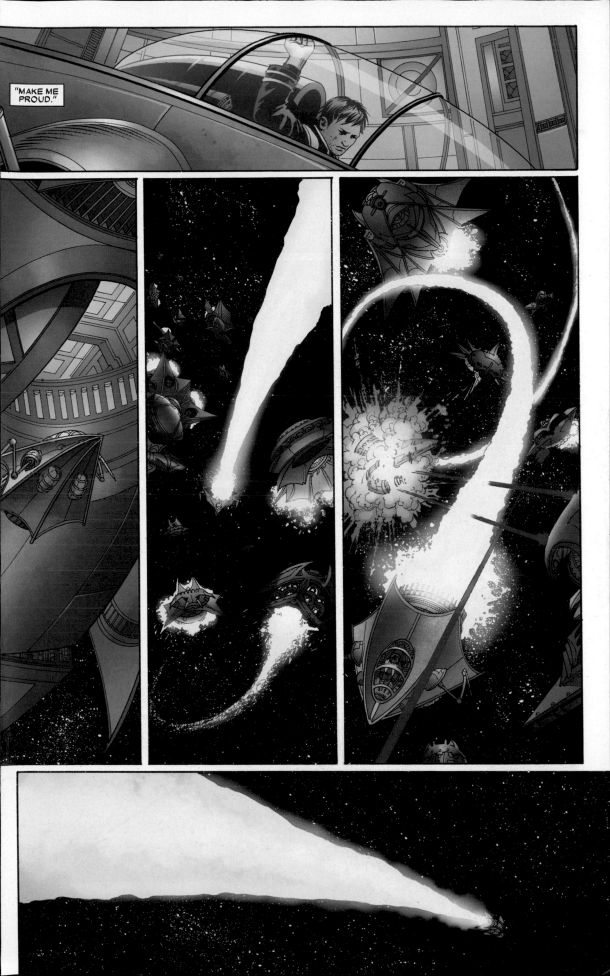

"MAKE ME PROUD."

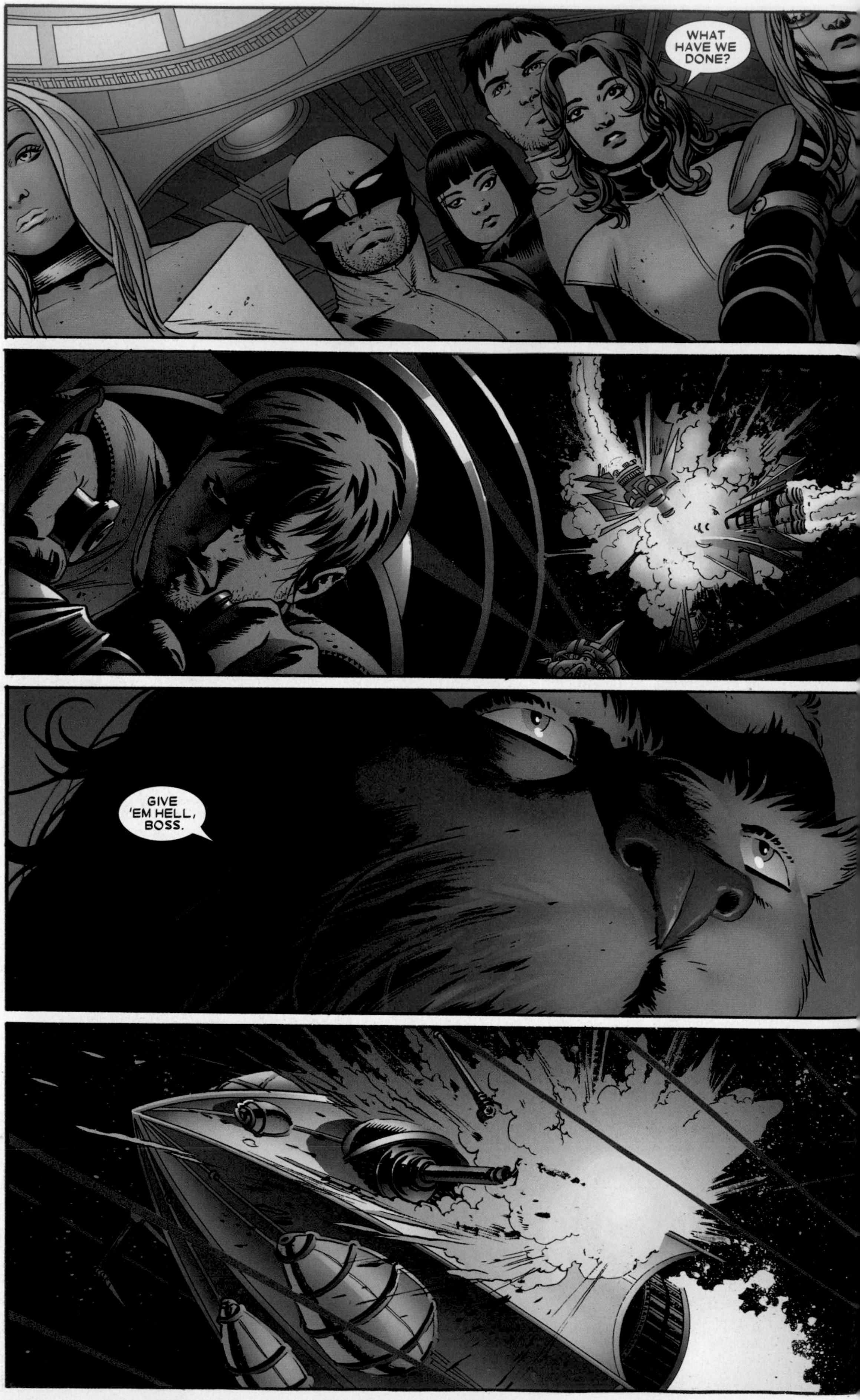
WHAT HAVE WE DONE?
GIVE 'EM HELL, BOSS.

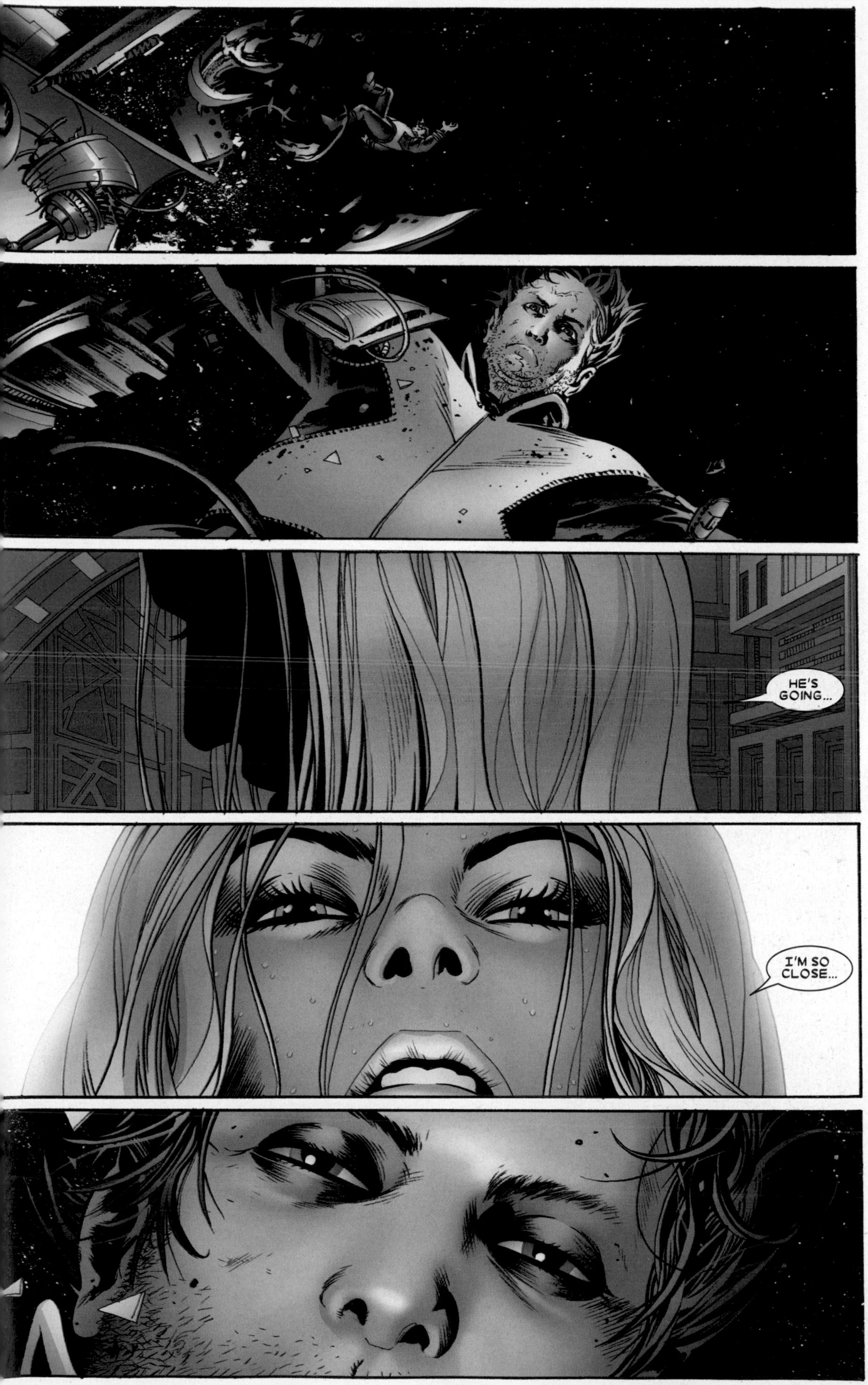
HE'S GOING...
I'M SO CLOSE...

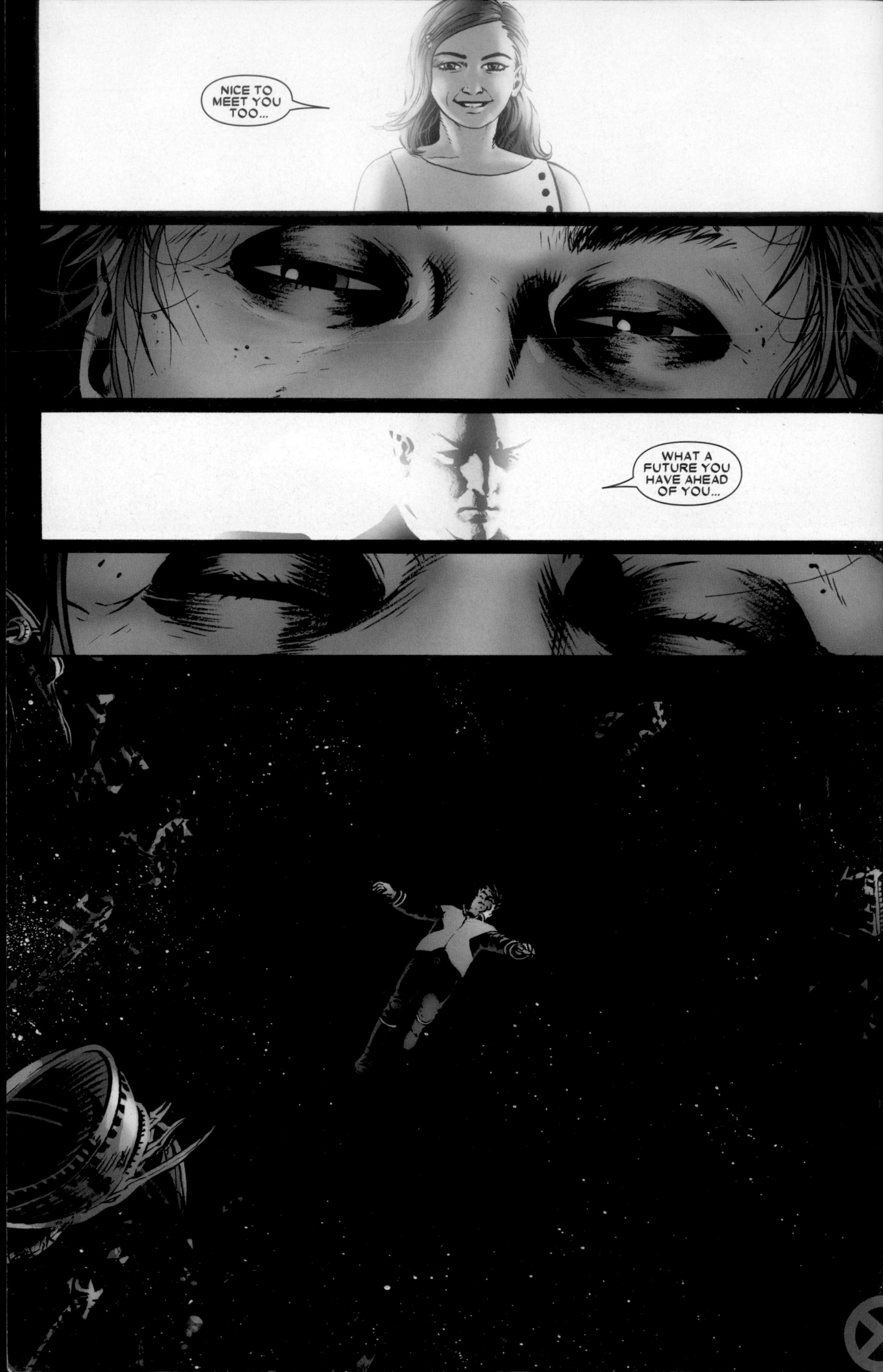
NICE TO MEET YOU TOO...
WHAT A FUTURE YOU HAVE AHEAD OF YOU...

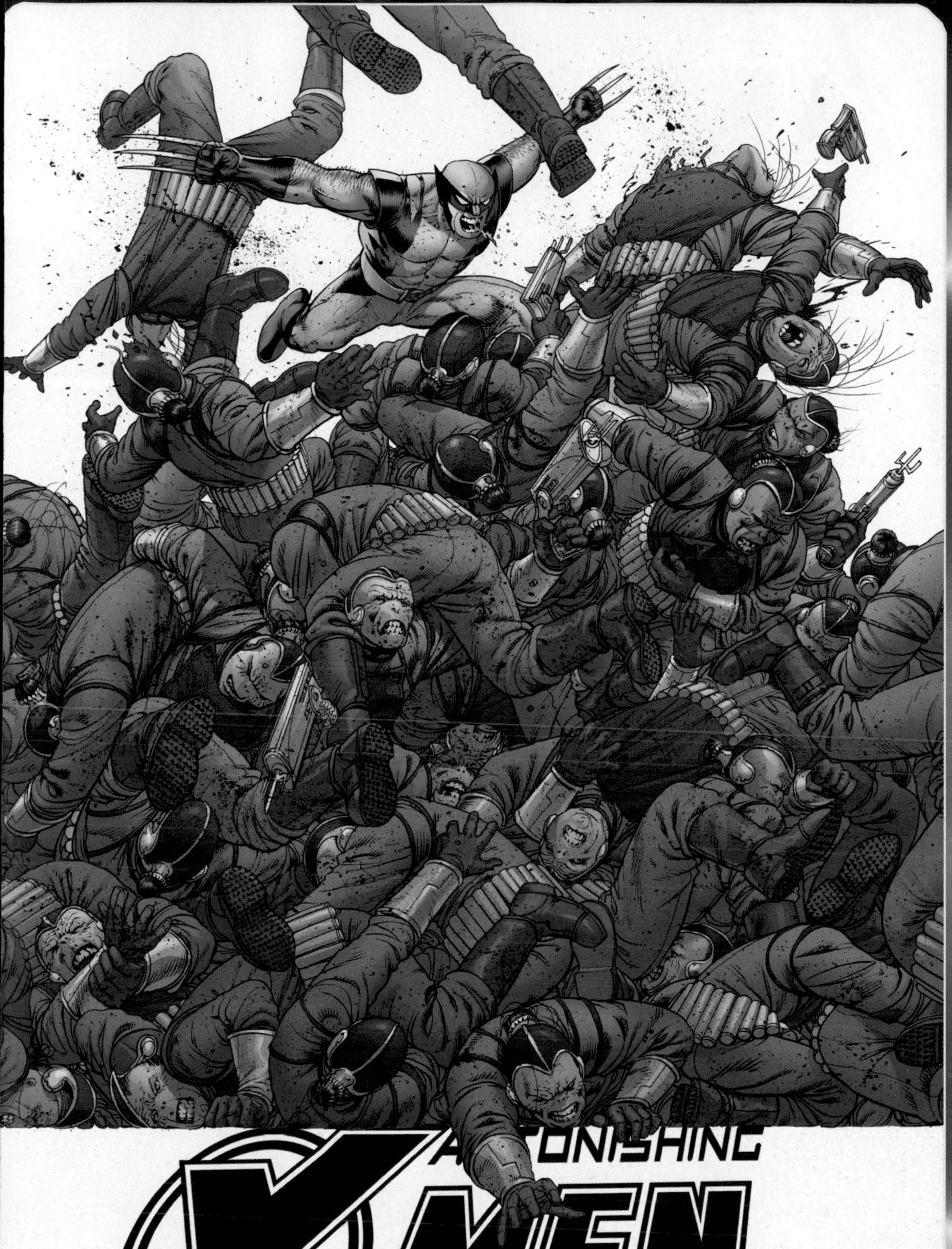
ASTONISHING
X-MEN

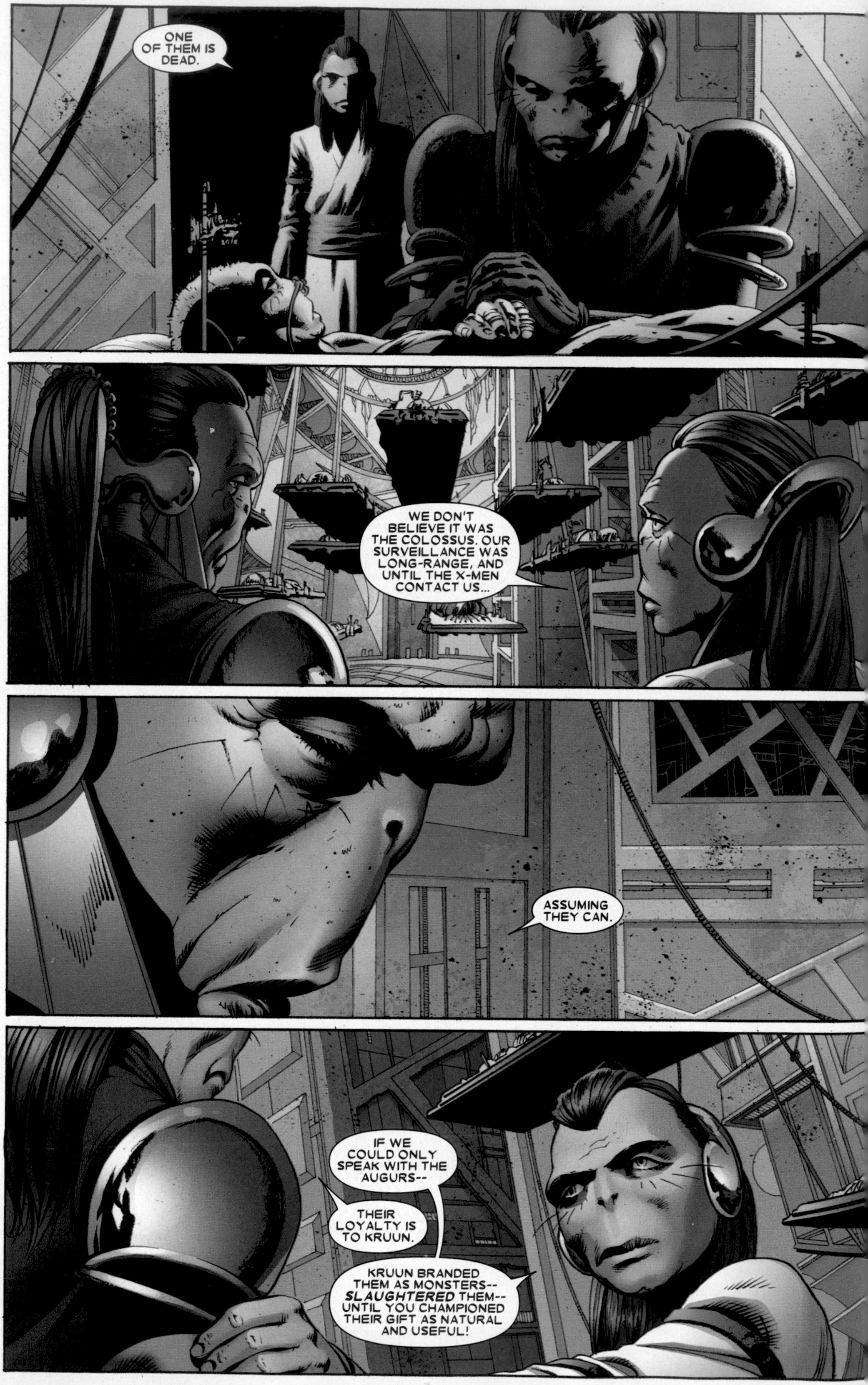
ONE OF THEM IS DEAD.
WE DON'T BELIEVE IT WAS THE COLOSSUS. OUR SURVEILLANCE WAS LONG-RANGE, AND UNTIL THE X-MEN CONTACT US...
ASSUMING THEY CAN.
IF WE COULD ONLY SPEAK WITH THE AUGURS--
THEIR LOYALTY IS TO KRUUN.
KRUUN BRANDED THEM AS MONSTERS-- *SLAUGHTERED* THEM-- UNTIL YOU CHAMPIONED THEIR GIFT AS NATURAL AND USEFUL!

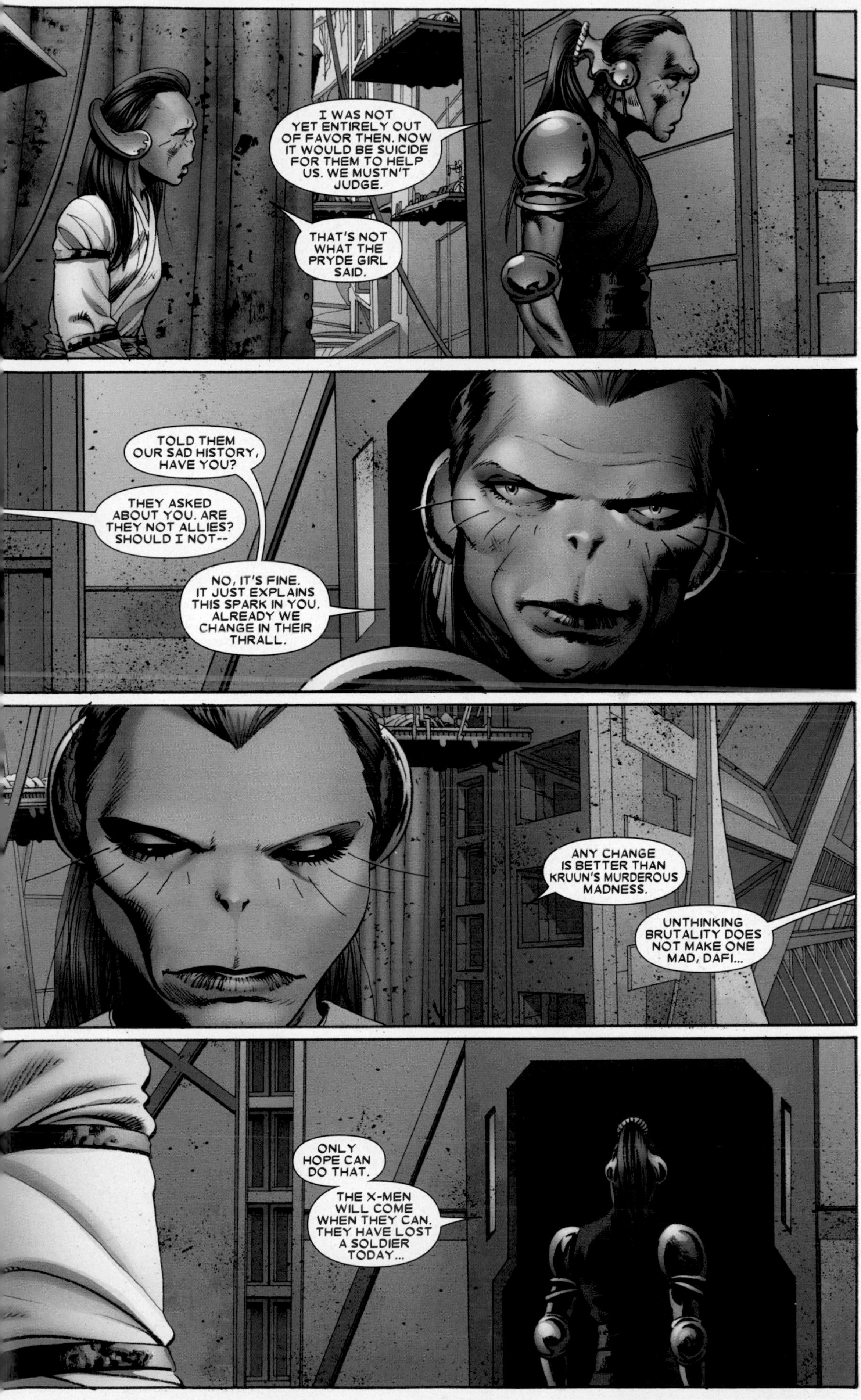
I WAS NOT YET ENTIRELY OUT OF FAVOR THEN. NOW IT WOULD BE SUICIDE FOR THEM TO HELP US. WE MUSTN'T JUDGE.
THAT'S NOT WHAT THE PRYDE GIRL SAID.
TOLD THEM OUR SAD HISTORY, HAVE YOU?
THEY ASKED ABOUT YOU. ARE THEY NOT ALLIES? SHOULD I NOT--
NO, IT'S FINE. IT JUST EXPLAINS THIS SPARK IN YOU. ALREADY WE CHANGE IN THEIR THRALL.
ANY CHANGE IS BETTER THAN KRUUN'S MURDEROUS MADNESS.
UNTHINKING BRUTALITY DOES NOT MAKE ONE MAD, DAFI...
ONLY HOPE CAN DO THAT.
THE X-MEN WILL COME WHEN THEY CAN. THEY HAVE LOST A SOLDIER TODAY...

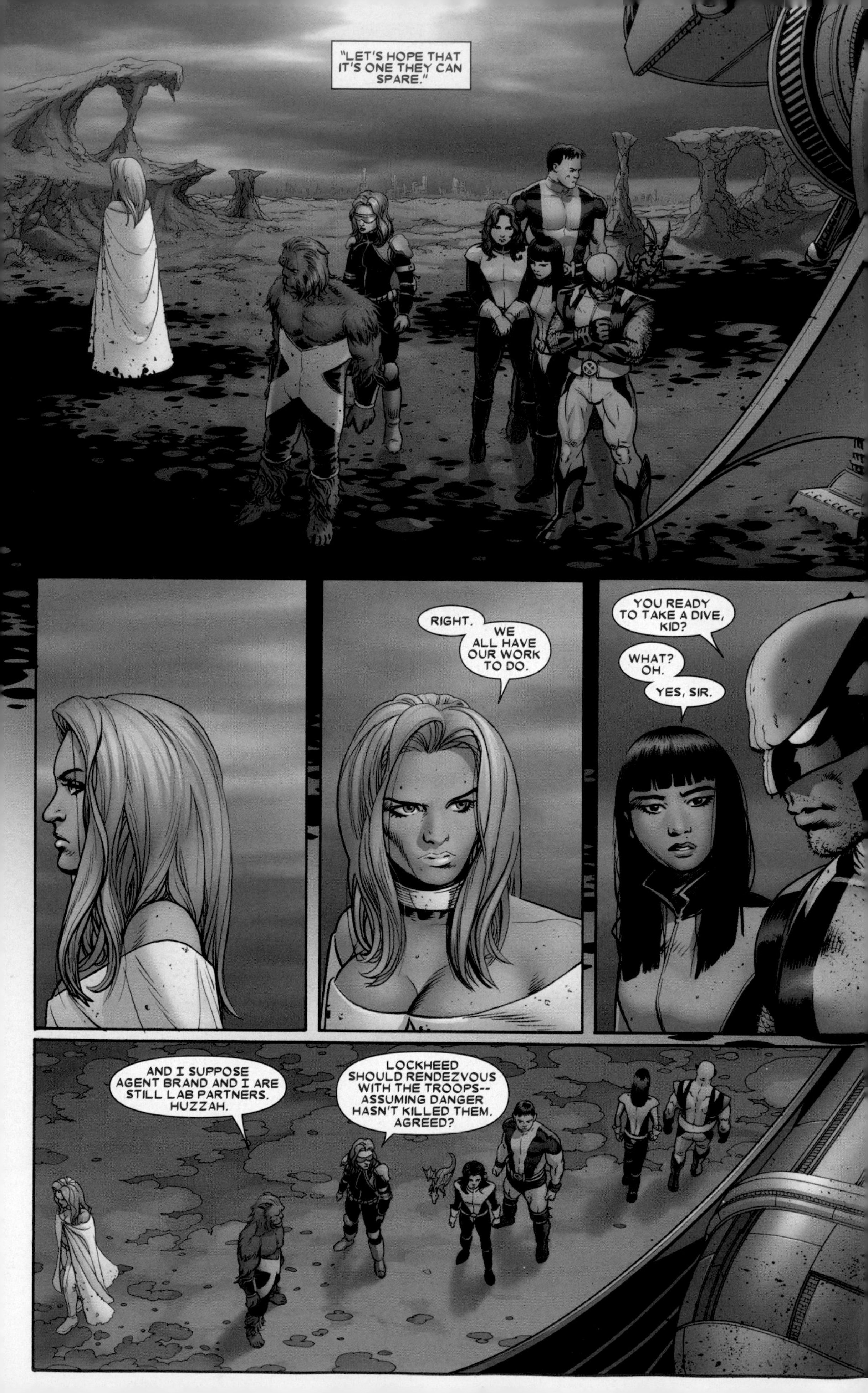
"LET'S HOPE THAT IT'S ONE THEY CAN SPARE."
RIGHT.
WE ALL HAVE OUR WORK TO DO.
YOU READY TO TAKE A DIVE, KID?
WHAT? OH.
YES, SIR.
AND I SUPPOSE AGENT BRAND AND I ARE STILL LAB PARTNERS. HUZZAH.
LOCKHEED SHOULD RENDEZVOUS WITH THE TROOPS-- ASSUMING DANGER HASN'T KILLED THEM. AGREED?

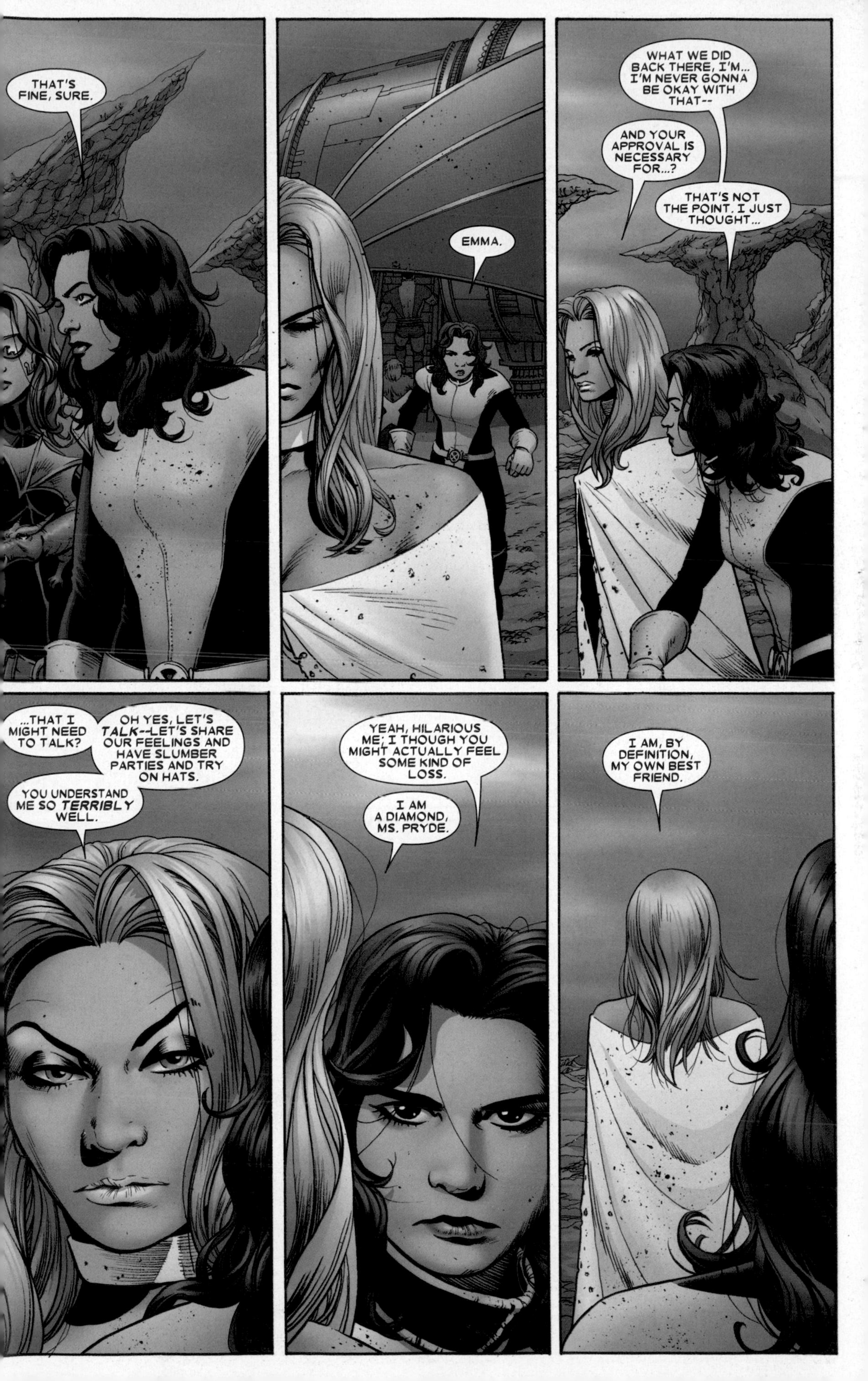
THAT'S FINE, SURE.
EMMA.
WHAT WE DID BACK THERE, I'M... I'M NEVER GONNA BE OKAY WITH THAT--
AND YOUR APPROVAL IS NECESSARY FOR...?
THAT'S NOT THE POINT. I JUST THOUGHT...
...THAT I MIGHT NEED TO TALK?
OH YES, LET'S TALK--LET'S SHARE OUR FEELINGS AND HAVE SLUMBER PARTIES AND TRY ON HATS.
YOU UNDERSTAND ME SO TERRIBLY WELL.
YEAH, HILARIOUS ME; I THOUGH YOU MIGHT ACTUALLY FEEL SOME KIND OF LOSS.
I AM A DIAMOND, MS. PRYDE.
I AM, BY DEFINITION, MY OWN BEST FRIEND.

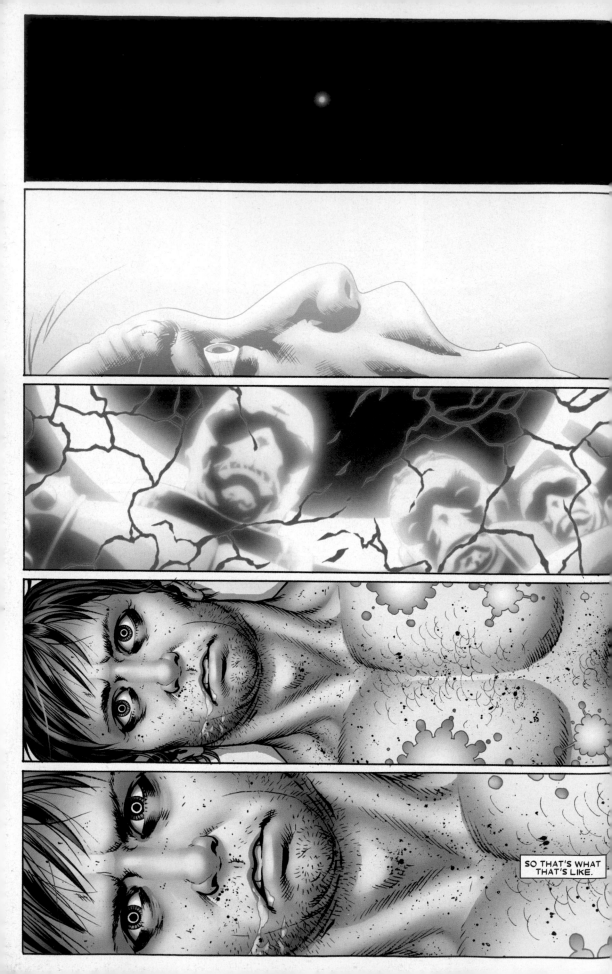

SO THAT'S WHAT
THAT'S LIKE.

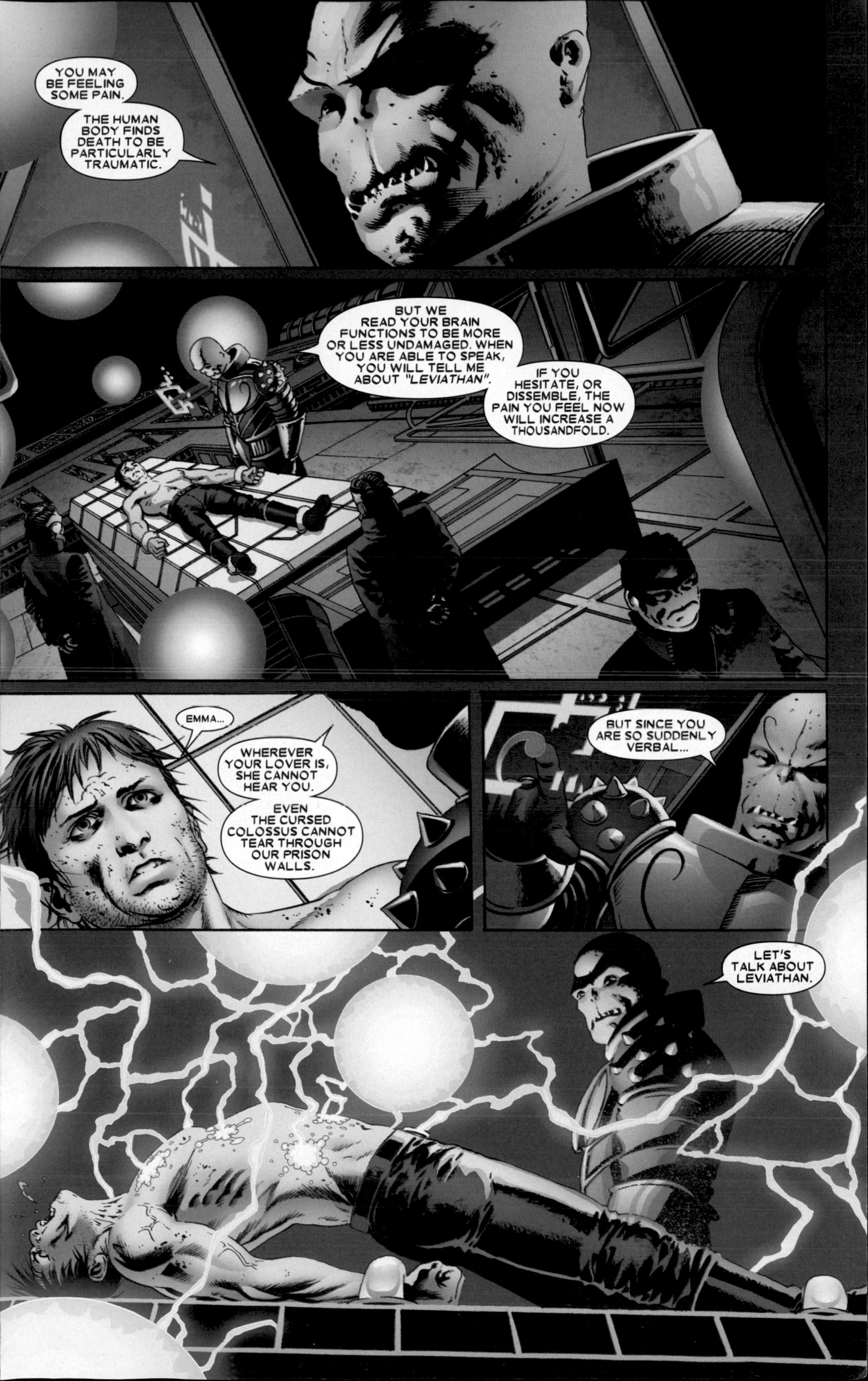
YOU MAY BE FEELING SOME PAIN.
THE HUMAN BODY FINDS DEATH TO BE PARTICULARLY TRAUMATIC.
BUT WE READ YOUR BRAIN FUNCTIONS TO BE MORE OR LESS UNDAMAGED. WHEN YOU ARE ABLE TO SPEAK, YOU WILL TELL ME ABOUT "LEVIATHAN".
IF YOU HESITATE, OR DISSEMBLE, THE PAIN YOU FEEL NOW WILL INCREASE A THOUSANDFOLD.
EMMA...
WHEREVER YOUR LOVER IS, SHE CANNOT HEAR YOU.
EVEN THE CURSED COLOSSUS CANNOT TEAR THROUGH OUR PRISON WALLS.
BUT SINCE YOU ARE SO SUDDENLY VERBAL...
LET'S TALK ABOUT LEVIATHAN.

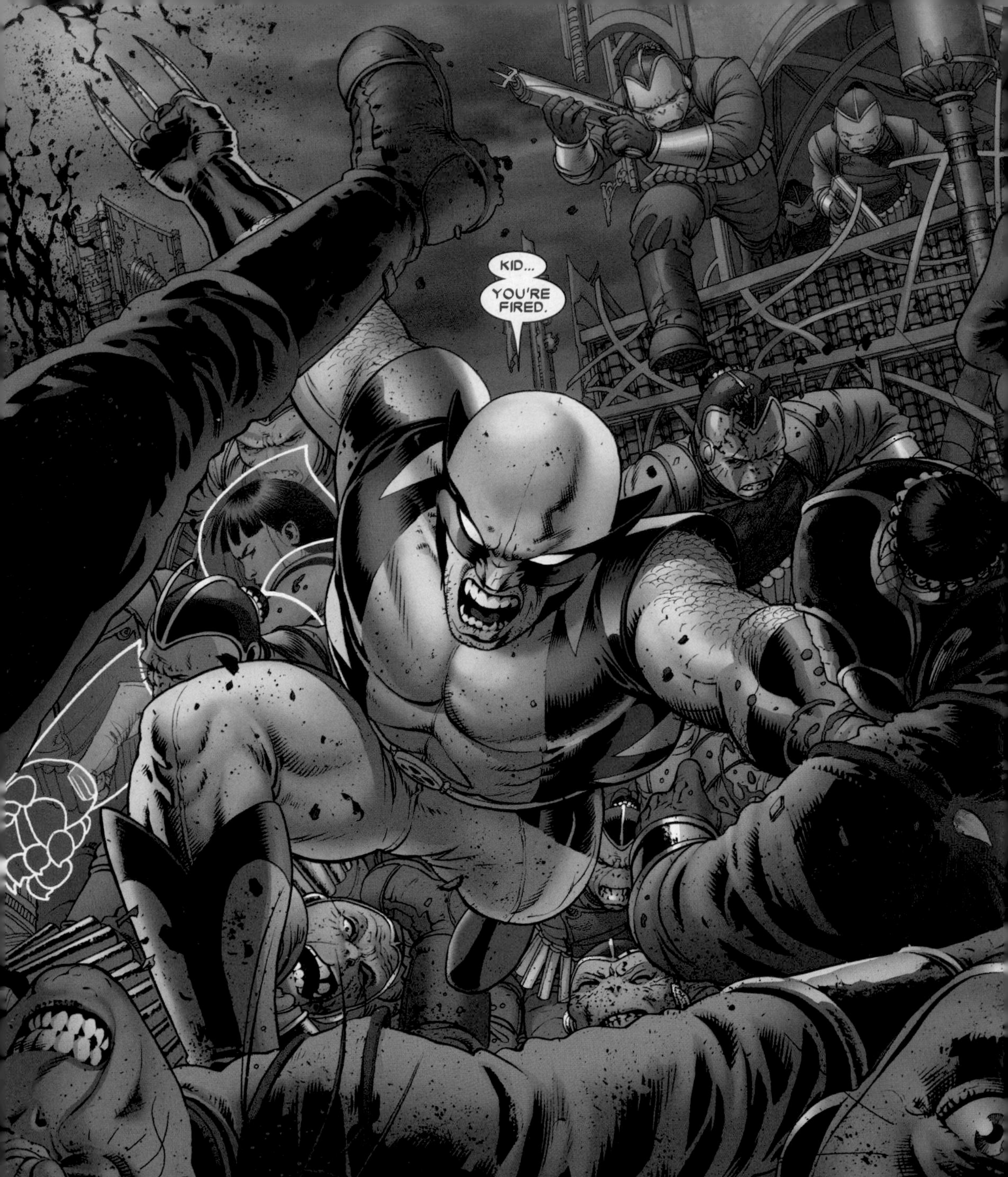
KID...
YOU'RE FIRED.

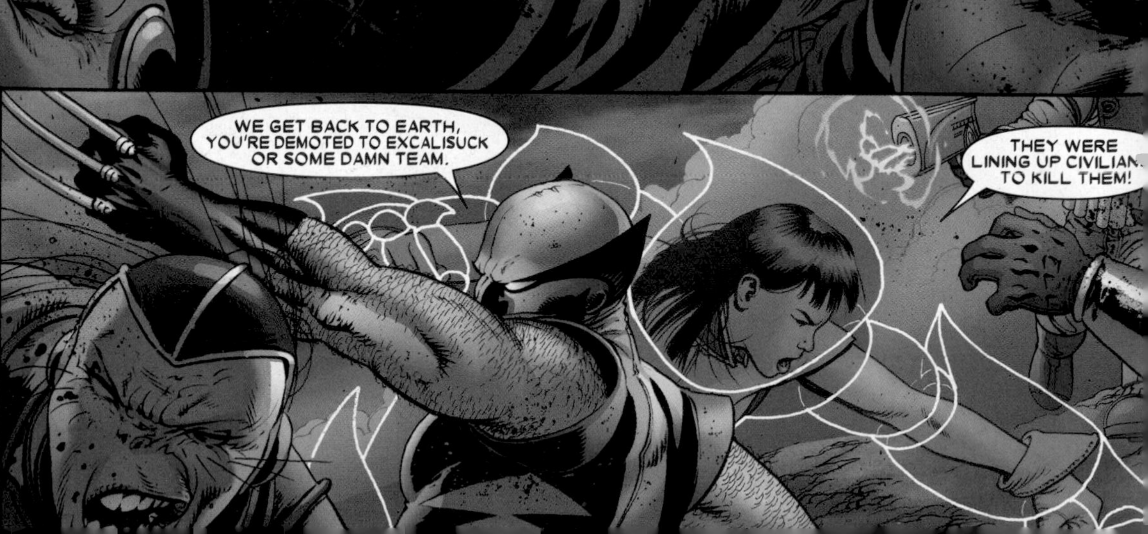
WE GET BACK TO EARTH, YOU'RE DEMOTED TO EXCALISUCK OR SOME DAMN TEAM.
THEY WERE LINING UP CIVILIAN TO KILL THEM!

THAT AIN'T THE MISSION.

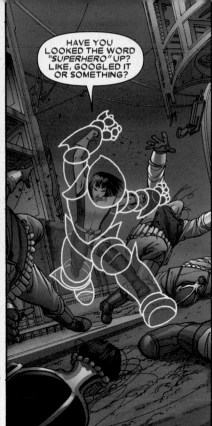

HAVE YOU LOOKED THE WORD "SUPERHERO" UP? LIKE, GOOGLED IT OR SOMETHING?

AAHHH!!!

LOGAN!

CLIK

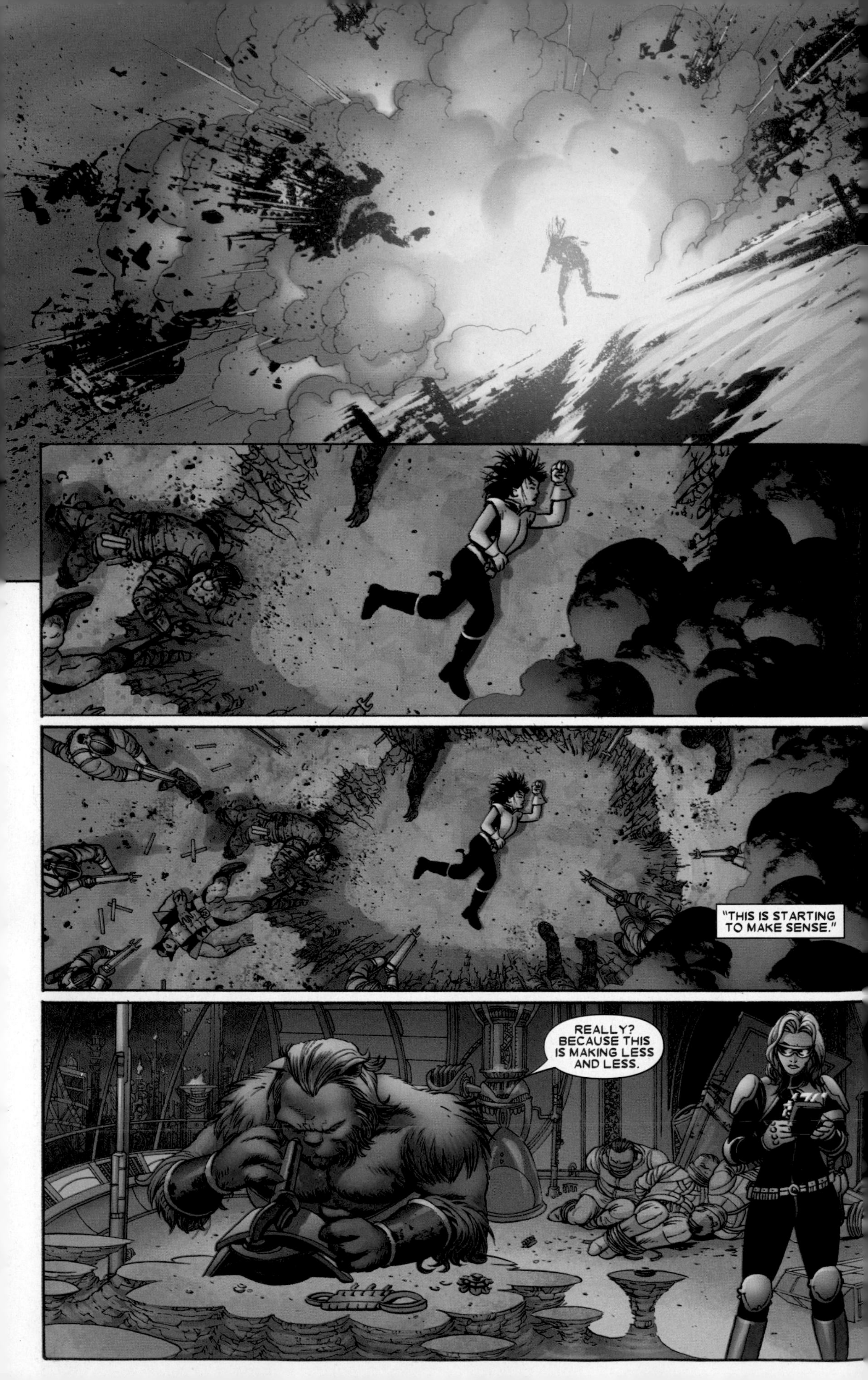
"THIS IS STARTING TO MAKE SENSE."
REALLY? BECAUSE THIS IS MAKING LESS AND LESS.

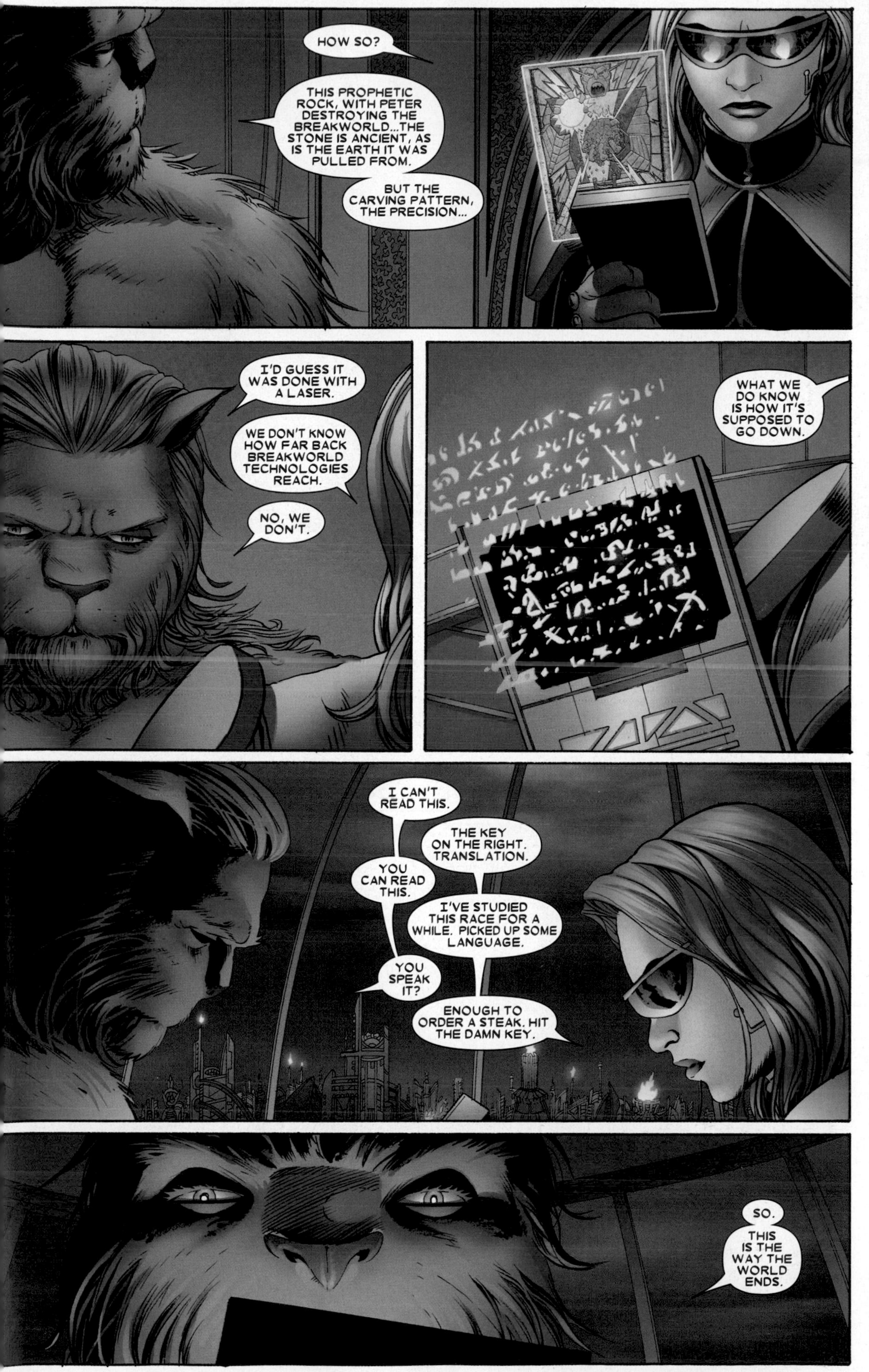
HOW SO?
THIS PROPHETIC ROCK, WITH PETER DESTROYING THE BREAKWORLD...THE STONE IS ANCIENT, AS IS THE EARTH IT WAS PULLED FROM.
BUT THE CARVING PATTERN, THE PRECISION...
I'D GUESS IT WAS DONE WITH A LASER.
WE DON'T KNOW HOW FAR BACK BREAKWORLD TECHNOLOGIES REACH.
NO, WE DON'T.
WHAT WE DO KNOW IS HOW IT'S SUPPOSED TO GO DOWN.
I CAN'T READ THIS.
THE KEY ON THE RIGHT. TRANSLATION.
YOU CAN READ THIS.
I'VE STUDIED THIS RACE FOR A WHILE. PICKED UP SOME LANGUAGE.
YOU SPEAK IT?
ENOUGH TO ORDER A STEAK. HIT THE DAMN KEY.
SO.
THIS IS THE WAY THE WORLD ENDS.

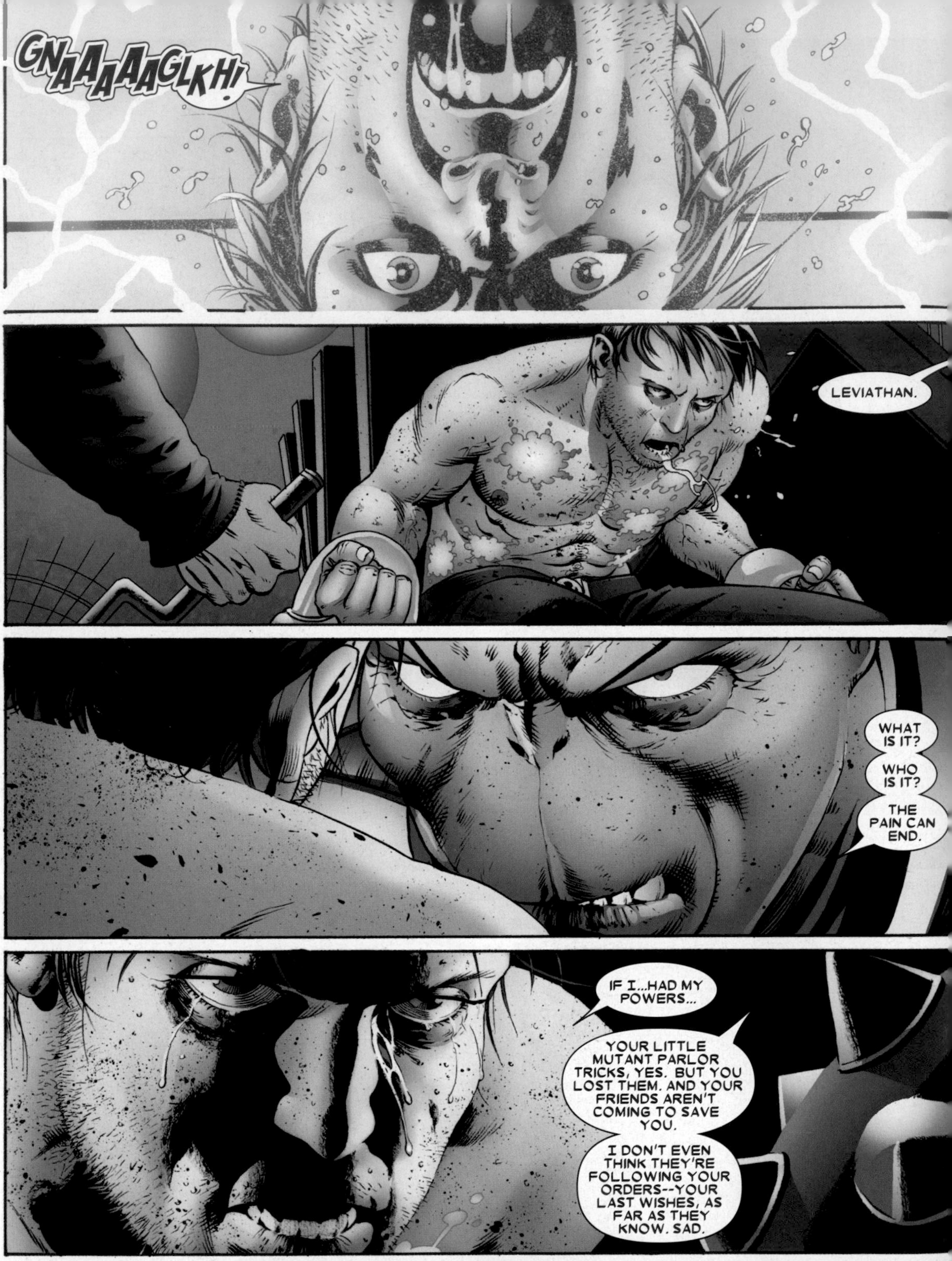
GNAAAAAGLKH!
LEVIATHAN.
WHAT IS IT?
WHO IS IT?
THE PAIN CAN END.
IF I...HAD MY POWERS...
YOUR LITTLE MUTANT PARLOR TRICKS, YES. BUT YOU LOST THEM. AND YOUR FRIENDS AREN'T COMING TO SAVE YOU.
I DON'T EVEN THINK THEY'RE FOLLOWING YOUR ORDERS--YOUR LAST WISHES, AS FAR AS THEY KNOW. SAD.
YOU... TRYING TO MAKE ME CRY?

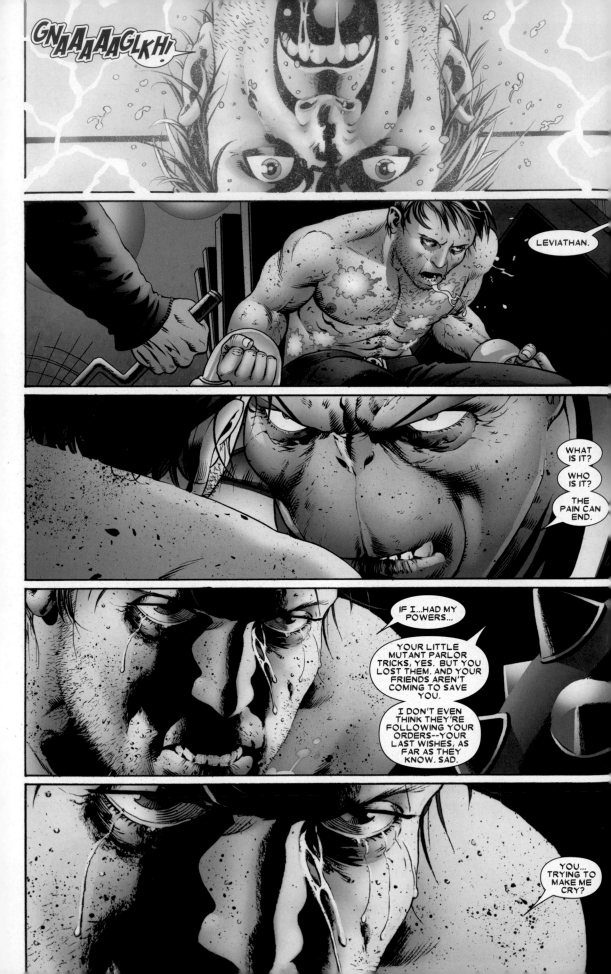

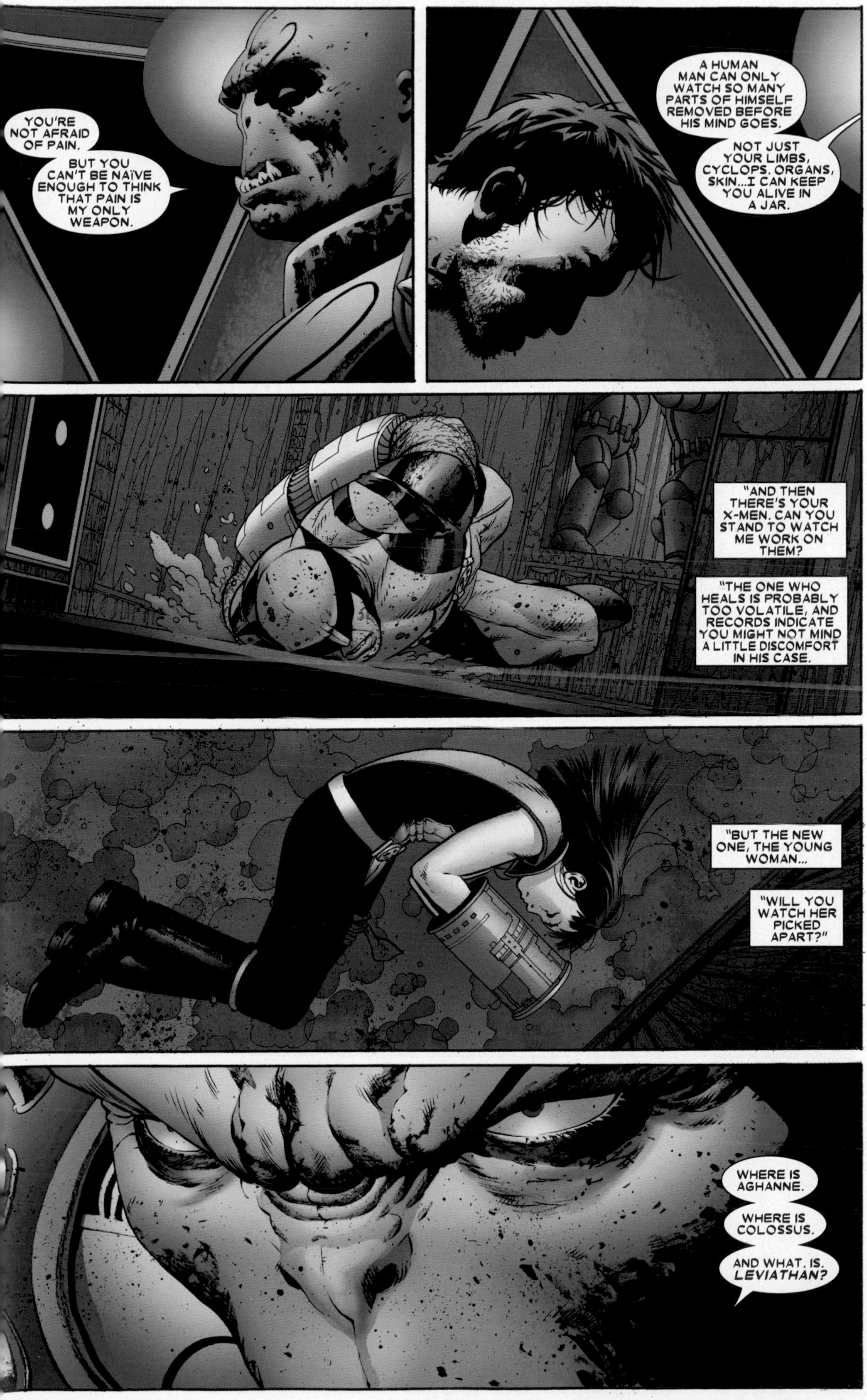
YOU'RE NOT AFRAID OF PAIN.
BUT YOU CAN'T BE NAÏVE ENOUGH TO THINK THAT PAIN IS MY ONLY WEAPON.
A HUMAN MAN CAN ONLY WATCH SO MANY PARTS OF HIMSELF REMOVED BEFORE HIS MIND GOES.
NOT JUST YOUR LIMBS, CYCLOPS. ORGANS, SKIN...I CAN KEEP YOU ALIVE IN A JAR.
"AND THEN THERE'S YOUR X-MEN. CAN YOU STAND TO WATCH ME WORK ON THEM?
"THE ONE WHO HEALS IS PROBABLY TOO VOLATILE, AND RECORDS INDICATE YOU MIGHT NOT MIND A LITTLE DISCOMFORT IN HIS CASE.
"BUT THE NEW ONE, THE YOUNG WOMAN...
"WILL YOU WATCH HER PICKED APART?"
WHERE IS AGHANNE.
WHERE IS COLOSSUS.
AND WHAT. IS. *LEVIATHAN?*

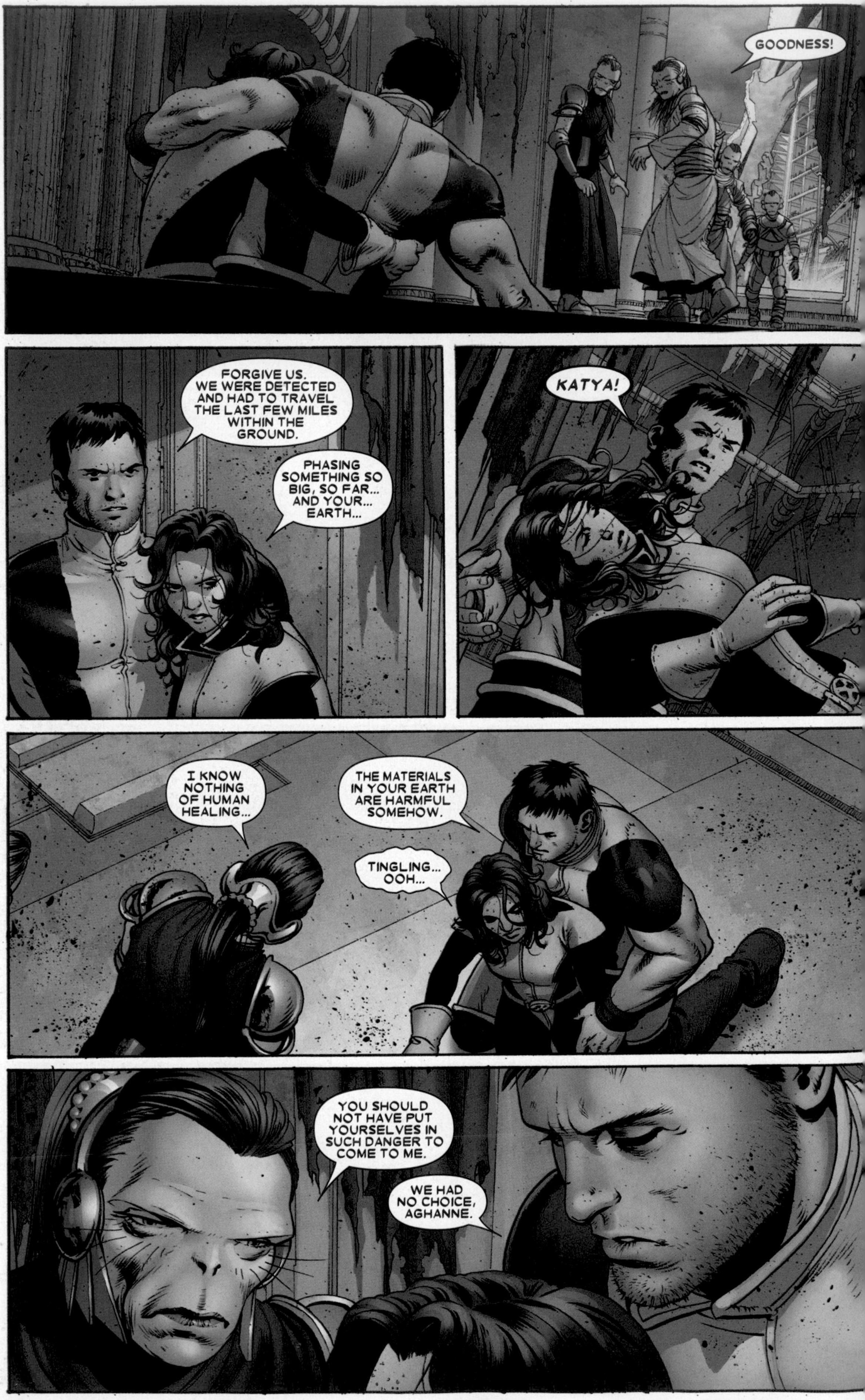
GOODNESS!
FORGIVE US. WE WERE DETECTED AND HAD TO TRAVEL THE LAST FEW MILES WITHIN THE GROUND.
PHASING SOMETHING SO BIG, SO FAR... AND YOUR... EARTH...
KATYA!
I KNOW NOTHING OF HUMAN HEALING...
THE MATERIALS IN YOUR EARTH ARE HARMFUL SOMEHOW.
TINGLING... OOH...
YOU SHOULD NOT HAVE PUT YOURSELVES IN SUCH DANGER TO COME TO ME.
WE HAD NO CHOICE, AGHANNE.

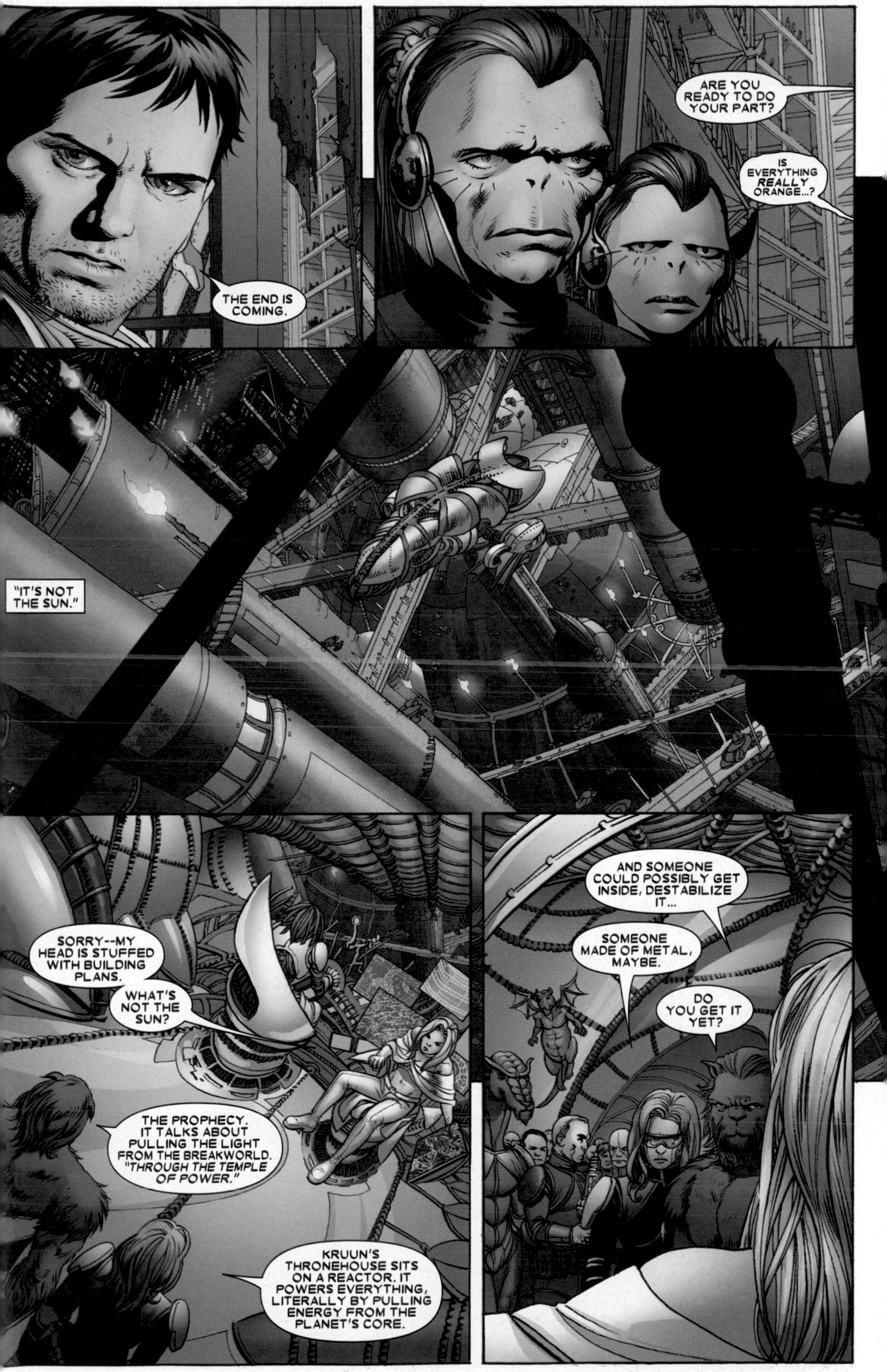
THE END IS COMING.
ARE YOU READY TO DO YOUR PART?
IS EVERYTHING *REALLY* ORANGE...?
"IT'S NOT THE SUN."
SORRY--MY HEAD IS STUFFED WITH BUILDING PLANS.
WHAT'S NOT THE SUN?
THE PROPHECY. IT TALKS ABOUT PULLING THE LIGHT FROM THE BREAKWORLD. *"THROUGH THE TEMPLE OF POWER."*
KRUUN'S THRONEHOUSE SITS ON A REACTOR. IT POWERS EVERYTHING, LITERALLY BY PULLING ENERGY FROM THE PLANET'S CORE.
AND SOMEONE COULD POSSIBLY GET INSIDE, DESTABILIZE IT...
SOMEONE MADE OF METAL, MAYBE.
DO YOU GET IT YET?

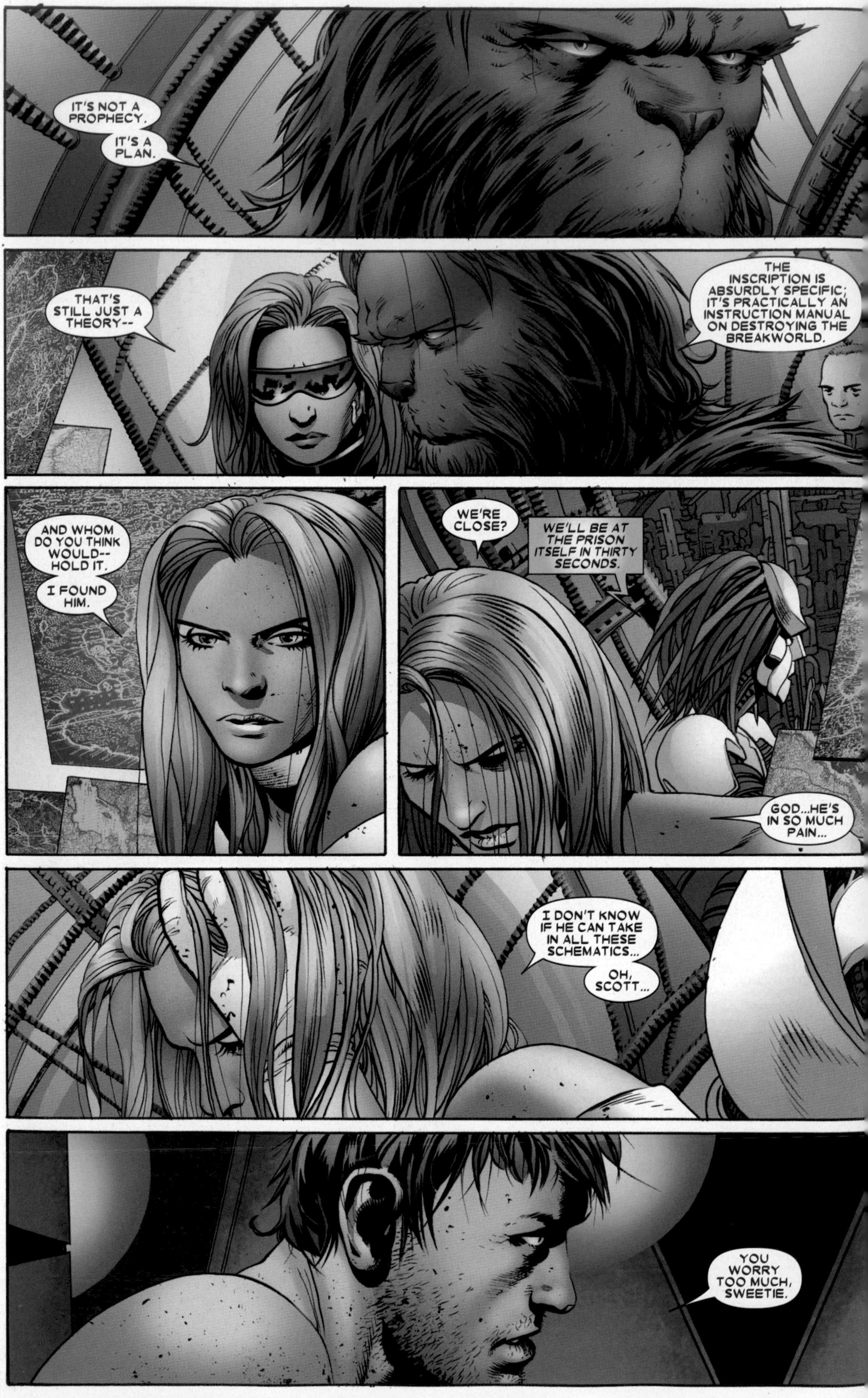
IT'S NOT A PROPHECY.
IT'S A PLAN.
THAT'S STILL JUST A THEORY--
THE INSCRIPTION IS ABSURDLY SPECIFIC; IT'S PRACTICALLY AN INSTRUCTION MANUAL ON DESTROYING THE BREAKWORLD.
AND WHOM DO YOU THINK WOULD-- HOLD IT.
I FOUND HIM.
WE'RE CLOSE?
WE'LL BE AT THE PRISON ITSELF IN THIRTY SECONDS.
GOD...HE'S IN SO MUCH PAIN...
I DON'T KNOW IF HE CAN TAKE IN ALL THESE SCHEMATICS...
OH, SCOTT...
YOU WORRY TOO MUCH, SWEETIE.

YOU CAN'T JUST HAVE CALLED ME "SWEETIE."

YOUR WITCH IS NEARBY. IT WILL AVAIL YOU NOTHING-- SHE CANNOT BREACH THESE WALLS.

THEY'RE NICE WALLS. WOULD YOU LIKE ME TO START ANSWERING YOUR QUESTIONS NOW?

"PETER--COLOSSUS-- IS WITH AGHANNE. SHOULD BE ON THEIR WAY."

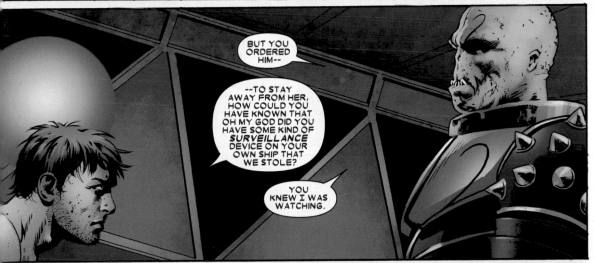

BUT YOU ORDERED HIM--

--TO STAY AWAY FROM HER, HOW COULD YOU HAVE KNOWN THAT OH MY GOD DID YOU HAVE SOME KIND OF *SURVEILLANCE* DEVICE ON YOUR OWN SHIP THAT WE STOLE?

YOU KNEW I WAS WATCHING.

EMMA, HELP ME.

I, UH...

RIGHT. I'M LINKING YOU ALL PSYCHICALLY. TRY TO KEEP TALKING NORMALLY.

WE NEED TO GET CLOSE TO KRUUN. THAT WON'T HAPPEN UNLESS HE THINKS WE'RE HELPLESS.

SO I'LL TAKE THE REPAIR SHIP AND GET MYSELF CAPTURED.

THERE'S A GOOD CHANCE THEY'LL KILL YOU, BOSS.

SUPPOSE THE LEADER.

THEY'RE GAINING...

THAT'S WHY I'M ACTING LIKE ONE.

THEY BROUGHT PETER BACK TO LIFE. THEY'LL DO THE SAME WITH ME IF THEY THINK I HAVE INFORMATION THEY NEED.

A SECRET WEAPON?

THAT WOULD WORK...

WE NEED A NAME: SOMETHING OMINOUS AND IMPOSING.

OUR ACE IN THE HOLE.

LEVIATHAN?

OH, HONEY, THAT'S IRRESISTIBLE! "LEVIATHAN."

KRUUN'LL WORK ME OVER FOR A WHILE TRYING TO GET THAT OUT OF ME. THE REST OF YOU GET TO WORK.

EMMA, I'LL NEED SCHEMATICS OF THE PRISON. LOGAN AND HISAKO, GET YOURSELVES CAPTURED IN A FEW HOURS SO WE'VE GOT A FORCE INSIDE.

I OBJECT!

WHAT?

BUGGER ME, WAS THAT ACTING?

IS NOT COURTROOM DRAMA, KATYA.

GONNA ALLOW YOU...

SHUT UP! I'M NOT GOOD AT HAVING TWO CONVERSATIONS AT ONCE. AND I HATE SCOTT'S PLAN!

YOU MEAN YOU "OBJECT" TO IT. BUT I'M GONNA ALLOW IT.

S#!%. I'M GONNA CRACK UP. I'M CRACKING UP.

SAY SOMETHING CYNICAL.

RIGHT. RIGHT.

EXCUSE ME, I'M THE ONE WHO'S GONNA

AGENT BRAND, YOU AND HANK WORK THAT PROPHECY. PETER, BRING AGHANNE INTO THE FOLD IF YOU CAN. BE OUTSIDE THE PRISON IN A FEW HOURS. BRING EVERYONE.

STA KR FR EVE

I'D BETTER GO BEFORE KITTY TRIES TO ACT AGAIN.

EMMA

SCOTT, IF KRUUN HAS YOU AT HIS MERCY...

DON'T WORRY, MY LOVE...

"LEVIATHAN" WILL SAVE ME.

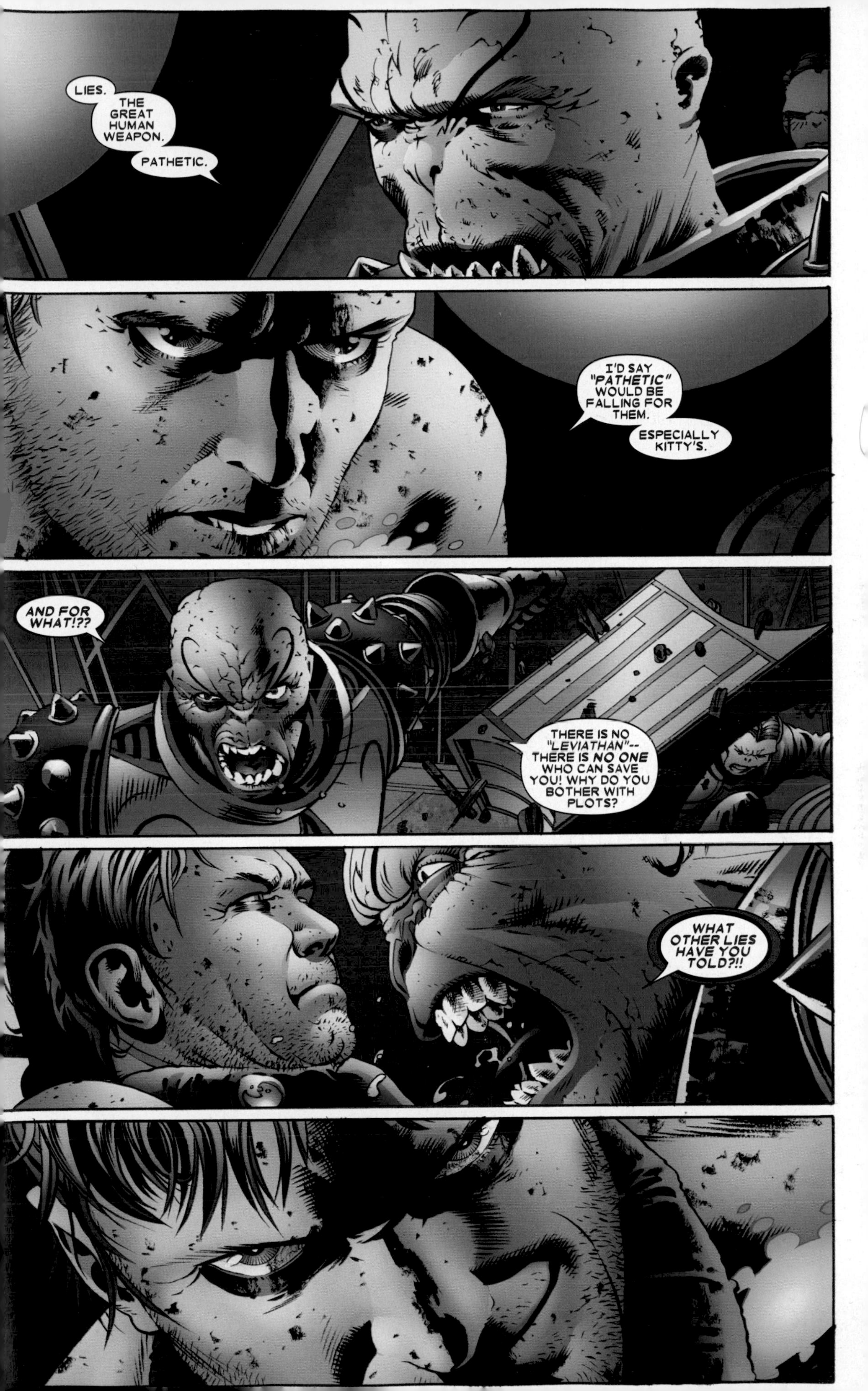
LIES.
THE GREAT HUMAN WEAPON.
PATHETIC.
I'D SAY "PATHETIC" WOULD BE FALLING FOR THEM.
ESPECIALLY KITTY'S.
AND FOR WHAT!??
THERE IS NO "LEVIATHAN"-- THERE IS NO ONE WHO CAN SAVE YOU! WHY DO YOU BOTHER WITH PLOTS?
WHAT OTHER LIES HAVE YOU TOLD?!!

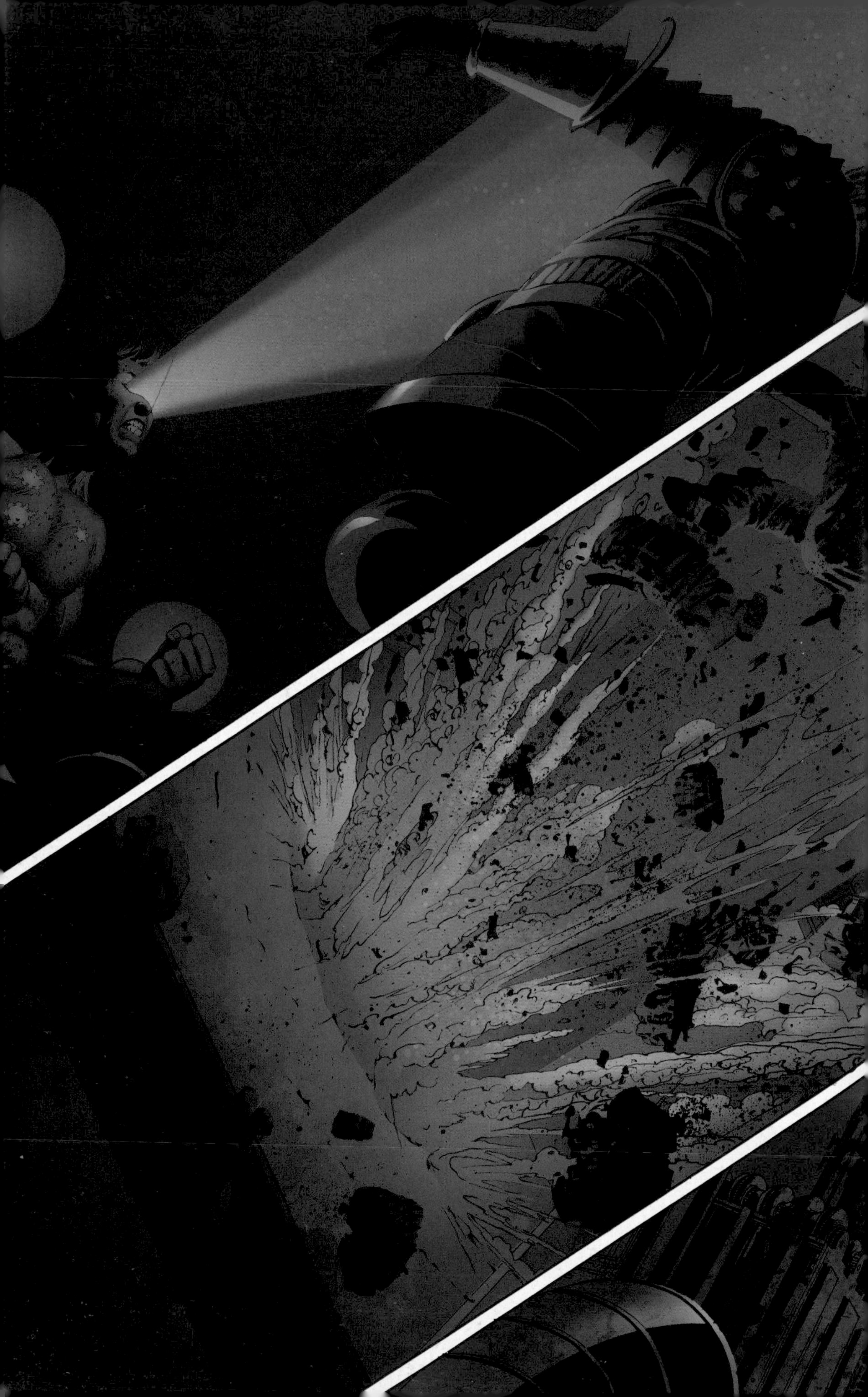

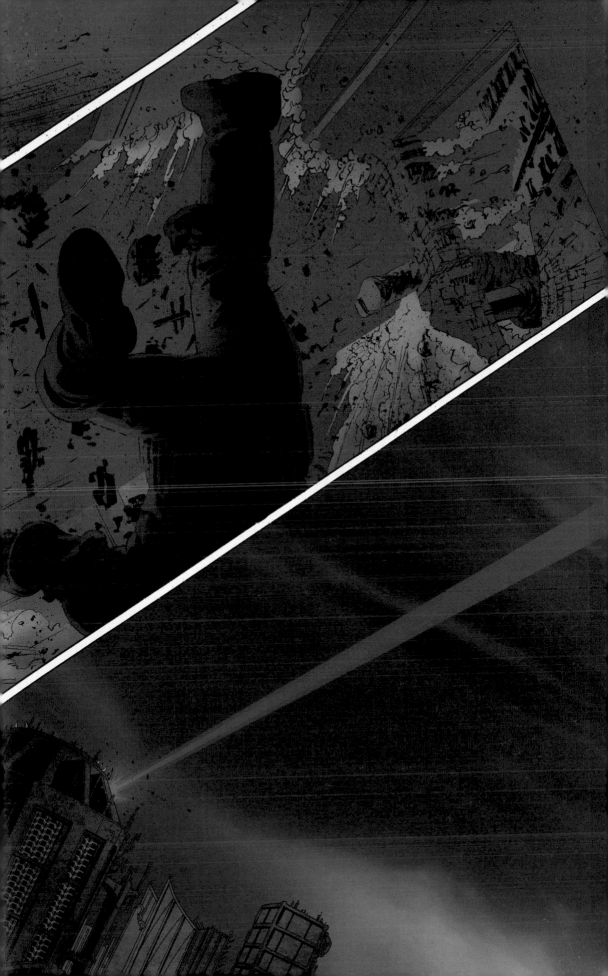

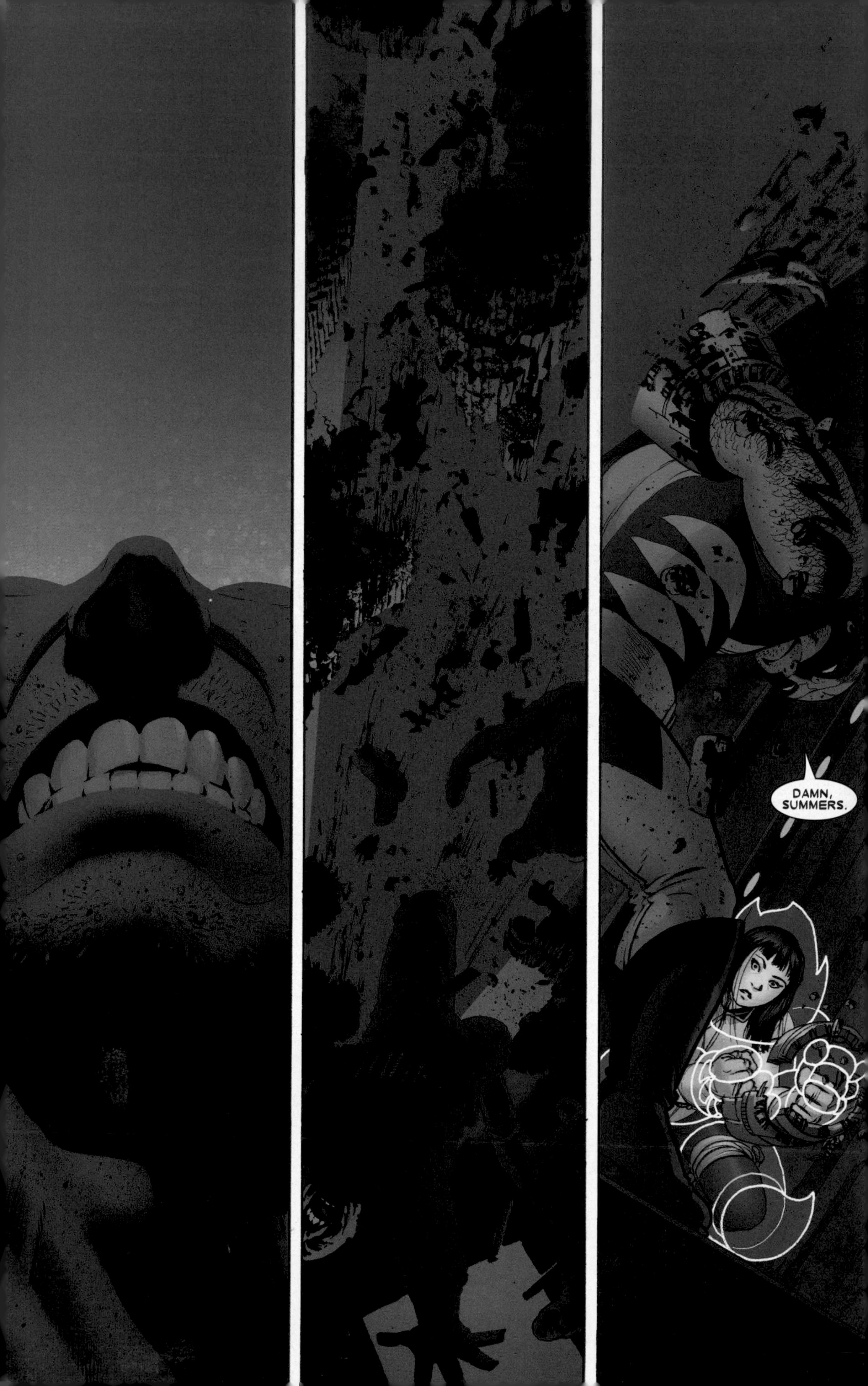
DAMN, SUMMERS.

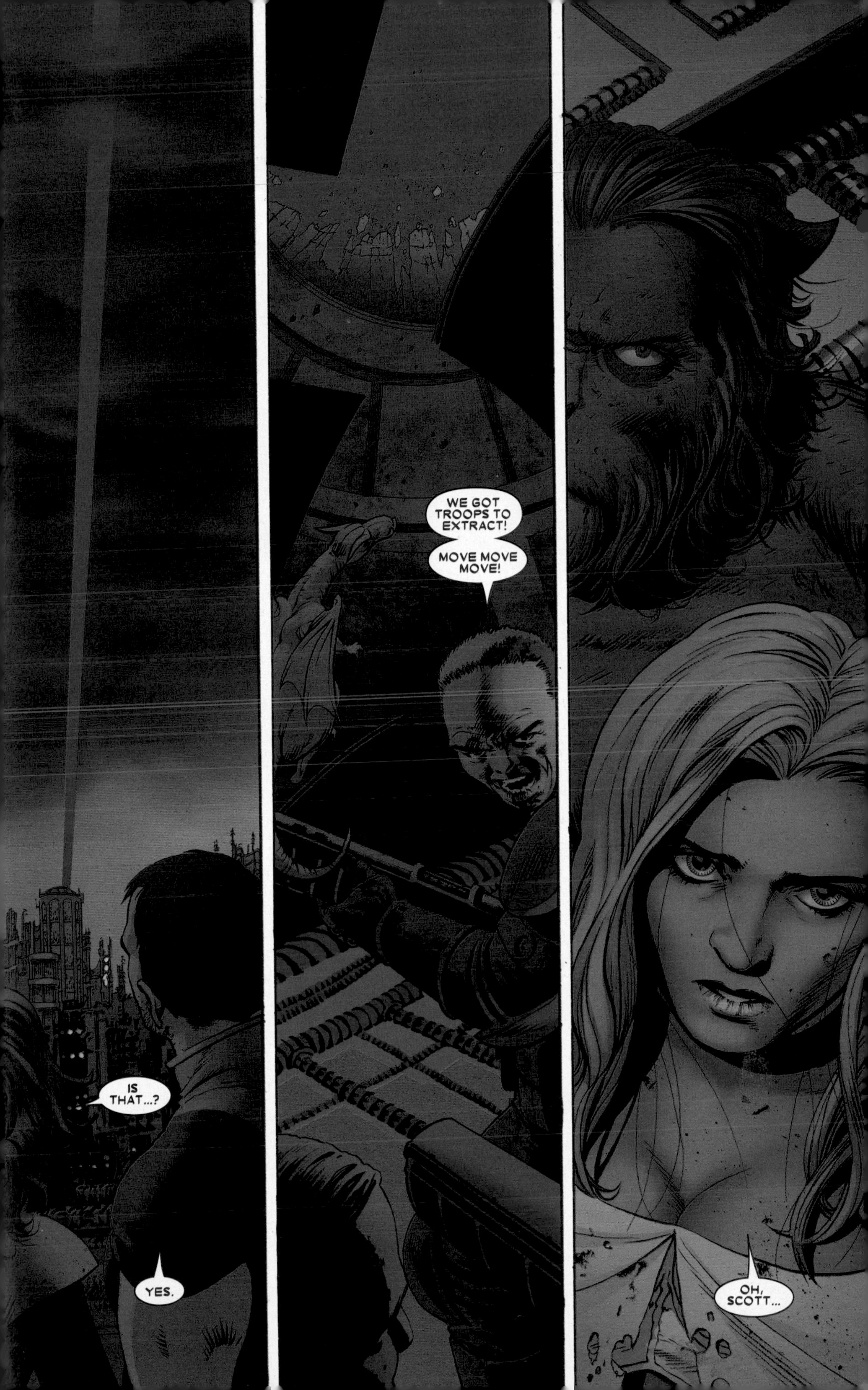
IS THAT...?
YES.
WE GOT TROOPS TO EXTRACT!
MOVE MOVE MOVE!
OH, SCOTT...

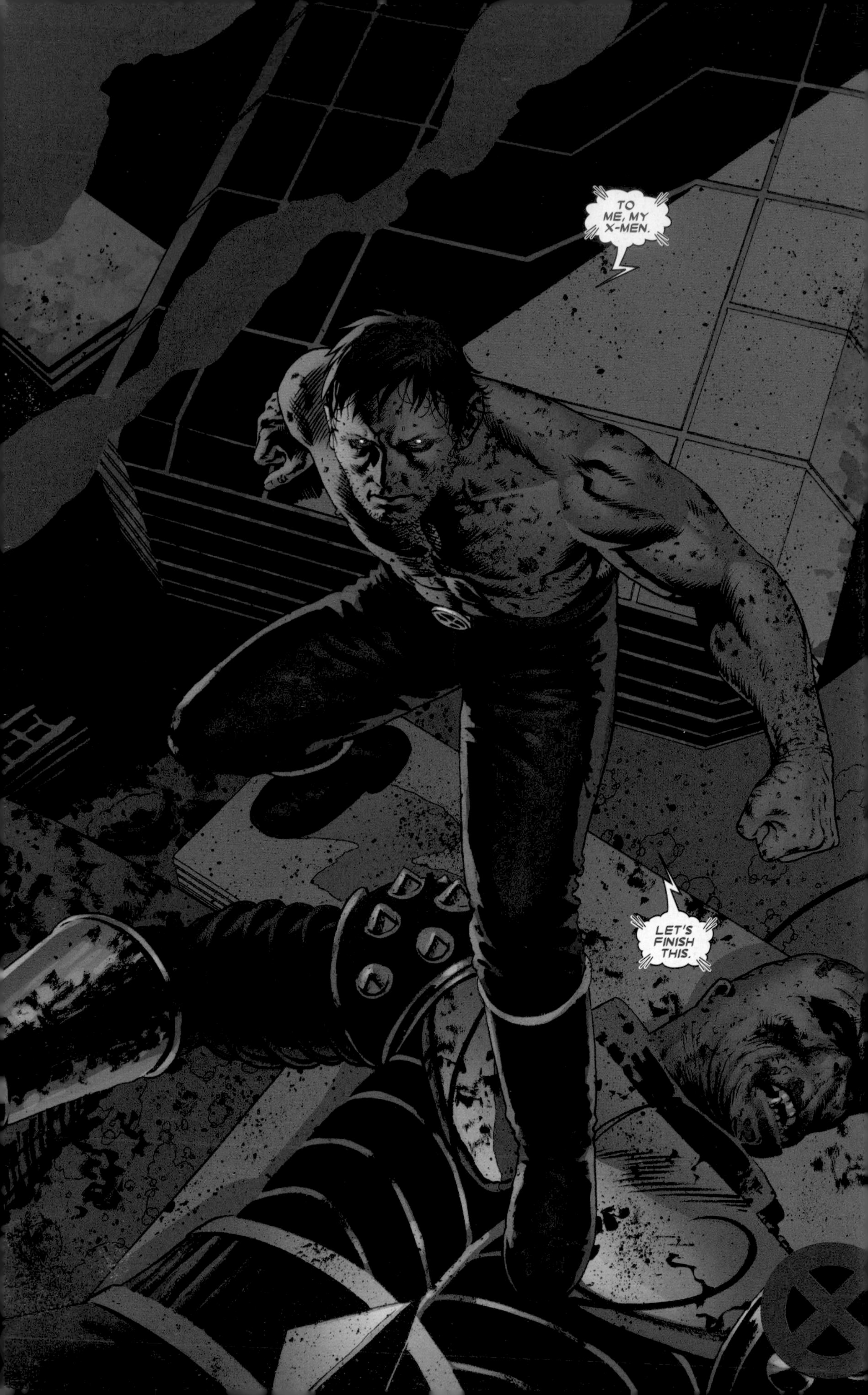
TO ME, MY X-MEN.
LET'S FINISH THIS.

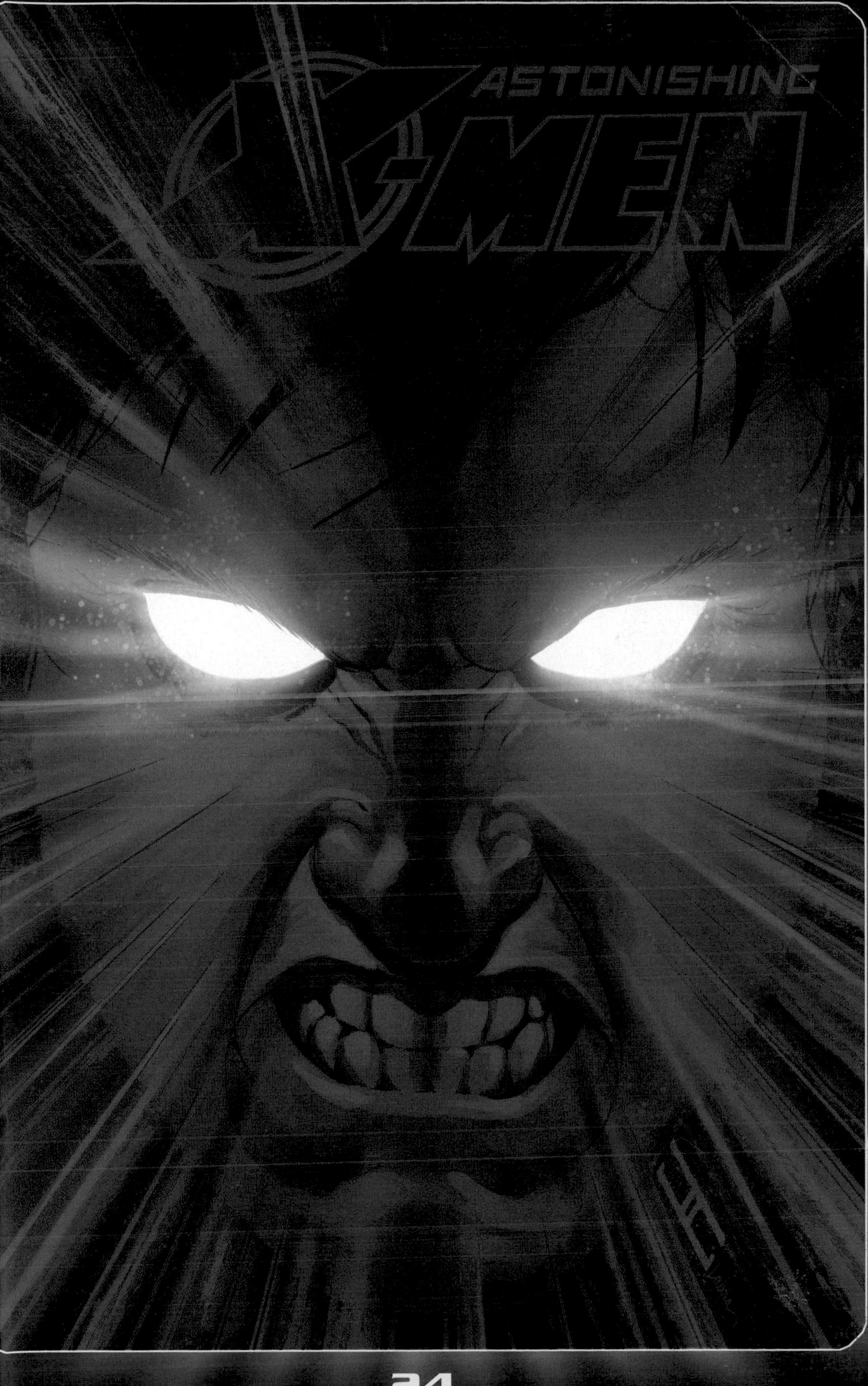
ASTONISHING
X-MEN

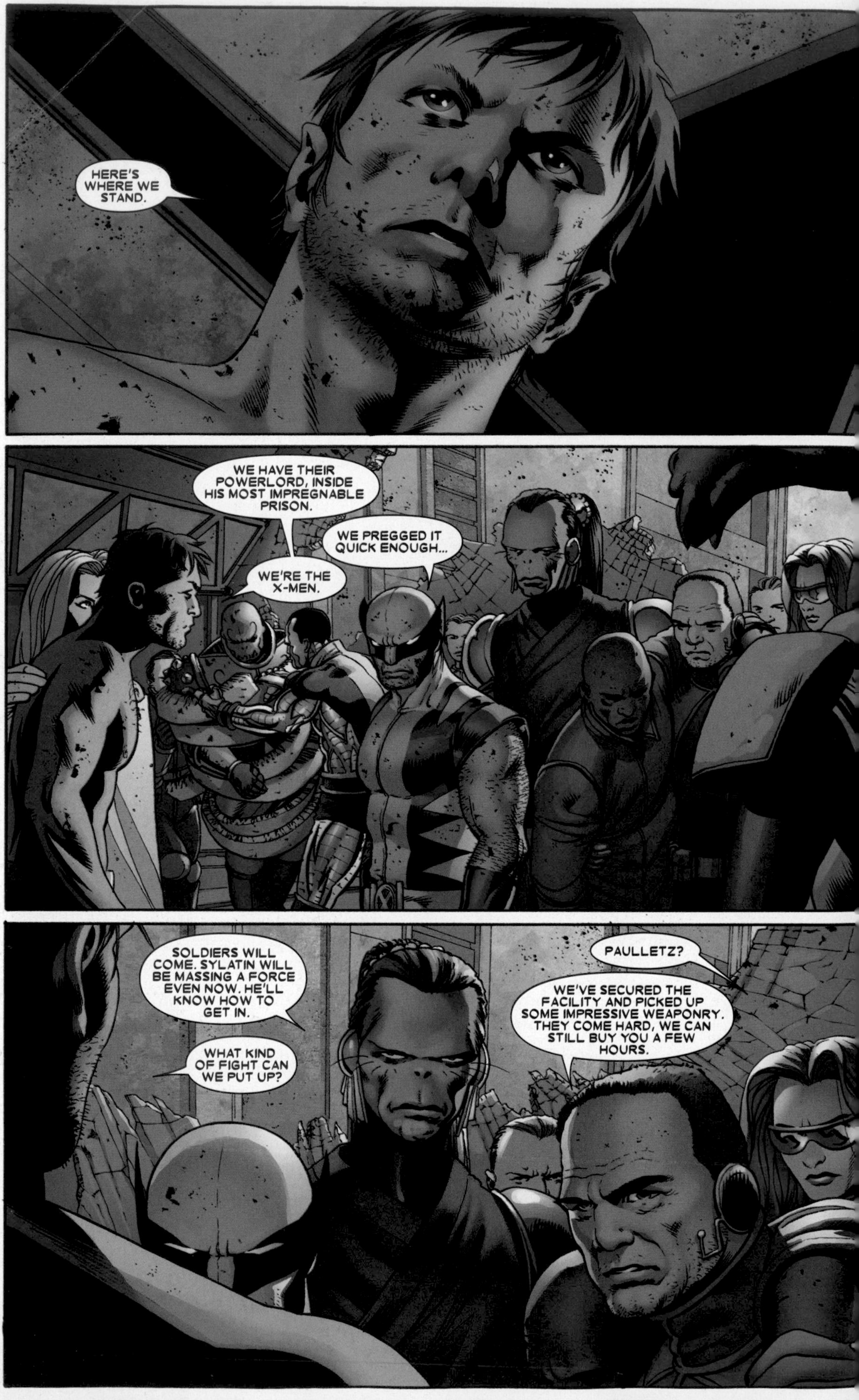
HERE'S WHERE WE STAND.
WE HAVE THEIR POWERLORD, INSIDE HIS MOST IMPREGNABLE PRISON.
WE'RE THE X-MEN.
WE PREGGED IT QUICK ENOUGH...
SOLDIERS WILL COME. SYLATIN WILL BE MASSING A FORCE EVEN NOW. HE'LL KNOW HOW TO GET IN.
WHAT KIND OF FIGHT CAN WE PUT UP?
PAULLETZ?
WE'VE SECURED THE FACILITY AND PICKED UP SOME IMPRESSIVE WEAPONRY. THEY COME HARD, WE CAN STILL BUY YOU A FEW HOURS.

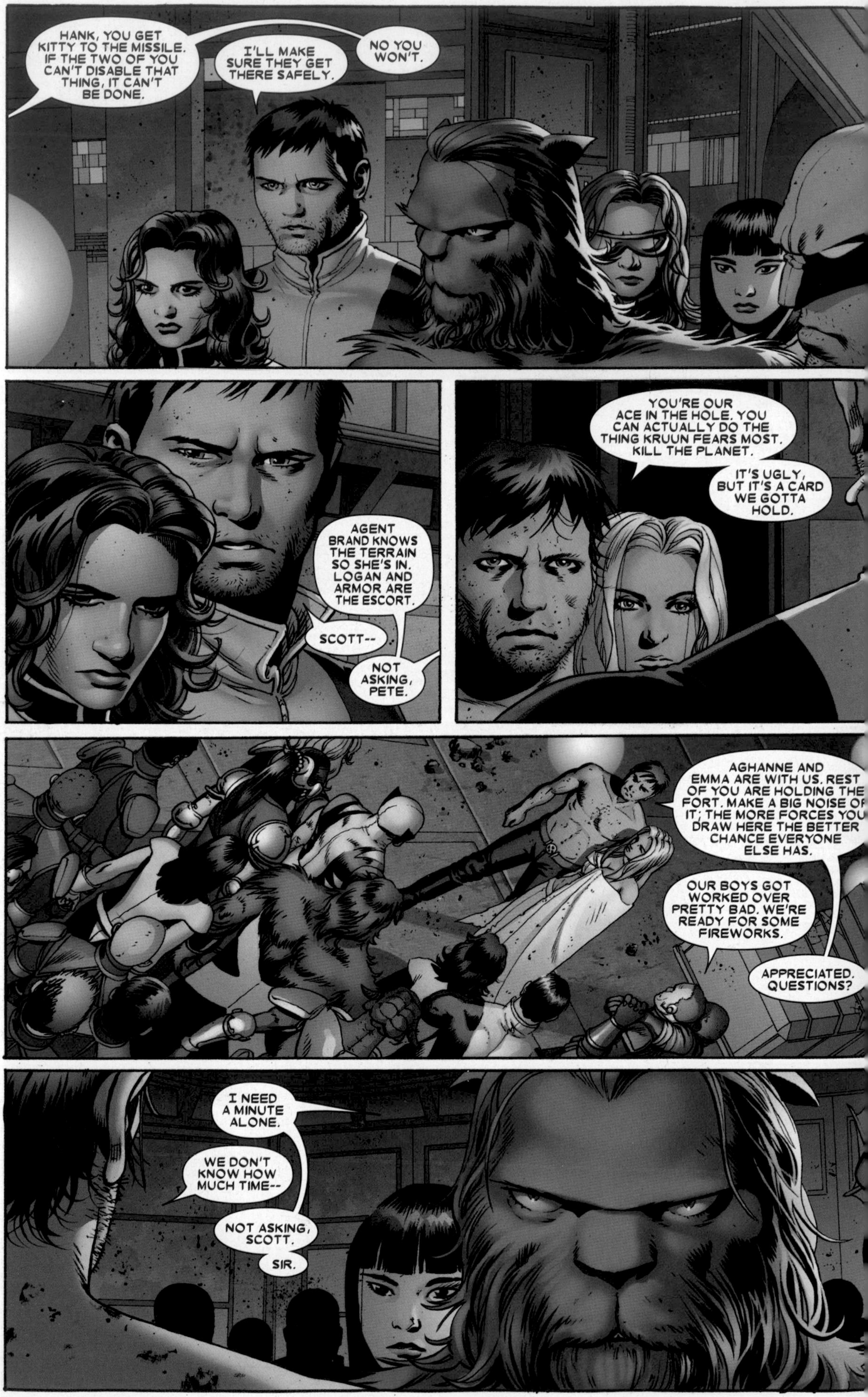
HANK, YOU GET KITTY TO THE MISSILE. IF THE TWO OF YOU CAN'T DISABLE THAT THING, IT CAN'T BE DONE.
I'LL MAKE SURE THEY GET THERE SAFELY.
NO YOU WON'T.
AGENT BRAND KNOWS THE TERRAIN SO SHE'S IN. LOGAN AND ARMOR ARE THE ESCORT.
SCOTT--
NOT ASKING, PETE.
YOU'RE OUR ACE IN THE HOLE. YOU CAN ACTUALLY DO THE THING KRUUN FEARS MOST. KILL THE PLANET.
IT'S UGLY, BUT IT'S A CARD WE GOTTA HOLD.
AGHANNE AND EMMA ARE WITH US. REST OF YOU ARE HOLDING THE FORT. MAKE A BIG NOISE OF IT; THE MORE FORCES YOU DRAW HERE THE BETTER CHANCE EVERYONE ELSE HAS.
OUR BOYS GOT WORKED OVER PRETTY BAD. WE'RE READY FOR SOME FIREWORKS.
APPRECIATED. QUESTIONS?
I NEED A MINUTE ALONE.
WE DON'T KNOW HOW MUCH TIME--
NOT ASKING, SCOTT.
SIR.

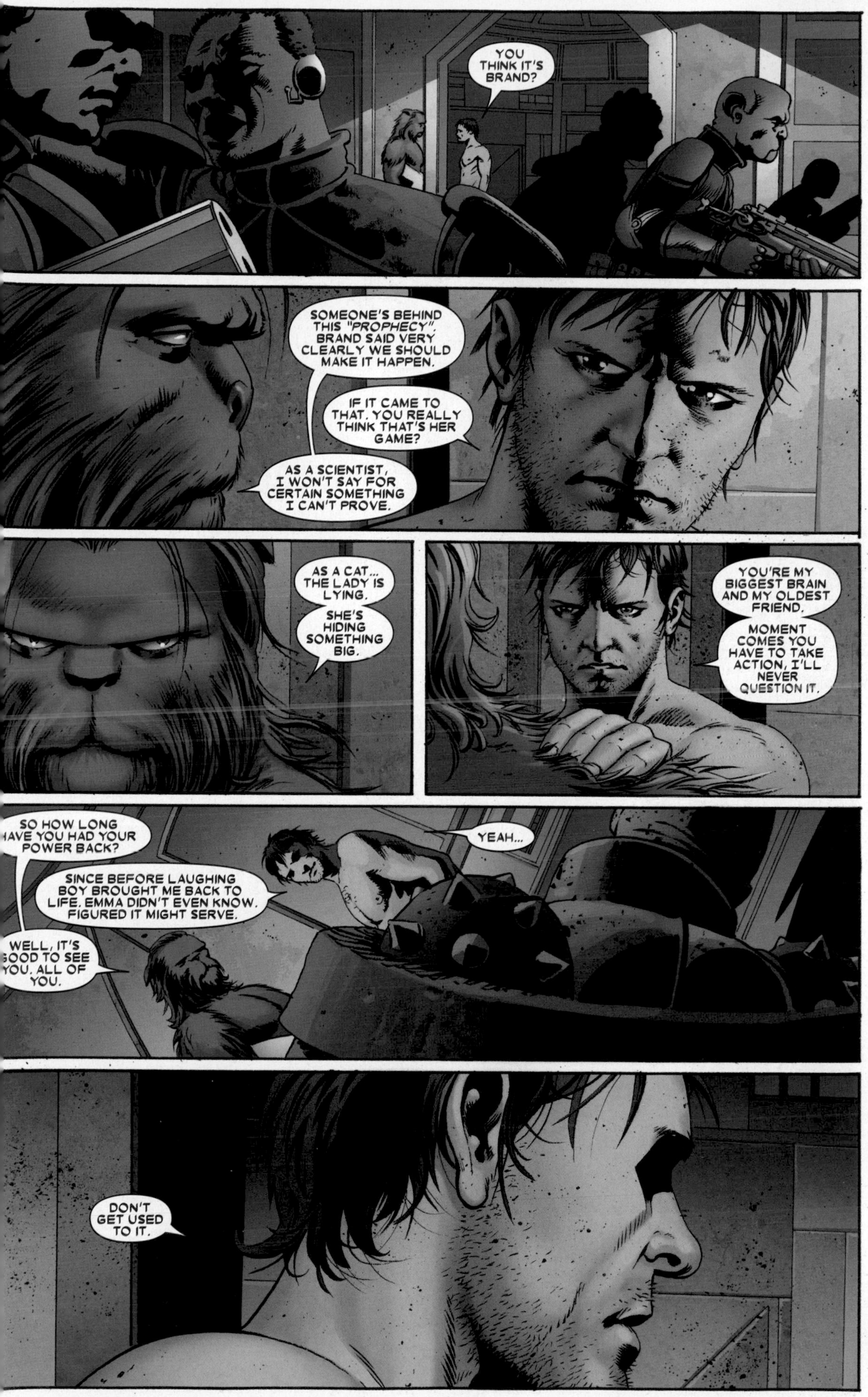
YOU THINK IT'S BRAND?
SOMEONE'S BEHIND THIS "PROPHECY". BRAND SAID VERY CLEARLY WE SHOULD MAKE IT HAPPEN.
IF IT CAME TO THAT. YOU REALLY THINK THAT'S HER GAME?
AS A SCIENTIST, I WON'T SAY FOR CERTAIN SOMETHING I CAN'T PROVE.
AS A CAT... THE LADY IS LYING.
SHE'S HIDING SOMETHING BIG.
YOU'RE MY BIGGEST BRAIN AND MY OLDEST FRIEND.
MOMENT COMES YOU HAVE TO TAKE ACTION, I'LL NEVER QUESTION IT.
YEAH...
SO HOW LONG HAVE YOU HAD YOUR POWER BACK?
SINCE BEFORE LAUGHING BOY BROUGHT ME BACK TO LIFE. EMMA DIDN'T EVEN KNOW. FIGURED IT MIGHT SERVE.
WELL, IT'S GOOD TO SEE YOU. ALL OF YOU.
DON'T GET USED TO IT.

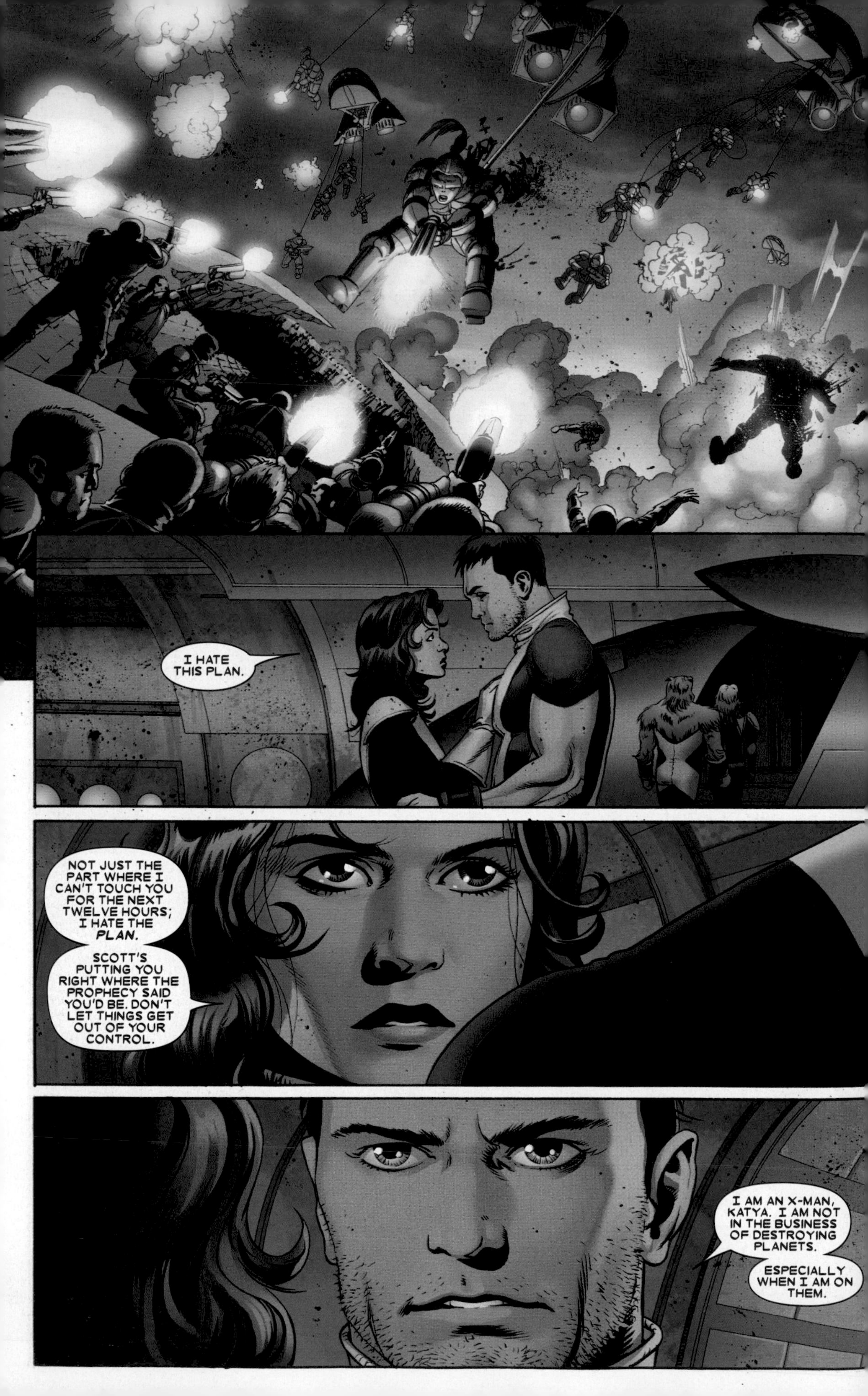
I HATE THIS PLAN.
NOT JUST THE PART WHERE I CAN'T TOUCH YOU FOR THE NEXT TWELVE HOURS; I HATE THE *PLAN*.
SCOTT'S PUTTING YOU RIGHT WHERE THE PROPHECY SAID YOU'D BE. DON'T LET THINGS GET OUT OF YOUR CONTROL.
I AM AN X-MAN, KATYA. I AM NOT IN THE BUSINESS OF DESTROYING PLANETS.
ESPECIALLY WHEN I AM ON THEM.

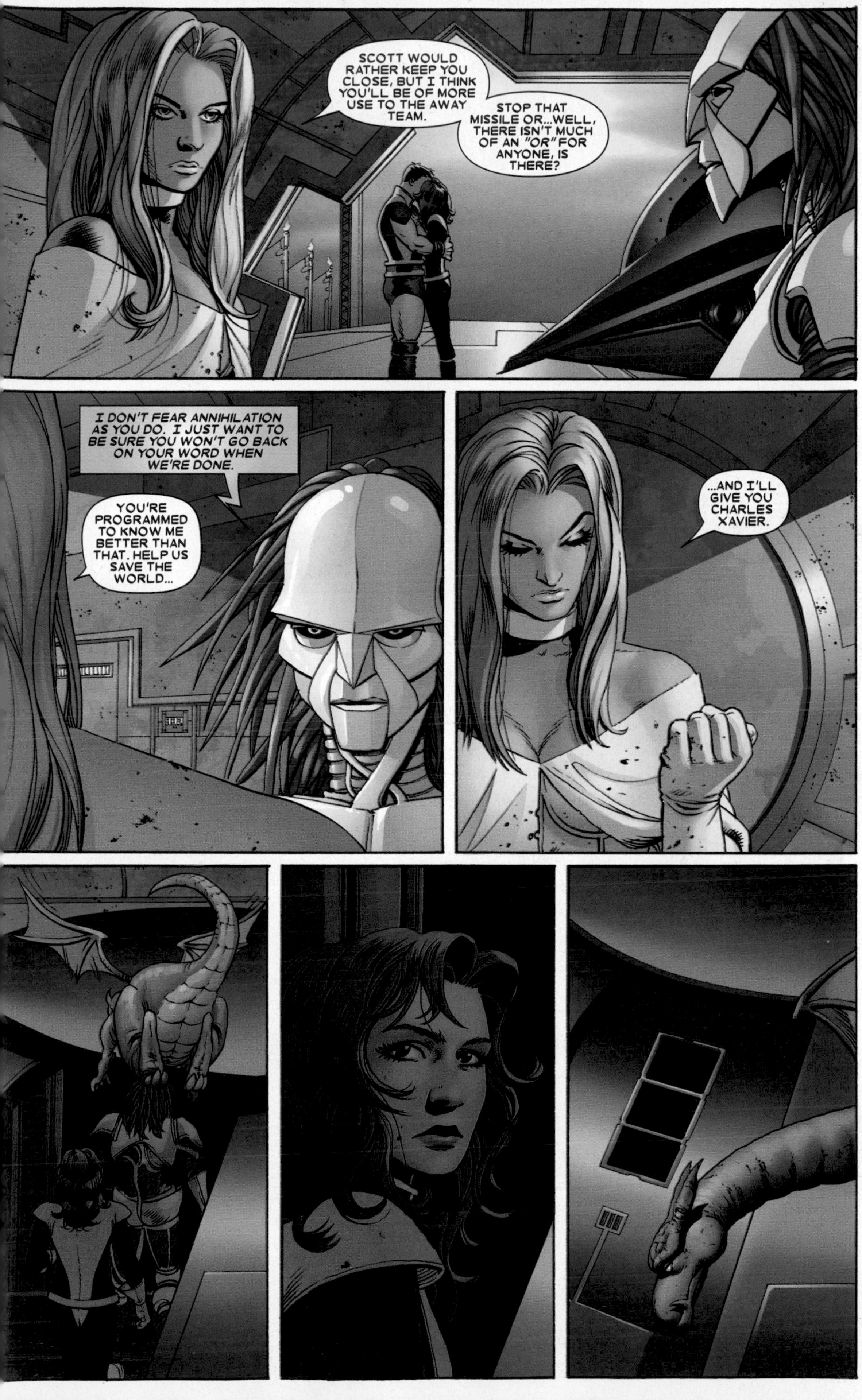
SCOTT WOULD RATHER KEEP YOU CLOSE, BUT I THINK YOU'LL BE OF MORE USE TO THE AWAY TEAM.
STOP THAT MISSILE OR...WELL, THERE ISN'T MUCH OF AN "OR" FOR ANYONE, IS THERE?
I DON'T FEAR ANNIHILATION AS YOU DO. I JUST WANT TO BE SURE YOU WON'T GO BACK ON YOUR WORD WHEN WE'RE DONE.
YOU'RE PROGRAMMED TO KNOW ME BETTER THAN THAT. HELP US SAVE THE WORLD...
...AND I'LL GIVE YOU CHARLES XAVIER.

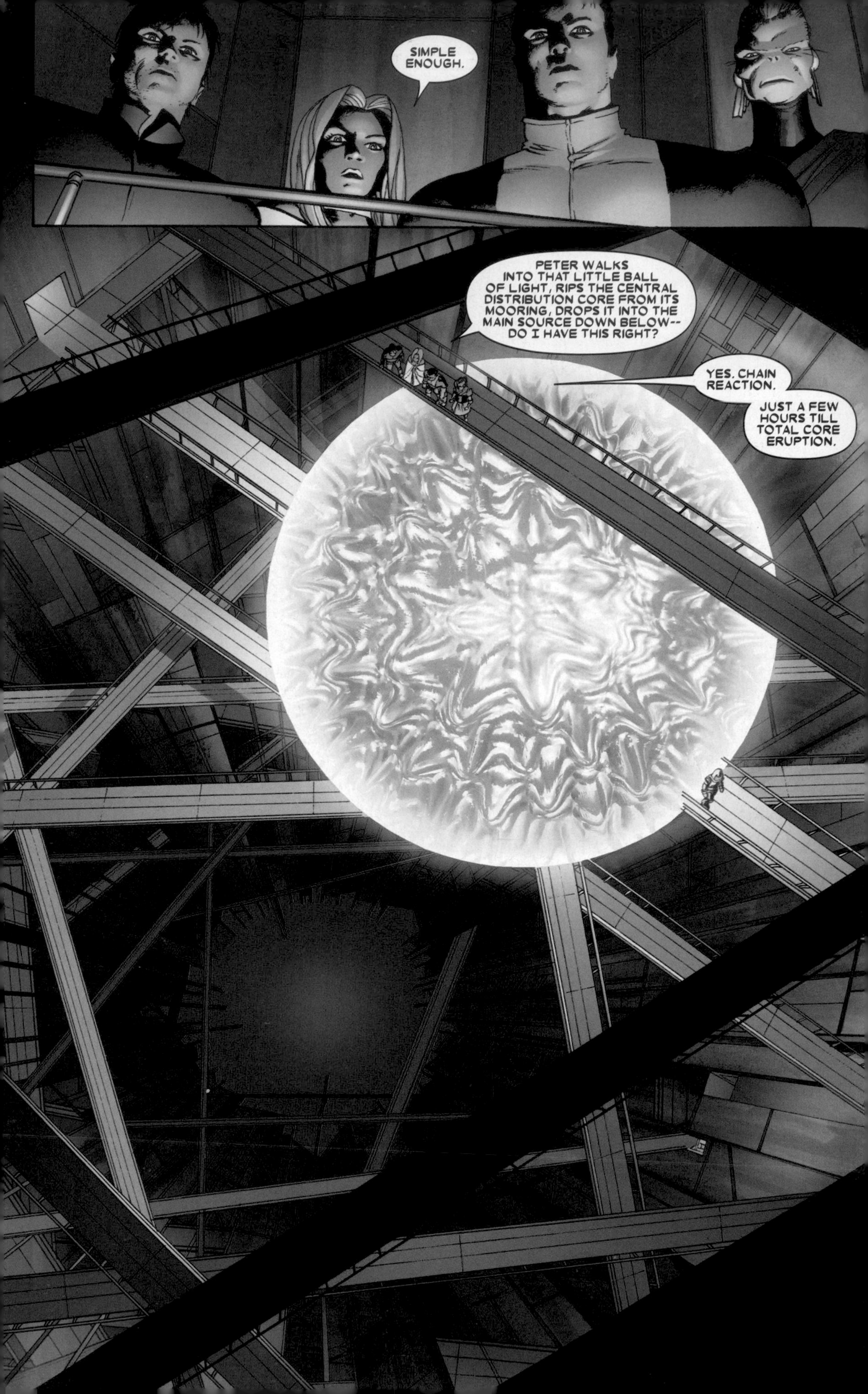
SIMPLE ENOUGH.
PETER WALKS INTO THAT LITTLE BALL OF LIGHT, RIPS THE CENTRAL DISTRIBUTION CORE FROM ITS MOORING, DROPS IT INTO THE MAIN SOURCE DOWN BELOW-- DO I HAVE THIS RIGHT?
YES. CHAIN REACTION.
JUST A FEW HOURS TILL TOTAL CORE ERUPTION.

IT MAKES NO SENSE. TO PUT YOUR WORLD AT RISK WITH SUCH A FRAGILE, UNSTABLE ENERGY SOURCE...

WE PRIZE EFFICIENCY OVER SAFETY. IS IT VERY DIFFERENT ON EARTH?

NOT AS MUCH AS WE'D LIKE. SHALL WE BEGIN? I BELIEVE HE'S WAKING UP.

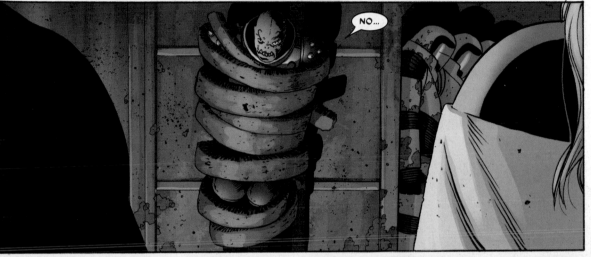

NO...

THIS IS VERY SIMPLE.

OUR WORLD FOR YOURS.

YOU DON'T KNOW WHAT YOU'VE DONE.

WE HAVEN'T DONE ANYTHING YET. DISABLE YOUR MISSILE AND WE FADE AWAY. YOU'RE THE HERO THAT SAVED THE BREAKWORLD.

THE RETALIATOR WILL FIRE AS SCHEDULED. NOTHING YOU DO CAN STOP IT.

SERIOUSLY: ARE YOU TRYING TO WIPE OUT YOUR WORLD?

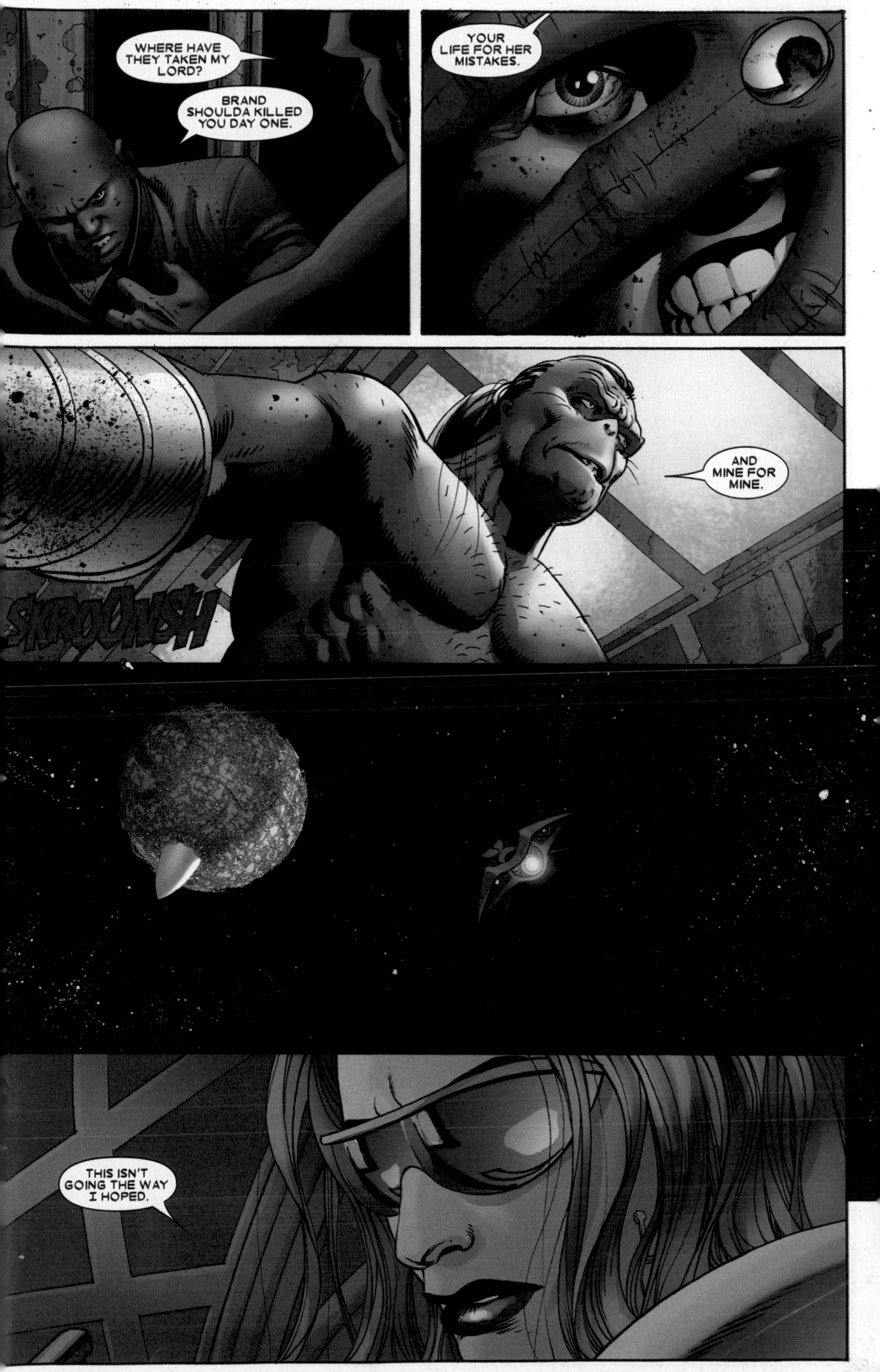
WHERE HAVE THEY TAKEN MY LORD?
BRAND SHOULDA KILLED YOU DAY ONE.
YOUR LIFE FOR HER MISTAKES.
AND MINE FOR MINE.
SKROONSH
THIS ISN'T GOING THE WAY I HOPED.

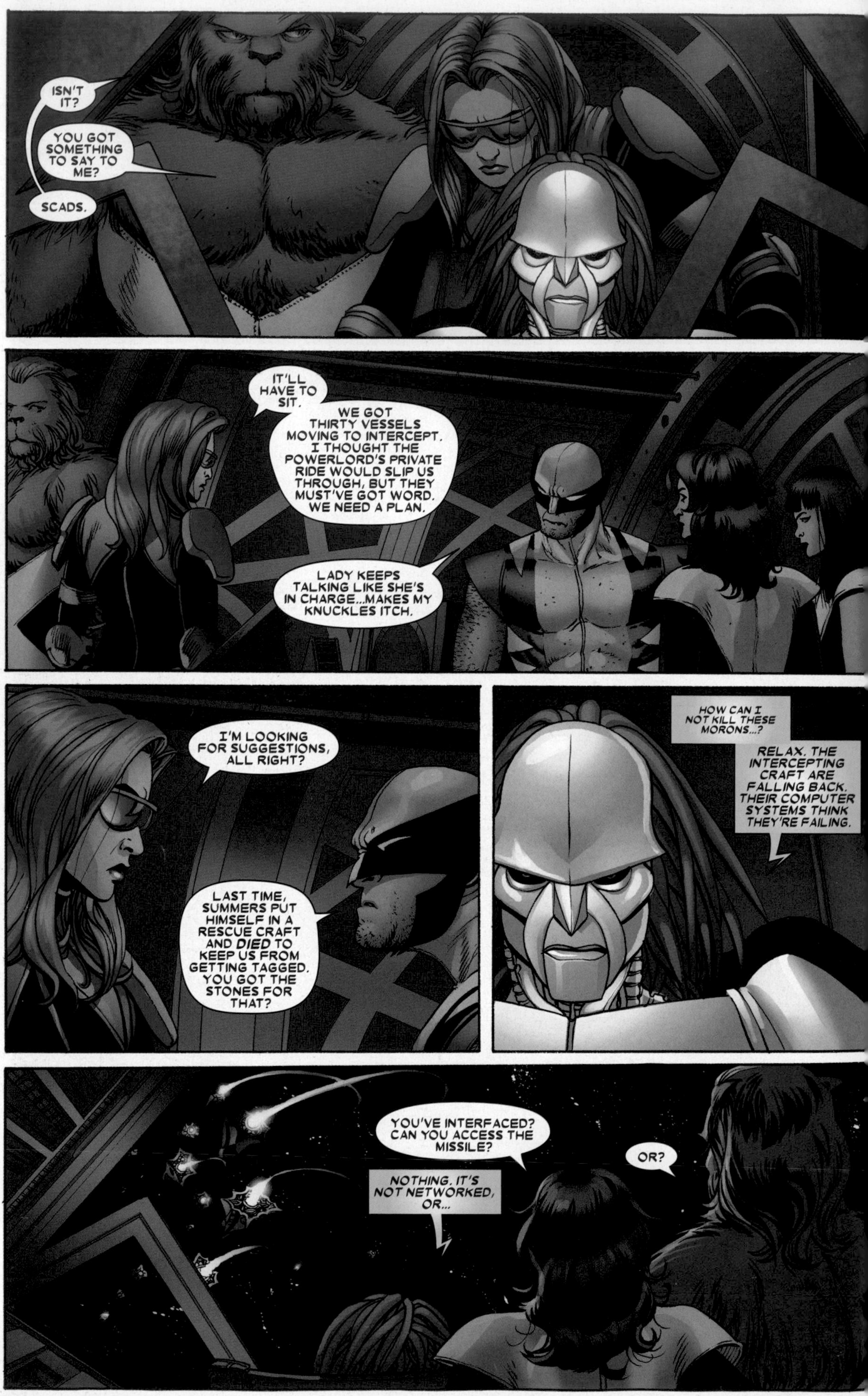
ISN'T IT?
YOU GOT SOMETHING TO SAY TO ME?
SCADS.
IT'LL HAVE TO SIT.
WE GOT THIRTY VESSELS MOVING TO INTERCEPT. I THOUGHT THE POWERLORD'S PRIVATE RIDE WOULD SLIP US THROUGH, BUT THEY MUST'VE GOT WORD. WE NEED A PLAN.
LADY KEEPS TALKING LIKE SHE'S IN CHARGE...MAKES MY KNUCKLES ITCH.
I'M LOOKING FOR SUGGESTIONS, ALL RIGHT?
LAST TIME, SUMMERS PUT HIMSELF IN A RESCUE CRAFT AND DIED TO KEEP US FROM GETTING TAGGED. YOU GOT THE STONES FOR THAT?
HOW CAN I NOT KILL THESE MORONS...?
RELAX. THE INTERCEPTING CRAFT ARE FALLING BACK. THEIR COMPUTER SYSTEMS THINK THEY'RE FAILING.
YOU'VE INTERFACED? CAN YOU ACCESS THE MISSILE?
NOTHING. IT'S NOT NETWORKED, OR...
OR?

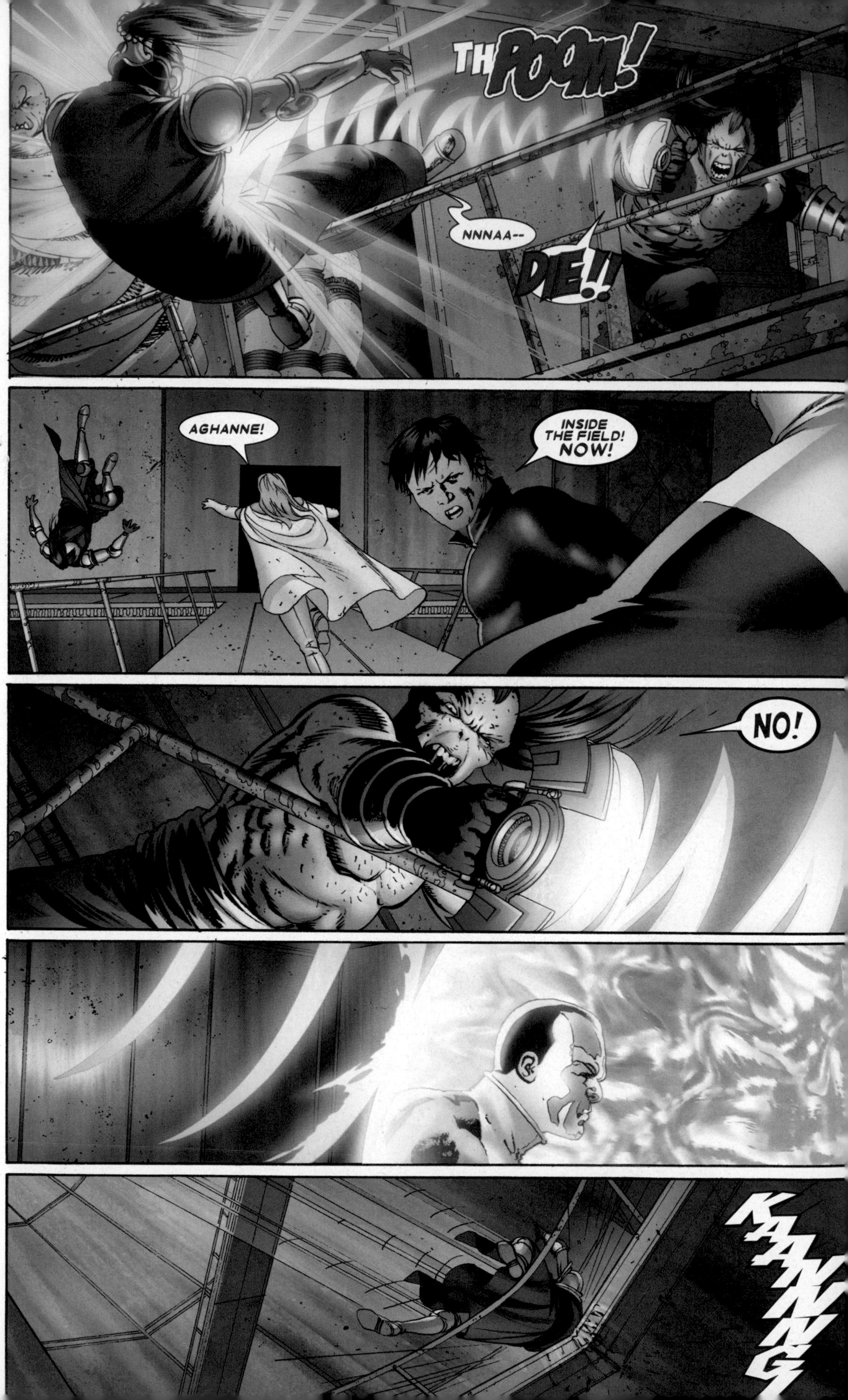
THPOOM!
NNNAA--
DIE!!
AGHANNE!
INSIDE THE FIELD! NOW!
NO!
KRAANNNG

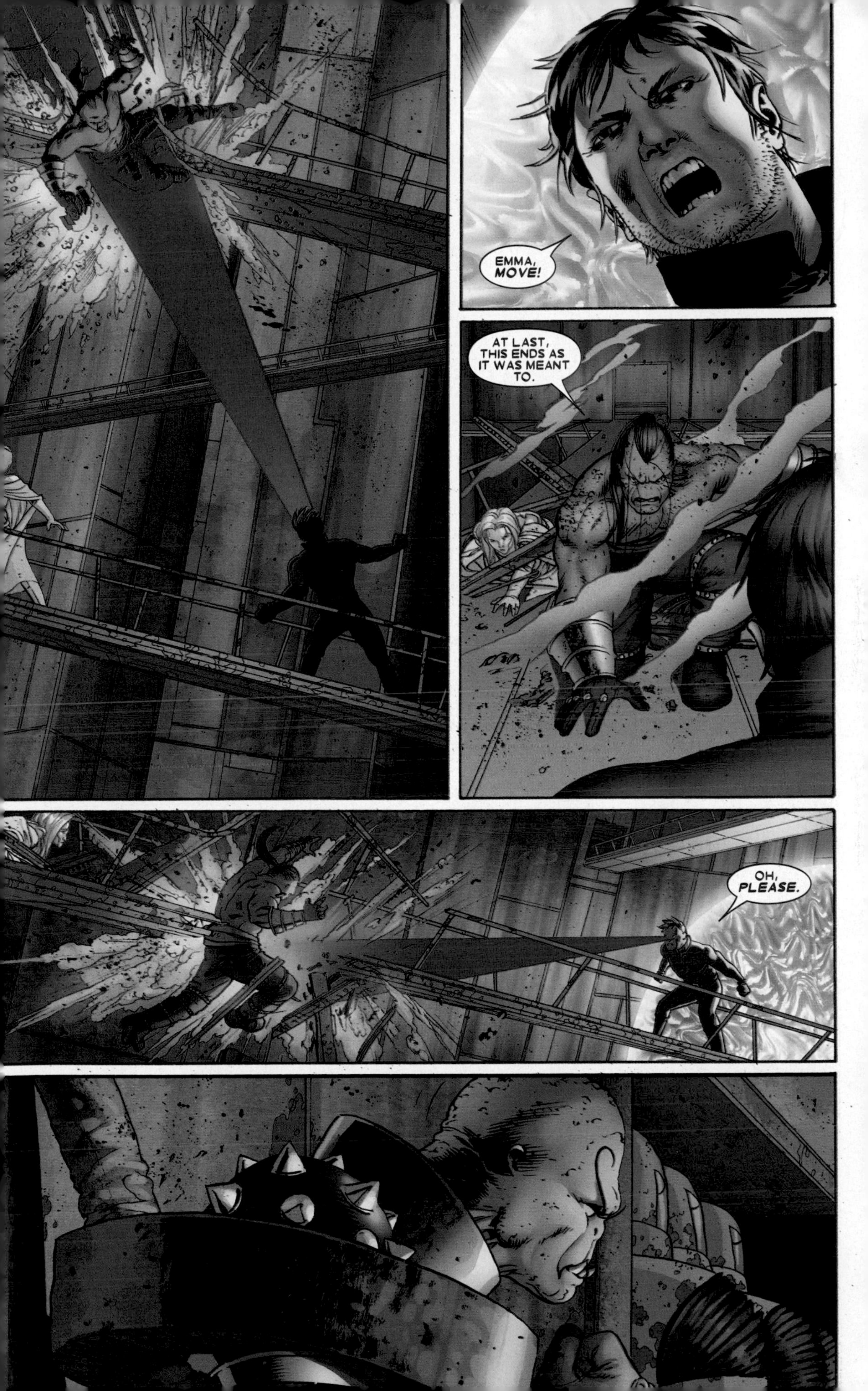
EMMA, MOVE!
AT LAST, THIS ENDS AS IT WAS MEANT TO.
OH, PLEASE.

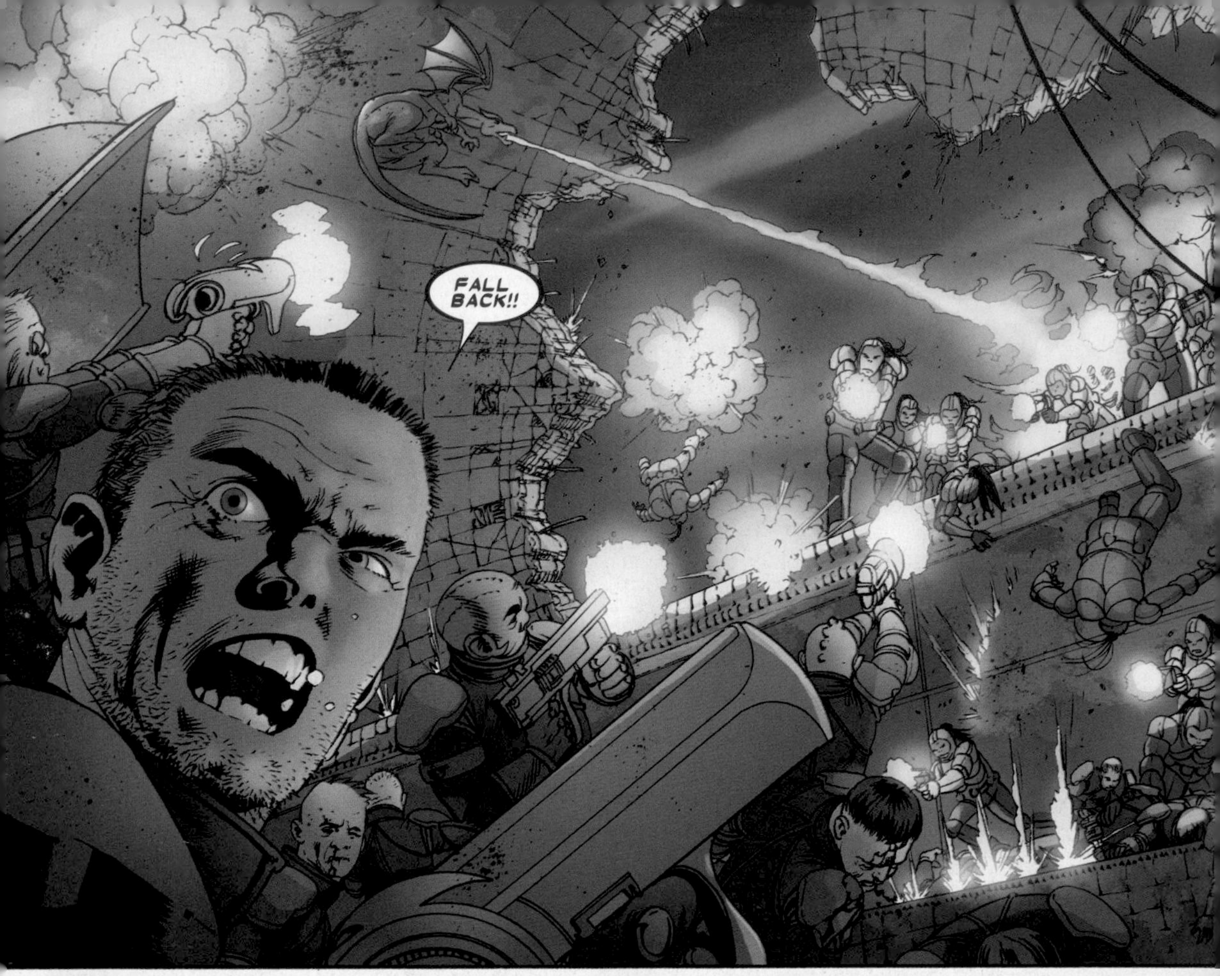
FALL BACK!!

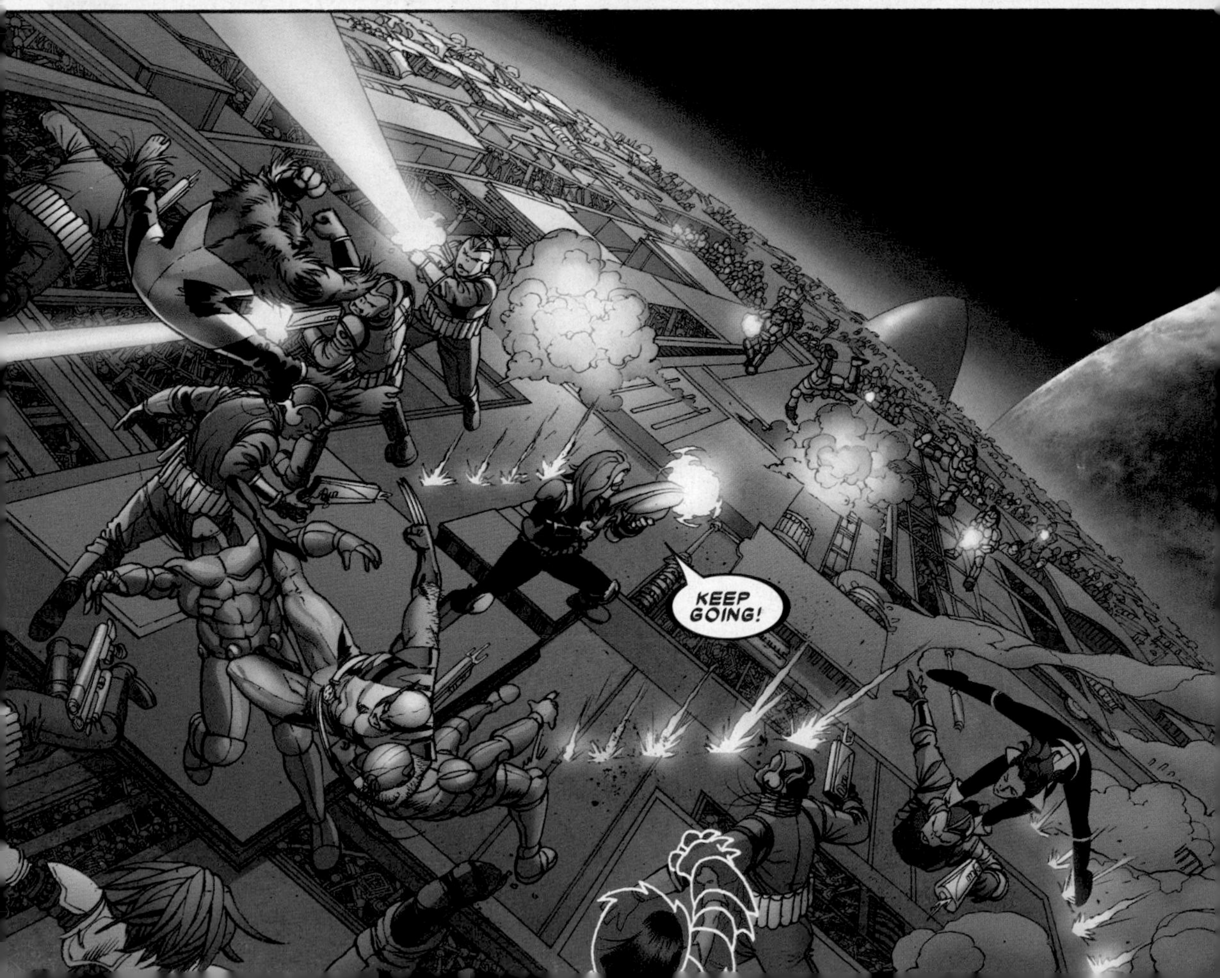
KEEP GOING!

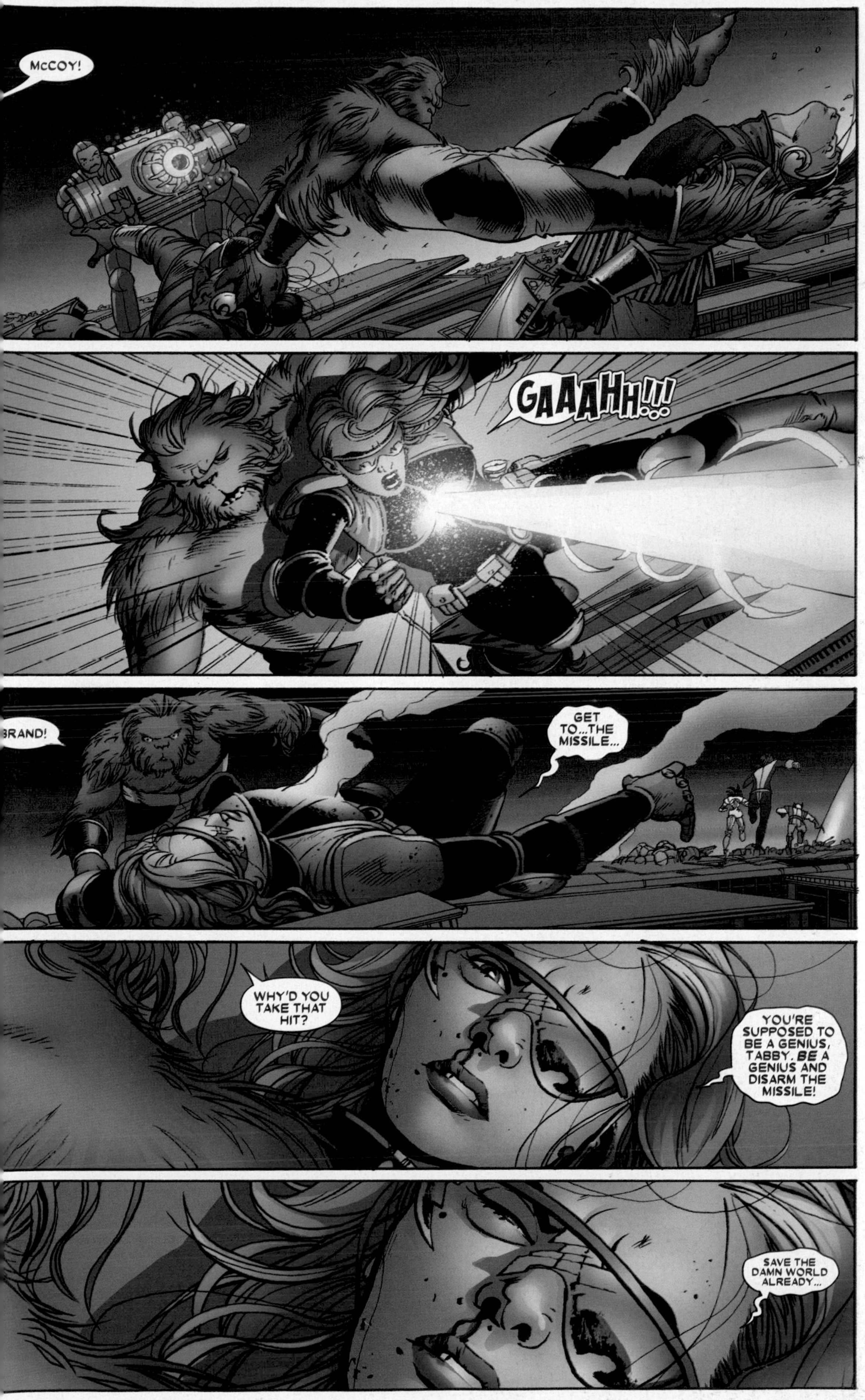
McCOY!
GAAAHH!!!
BRAND!
GET TO...THE MISSILE...
WHY'D YOU TAKE THAT HIT?
YOU'RE SUPPOSED TO BE A GENIUS, TABBY. BE A GENIUS AND DISARM THE MISSILE!
SAVE THE DAMN WORLD ALREADY...

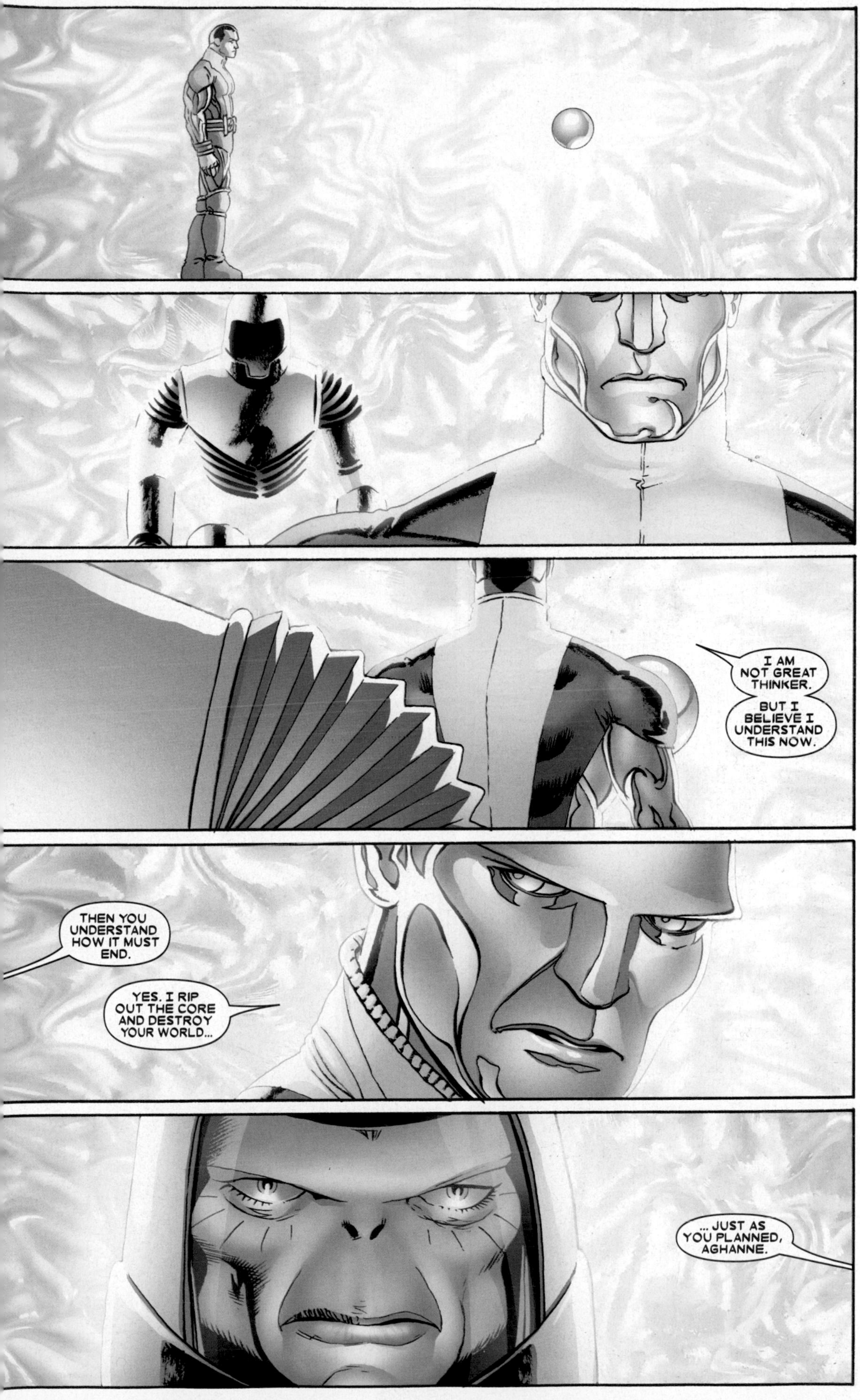
I AM NOT GREAT THINKER.
BUT I BELIEVE I UNDERSTAND THIS NOW.
THEN YOU UNDERSTAND HOW IT MUST END.
YES. I RIP OUT THE CORE AND DESTROY YOUR WORLD...
...JUST AS YOU PLANNED, AGHANNE.

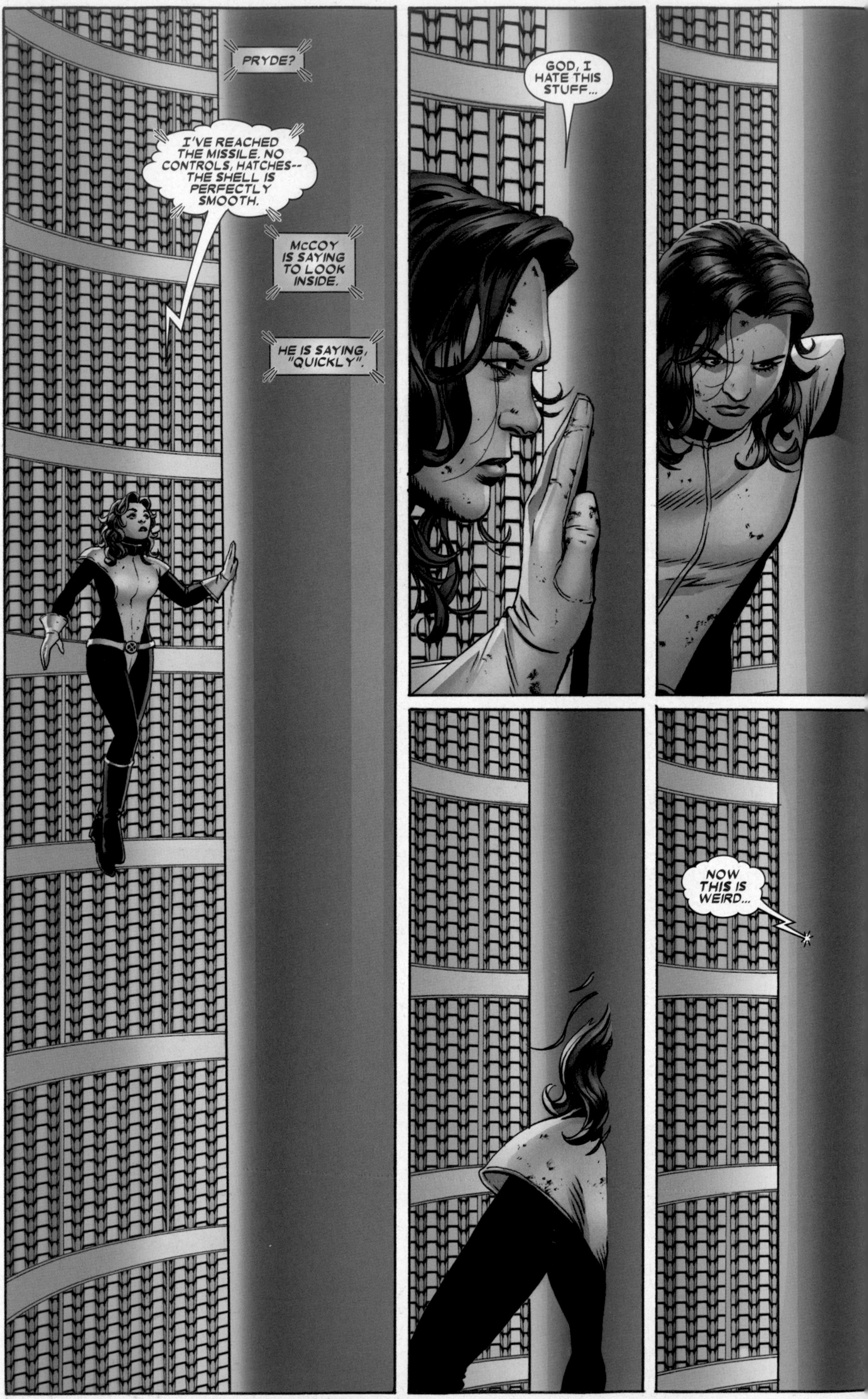
PRYDE?
I'VE REACHED THE MISSILE. NO CONTROLS, HATCHES-- THE SHELL IS PERFECTLY SMOOTH.
McCOY IS SAYING TO LOOK INSIDE.
HE IS SAYING, "QUICKLY".
GOD, I HATE THIS STUFF...
NOW THIS IS WEIRD...

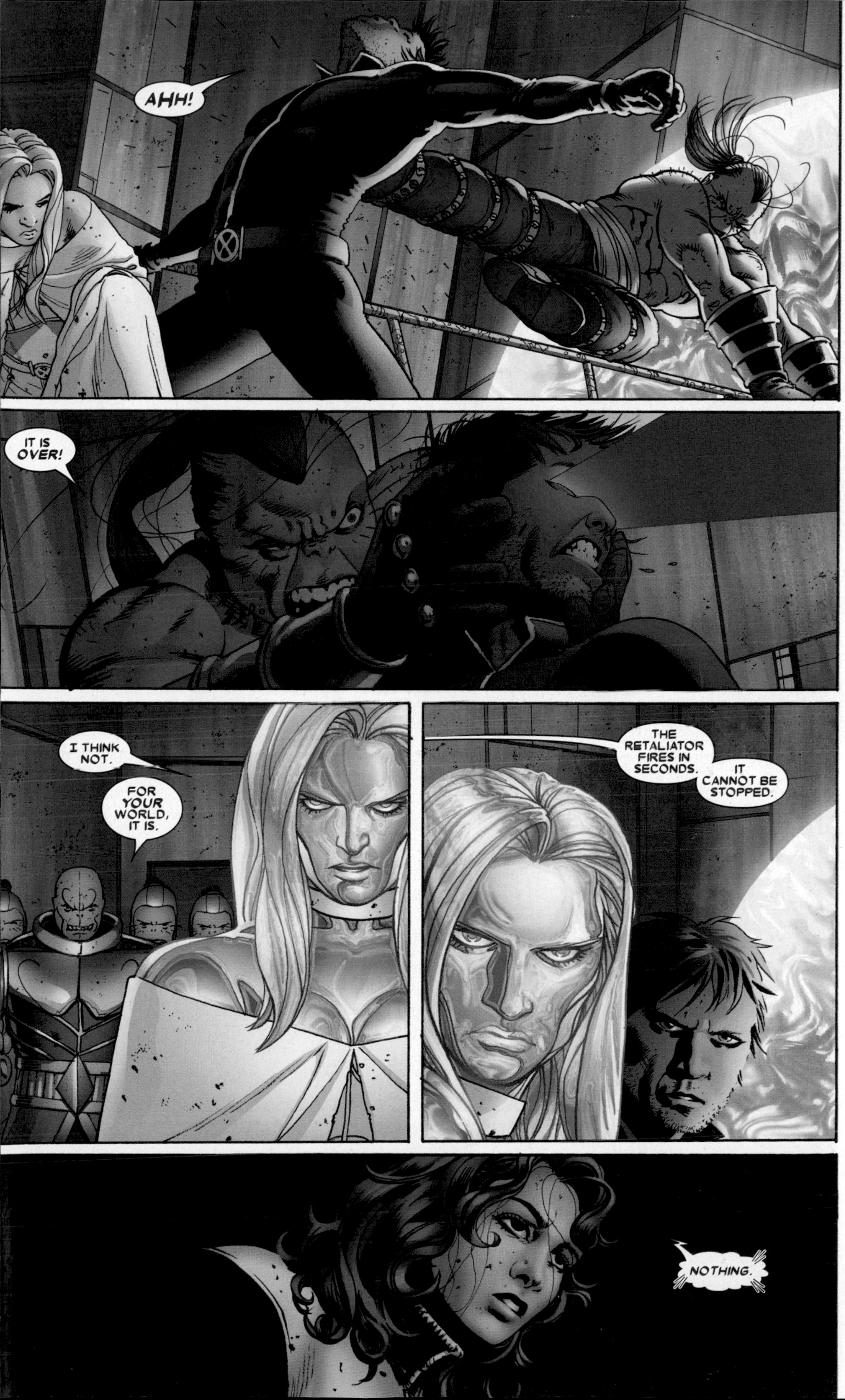
AHH!
IT IS OVER!
I THINK NOT.
FOR YOUR WORLD, IT IS.
THE RETALIATOR FIRES IN SECONDS.
IT CANNOT BE STOPPED.
NOTHING.

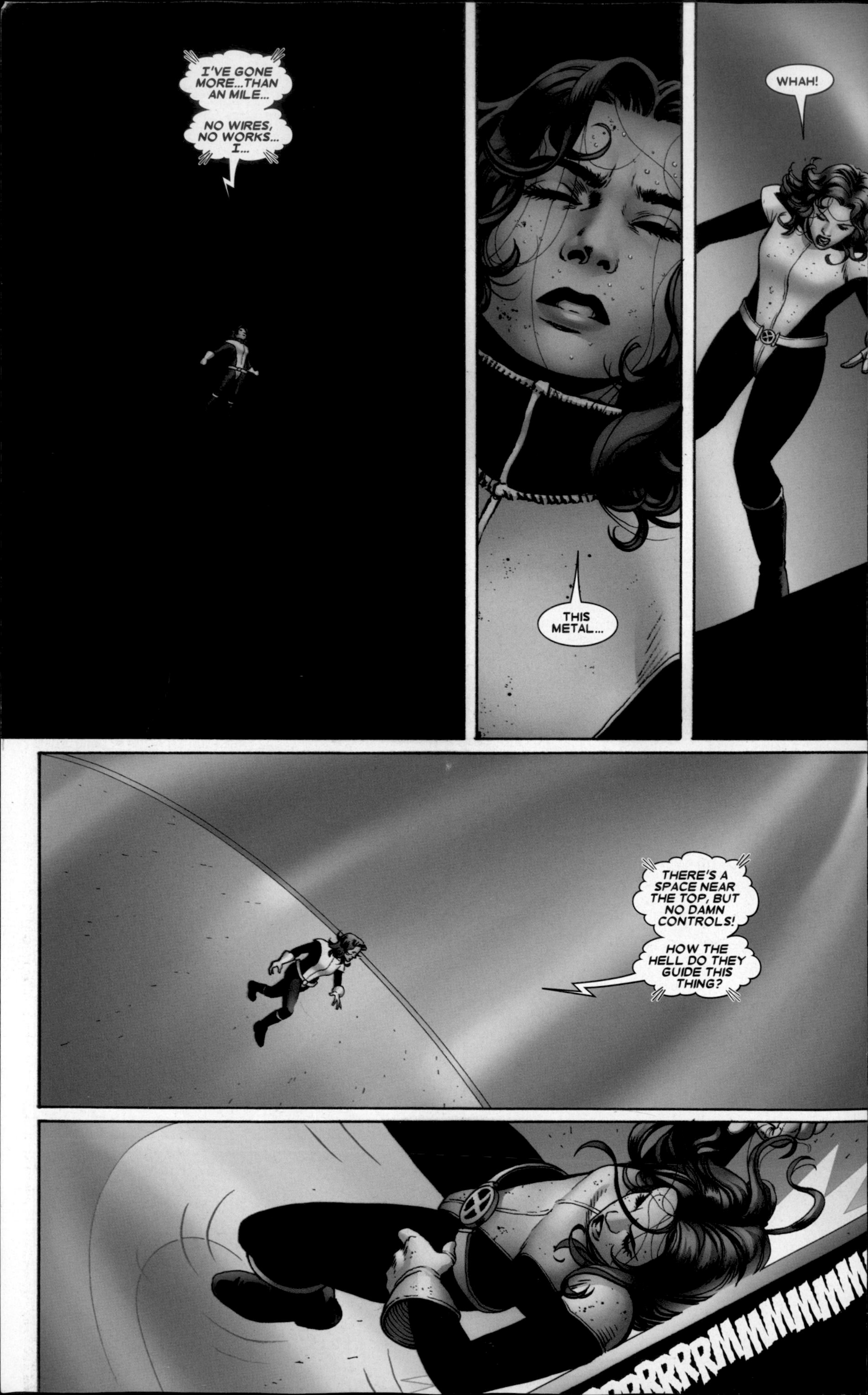
I'VE GONE MORE...THAN AN MILE...
NO WIRES, NO WORKS... I...
THIS METAL...
WHAH!
THERE'S A SPACE NEAR THE TOP, BUT NO DAMN CONTROLS!
HOW THE HELL DO THEY GUIDE THIS THING?

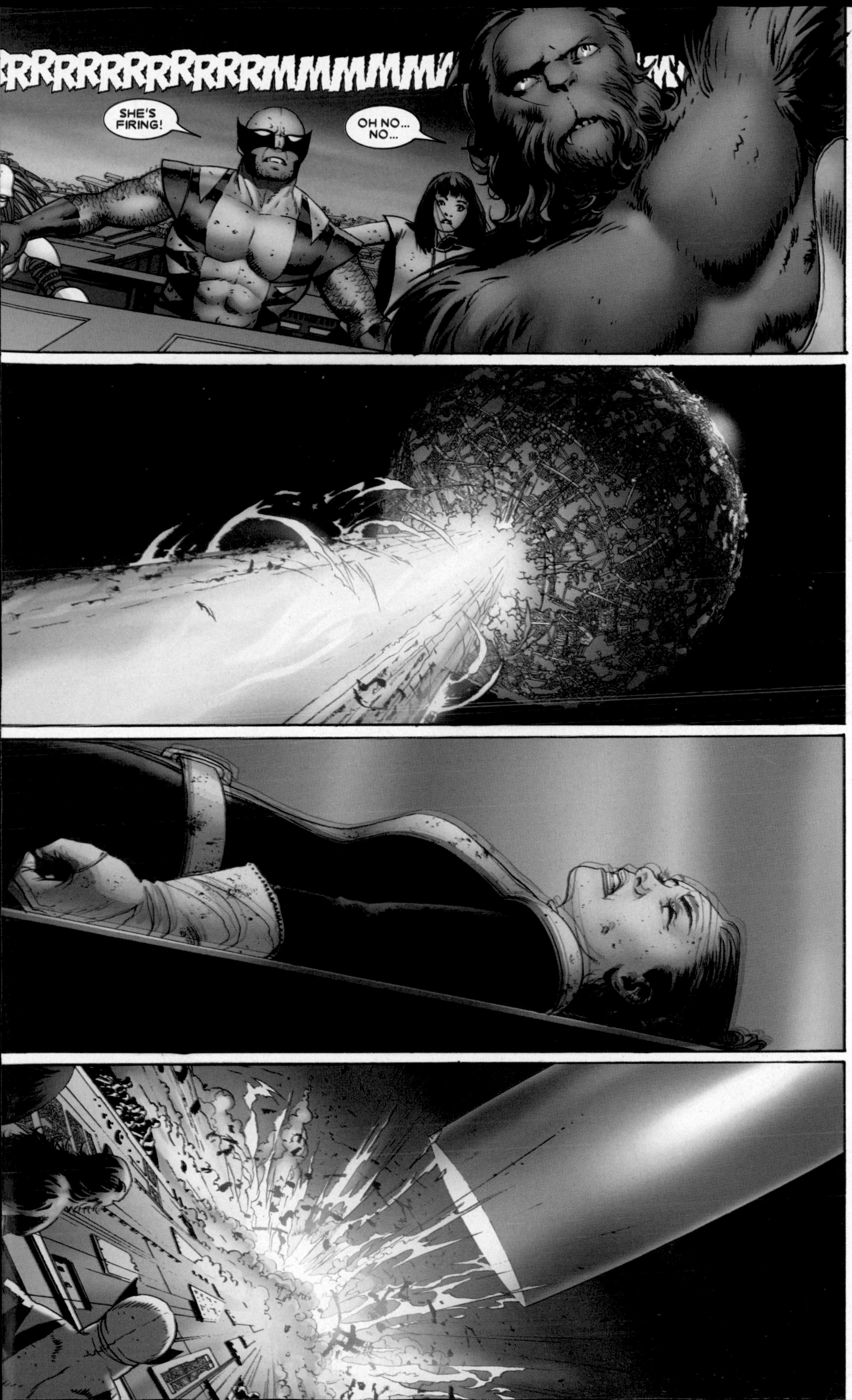

RRRRRRRRRRRRRRRMMMMMM
SHE'S FIRING!
OH NO... NO...

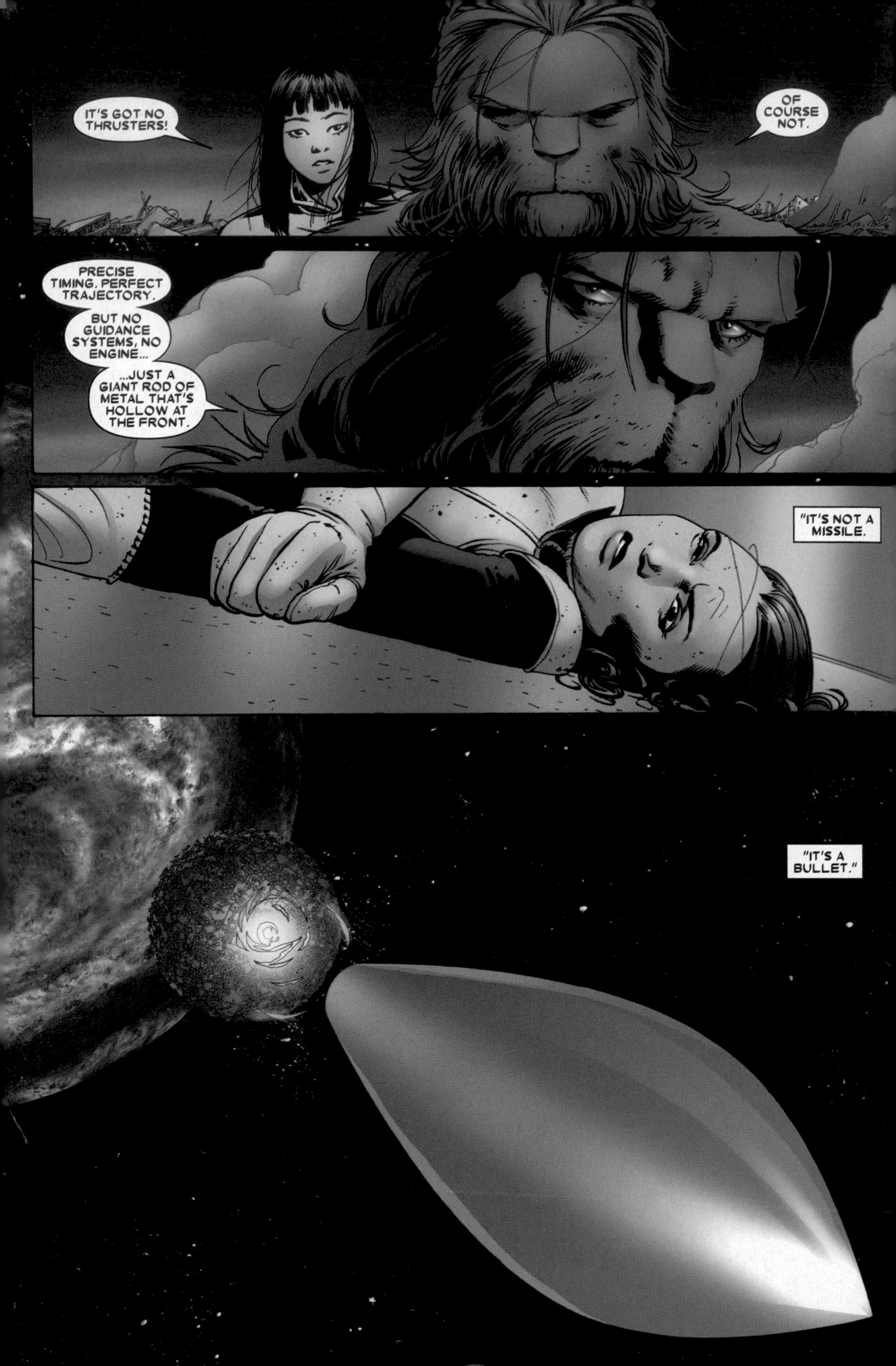
IT'S GOT NO THRUSTERS!
OF COURSE NOT.
PRECISE TIMING, PERFECT TRAJECTORY.
BUT NO GUIDANCE SYSTEMS, NO ENGINE...
...JUST A GIANT ROD OF METAL THAT'S HOLLOW AT THE FRONT.
"IT'S NOT A MISSILE.
"IT'S A BULLET."

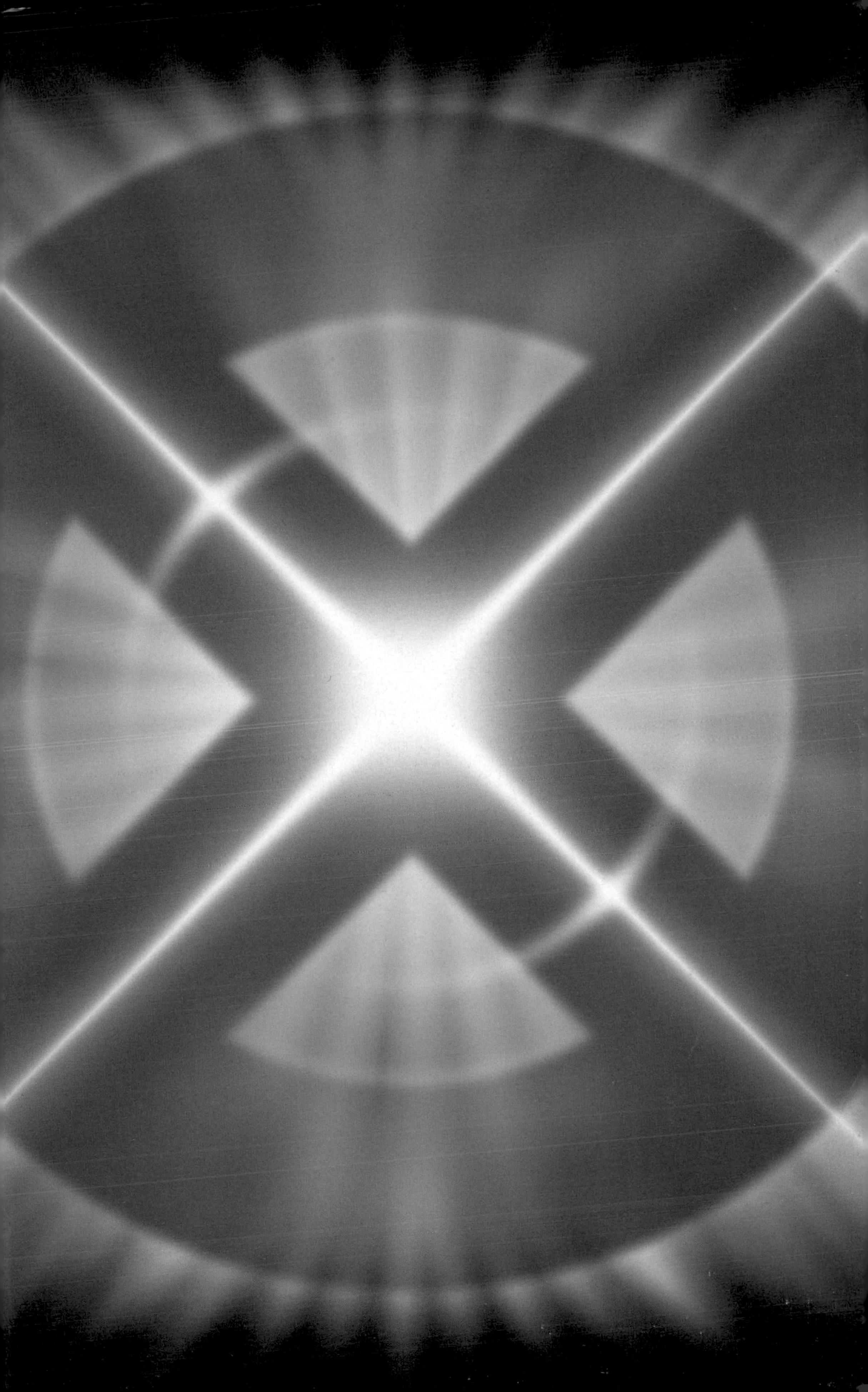

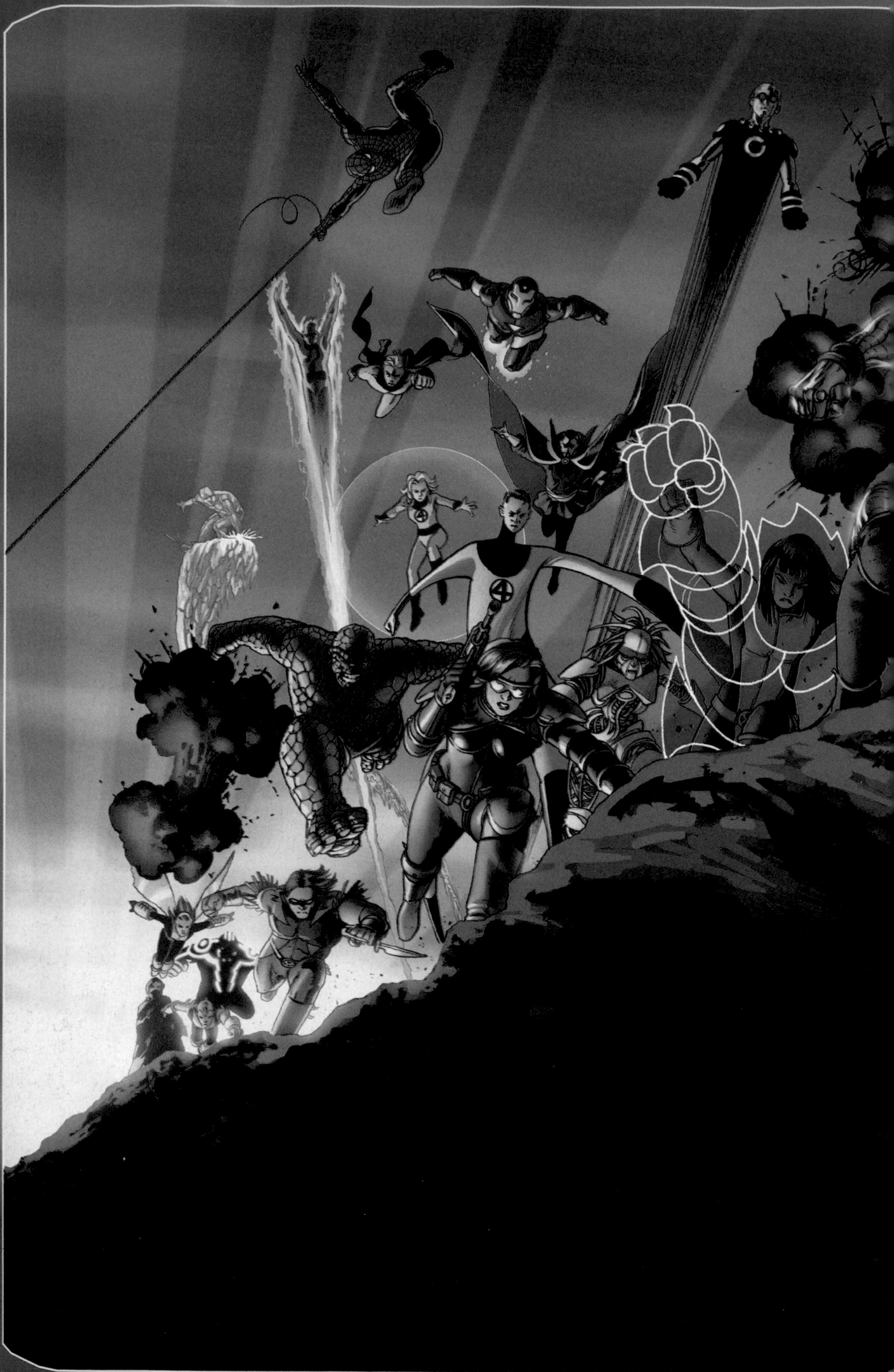

GIANT-SIZE 1

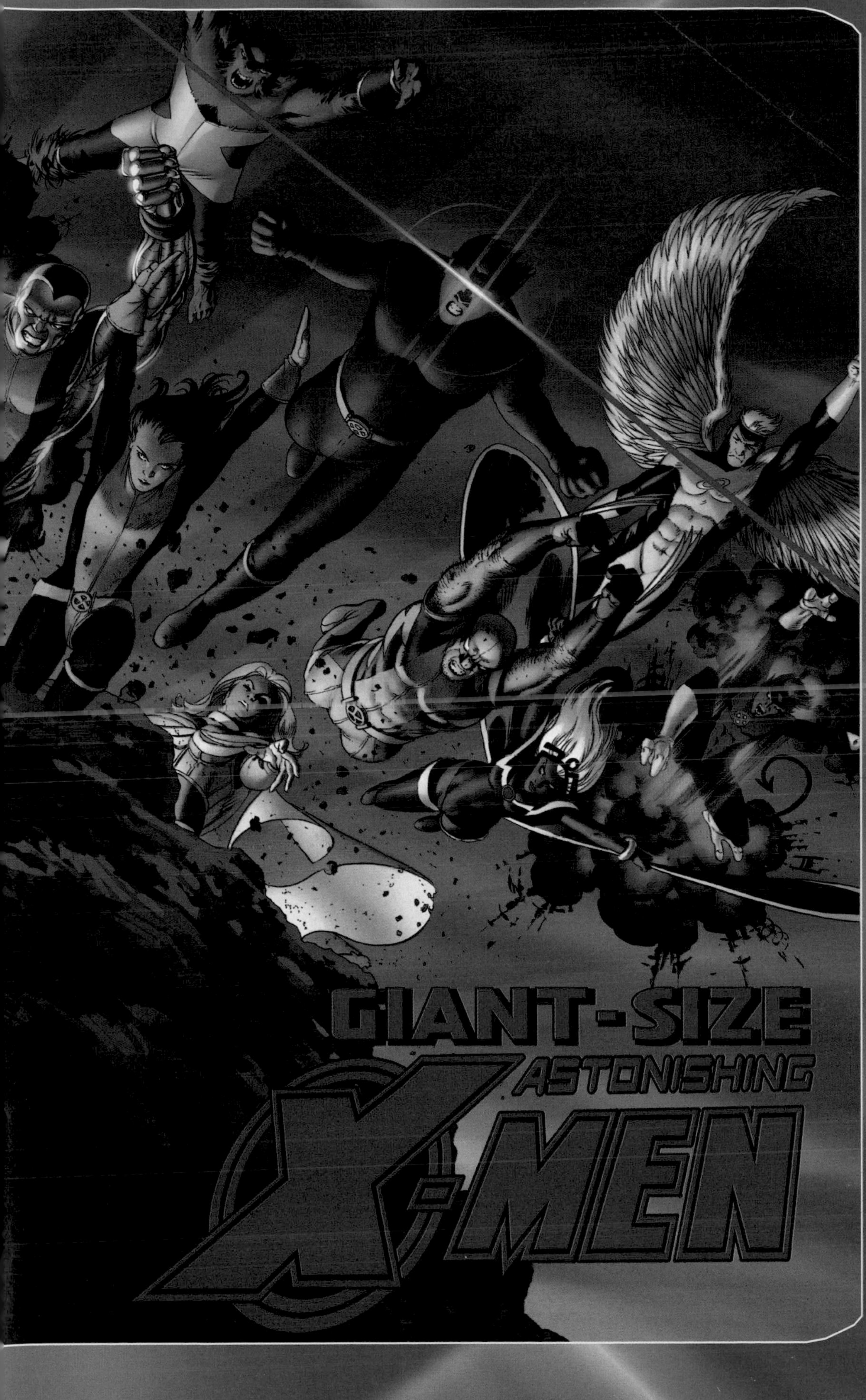
GIANT-SIZE
ASTONISHING
X-MEN

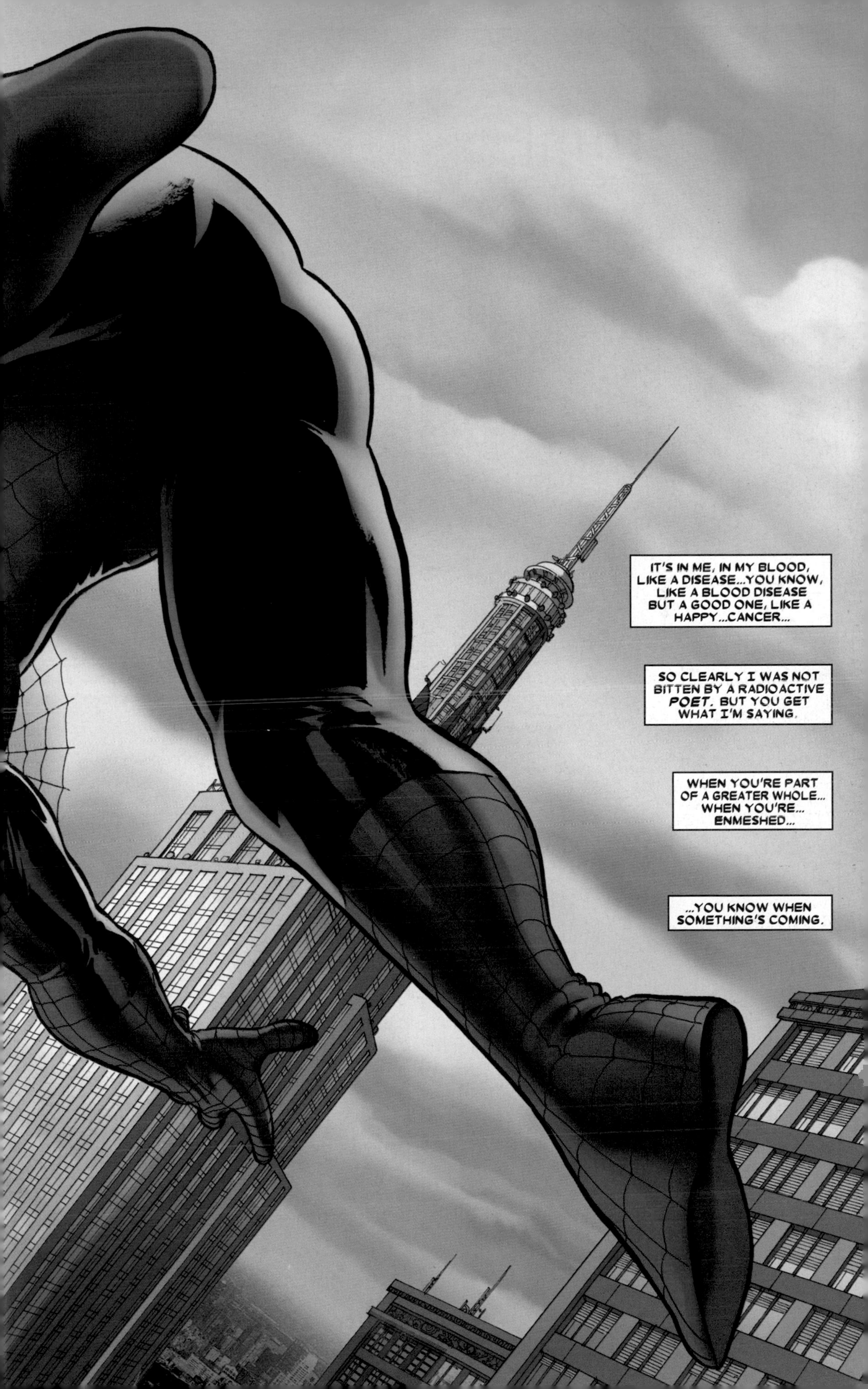
IT'S IN ME, IN MY BLOOD, LIKE A DISEASE...YOU KNOW, LIKE A BLOOD DISEASE BUT A GOOD ONE, LIKE A HAPPY...CANCER...
SO CLEARLY I WAS NOT BITTEN BY A RADIOACTIVE *POET*. BUT YOU GET WHAT I'M SAYING.
WHEN YOU'RE PART OF A GREATER WHOLE... WHEN YOU'RE... ENMESHED...
...YOU KNOW WHEN SOMETHING'S COMING.

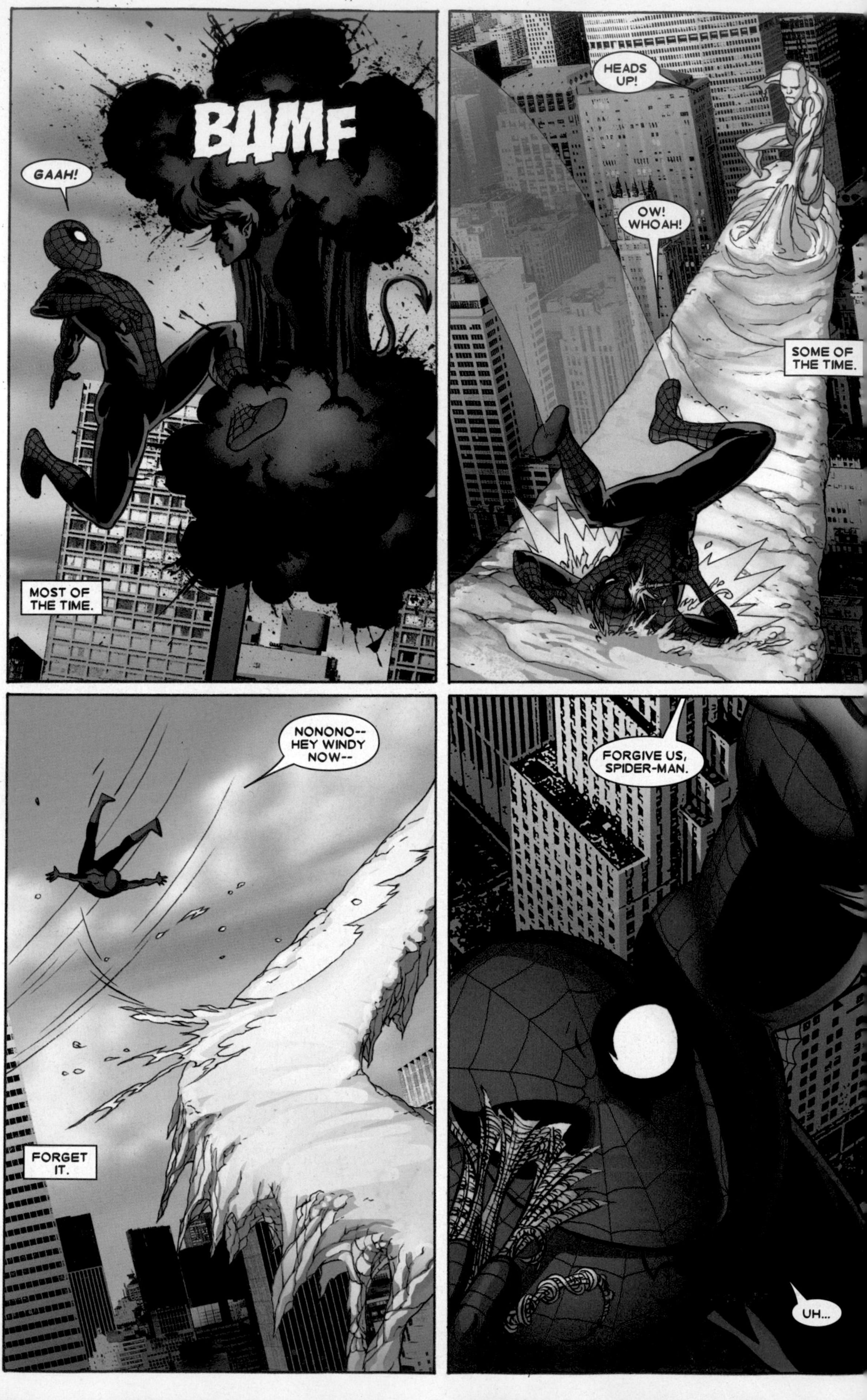
BAMF
GAAH!
MOST OF THE TIME.
HEADS UP!
OW! WHOAH!
SOME OF THE TIME.
NONONO-- HEY WINDY NOW--
FORGET IT.
FORGIVE US, SPIDER-MAN.
UH...

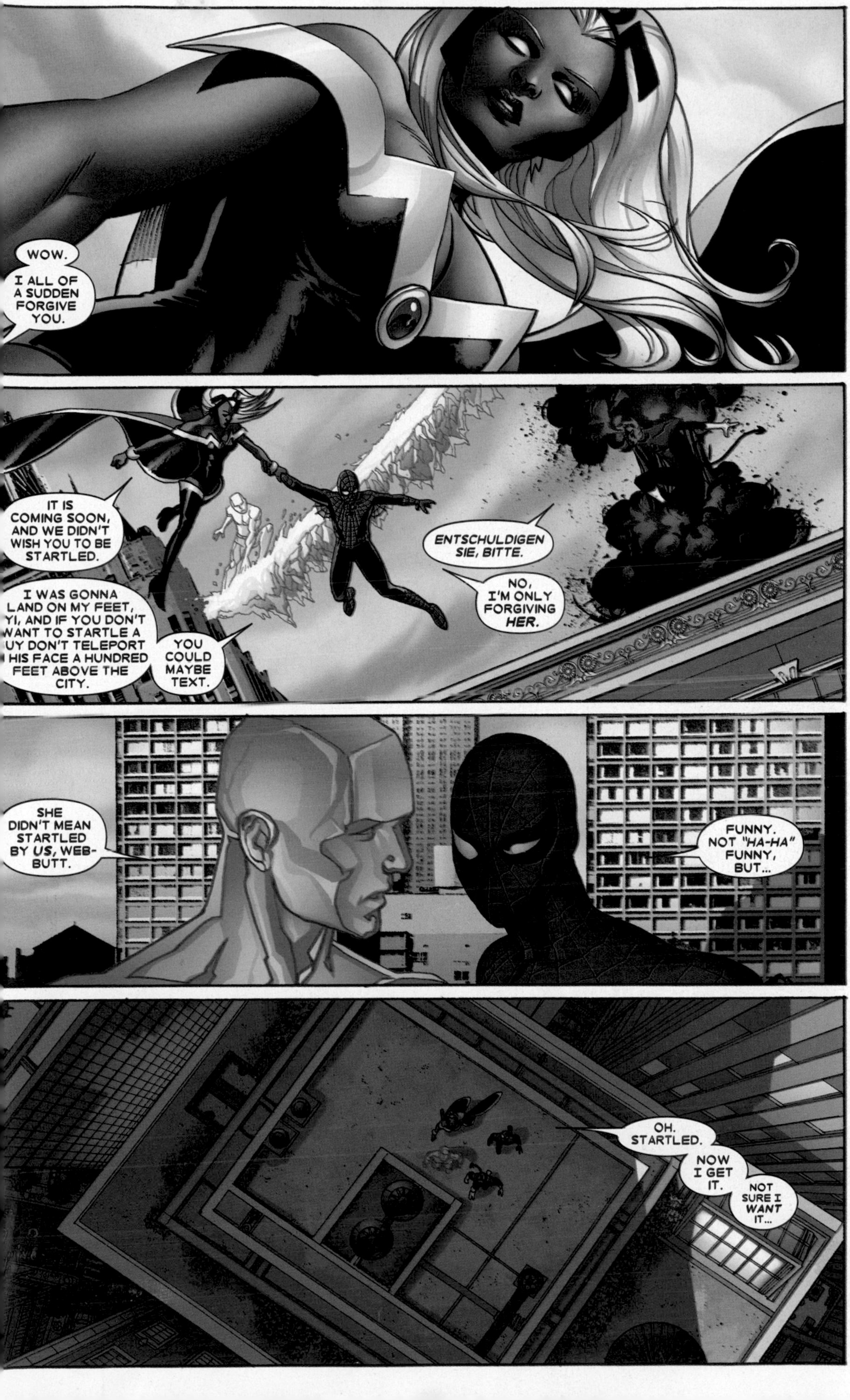

WOW.
I ALL OF A SUDDEN FORGIVE YOU.
IT IS COMING SOON, AND WE DIDN'T WISH YOU TO BE STARTLED.
I WAS GONNA LAND ON MY FEET, YI, AND IF YOU DON'T WANT TO STARTLE A UY DON'T TELEPORT HIS FACE A HUNDRED FEET ABOVE THE CITY.
YOU COULD MAYBE TEXT.
ENTSCHULDIGEN SIE, BITTE.
NO, I'M ONLY FORGIVING HER.
SHE DIDN'T MEAN STARTLED BY US, WEB-BUTT.
FUNNY. NOT "HA-HA" FUNNY, BUT...
OH. STARTLED.
NOW I GET IT.
NOT SURE I WANT IT...

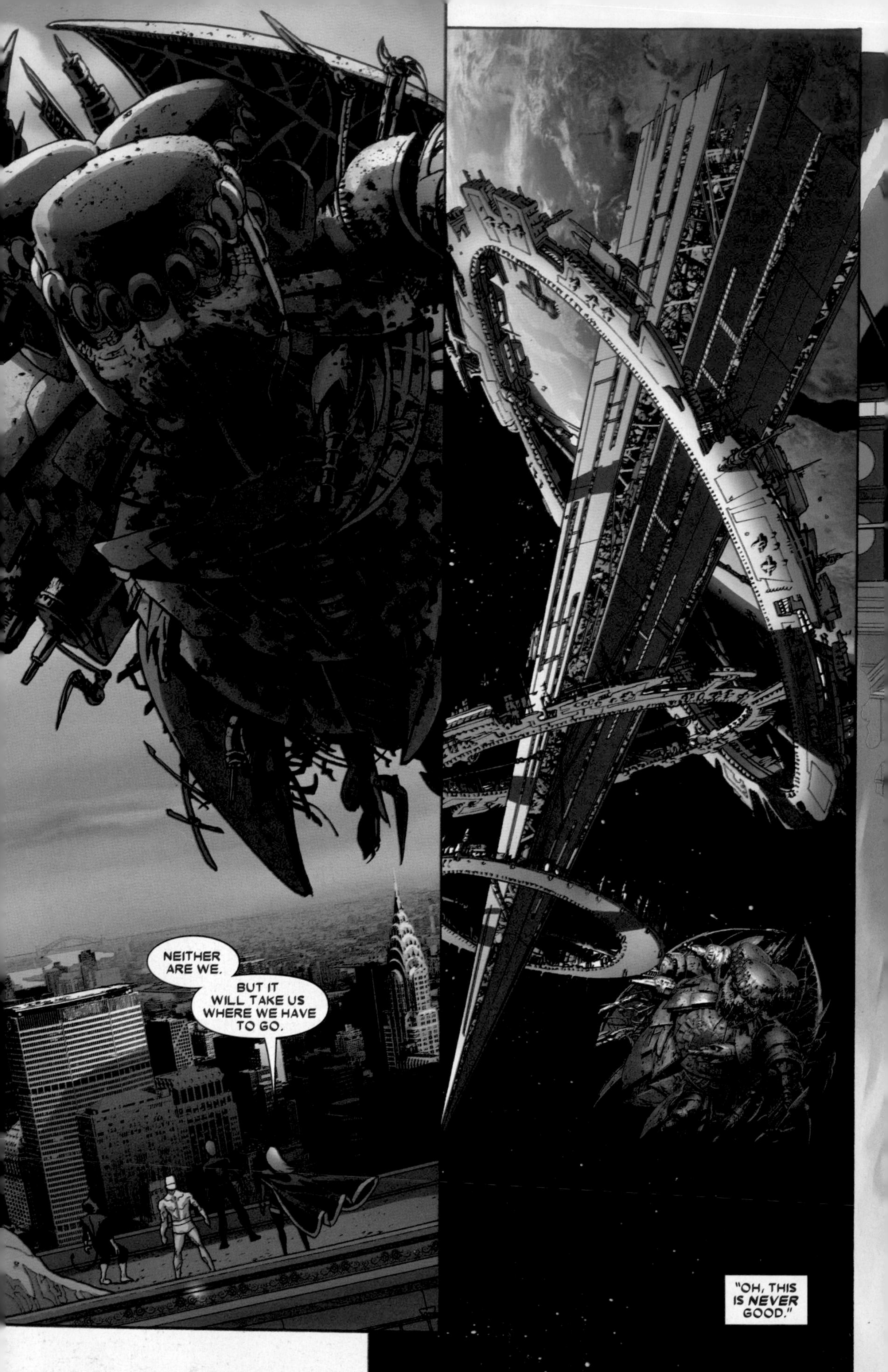
NEITHER ARE WE.
BUT IT WILL TAKE US WHERE WE HAVE TO GO.
"OH, THIS IS NEVER GOOD."

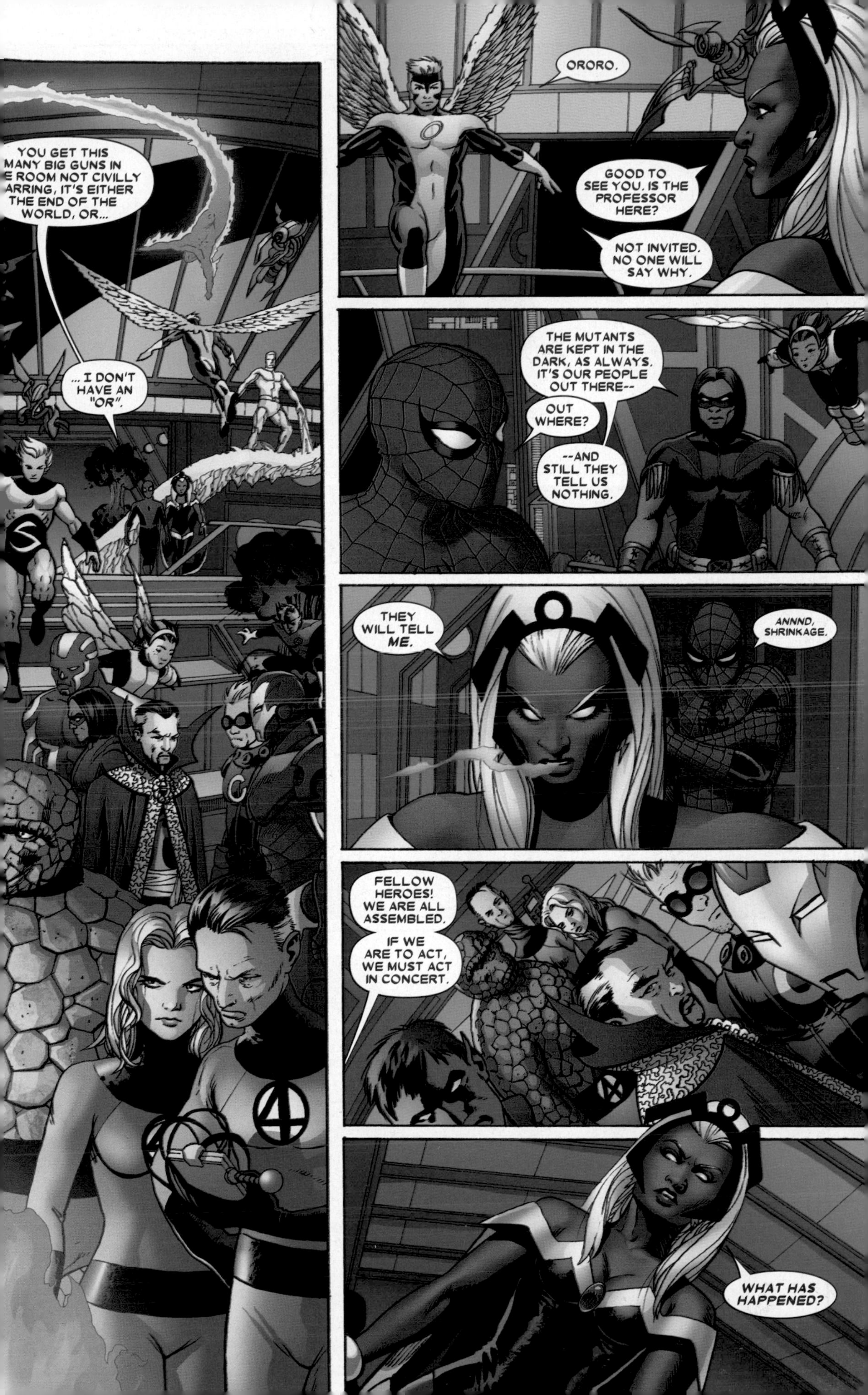
YOU GET THIS MANY BIG GUNS IN E ROOM NOT CIVILLY ARRING, IT'S EITHER THE END OF THE WORLD, OR...
...I DON'T HAVE AN "OR".
ORORO.
GOOD TO SEE YOU. IS THE PROFESSOR HERE?
NOT INVITED. NO ONE WILL SAY WHY.
THE MUTANTS ARE KEPT IN THE DARK, AS ALWAYS. IT'S OUR PEOPLE OUT THERE--
OUT WHERE?
--AND STILL THEY TELL US NOTHING.
THEY WILL TELL *ME*.
ANNND, SHRINKAGE.
FELLOW HEROES! WE ARE ALL ASSEMBLED.
IF WE ARE TO ACT, WE MUST ACT IN CONCERT.
WHAT HAS HAPPENED?

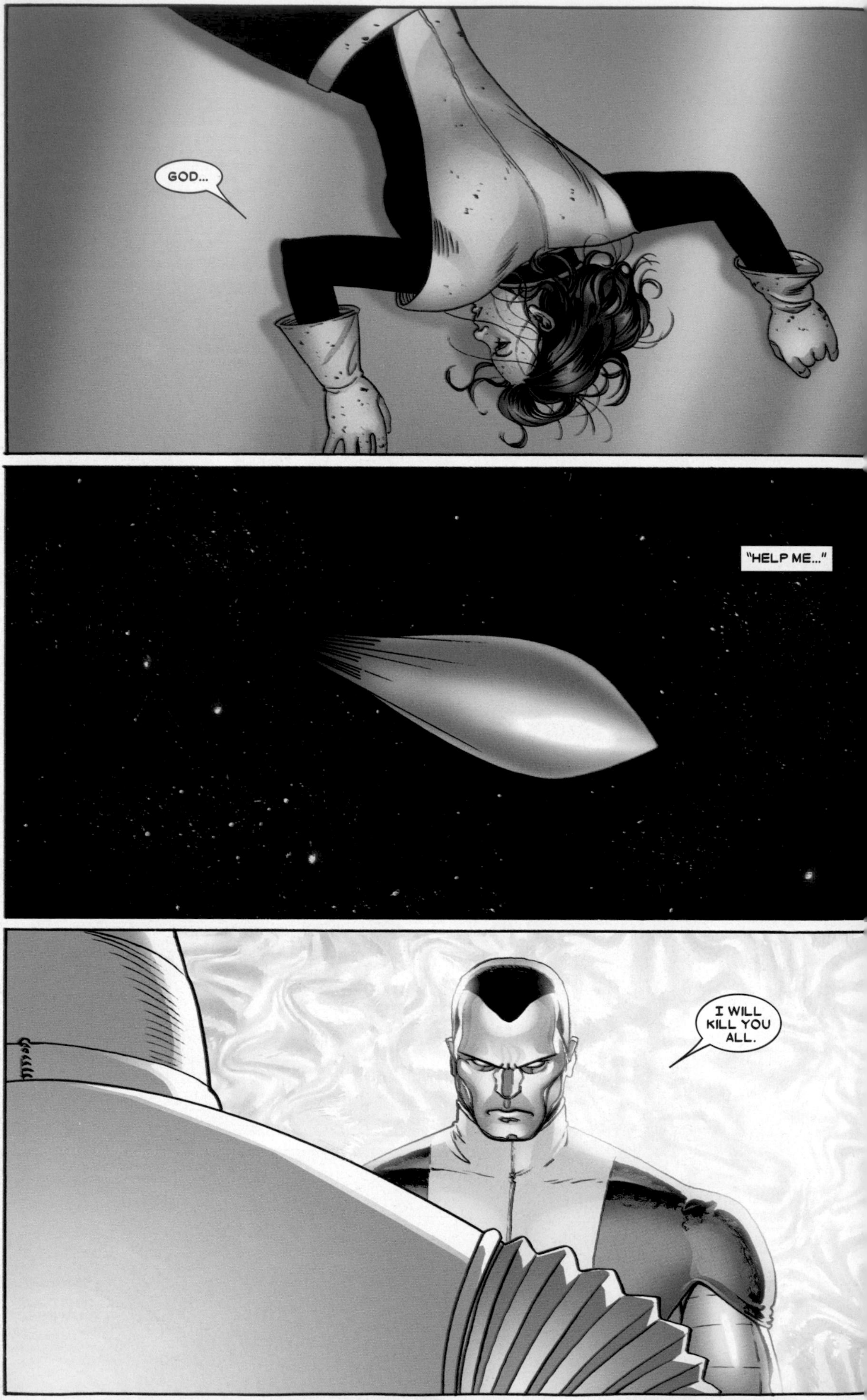
GOD...
"HELP ME..."
I WILL KILL YOU ALL.

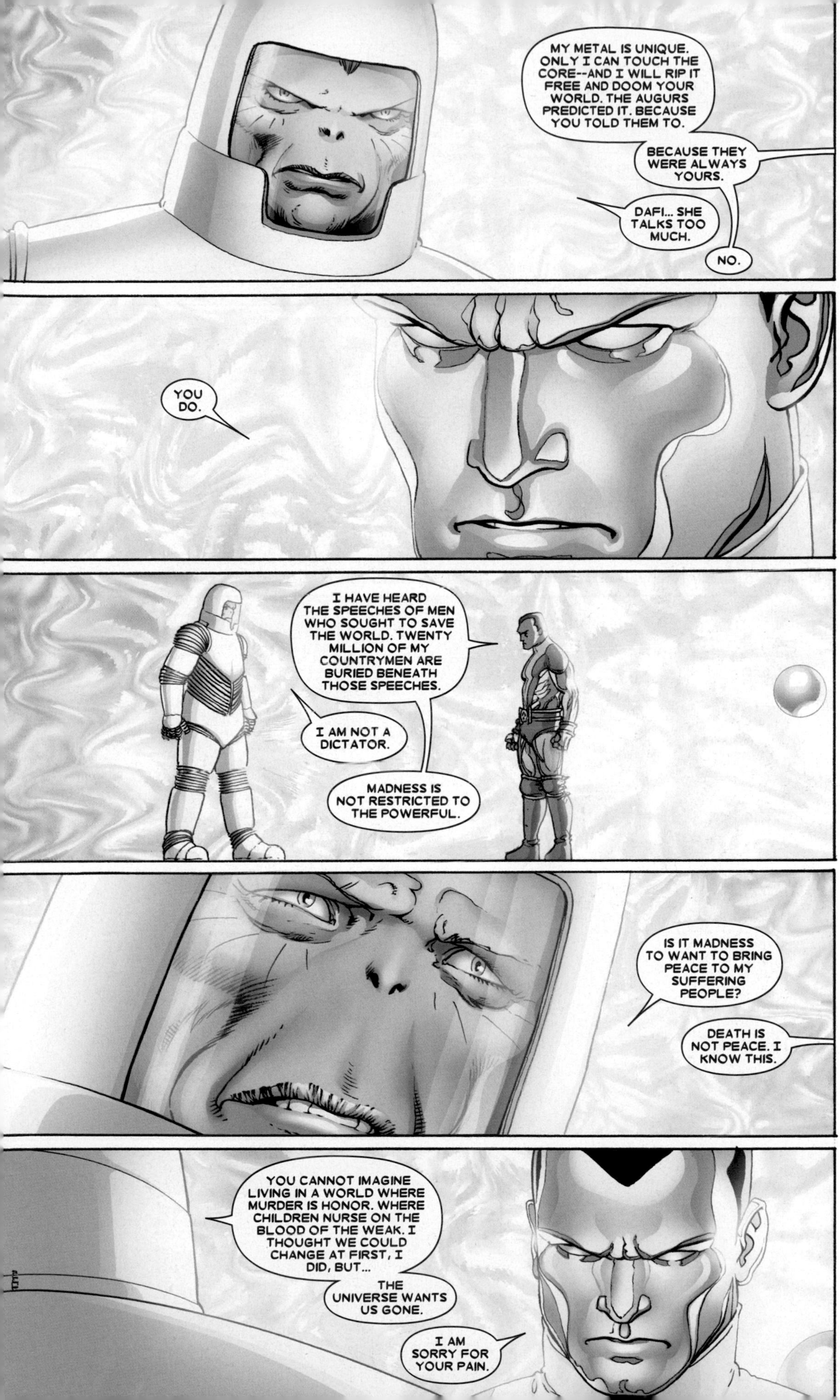
MY METAL IS UNIQUE. ONLY I CAN TOUCH THE CORE--AND I WILL RIP IT FREE AND DOOM YOUR WORLD. THE AUGURS PREDICTED IT. BECAUSE YOU TOLD THEM TO.
BECAUSE THEY WERE ALWAYS YOURS.
DAFI... SHE TALKS TOO MUCH.
NO.
YOU DO.
I HAVE HEARD THE SPEECHES OF MEN WHO SOUGHT TO SAVE THE WORLD. TWENTY MILLION OF MY COUNTRYMEN ARE BURIED BENEATH THOSE SPEECHES.
I AM NOT A DICTATOR.
MADNESS IS NOT RESTRICTED TO THE POWERFUL.
IS IT MADNESS TO WANT TO BRING PEACE TO MY SUFFERING PEOPLE?
DEATH IS NOT PEACE. I KNOW THIS.
YOU CANNOT IMAGINE LIVING IN A WORLD WHERE MURDER IS HONOR. WHERE CHILDREN NURSE ON THE BLOOD OF THE WEAK. I THOUGHT WE COULD CHANGE AT FIRST, I DID, BUT...
THE UNIVERSE WANTS US GONE.
I AM SORRY FOR YOUR PAIN.

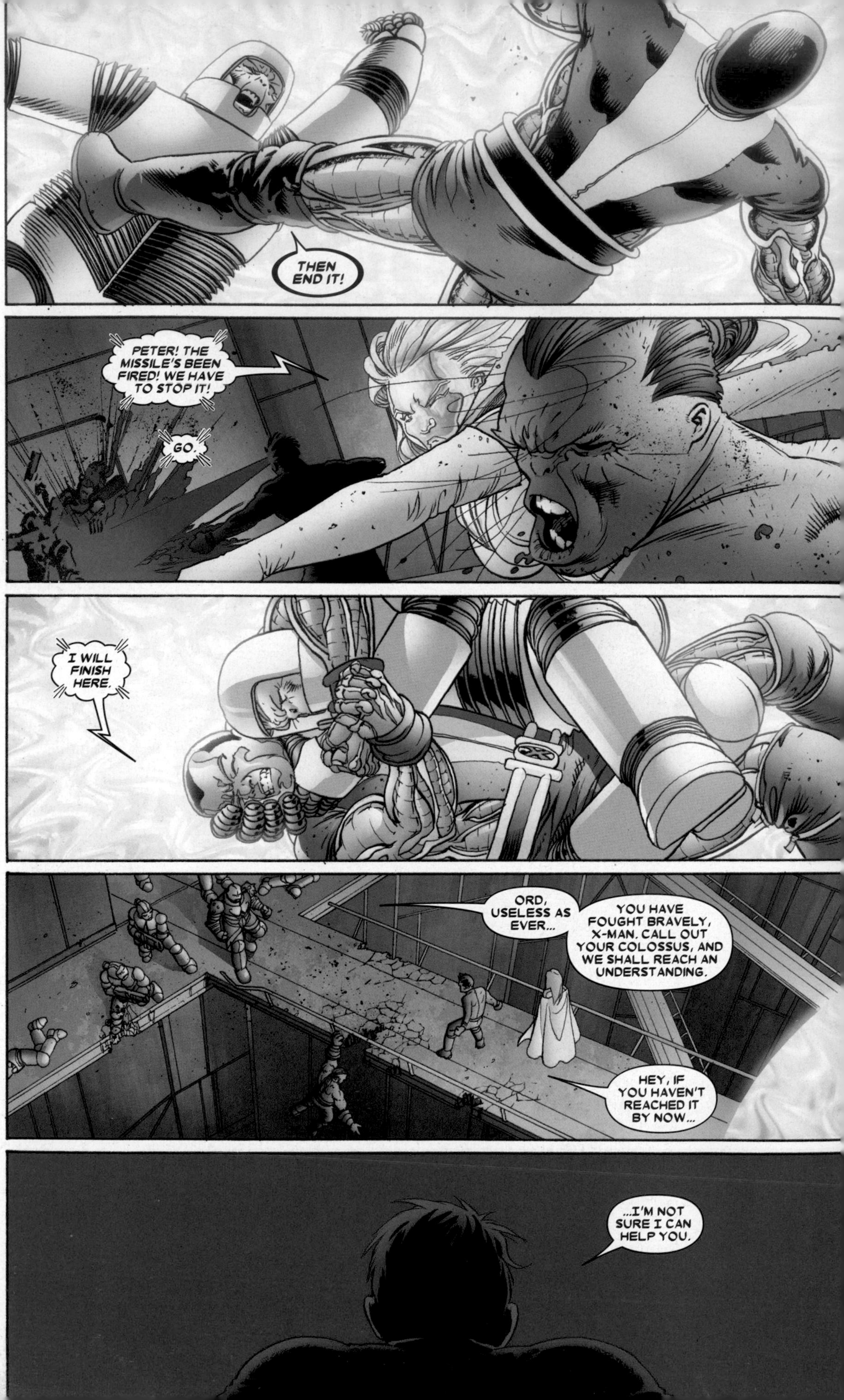
THEN END IT!
PETER! THE MISSILE'S BEEN FIRED! WE HAVE TO STOP IT!
GO.
I WILL FINISH HERE.
ORD, USELESS AS EVER...
YOU HAVE FOUGHT BRAVELY, X-MAN. CALL OUT YOUR COLOSSUS, AND WE SHALL REACH AN UNDERSTANDING.
HEY, IF YOU HAVEN'T REACHED IT BY NOW...
...I'M NOT SURE I CAN HELP YOU.

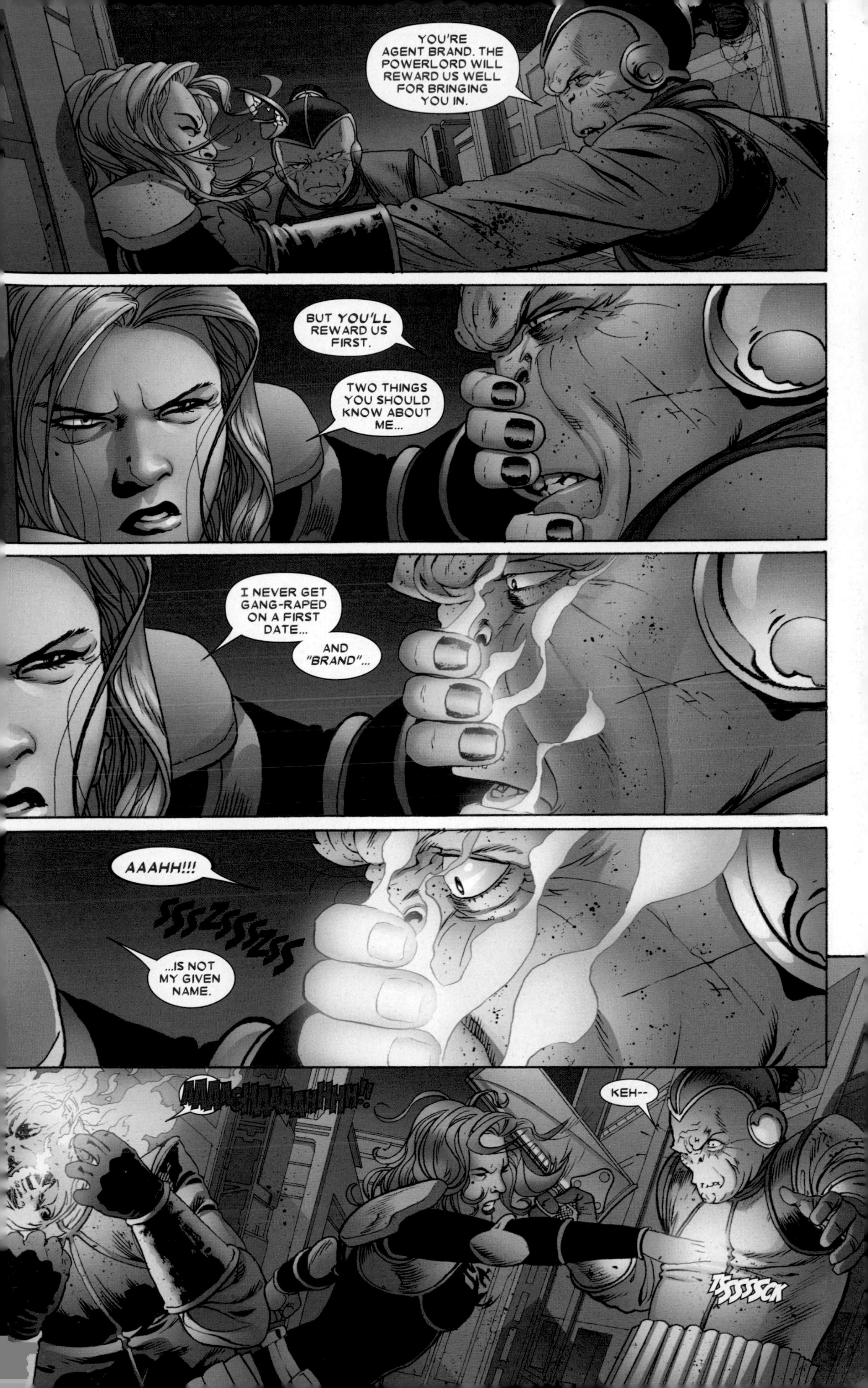
YOU'RE AGENT BRAND. THE POWERLORD WILL REWARD US WELL FOR BRINGING YOU IN.
BUT YOU'LL REWARD US FIRST.
TWO THINGS YOU SHOULD KNOW ABOUT ME...
I NEVER GET GANG-RAPED ON A FIRST DATE...
AND "BRAND"...
AAAHH!!!
...IS NOT MY GIVEN NAME.
KEH--
TSSSSCK

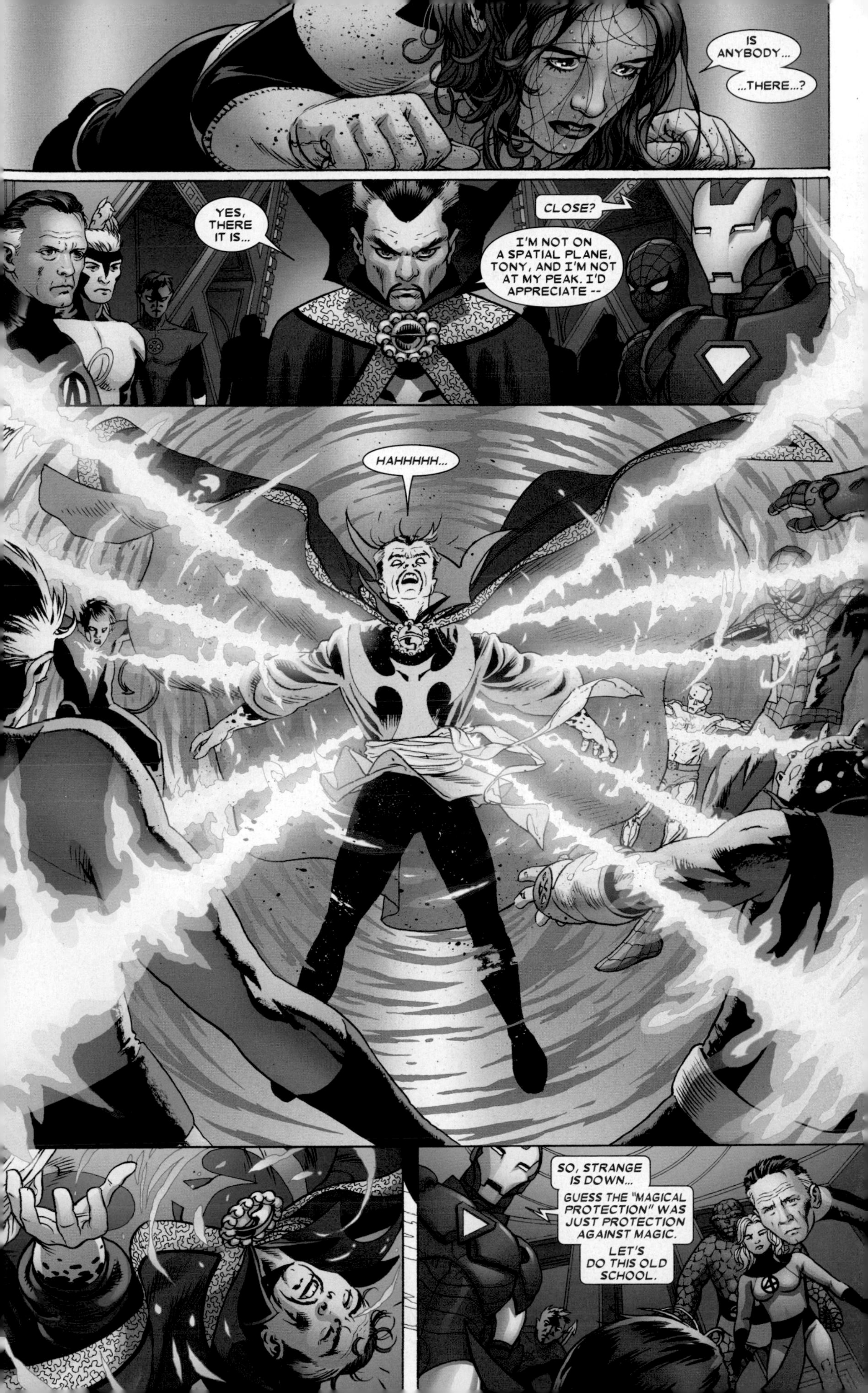
IS ANYBODY...
...THERE...?
YES, THERE IT IS...
CLOSE?
I'M NOT ON A SPATIAL PLANE, TONY, AND I'M NOT AT MY PEAK. I'D APPRECIATE --
HAHHHHH...
SO, STRANGE IS DOWN...
GUESS THE "MAGICAL PROTECTION" WAS JUST PROTECTION AGAINST MAGIC.
LET'S DO THIS OLD SCHOOL.

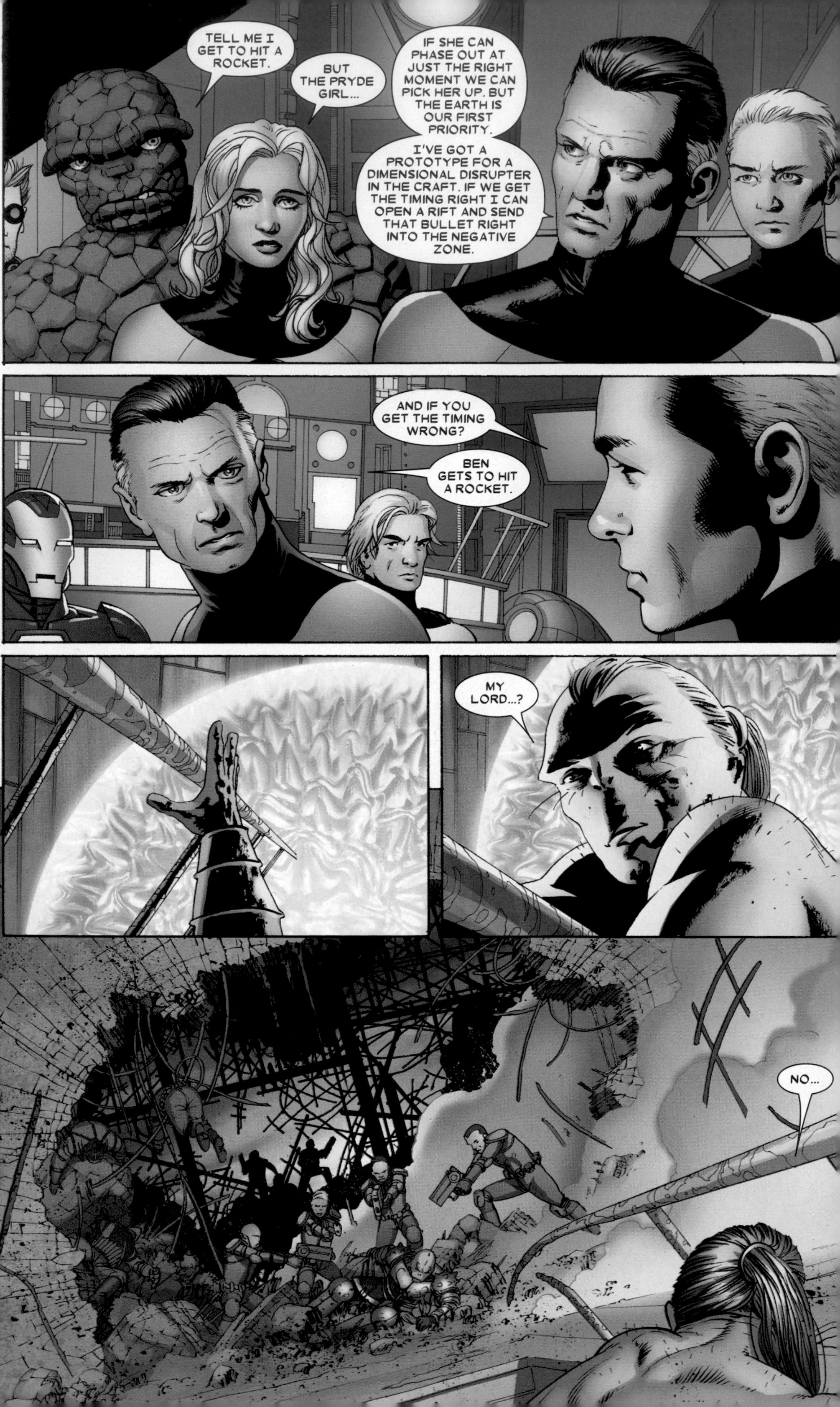
TELL ME I GET TO HIT A ROCKET.
BUT THE PRYDE GIRL...
IF SHE CAN PHASE OUT AT JUST THE RIGHT MOMENT WE CAN PICK HER UP. BUT THE EARTH IS OUR FIRST PRIORITY.
I'VE GOT A PROTOTYPE FOR A DIMENSIONAL DISRUPTER IN THE CRAFT. IF WE GET THE TIMING RIGHT I CAN OPEN A RIFT AND SEND THAT BULLET RIGHT INTO THE NEGATIVE ZONE.
AND IF YOU GET THE TIMING WRONG?
BEN GETS TO HIT A ROCKET.
MY LORD...?
NO...

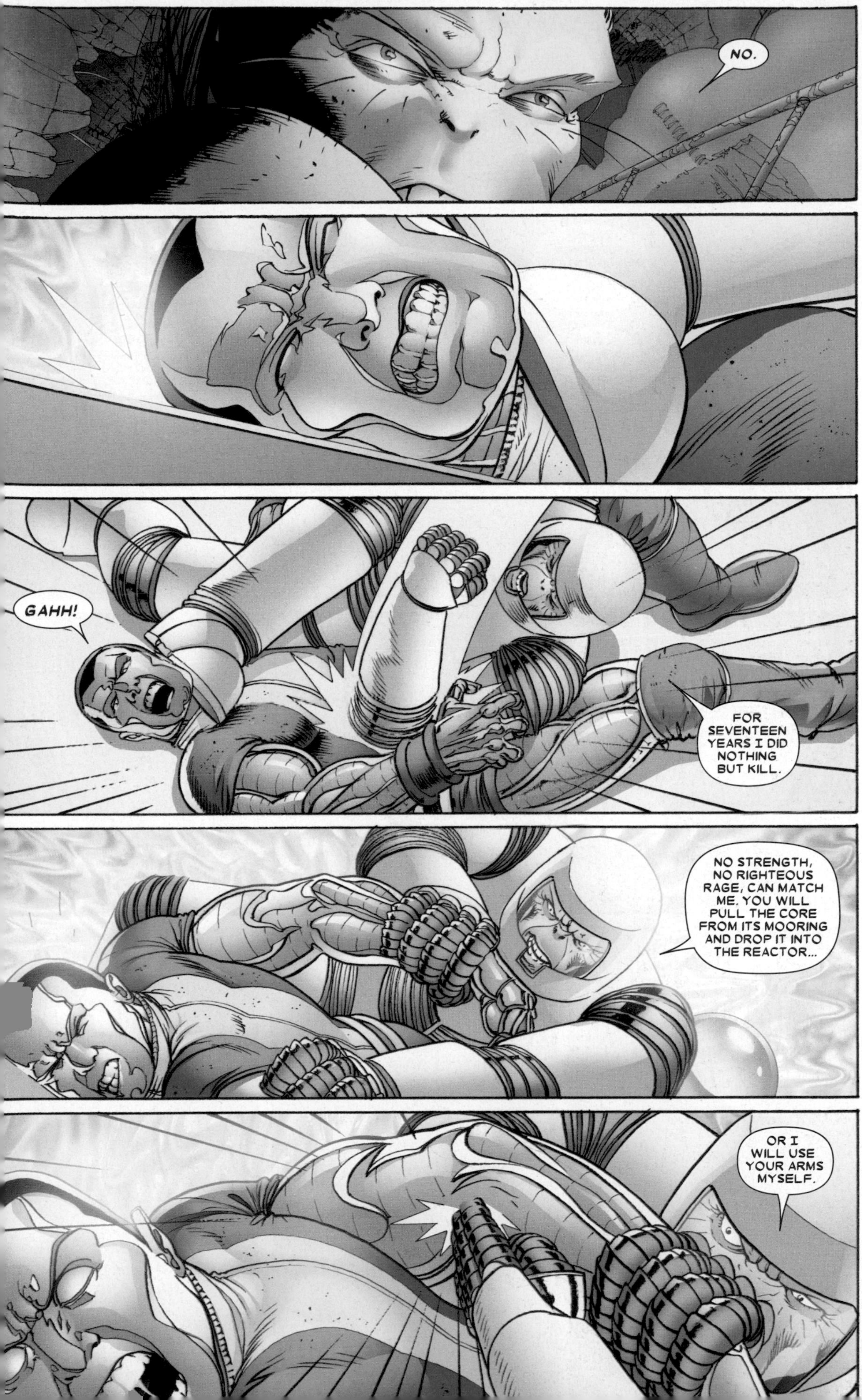
NO.
GAHH!
FOR SEVENTEEN YEARS I DID NOTHING BUT KILL.
NO STRENGTH, NO RIGHTEOUS RAGE, CAN MATCH ME. YOU WILL PULL THE CORE FROM ITS MOORING AND DROP IT INTO THE REACTOR...
OR I WILL USE YOUR ARMS MYSELF.

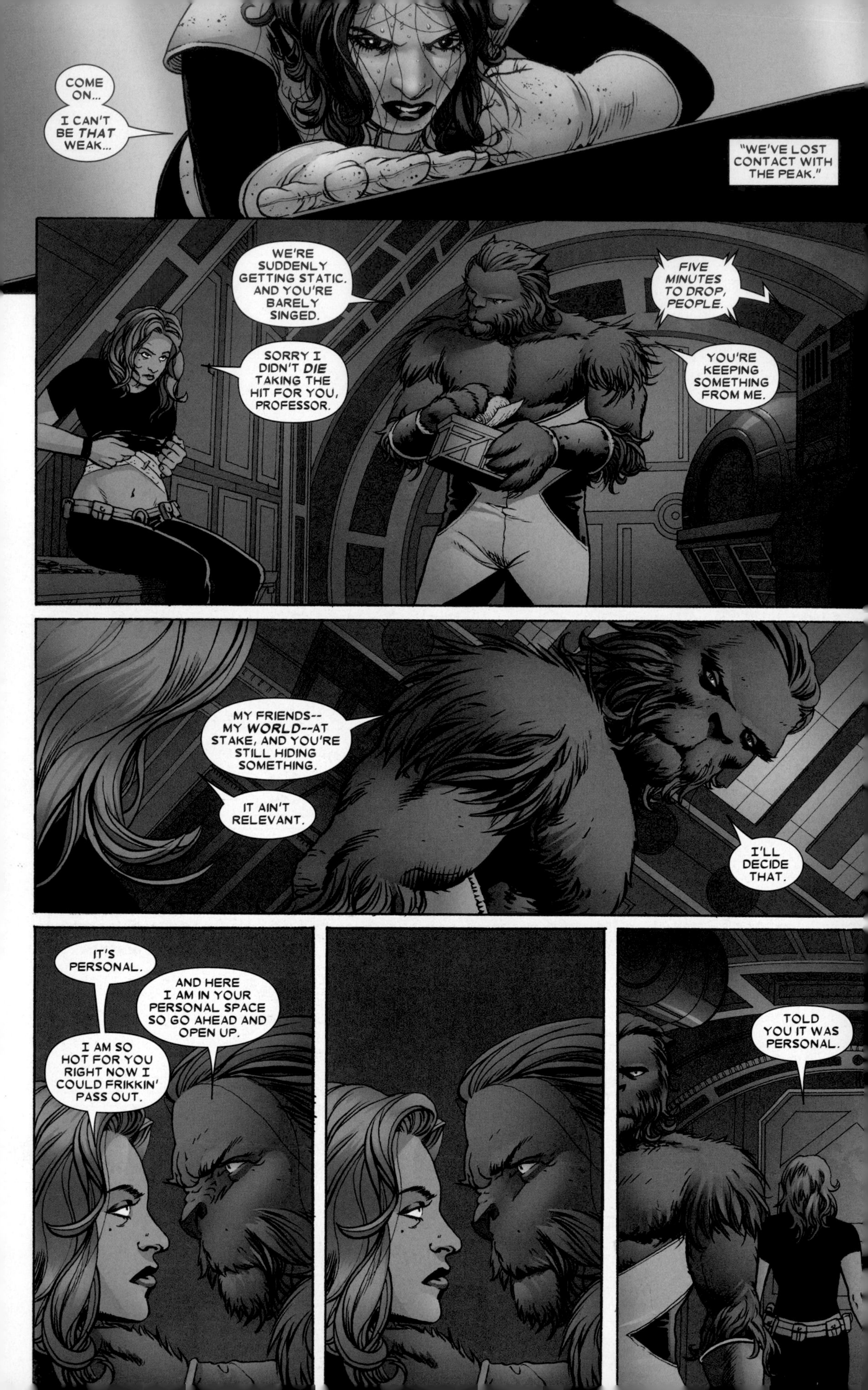
COME ON...
I CAN'T BE *THAT* WEAK...
"WE'VE LOST CONTACT WITH THE PEAK."
WE'RE SUDDENLY GETTING STATIC. AND YOU'RE BARELY SINGED.
FIVE MINUTES TO DROP, PEOPLE.
SORRY I DIDN'T *DIE* TAKING THE HIT FOR YOU, PROFESSOR.
YOU'RE KEEPING SOMETHING FROM ME.
MY FRIENDS-- MY *WORLD*--AT STAKE, AND YOU'RE STILL HIDING SOMETHING.
IT AIN'T RELEVANT.
I'LL DECIDE THAT.
IT'S PERSONAL.
AND HERE I AM IN YOUR PERSONAL SPACE SO GO AHEAD AND OPEN UP.
I AM SO HOT FOR YOU RIGHT NOW I COULD FRIKKIN' PASS OUT.
TOLD YOU IT WAS PERSONAL.

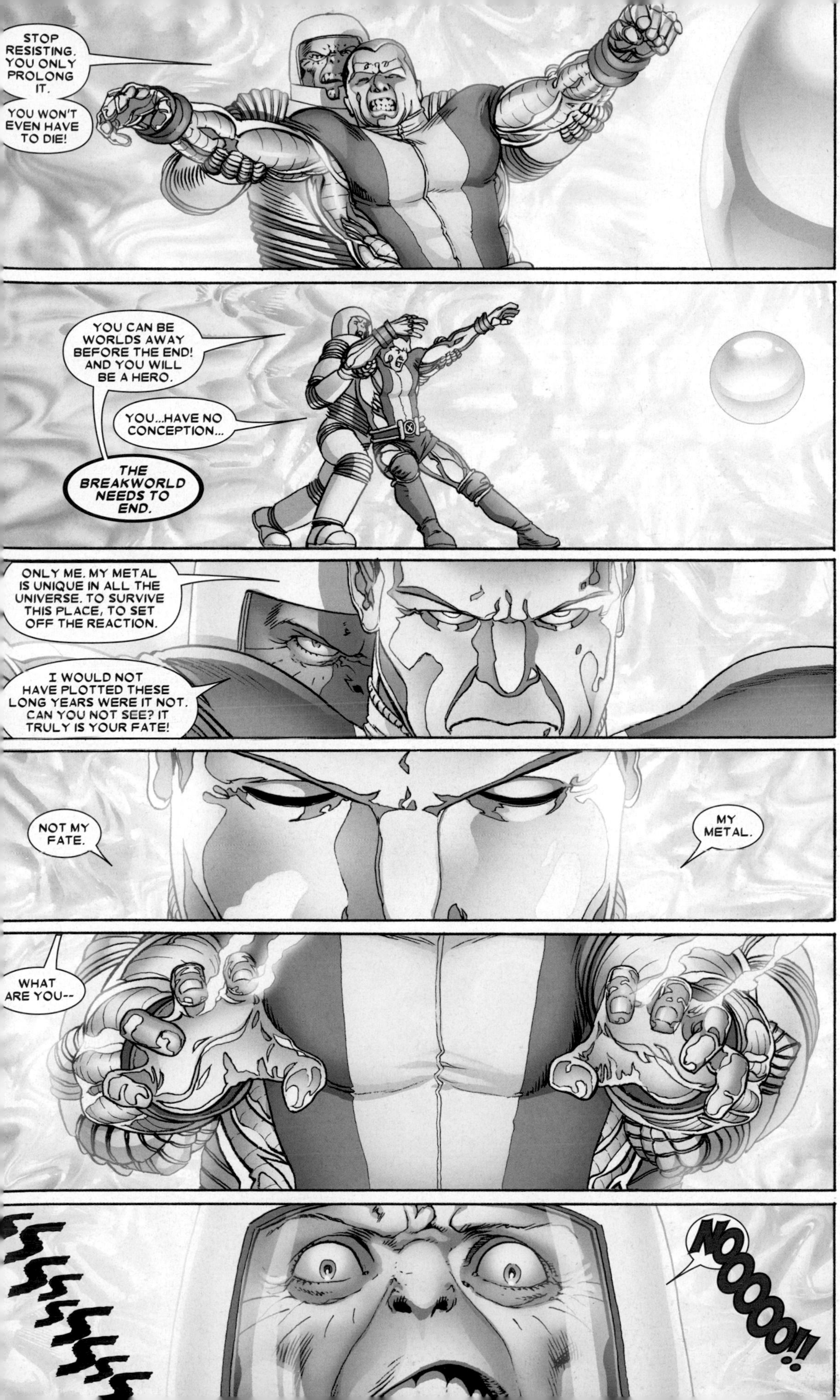
STOP RESISTING. YOU ONLY PROLONG IT.
YOU WON'T EVEN HAVE TO DIE!
YOU CAN BE WORLDS AWAY BEFORE THE END! AND YOU WILL BE A HERO.
YOU...HAVE NO CONCEPTION...
THE BREAKWORLD NEEDS TO END.
ONLY ME. MY METAL IS UNIQUE IN ALL THE UNIVERSE. TO SURVIVE THIS PLACE, TO SET OFF THE REACTION.
I WOULD NOT HAVE PLOTTED THESE LONG YEARS WERE IT NOT. CAN YOU NOT SEE? IT TRULY IS YOUR FATE!
NOT MY FATE.
MY METAL.
WHAT ARE YOU--
SSSSSSSS
NOOOOO!!

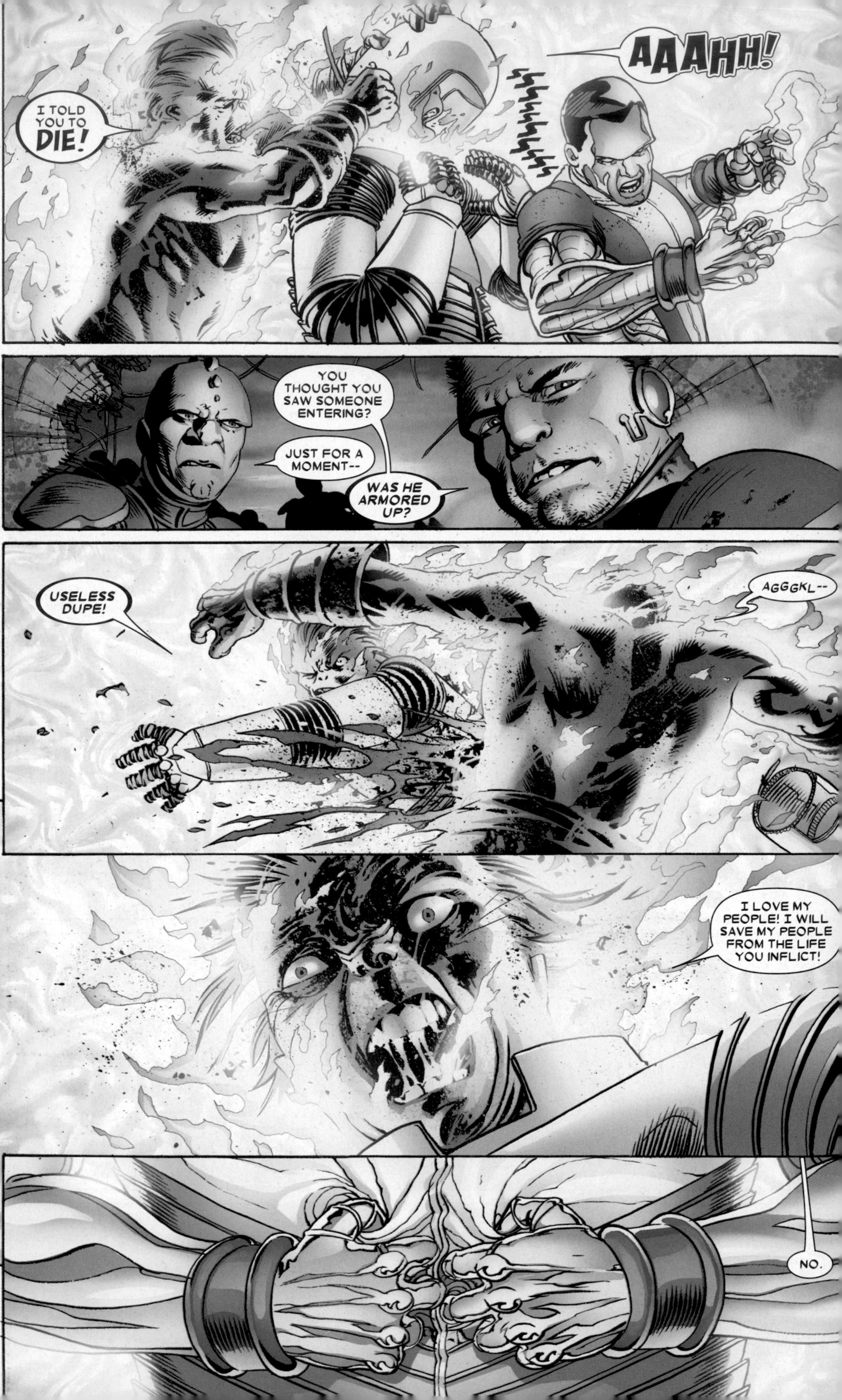
I TOLD YOU TO DIE!
AAAHH!
YOU THOUGHT YOU SAW SOMEONE ENTERING?
JUST FOR A MOMENT--
WAS HE ARMORED UP?
USELESS DUPE!
AGGGKL--
I LOVE MY PEOPLE! I WILL SAVE MY PEOPLE FROM THE LIFE YOU INFLICT!
NO.

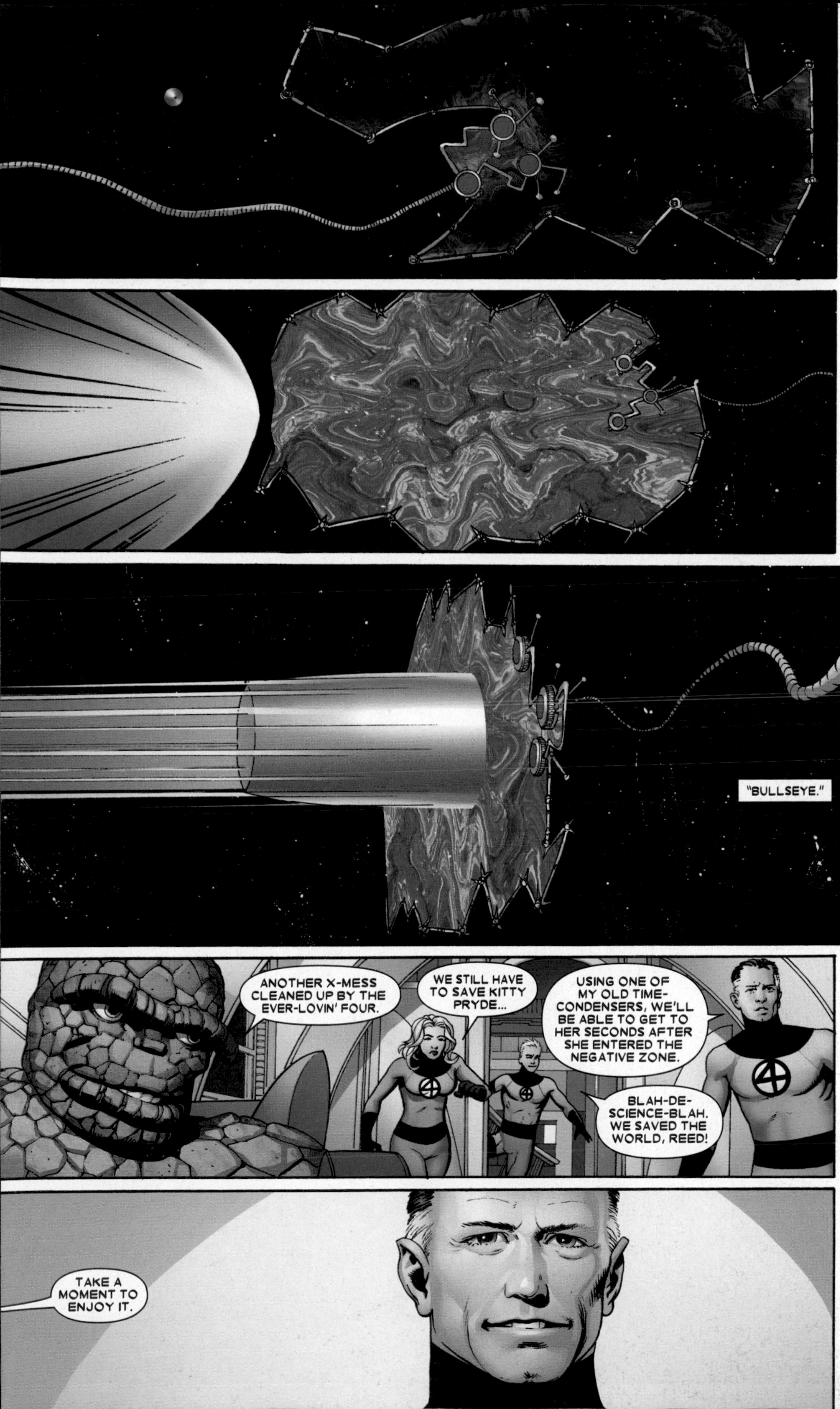
"BULLSEYE."
ANOTHER X-MESS CLEANED UP BY THE EVER-LOVIN' FOUR.
WE STILL HAVE TO SAVE KITTY PRYDE...
USING ONE OF MY OLD TIME-CONDENSERS, WE'LL BE ABLE TO GET TO HER SECONDS AFTER SHE ENTERED THE NEGATIVE ZONE.
BLAH-DE-SCIENCE-BLAH. WE SAVED THE WORLD, REED!
TAKE A MOMENT TO ENJOY IT.

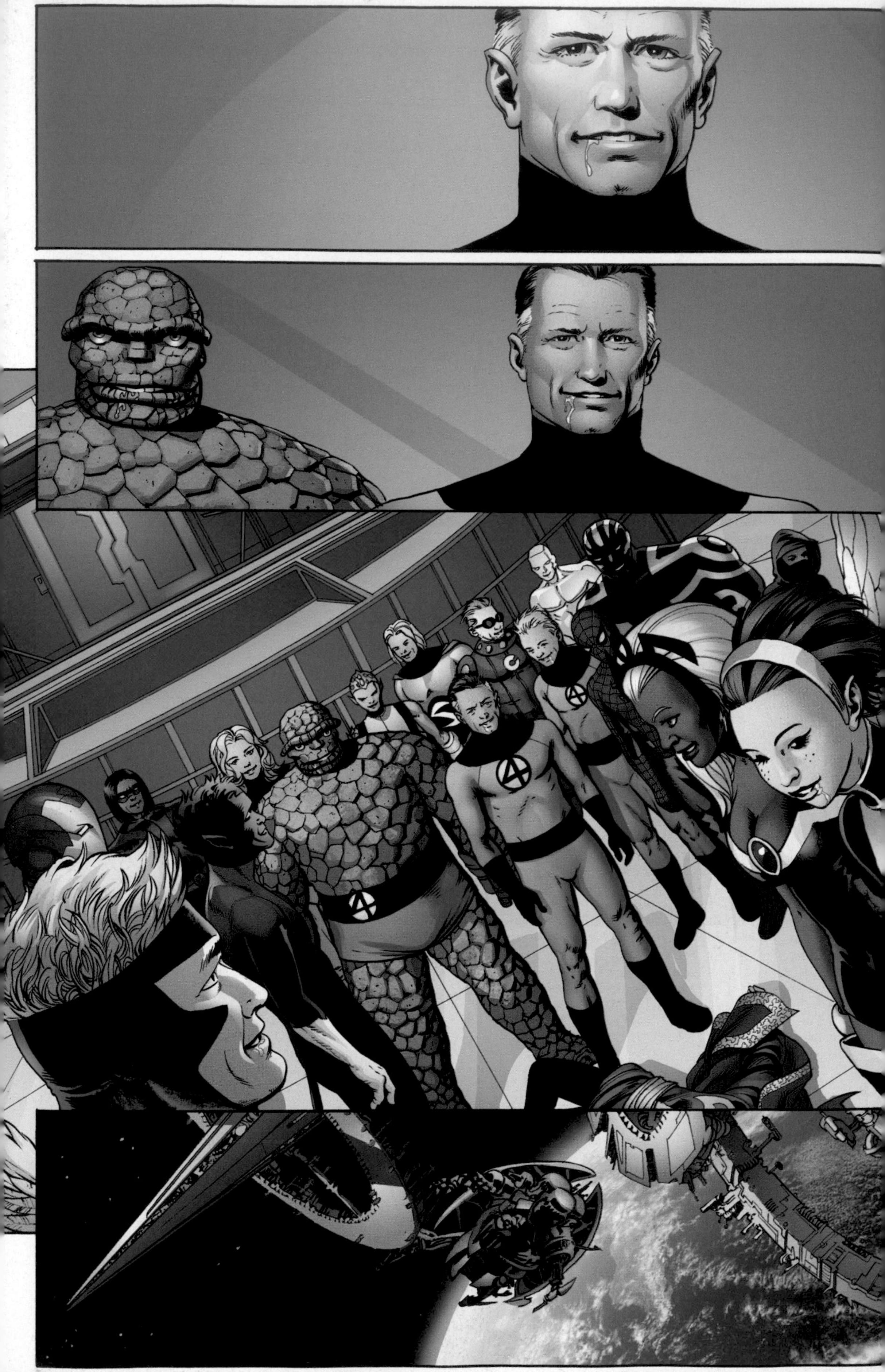

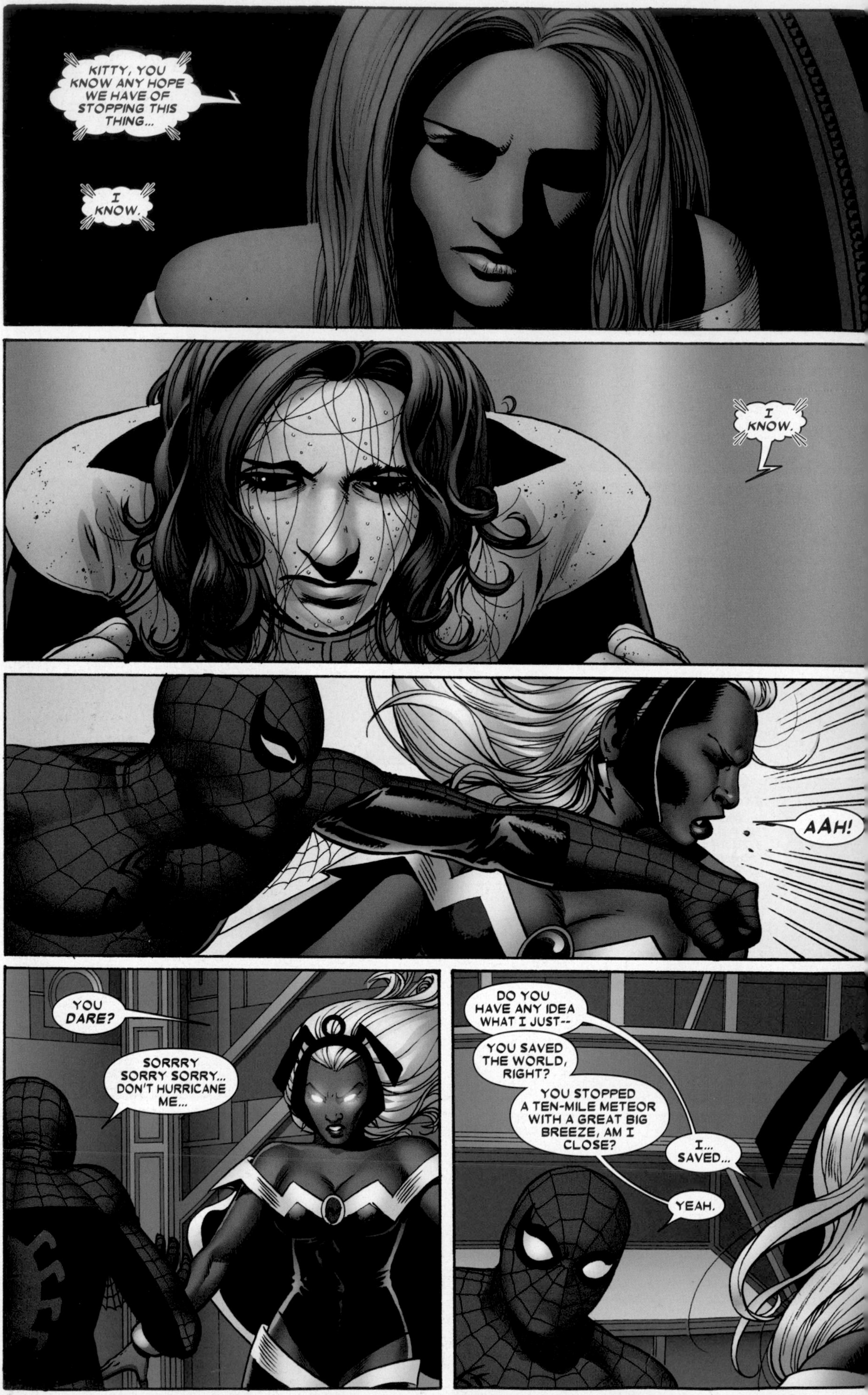
KITTY, YOU KNOW ANY HOPE WE HAVE OF STOPPING THIS THING...
I KNOW.
I KNOW.
AAH!
YOU DARE?
SORRRY SORRY SORRY... DON'T HURRICANE ME...
DO YOU HAVE ANY IDEA WHAT I JUST--
YOU SAVED THE WORLD, RIGHT?
YOU STOPPED A TEN-MILE METEOR WITH A GREAT BIG BREEZE, AM I CLOSE?
I... SAVED...
YEAH.

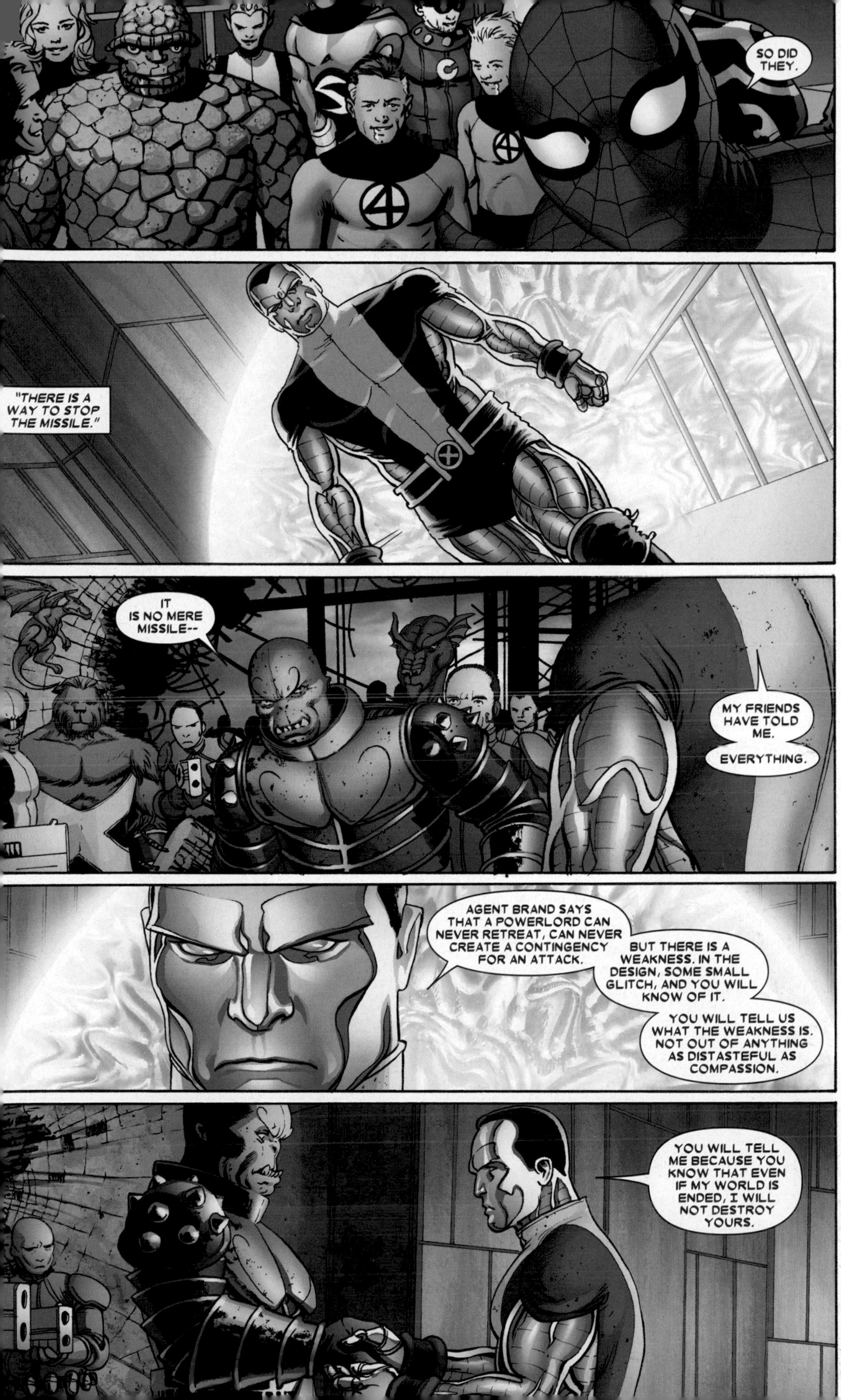
SO DID THEY.
"THERE IS A WAY TO STOP THE MISSILE."
IT IS NO MERE MISSILE--
MY FRIENDS HAVE TOLD ME.
EVERYTHING.
AGENT BRAND SAYS THAT A POWERLORD CAN NEVER RETREAT, CAN NEVER CREATE A CONTINGENCY FOR AN ATTACK.
BUT THERE IS A WEAKNESS. IN THE DESIGN, SOME SMALL GLITCH, AND YOU WILL KNOW OF IT.
YOU WILL TELL US WHAT THE WEAKNESS IS. NOT OUT OF ANYTHING AS DISTASTEFUL AS COMPASSION.
YOU WILL TELL ME BECAUSE YOU KNOW THAT EVEN IF MY WORLD IS ENDED, I WILL NOT DESTROY YOURS.

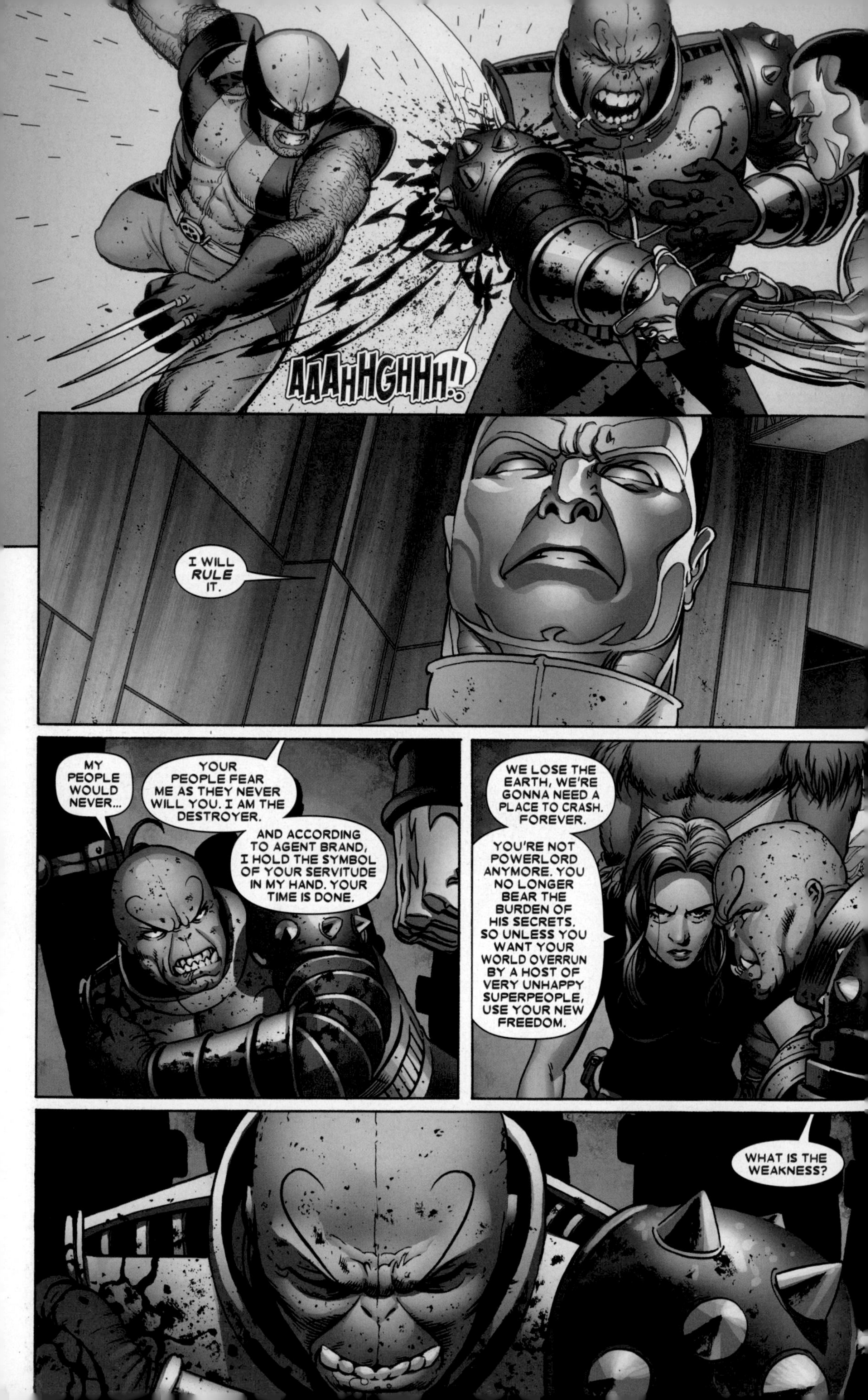
AAAHHGHHH!!
I WILL RULE IT.
MY PEOPLE WOULD NEVER...
YOUR PEOPLE FEAR ME AS THEY NEVER WILL YOU. I AM THE DESTROYER.
AND ACCORDING TO AGENT BRAND, I HOLD THE SYMBOL OF YOUR SERVITUDE IN MY HAND. YOUR TIME IS DONE.
WE LOSE THE EARTH, WE'RE GONNA NEED A PLACE TO CRASH. FOREVER.
YOU'RE NOT POWERLORD ANYMORE. YOU NO LONGER BEAR THE BURDEN OF HIS SECRETS. SO UNLESS YOU WANT YOUR WORLD OVERRUN BY A HOST OF VERY UNHAPPY SUPERPEOPLE, USE YOUR NEW FREEDOM.
WHAT IS THE WEAKNESS?

YOU CAN'T WAKE ANYONE?

THE MOST POWERFUL SEEM TO BE THE MOST POWERFULLY HIT. SPIDER-MAN IS STILL TRYING TO ROUSE DR. STRANGE...

AT LEAST, I THINK THAT'S WHY HE'S HITTING HIM...

IT'S GOT TO BE DEAD ON.

ORORO, WE'RE GETTING VERY CLOSE. WE'VE BEEN TOLD THAT A DIRECT HEAD-TO-HEAD HIT BY SOMETHING BIG ENOUGH MIGHT BUCKLE THE BULLET, OR AT THE VERY LEAST DIVERT IT.

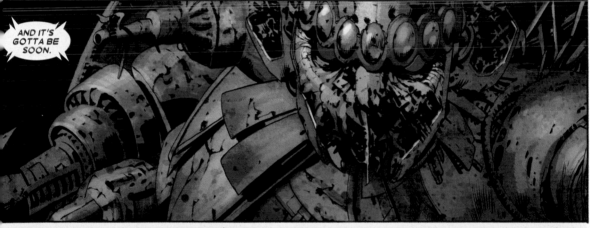

AND IT'S GOTTA BE SOON.

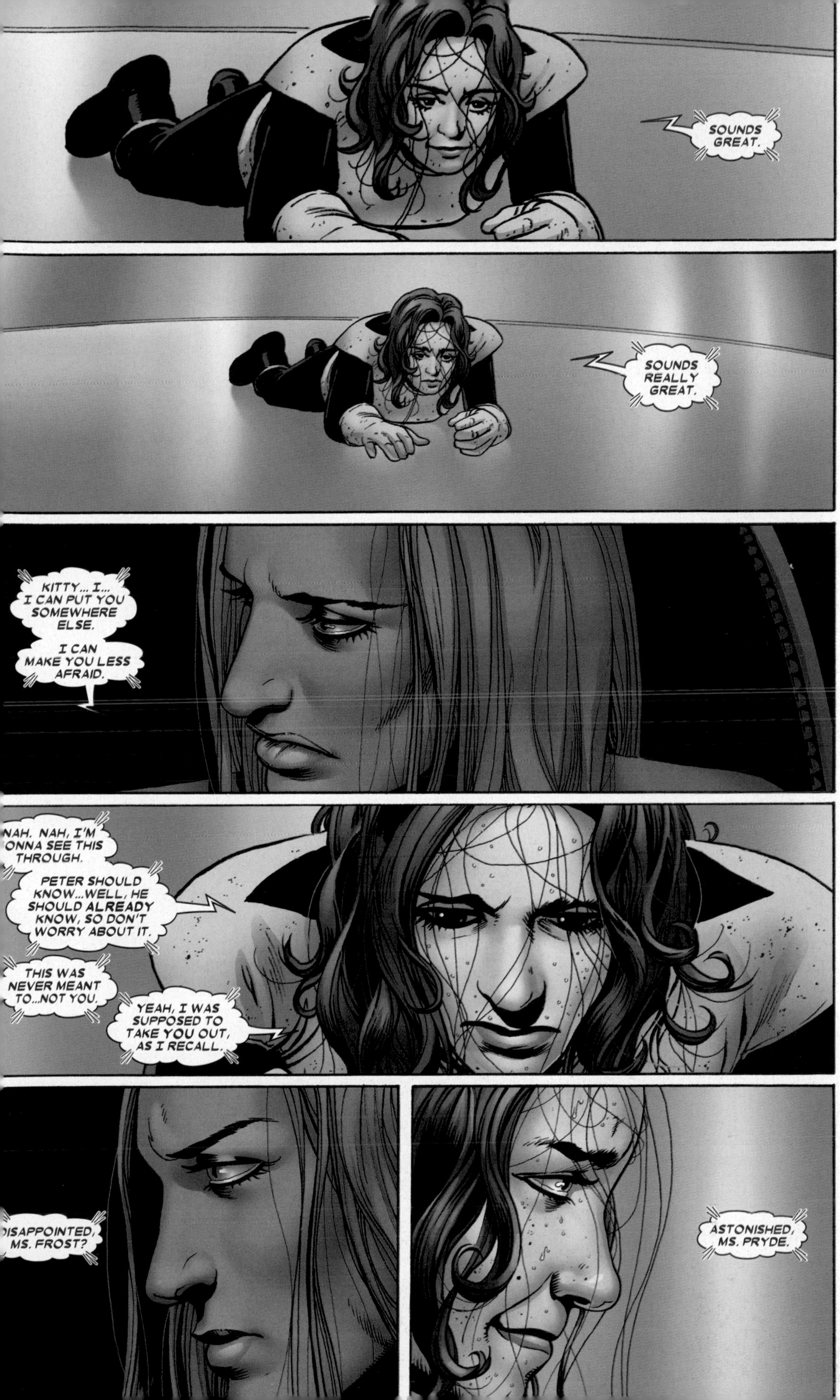
SOUNDS GREAT.
SOUNDS REALLY GREAT.
KITTY... I... I CAN PUT YOU SOMEWHERE ELSE.
I CAN MAKE YOU LESS AFRAID.
NAH. NAH, I'M ONNA SEE THIS THROUGH.
PETER SHOULD KNOW...WELL, HE SHOULD ALREADY KNOW, SO DON'T WORRY ABOUT IT.
THIS WAS NEVER MEANT TO...NOT YOU.
YEAH, I WAS SUPPOSED TO TAKE YOU OUT, AS I RECALL.
ISAPPOINTED, MS. FROST?
ASTONISHED, MS. PRYDE.

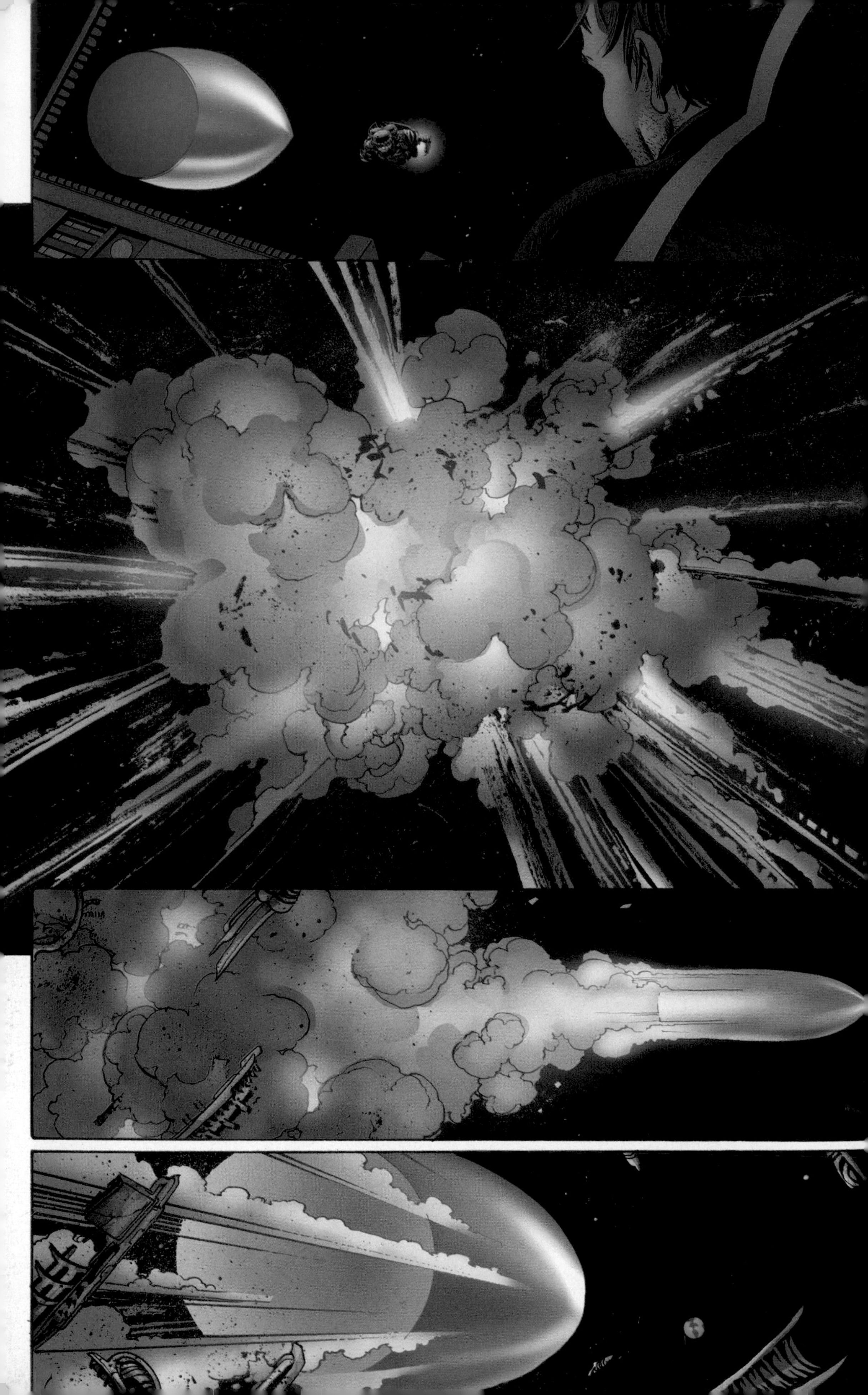

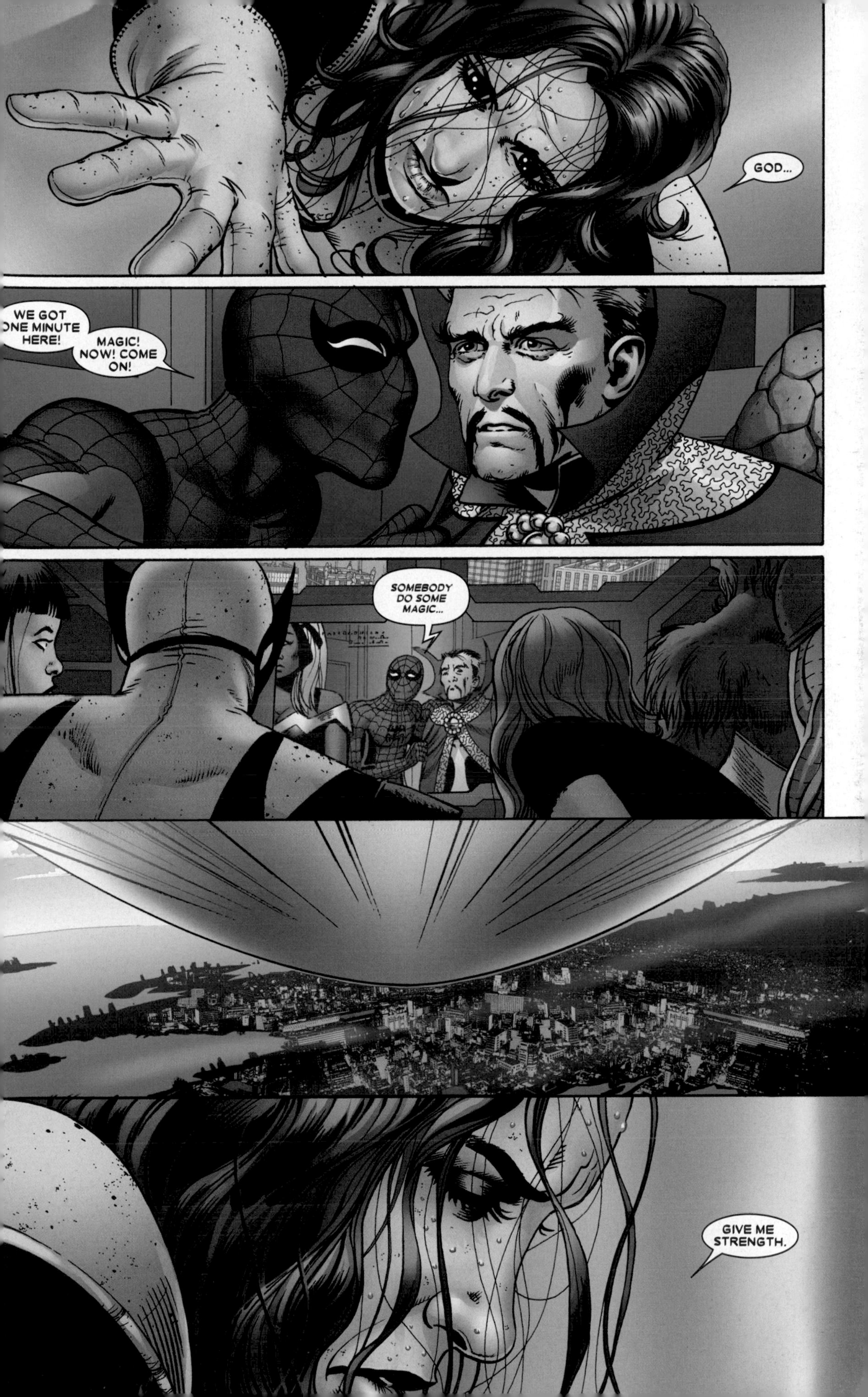
GOD...
WE GOT ONE MINUTE HERE!
MAGIC! NOW! COME ON!
SOMEBODY DO SOME MAGIC...
GIVE ME STRENGTH.

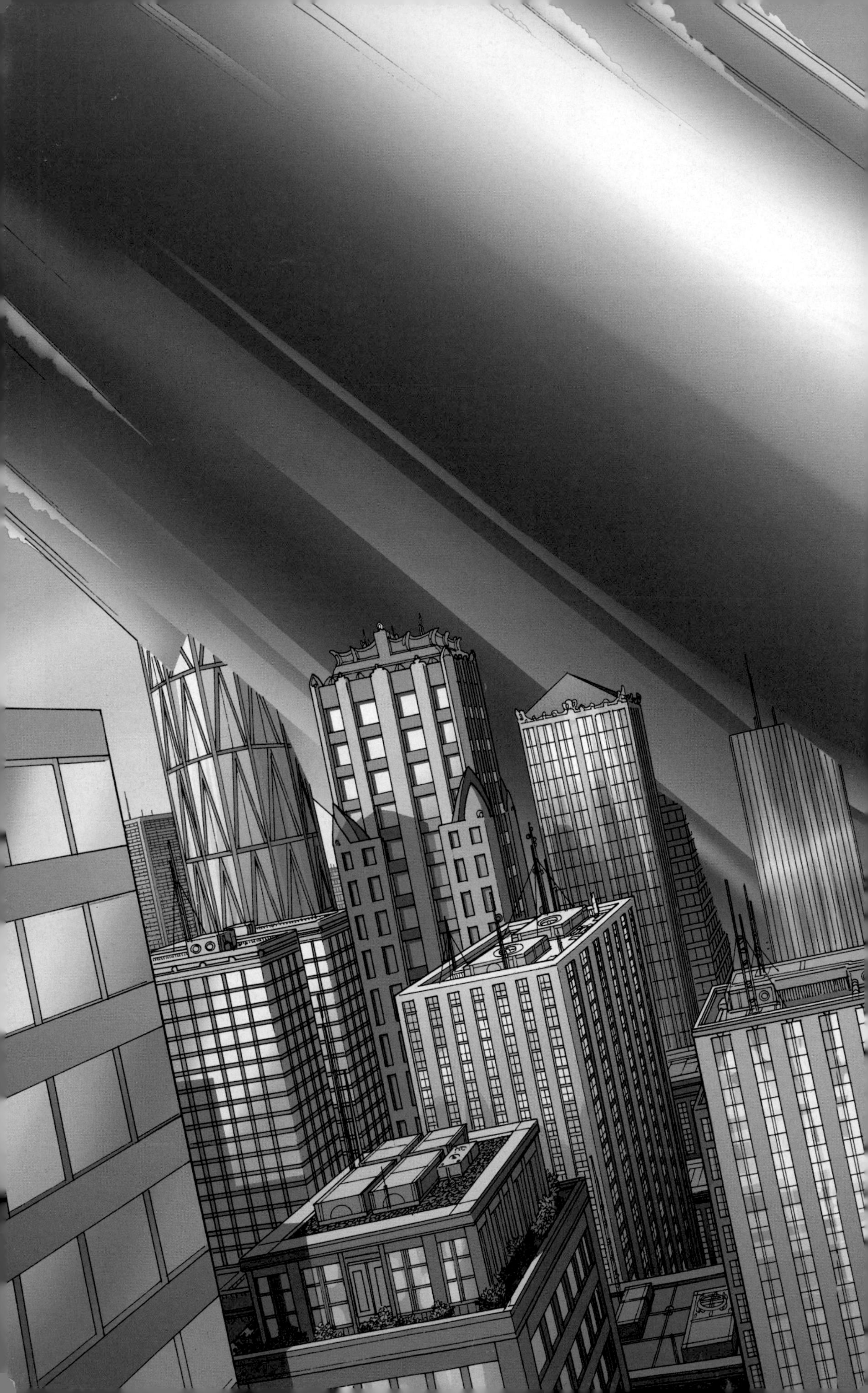

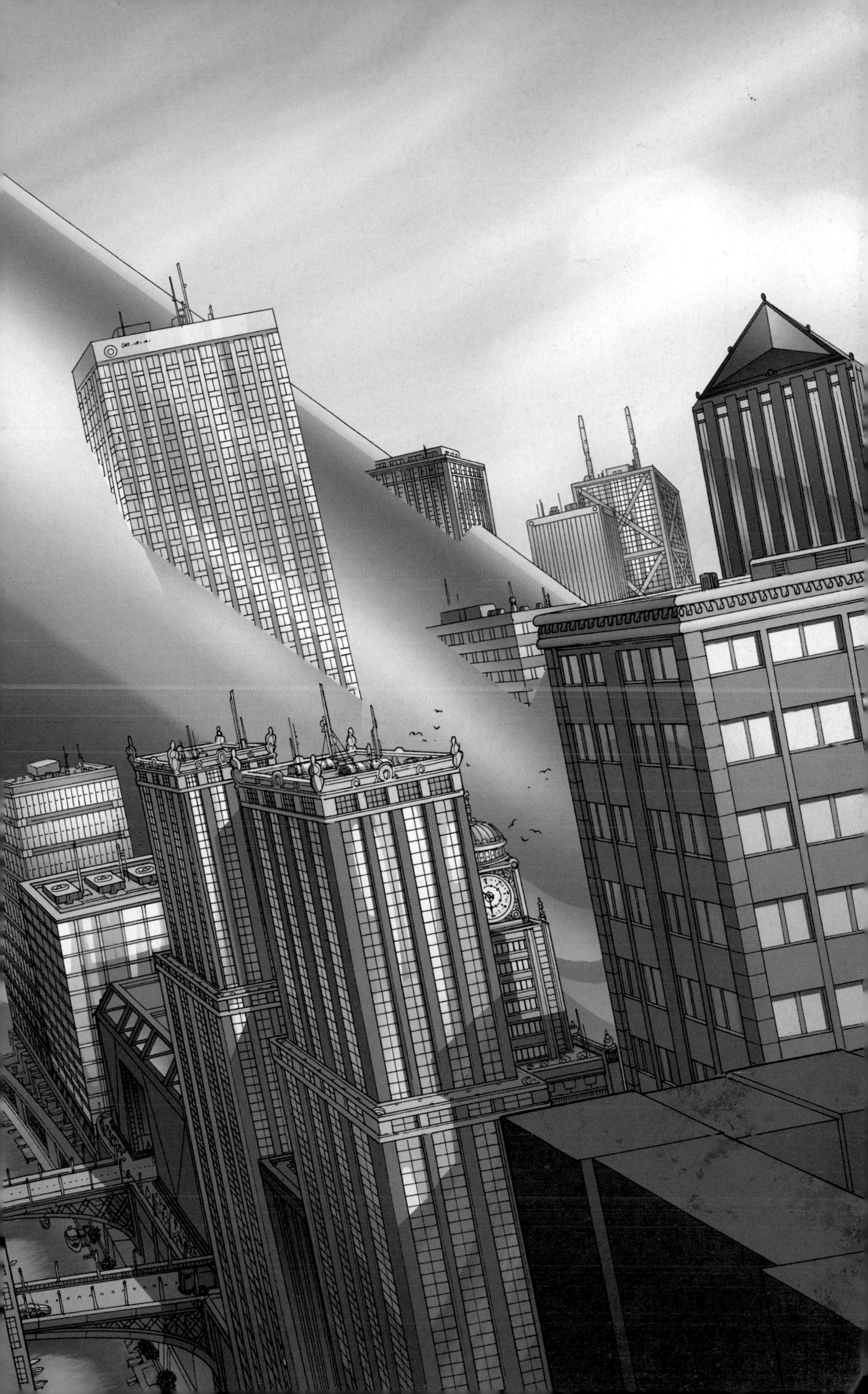

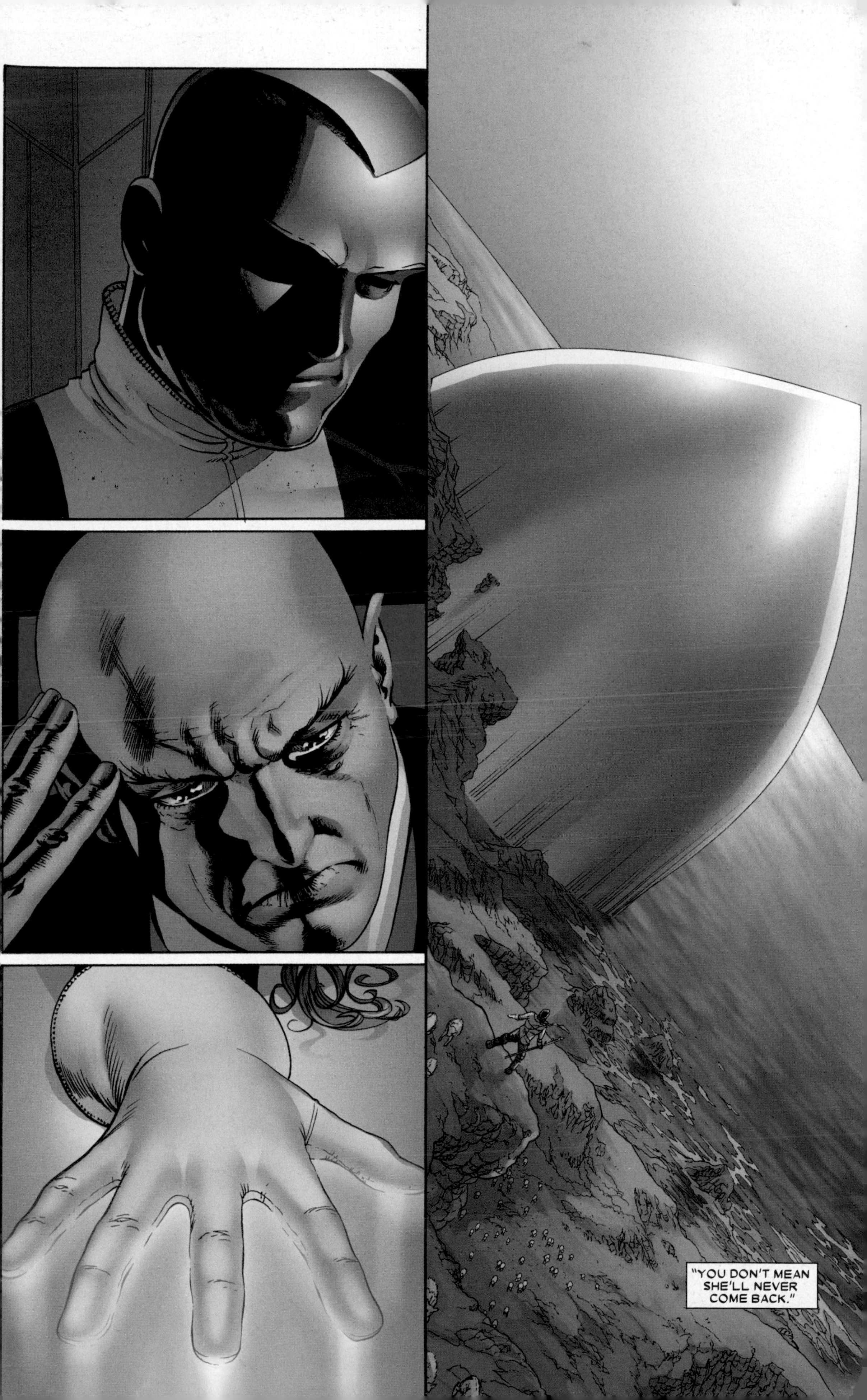
"YOU DON'T MEAN SHE'LL NEVER COME BACK."

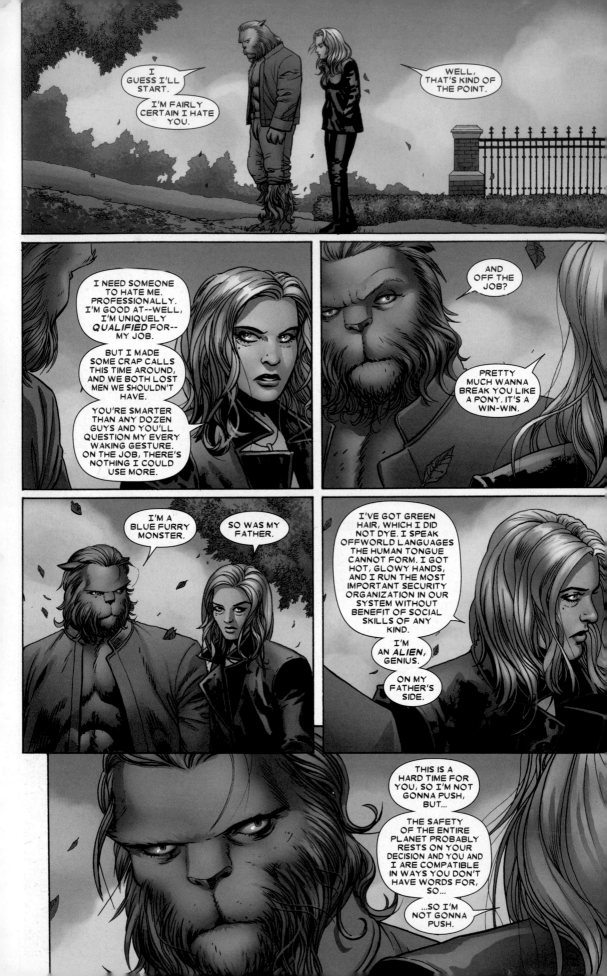

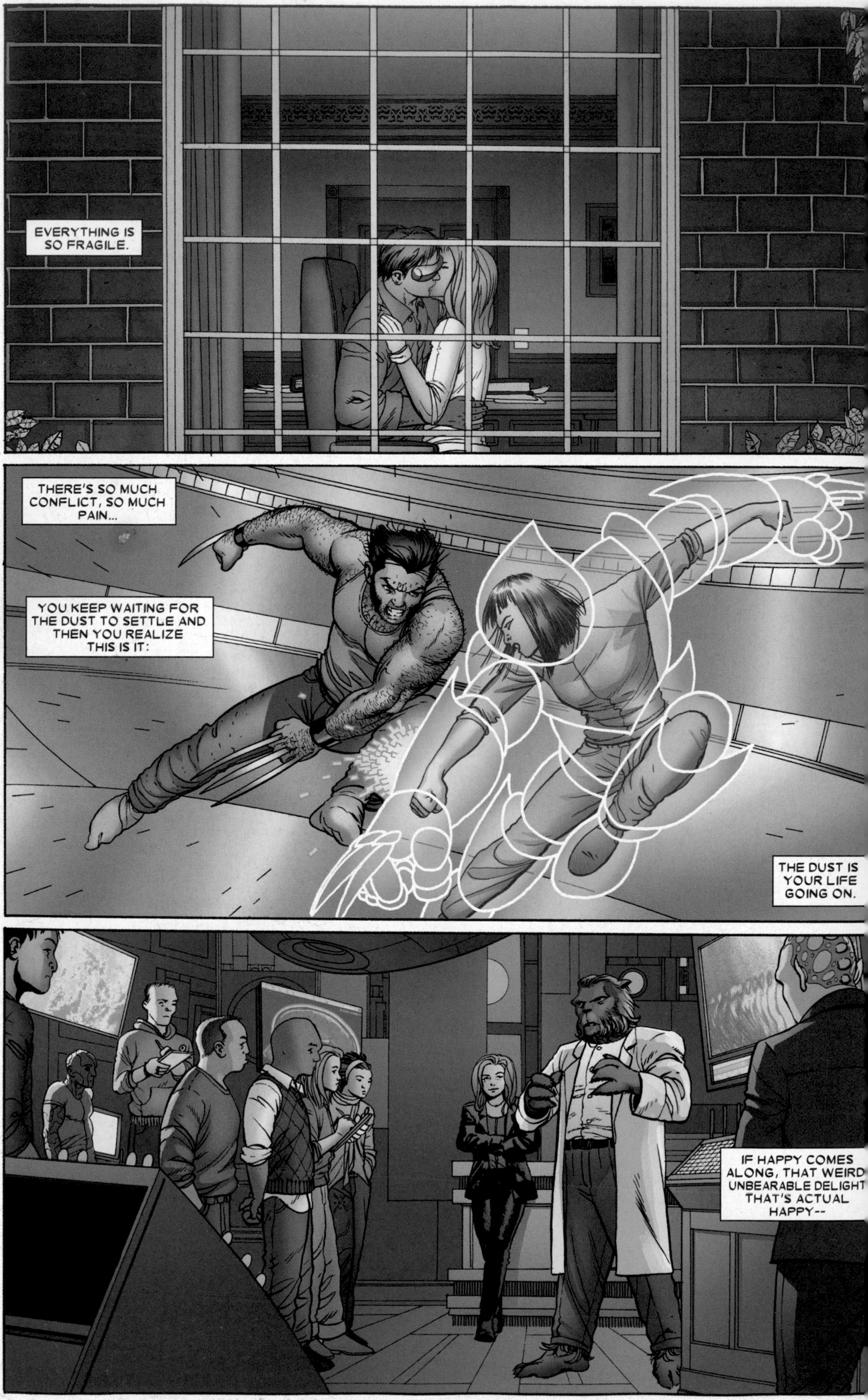
EVERYTHING IS SO FRAGILE.
THERE'S SO MUCH CONFLICT, SO MUCH PAIN...
YOU KEEP WAITING FOR THE DUST TO SETTLE AND THEN YOU REALIZE THIS IS IT:
THE DUST IS YOUR LIFE GOING ON.
IF HAPPY COMES ALONG, THAT WEIRD UNBEARABLE DELIGHT THAT'S ACTUAL HAPPY--

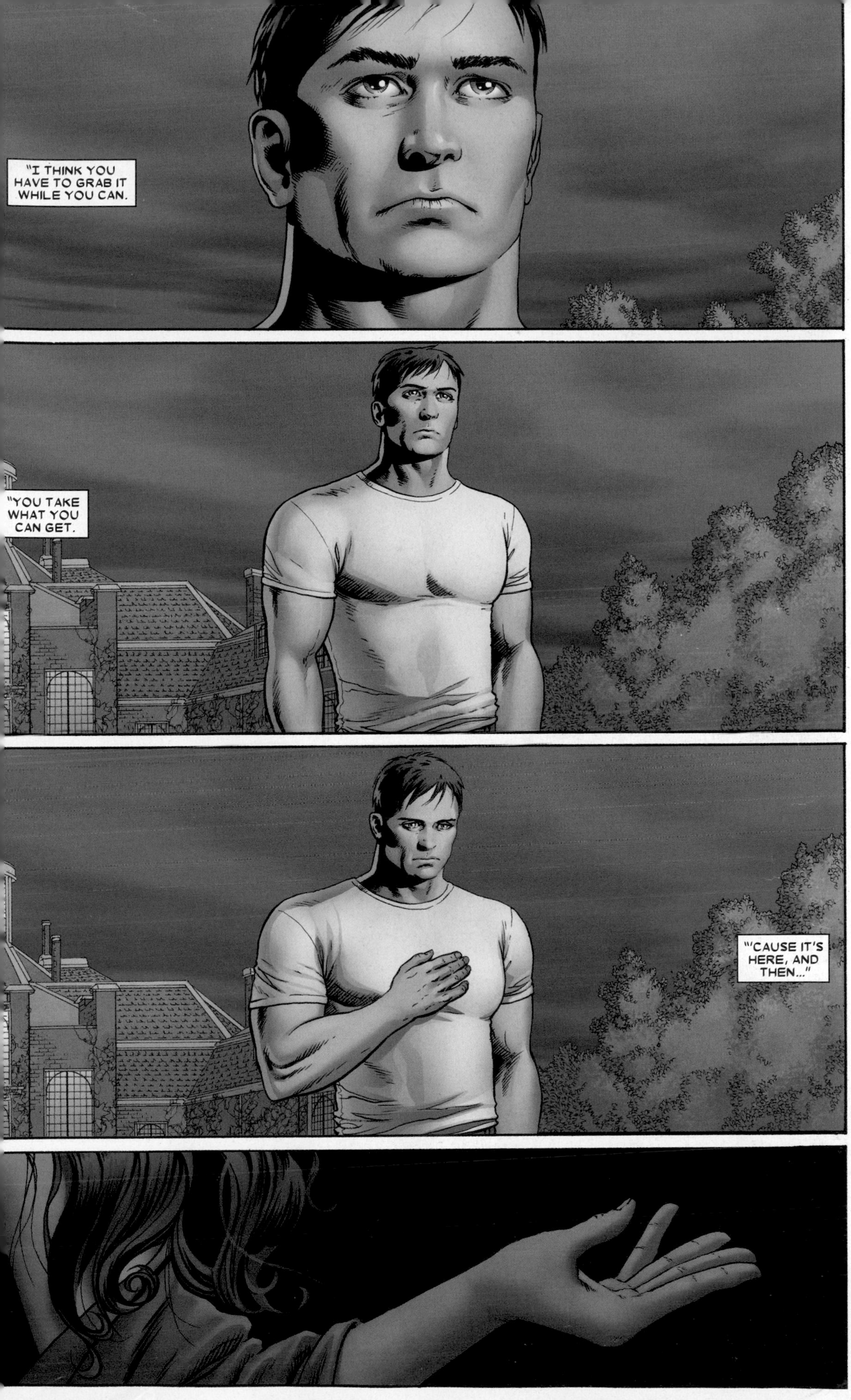
"I THINK YOU HAVE TO GRAB IT WHILE YOU CAN.
"YOU TAKE WHAT YOU CAN GET.
"'CAUSE IT'S HERE, AND THEN..."

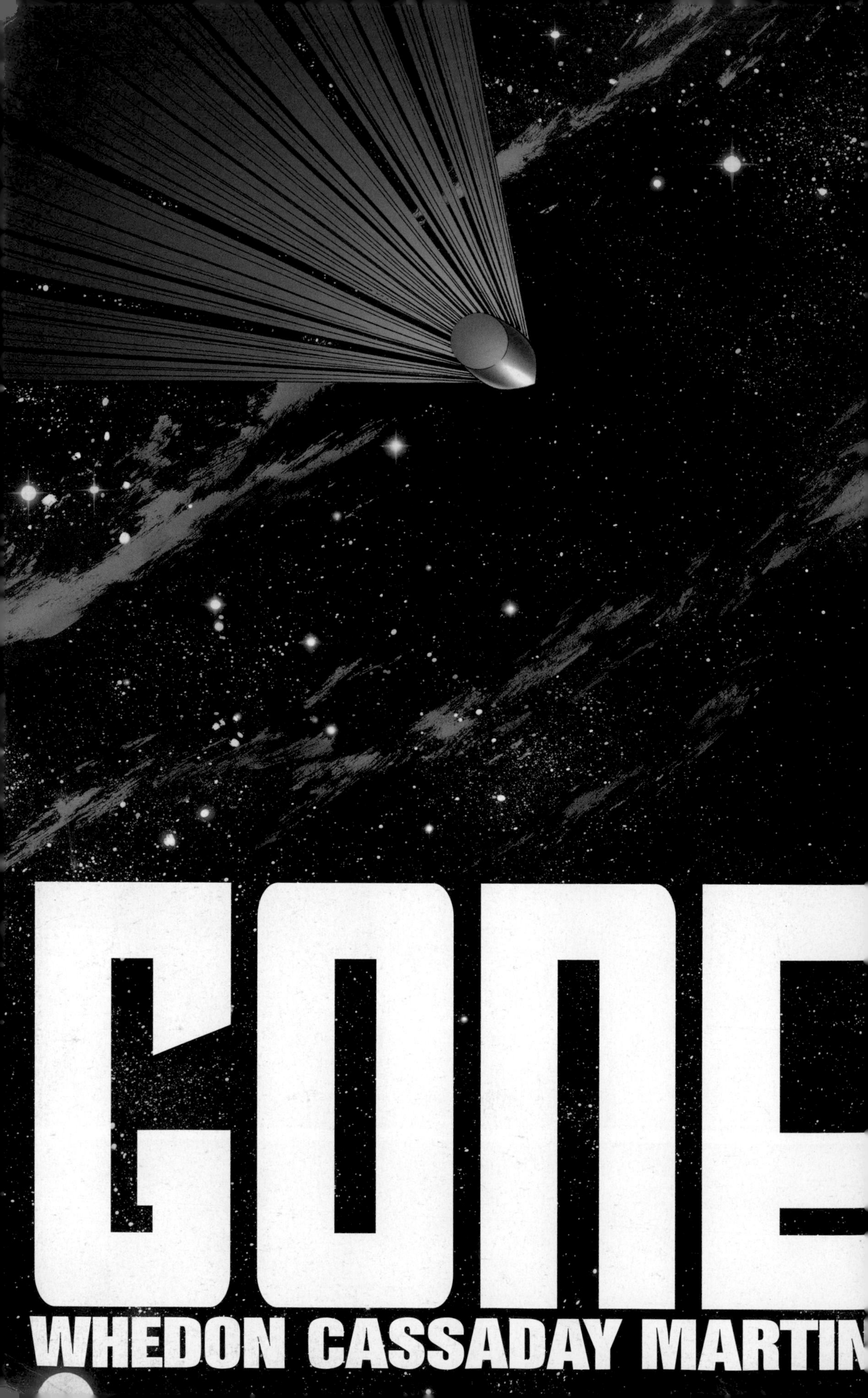
GONE
WHEDON CASSADAY MARTI

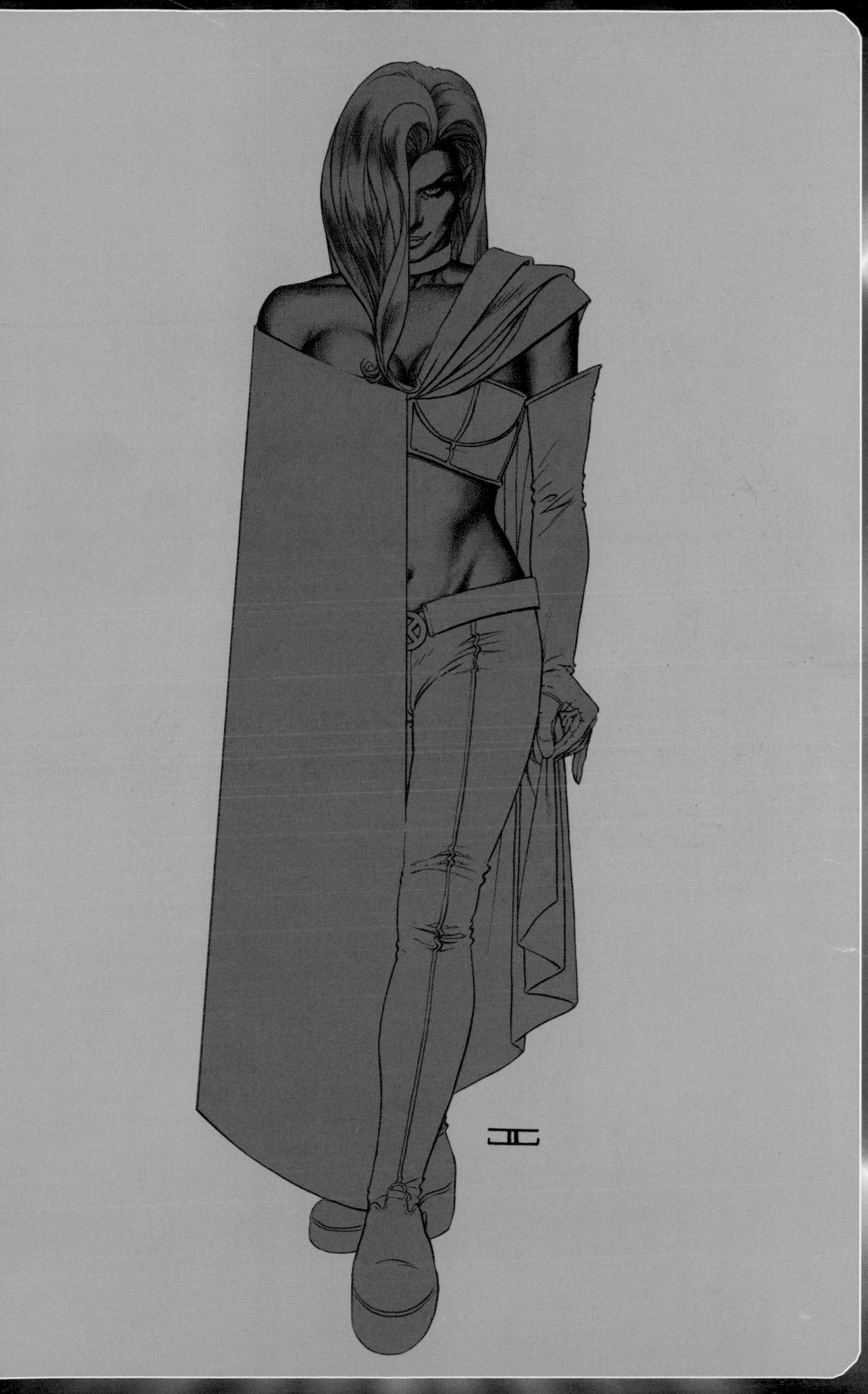

21 VARIANT

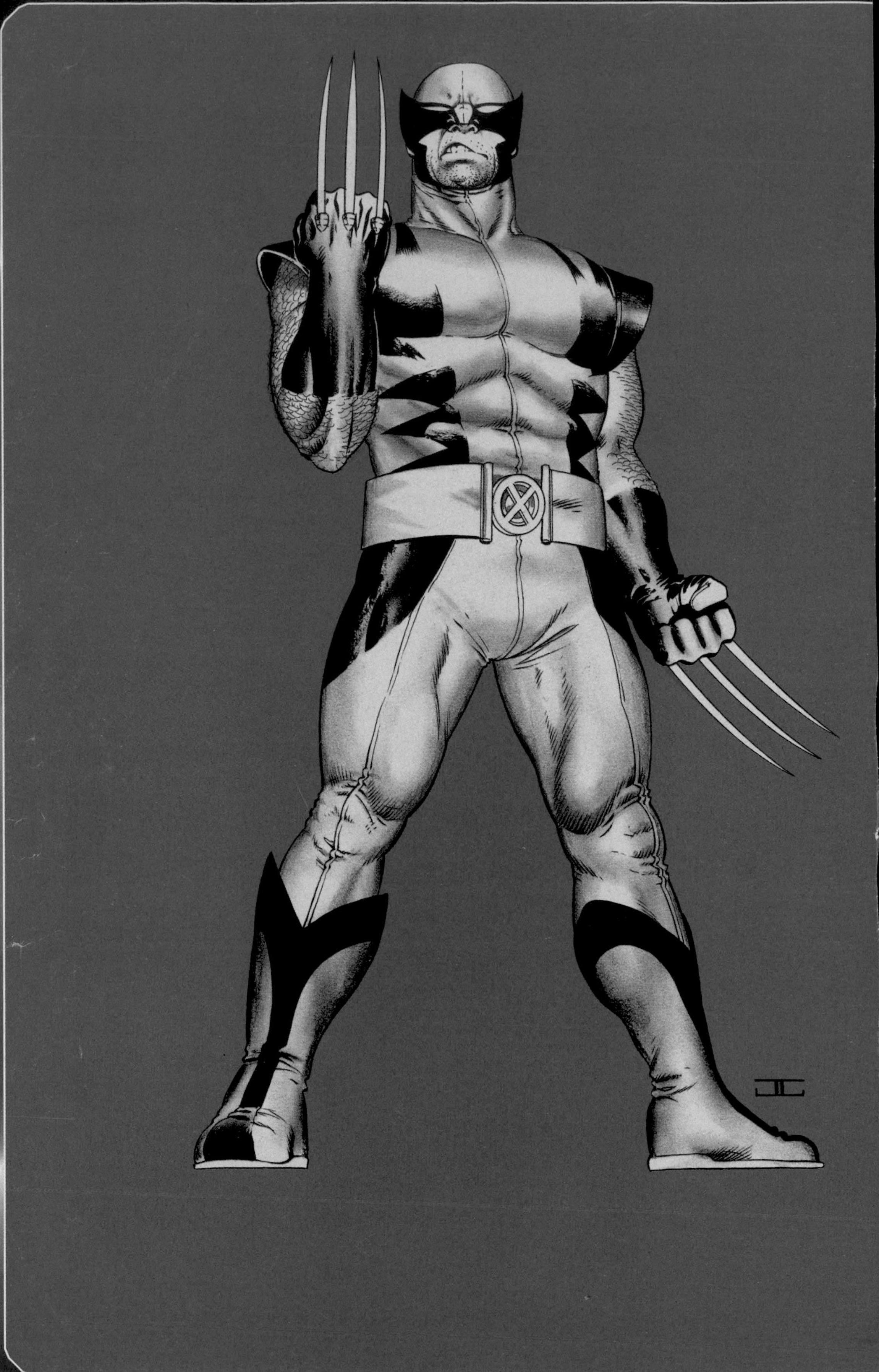

22 VARIANT

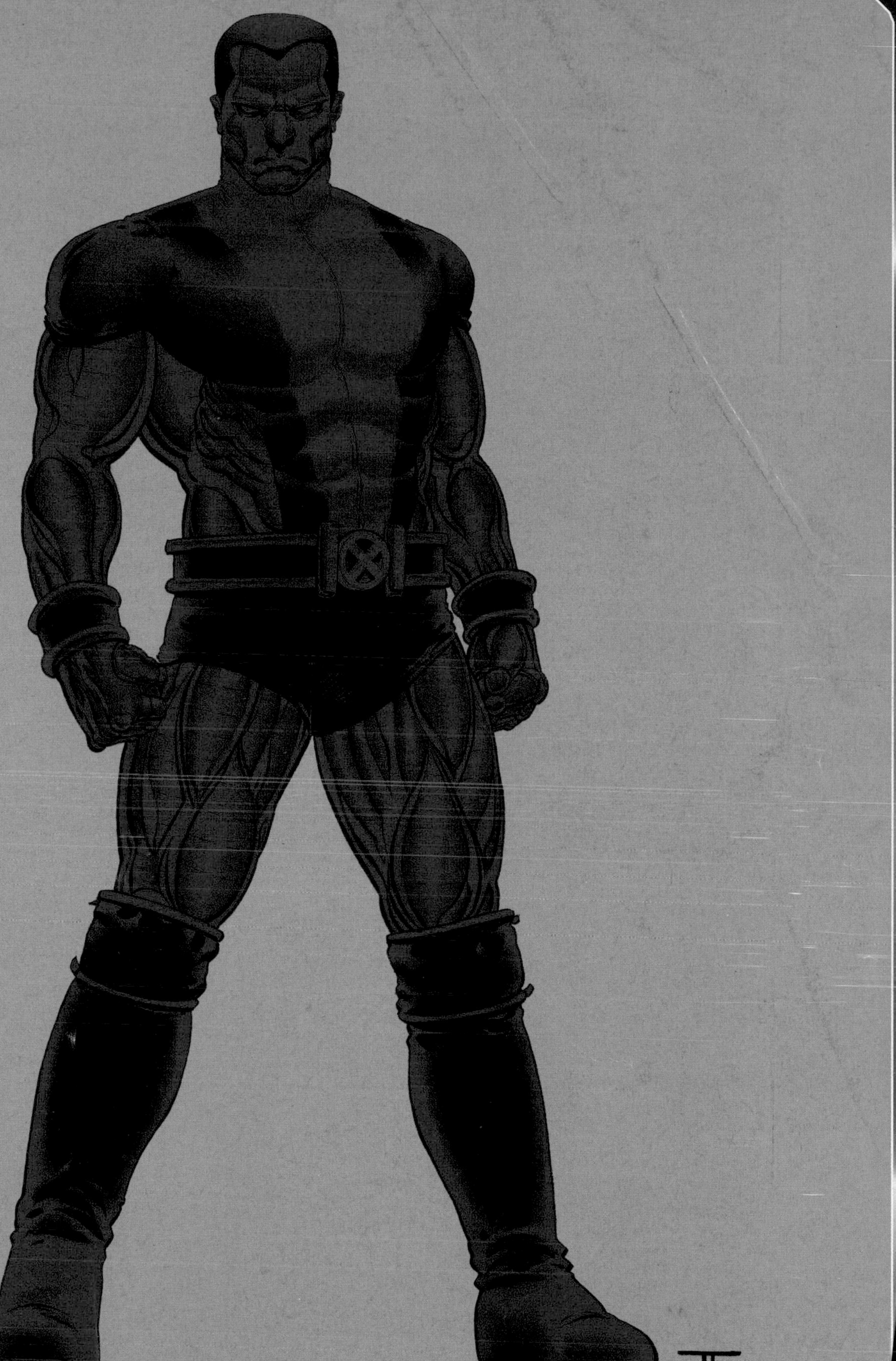

23 VARIANT

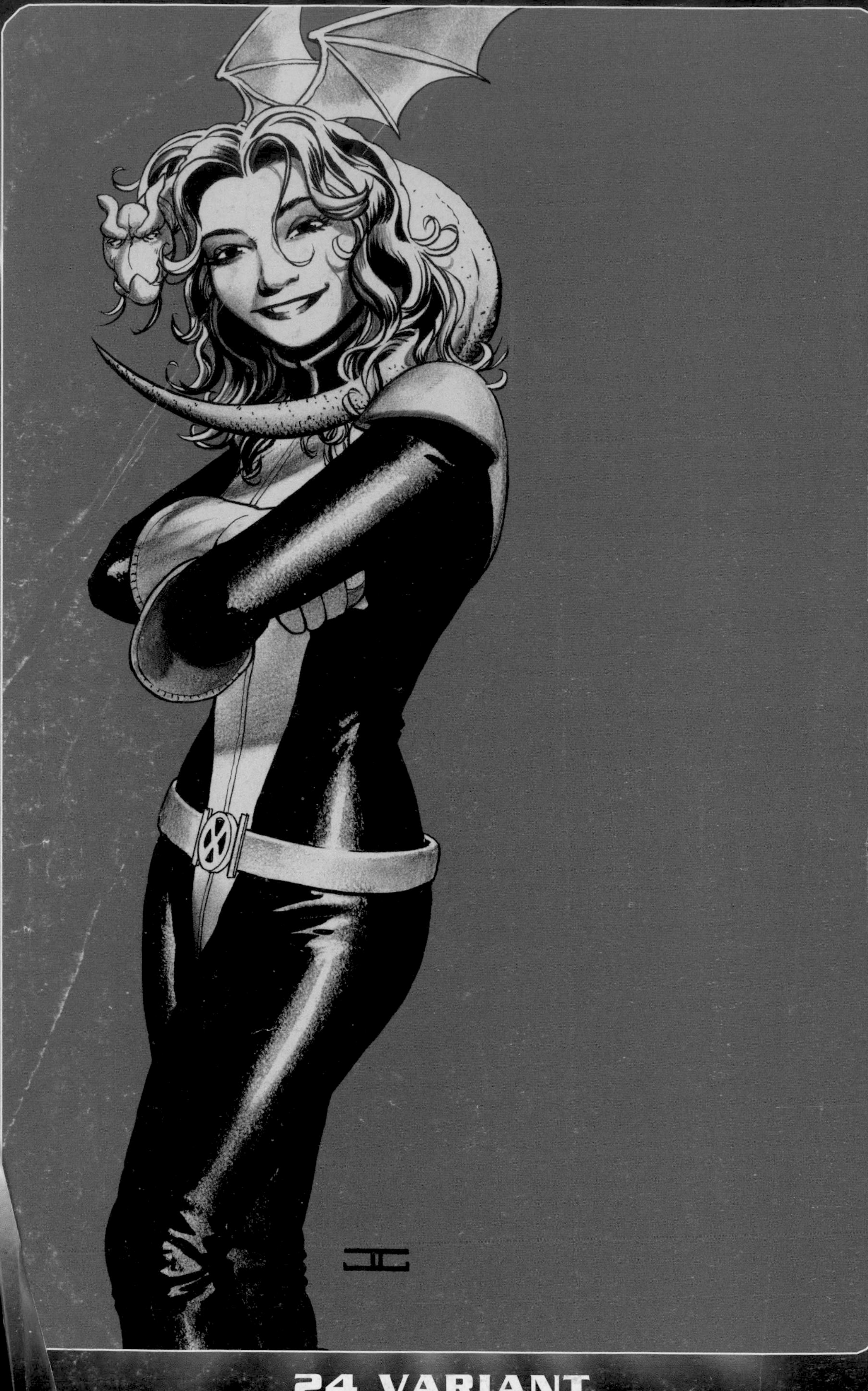

24 VARIANT